WHAT IS IT LIKE TO BE WITH XAVIERA?

"Who am I? I often ask myself that question. People ask me if I'm happy, satisfied or content. Or they ask me if I'm a lesbian, or if I hate men, or am I a masochist, or a sadist. My answer is that I'm a little bit of everything. I am happy at times and sad occasionally. I'm emotional and sensitive, very much so, but I can also be tough as nails. I'm an exhibitionist because I like to walk around in the nude, as long as I'm young and well put together, and feel comfortable that way. I'm not ashamed of people seeing me in Eve's costume."

And Xaviera goes on with:

★ The X-rated movie producer

★ New York's most notorious phone number (the guy who got Xaviera's old number)

★ Girls in her life

★ New men in her life

★ This country's most outrageous publicity tour (Xaviera on the road)

★ Do you have any questions of me? (Questions To The Happy Hooker)

D0926260

Xaviera!

HER CONTINUING ADVENTURES

By

Xaviera
Hollander

The Author Of

"The Happy Hooker"

WARNER
PAPERBACK
LIBRARY

A Warner Communications Company

WARNER PAPERBACK LIBRARY EDITION

First Printing: February, 1973
Second Printing: February, 1973
Third Printing: February, 1973
Fourth Printing: March, 1973
Fifth Printing: May, 1973

Lines on page 40 Copyright © 1965 by Beechwood
Music Corp. Words and Music by Terry Kirkman.

Cover photo by Neal Slavin

Warner Paperback Library is a division of Warner Books, Inc.,
315 Park Avenue South, New York, N.Y. 10010.

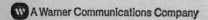 A Warner Communications Company

"The only unnatural sex act is that which you cannot perform."

—*Dr. Alfred Kinsey*

"Love, like butter, goes well with bread."

—*Yiddish proverb*

"Men always want to be a woman's first love. That is their clumsy vanity. Women have a more subtle instinct about things: What they like is to be a man's last romance."

—*Oscar Wilde*

EDITOR'S NOTE: The material in this book is not being presented in any specific chronological order. Some of these things occurred at the same time. Such is the style of Ms. Hollander's life.

In response to several billion inquiries, the correct pronunciation of her name is Xaviera like in Riviera, but with a *"zah"* sound in front. Zah-viera.

INTRODUCTION

Since I've never had a baby, it may be presumptuous of me to say that writing a book is like giving birth to a child. Especially when the book is a wildly sensational affair entitled *The Happy Hooker*. But it was my first book, and I'm reasonably proud of its creation. I do wish there had been more time for me to edit it in its final version, but the publisher was anxious—as was I—to have the book out in time to take advantage of the Knapp Commission publicity. And given the book's wonderful sales, I can't really complain. On the other hand, I'm delighted that *this* book did not go to the printer's without my having approved every sentence, word, and syllable. This time, they're all mine, as there are no collaborators on this book.

I don't know if people judged my first book by its cover. I do know, after talking with so many people who've read it, that while the title surely helped to sell the book, it may not have been the happiest of titles. There's a little story behind this, and I'm telling it here, for the first time.

As I recall, I met Robin Moore in December of 1970. In January, we began the manuscript that was to be *The Happy Hooker*. At the time, however, the book had no title. We thought it might end up being *Just Call Me Anytime* or *Madam X*, but the latter had been used a few million times and the former lacked zap. So, in what I thought was an inspired moment, I suggested calling the book *Come and Go*. It was funny, and described what gentlemen who paid house calls at my establishment actually did. But Robin leaned toward *The Happy Hooker* as an even jollier title.

Well, that title didn't give me any jollies. As New York's most successful madam, I certainly didn't consider myself a streetwalker who belongs at the bottom of the hooker hierarchy.* As for the "happy" part of the title, I wasn't exactly ecstatic at the time because of the incredible police harassment I was suffering. However, as you well know, the title of the book, the happiest choice or not, became *The Happy Hooker*. It had good alliteration and made the book seem light and funny. Besides, my publisher was all for it because that title had already gained considerable publicity due to my connections with the Knapp Commission investigations.

Of course the proof of this particular publishing pudding is the book's sales record: as this is being written, in mid-October of 1972, *The Happy Hooker* is approaching four million copies in print and is expected eventually to sell over five million copies in America and Canada alone. Not bad for a gullible little Dutch girl who came here to marry Mr. Right—a wrong move that turned out right.

But I still think I might have been—whoops—right about the other title. For one thing, *The Happy Hooker* kept me off the top evening TV talk shows. Dick Cavett was interested but settled instead for an elderly ex-madam who was now heavy into needlework or something. I was on "The Kup Show" in Chicago with superstud Burt Reynolds, and when he later hosted "The Tonight Show" when Johnny Carson was on vacation, he tried three times to get me on the show—to no avail. Supposedly the FCC was afraid I'd come out with four-letter words—and thereby shock the

---

* By the way, the ancient Greek term *hataera* referred to the courtesans of the day who gave inspiration and solace to tired philosophers and were much admired, as witnessed by Greek temple art. But the current usage of the term *hooker* goes back to General Joseph Hooker who, during the Civil War, allowed his men to do battle with camp followers —who became known as "Hooker's girls." He may not have earned immortality as a general, but he certainly earned himself a permanent place in the language.

nation—and sponsors of the program were just plain afraid I'd besmirch their image.

The hypocritical aspects of this are also worth mentioning: it was all right for me to be on morning and afternoon television when the audience would mostly be female, but not okay for me to appear on TV when the big boys were home. How adult is television anyway, given this kind of thinking?

Don't get me wrong—I'm grateful for the terrific TV and radio exposure I did receive, and I'm especially grateful that people seemed to find me intelligent and charming and even capable of an eloquent statement now and then. I think they somehow expected me to be vulgar or cross, and just a "Fun City" girl instead of someone who has thought a great deal in recent years about human relationships and is willing to be candid and outspoken—at the risk of controversy and even abuse—about them.

So at the risk of blowing my own horn too loudly, I'd like to say, however immodestly, that writing a book that is so candid is not an easy experience. It's like giving away a lot of yourself. Before publication of *The Happy Hooker,* there were many, many secrets in my life, and suddenly there they were, in print. My own life story, full of confessions—if that's the way you want to look at my revelations—cut out of my own flesh and blood and set in type. It was often an unsettling experience to be the author of a best-selling book as this book will make perfectly clear. (Thank you, Tricky Dicky.)

Still, a lot of it was very nice indeed. People would ask me, "Xaviera, do you still have that scar on your leg?" Or, "Xaviera, is it really true you don't drink?" I'd immediately wonder how they knew *that* about me, and then came the answer. They'd tell me, "It's on page so-and-so." Or, "Your parents did this or that." Or, "Your first girlfriend's name was Helga." So there are not many secrets I've kept. And perhaps that's something to regret about having written a book so open and so honest.

Not surprisingly, many people ask me if the incidents I related in the first book—and am about to relate in this sequel to *The Happy Hooker*—are really true. They insist I must have exaggerated or fantasized a lot of it to make the

book a commercial success. They can't believe I could have
lived through all of those weird experiences. Well, I did—
and I was honest enough to reveal them without shame.

Actually I had originally intended to write my book as
"X"—*a la The Sensuous Woman* by "J" and *The Sensuous
Man* by "M"—but it now made great sense to take advantage of the worldwide publicity given my testimony for
the Knapp Commission. Besides, my profession was not
precisely a secret anymore. And, probably most important,
by using my name, the book would be identified with a real
person and my ability to promote it would be enormously
enhanced.

If I do have any serious cause for reflection about what
was revealed in the first book, it deals with my parents and
my early youth. And, yes, the business with my brother-in-
law. And, yes, bow-wow, the doggy scene! I thought it was
playful. Some people were shocked. That's their problem.
At least I haven't heard from the American Kennel Society
or the ASPCA.

However, I really do sincerely regret a certain amount
of embarrassment the book has caused some of my relatives. These things happened a long time ago, and far
away from America, but the attention the book received
brought it to my family's attention and made my long-held
secrets public knowledge, even in South Africa where, I
knew, the book was sure to be banned. So the irony about
the book's success is that if I'd known it would do so well, I
probably wouldn't have been so frank about my family
affairs. My sister read about the book in the South African
newspapers and almost divorced her husband. But they're
okay now. And, closer to home, my parents forgave me
because they know the kind of honest straight-forward person I am; and of course they were so relieved that I'd
pulled out (I can resist lots of men but never a chance to
pun) of my previous occupation.

Speaking of childhood experiences, Doctor Sigmund
Freud, the old couchmaster himself, pointed out that in
order to judge or evaluate adult behaviour, you must study
a person's youthful experiences. So when I look at someone
like my ex-fiancé, Carl, who everyone (except me) agrees
was a lousy son of a bitch, well, I can feel sorry for a man

like that. This poor bugger has no soul and no awareness of himself—he simply *has* to think of himself as a superman who can do no wrong, who has no flaws. But a man like this is basically insecure and unhappy because he doesn't know how to love, or be loved, because he grew up in a loveless atmosphere.

At least I know I'm different in that department. I knew as a child what it was to be loved. In fact, sometimes I think I was loved too much. My mother used to treat me like her little baby chick, and even now she would like to treat me like a teenager. She certainly means the best for me; but too much affection or pampering isn't good for you. You have to grow up on your own and learn to live with yourself. That's why I ran away from Holland in the first place. I guess I just outgrew the tender loving care. But don't get me wrong—I'm all for making love! That's what makes my world go round.

Which brings me to one of my favorite topics. Psychiatrists and psychologists—particularly Dr. David Reuben—seem to see prostitutes as poor deprived girls from broken families who turn to hooking as an escape from reality. *Merde,* as the French say. One can't make such broad generalizations. To judge a prostitute, you have to be familiar with the intelligence and personality of the girl and exactly what her background was. In my case, I certainly didn't come from a deprived, broken home. My parents didn't neglect me or fail to give me affection. Quite the opposite! And I'm not taking revenge on men, either. (Although there *are* a few swine to whom I wouldn't mind giving a genteel clout on the head.) And, as I'm going to point out in this book, there are many, many girls like me who didn't get into prostitution because they were outcasts of society.

Ah, *this* book. As in *The Happy Hooker,* I've written it in the first person, as though I'm talking to the reader as a friend—a personal, even intimate, conversation. I also have tried to make it as truthful and exciting as possible. As you may have suspected, there haven't been very many dull moments in my life since I finished writing *The Happy Hooker.* "Expect the unexpected," as it says in the New York subway system.

So . . . on to the continuing adventures of the new me, the ex-Happy Hooker. I'm no longer playing for pay, but in the grand tradition—the play must go on!

PREFACE

TORONTO, October 1972—I am temporarily residing in this lovely Canadian city with its friendly, hospitable people. I have come here to appear on several television programs—in particular a major discussion show called "Under Attack," where I debated my book both with a panel and with what seemed like the entire student body of Waterloo University—and to complete this book.

Nearly a year has gone by since I delivered the manuscript of *The Happy Hooker* to my publisher. And this book deals with part of that year—a period that was part triumph, part disaster, but certainly never boring.

In the beginning it was a bit difficult to get used to phones which did not keep ringing till the early morning hours, to a few friends visiting instead of the small hordes of visiting firemen, to a good night's sleep instead of a long, *hard* day-long night with only four hours of actual sleep. But with the friendly cooperation of the New York law enforcement Establishment, the earnest Internal Revenue Service, and the amicable Immigration Department, a little spice soon came into my life. Then came my wild publicity trek through America, very nicely spiced with private encounters. Then, too, Xaviera—the ex-Happy

Hooker—is just a little capable of putting her own brand of
spice into her life. . . .

This, then, is what my new book is all about. An entire
lifetime lived in half a year. A lifetime that ended with my
rude departure from the United States, accompanied by
dozens of journalists and other media people who literally
followed me step by step from my penthouse apartment to
my plane for Amsterdam. That night I was on at least five
New York television stations, saying an unwilling goodbye
to America with my much-quoted last words: "I am leaving
as a lady of the night, but would like to come back as a
lady."

But, as the British say, "Not to worry." I've learned to
enjoy my new freedom. And let it be, let it be, as a certain
quartet of British gentlemen has advised. Xaviera Hollander, free as a wind-blown nymph, will continue to have
her own say, will keep on communicating with the people
she loves. Differently now. Not by supplying girls. Rather
by supplying stories—entertaining stories and, hopefully,
educational at times. Some of these stories will be sexily
educational. Others educationally sexy. Others are intended
to strike your funny bone. And others get you where you
live—in your heart of hearts, your soul of souls, wherever
it is we must all live . . . together.

I. A NEW LIFE

THE HAPPY HOOKER HOOKED

It happened again. Love came into my life. And at just the right time. I was getting slightly bored in my retirement.

I'd been invited to a party given by Polly, who was a good friend of mine although I'd only known her for about four months. She is a remarkable person, a woman with a phenomenal always-cheerful personality who jokingly calls herself "Auntie Mame." Whenever I felt depressed and wanted to be cheered up, I'd give her a call and she'd talk me into a happier mood with a good joke or humorous story.

Polly likes to describe herself in the following way: "I'm a legend, honey. I will never be too old, just as I never was too young. I'm just a legend. I am pure sex and I love to fuck faggots. I am flamboyant and an extremely good dresser. I just love sex and cock and men. I am the only woman alive who has ever fucked so many gay boys. If I were to have a son, I would definitely pop his cherry."

So it was no surprise that whenever I visited Polly's house, there was a gay atmosphere—with the accent on "gay," since Polly occasionally sends out some male prostitutes on a job and even in her free time associates mostly with gay boys, most of them young, stunning, professional hustlers. In other words, they work for either male or female madams. In her case, Polly manages to combine tender loving care for her "boys" with an amazingly astute business sense.

Polly is one of those ageless women. Not only is she young at heart but she has a fantastic body. Big boobs that are strong and firm as rocks, without the help of silicone. Amazing! She must be in her late forties, maybe even early fifties. I don't think she herself is gay, although with her short, blonde hair and her twinkling blue eyes, she could easily be mistaken for a handsome "butch." In any case, she has never approached me, nor I her. I respect her as a friend and get far more turned on to her as a fun person to be with rather than as a love object.

This party to which I'd been invited was a so-called "picture party," where Polly was to show slides and color pictures taken during her two-month vacation through Europe the previous summer. I invited my steady boyfriend, Larry, who has been with me for the last three years. Larry, a forty-three-year-old straight Jewish businessman, seemed a bit hesitant when I told him that there would be at least twenty-five faggots rallying around good old Polly.

The party was kind of fun, with Polly's small army of cute gay boys jumping all over the place, jeering and heckling as they watched themselves in odd poses in Italy, Austria, and Yugoslavia. Polly was not only the tour guide for this group of gay blades but also the only female member of the party. This entourage must have turned a few heads on the Continent.

After a while, though, I was getting a mite weary of all the pictures of gay Vienna and I started looking around the room to see if there was anyone there who might be worth talking to—anyone who wasn't being enthralled by the slides being projected on the screen. Sitting in one of the big fluffy chairs was, to my surprise, a very good-looking—and masculine-looking—man. He was a big man, well-built, and his very manner seemed to command respect. I soon learned from Polly that this handsome gent was her private lover—a fireman from Queens—and just as straight and square as they come. He was a devout Catholic, and after every night spent in Polly's bed, he went straight to confession.

In any case, he was being admired by all the slim-hipped queers and appeared quite pleased when Larry and I introduced ourselves to him and began a conversation. He even seemed to be flirting with me a little, and Polly came over and asked if she could speak with me privately for a moment. Since she'd already answered my inquiries about who the good-looking man was, I was sure now she was going to tell me to keep hands off. But no, not crazy wonderful Polly! Instead she told me that her fiery fireman managed to spout fire six times within two hours and that he was shaped like a horse. And that I should definitely try him!

This invitation and information certainly kindled my interest in her fireman and his wonderful hose, but I found, after chatting with him some more, that he simply wasn't that interesting. There are times when men can turn me off in a minute, and this was one of those times. Anyhow, since there was no fire in my pants, I preferred to stick to good old Larry.

The time passed slowly and the slides continued to be shown—seemingly an endless array of slides. Despite my growing boredom, or maybe because of it, I almost did a double-take when Polly appeared on the screen, stark naked, riding on top of a gorgeous, sun-tanned Don Juan from Spain. She was riding him as though she planned never to let go. Her breasts covered his eyes, his nose, and half his face, although another shot showed his romantic big hazel eyes admiring this wild woman in action.

Another shot showed Polly getting out of the shower, grasping her young friend's enormous penis, which was protruding out of the yellow towel wrapped around his sun-tanned body. The gaping crowd of young men really got inspired, screaming and laughing, by this shot. They all pointed at Polly doing her thing.

"Wow, where did you pick up that cutie pie, Polly?"

"Wish I had his prick up my ass!"

"What did you do-oooo to him? You spoilt him, he'll never want to make it with the boys again."

"I wish my cock was as big as his. Gosh, and I thought I was tremendous down there. Oh . . . if only I could suck his cock for just a second!"

"Polly, you never stopped, did you? You had more fun and action than any of us."

As the evening wore on, Polly, in her expensive Pucci outfits or else bare-assed as a new-born baby, continued to parade through another four dozen pictures—elegant and charming, dressed or undressed.

As I sat between the soft pillows on her couch, I observed an attractive, young, Latin-looking lad sitting in a corner, making hand gestures to another man who looked to be in his forties. At first I thought they were using deaf and dumb language in order not to disturb the other people watching the pictures. I couldn't quite make out what was happening. Then I began to realize that they *were* deaf mutes. A loving couple who'd met at a school for the deaf and dumb, as I later found out.

By this time I'd become so intrigued by the sign-language conversation of those two men that I got up and joined them. They seemed delighted by the attention and before very long had taught me a few of their gestures. Soon we had a regular "silent conversation" of our own going on. It was the best part of the evening and would have been at many a livelier party. The party itself had been something of a drag, ending with a big cat fight over who owned what slides or pictures, but I'd long remember my two deaf-mute friends.

A few days after the great slide show, Polly and I decided to get together again. Larry came along, but the minute I entered her apartment my eyes centered on a young boy moving restlessly around the place. I suppose he was about nineteen. He had an innocent, yet finely masculine, face. His hair was brown and straight—long over his forehead but cut short in the back and around his ears, meticulously cut, almost like a soldier's. He moved like a young stallion. In a brief moment I realized that I really could dig this guy.

As it turned out, David was twenty-one and was indeed in the army. He came from Tennessee and I immediately fell in love with his crazy, hillbilly accent, something I wouldn't usually dig. David was soon to be discharged from

the service after spending a tour of duty in Vietnam, where
he had been wounded in the arm.

Electricity. David kept staring directly at me with his
lovely big hazel eyes and it didn't seem to matter to him
that Larry and Polly were watching the two of us. It might
have become awkward, but we soon had a big discussion
going about where to go for dinner. Larry and I had intended to stay in the neighborhood since it was a cold
evening, but David was now insisting that we go to the
Adam's Apple on First Avenue, where they supposedly had
the best roast beef and steaks in town for the least money.

We apparently all decided that David's opinion about a
restaurant demanded serious attention, and although we
tried to argue him out of going to a restaurant so far from
the apartment, he had his way and we finally agreed to his
choice. David, it turned out, had a car, and that promised
to make the cold weather less of a problem.

It was a wild ride to the Adam's Apple. The car needed
a new muffler and David drove like a dedicated maniac in
his beaten-up reconditioned red Ford. And I later learned
that he drove so crazily that a few times he'd actually
eluded police who were chasing him for speeding.

Anyhow, if David's driving was one kind of surprise, his
choice of restaurant was another. The Adam's Apple turned
out to be a lovely restaurant, decorated like a park. There
were trees all over, plus some artificial greenery. The seats
were made out of tree trunks. There was a giant buffet
table where you helped yourself to salads and dressing,
and the roast beef served at the table was the best I'd eaten
in a long time. The clientele was basically young, in their
twenties and thirties, and a pleasant crowd to be amongst,
quiet, but obviously enjoying the meal and the place.

At one point, David was just sitting there in his grey
slacks and checkered shirt, over which he wore his olive
drab military field jacket, while Polly was whispering "sweet
nothings" (or dirty thoughts) into his ear. Larry and I
continued our meal, but I was feeling a familiar warmth
creep through my body and I suddenly was aware that I
felt very jealous of Polly. It was the way she fondled him
that bothered me and I remembered how, earlier that evening, she had told me how often they made love. I secretly

hoped she had been lying, even though she was a lovely and gracious woman. I thought: "How can he do it? Doesn't he find her slightly ridiculous? A woman her age, old enough to be his mother."

My wishful thinking was disturbed, and I became even more upset when a lovely young brunette walked over to our table. She greeted David warmly and, apparently just kidding around, hugged and kissed him from behind his chair. He grinned broadly and got up to continue their embrace. As I watched the girl and David embrace, my mood changed—I no longer had nightmare fantasies about David making it with Polly, fondling those big boobs of hers. Now I turned to Polly and began to whisper in her ear, trying to find out what David and this girl meant to each other. Polly had no bright ideas on the subject, nor did Larry, who wasn't at all interested in David's behavior. Interestingly enough, we both were ready to condemn him as being completely unfaithful, but all he'd actually done was to kid around with the girl.

But, my God . . . how I desired that boy, David. I loved everything about him—his wide square shoulders, his tallness, his wonderful high cheekbones, and his funny boyish conversation. I recalled Polly offering me her fireman, but I'd refused since I wasn't attracted to him. Ah, how different it was this time!!!

After David's lovely young friend had finally left, with a cheerful *"Ciao"* to all of us, Polly and I breathed a sigh of relief. Our baby boy had been saved, after having almost been stolen from the aging Polly and the mature Xaviera, both of whom were determined to give him further lessons in sex education . . . that is, if he needed any.

Fortunately for me, this night Larry had to leave early to see some people on business matters. While he knows how I love to seduce young boys, he didn't realize how much I'd been turned on by David. So far as I knew, nobody else guessed my feelings except, surely, Polly. David certainly didn't have any idea of how I felt about him. He seemed basically a conservative, square kid and not terribly perceptive—but that's precisely what turned me on so tremendously. His innocence fairly cast a glow about him. With Polly he'd had an almost doglike obedience—to this boy she was an absolutely marvelous person and everyone else faded into limbo when he was with her.

However, as it happened he was also very proud, and this pride of his became obvious very soon. When Larry had left, David called for the check, and I offered to pay half because I didn't want David to pay the entire bill. He was adamant. He'd suggested the restaurant. Still, I discreetly pushed a ten-dollar bill under his plate, and he accepted it. I knew the poor kid didn't have much money and what little he did have had to last him long enough to drive his car back to Fort Campbell, Kentucky, to get his discharge from the service.

David offered to drive Polly and me home, but of course not in that order. On the way home David once again drove like a complete jackass and I got very nervous and asked him to take it a little bit slower. But it didn't do any good. I nearly had a heart attack every few blocks as he screeched around corners or zipped through red lights, constantly alternating between the gas pedal and the brake.

On the other hand, despite my genuine fright, I was getting more and more turned on by David. My own youth —those "I don't give a damn" days—seemed far behind me as I drove with this beautiful young nut with his big childlike eyes and perfect, sensuous mouth. He was driving this car as though he were riding a horse in a cowboy movie, enjoying the hell out of it.

Suddenly, somehow, his very craziness at the wheel made him as desirable as he was cuckoo, and I stopped being so afraid. And since Polly was sitting comfortably in the back seat, I put my hands in David's lap and I felt his cock pushing against his woolen trousers. I was astonished by its size. It felt almost as thick, or even thicker, as my wrist. It was hard to believe.

Still, I was dropped off at my apartment and David drove off with Polly, now in the front seat and probably feeling the hell out of him—just as I'd done. I went upstairs, sad, but somehow knowing I hadn't seen the last of young David. I sure hadn't. An hour later he was ringing my doorbell. I embraced him—just old friends, you know —and invited him inside. I didn't ask him about Polly, and he didn't offer any information.

We clicked right off. I poured him a soft drink. We talked and admired the panoramic view from my apartment, the twinkling lights of Manhattan by night, a city looking so peaceful and beautiful. My apartment really offered a serene study of the usually bustling city and we both grooved on it.

We played a lot of records that night. I recall that the music of Astrid Gilberto, in particular, put us both in a very tender frame of mind. We danced for a while, completely enthralled with one another, and then we slowly moved toward my bedroom. My Cardin sheets were fresh and clean and inviting; my "black" neon light accentuated the multicolored posters and paintings on the walls. The white phone next to my bed was amazingly quiet that night, as though trained to shut up when I wanted it to. When David wasn't clinging to me like a baby, he was following me around like a little puppy. He seemed to worship me, and my ego soared. I need to be needed. Who doesn't. . . ?

When I undressed him, I saw how truly gorgeous his body was. He had an almost hairless chest, with a strong torso and sinewy arms. His belly was completely flat and his legs were long and muscular. His penis was magnificently large, bigger than I had seen in quite some time. The head looked almost as big as my fist.

We decided to take a shower together. I loved rubbing his body with my favorite men's soap, Aramis. "Up, up, up," I told him, as he lifted his arms so I could soap his armpits thoroughly. By this time, he was clean twice over, but I loved just standing under the shower with him. My shower stall had become a cozy little room with a glass door separating me and David from the rest of the world. I massaged his hard cock and got it all soapy. It was so tremendous I could hardly hold it in my hand. He took his hard-on and rubbed it against my buttocks for a little while, pushing it in between my legs while embracing me gently, the water running down our bodies. He then turned me around and taking his huge cock in one hand, rubbed it against my pubic hair, which was full of soap lather. My passion soared. I was so eager to make love to him.

We ran out of the shower and got into bed, not even bothering to dry off. David was very gentle and certainly not as naive or innocent as he appeared to be. He turned out to be one of my most exciting lovers, extremely knowledgeable, and I quickly gave up my ideas about teaching this kid anything about the art of making love.

He caressed me gently, yet firmly, and kissed me all over my body, sending chills racing through my entire being. He spread my legs and put his head between them. I went into ecstasy! He planted his strong shoulders under my thighs and held me tightly as his mouth sought its way through my lower lips of desire. I felt myself becoming moist, so moist. My body was warm and tingling. My nipples stood erect as his supple fingers and skillful tongue found my clitoris. I knew I was about to come—oh, *how* I was about to come! My legs clamped around his head and my body almost went out of control. I screamed from utter joy, and I came and came and came, my thighs holding his face almost inside my body.

Exhausted, I softly pushed his head away with my hand and lay beside him. I felt a bit embarrassed about letting myself go as much and as quickly as I had. I wiped his mouth and cheeks, moist with my juices, with the back of my hand. I guess every woman at the point of climax gets a bit embarrassed when her vagina becomes a veritable "Niagara Falls of love juices."

After we'd relaxed for a while, it was my turn to please him. I fondled and kissed his nipples and his navel and his groin and, eventually, I put my eager mouth around his big cock—it was so big I could barely contain much of it. But David didn't let me go down on him for long. He turned me around so that we were in a 69 position. I was still very sensitive from my first climax, but he was so gentle that it was even more delightful the second time. While caressing each other, I could feel his cock grow and move in my mouth, surely almost ready to explode and this, combined with his warm tongue arousing me, started my body shaking and quivering again, this time even more fiercely because I was even more turned on than the first time.

Incredibly aroused, I began licking the entire shaft of his penis and his balls, all the while my hand was stroking his buttocks and back. David made moaning sounds and I realized he was holding back, or at least trying to hold back, as long as possible. But I, who pride myself on my control, was once again out of this world. With David eating me so divinely, I had another sensational orgasm.

Now David turned me around and put himself into my body as though he'd always been there. What was particularly wonderful was that despite his being built so big, I didn't feel any pain because I was so well lubricated and aroused by him. Sometimes men who are very big are rough in bed; they can virtually bang your ovaries out. But not so my David, he was one of the gentlest lovers and, for a boy his age, very mature in bed. He knew instinctively what excited me, which parts of my body to touch, kiss, or lick.

When we first started to make love, he softly stroked the back of my neck with his strong but gentle hands. He kissed my neck and caressed my back and my lower spine and my buttocks. But what I remember so vividly was his being inside of me; he filled me up completely and his movements were so graceful. He lifted my body up and penetrated even deeper inside me. I felt I was in Seventh Heaven revisited, when suddenly he slipped out of me, causing me to beg him to stay inside.

But our bodies didn't desert one another for long. Seconds after he had pulled out of me, he turned me on my stomach and put two big pillows under my belly. I rested on my knees with my bottom up in the air (semi-dogstyle), my head and shoulders resting flat above the piled-up pillows. He moved behind me and put his knees between my legs and inserted that marvelous huge organ of his. This, by the way, is an absolutely divine position, except for the fact that you are not able to face your lover or hold his body. It does, however, afford you every other exciting feeling. I clutched the pillows that were spread to the left and right of me, and when we reached our climax simultaneously, I screamed for joy and pleasure. I grabbed one of the other pillows on the bed and bit into it and almost ripped it apart. David's nails were digging into my hot flesh and I loved the momentary pain it gave me. I felt his cock throbbing and my body so hot and wet inside from his semen.

I moved the pillows from under my belly and we both

lay back exhausted, yet ecstatic, still caressing one another. The nicest things about making love are the emotional build-up before and the extreme contentment afterwards. If those are perfect, then you can be assured that the act of love has been something more than just a good fuck. David smoked a cigarette, slowly blowing the smoke into the warm room. I got up and got us some apple juice. Completely satisfied, we turned off the lights and turned on our right sides in a close embrace. David put his arms around my shoulders, with his face against the back of my head. We fell asleep like two little kids, with our bodies curved in an almost embryonic position—legs curled up, heads bent forward, and his arms around mine.

The next morning, we awoke in an extremely good mood —no temper tantrum for either one of us. I made breakfast. Mmmmm . . . did I ever make breakfast . . . tons of waffles with butter and jam and bacon, black coffee for David, and orange juice for me.

While we ate, I yearned to ask him a few things about his relationship with Polly and if he had any involvement in her gay scene. But after our tender night together, I certainly didn't believe that "my David" would be a male stud in Polly's stable, servicing men and Polly on the side.

As though he could read my mind, David himself brought up the subject and denied being anything but a friend of Polly's. As we pursued the subject a bit, he did seem to know an awful lot of her boys and also several male madams, such as Joe Roberts and Bob Lang.

I'd met Bob Lang on several occasions. He owns two tremendous Great Danes who've been trained to perform sexually with men. Besides being moneymakers, these dogs are extremely devoted to him and would attack anyone if the occasion called for it.

Bob, although several years older than David, had come from the same town in Tennessee, and that's how David happened to know Lang, David told me, apparently a bit embarrassed to speak about their relationship.

He told me he could never be a male prostitute because the thought of making it with a man revolted him. If ever he got involved in such a situation, the most he'd let a man do was to suck his cock; he'd refuse to have any men fuck him up the rear end, and he'd certainly refuse to blow another man.

David clearly wanted to change the subject and began to tell me about his childhood. He had been a sensitive and high-strung youth but not much of a student. When his parents offered to send him to college, he enlisted in the army. But before he went into the service, he met and fell head over heels in love with a seventeen-year-old girl. Since it was his first love affair, he rushed headlong into marriage. He was only eighteen himself, and shortly after he married the girl, he went into the army. On weekends, he'd come home and make love to her all weekend long. One weekend she told him she was pregnant. Instead of being upset, David was terribly pleased because he loved children and the thought of being a father filled him with happiness. Nine months later, his wife gave birth to a healthy, handsome little boy, and David's face positively glowed when he described his feelings at seeing his tiny son for the first time.

When the child was four months old and David was home on a weekend pass, his wife sobbingly confessed to him that the baby was not his. She'd had an affair with his best friend, who was also in the army, and since David's schedule and his friend's didn't overlap, she managed her cheating very well. She swore the affair was over. Even though David was deeply hurt by her revelation, he forgave her because of his love for her and for the baby, his real son or not. Yet the very next time David came home, having unexpectedly gotten a weekend pass, he caught them together in bed.

There was the real father of the child David loved so much, screwing the wife he loved so much. David, to this day still bothered by the memory of this scene, said that if he had had a gun with him at the time, he would have shot the two of them in their love bed and then shot himself. I could well believe him. Luckily for him, and everyone else concerned, there was no gun available, so David managed to control himself after a big scene, which ended with him insisting upon a divorce. Within a few months the marriage was over legally, and David had to live with the fact that he'd been cheated so badly. No son—and no marriage.

To add to his troubles, the army sent him to Vietnam shortly after his divorce, but he didn't give a damn any more. Since nothing was keeping him in America, he was almost glad to fight in the jungles of Southeast Asia. He became a man there, and in one of several heavy skirmishes he was badly wounded in his left arm. However, thanks to good medical treatment, the only reminders he has of Vietnam are some kind of interesting scars on his left arm and hand.

So this had been the coming-of-age of young David, who'd quickly grown from boy to man, and had certainly suffered more than most boys his age. His parents had more or less disowned him because they adored his ex-wife and didn't believe the story of his bastard child. In any case, his ex-wife was telling two different stories. To some people, she declared that the child *was* David's, and to others, she denied it.

After David returned from Vietnam, but was still in the service at Fort Dix, he began to come to New York on weekends and this is where he bumped into Bob Lang, whom he had known back in Tennessee. He'd been Bob's guest on several weekends, David told me, and this was how he became friendly with Polly. I thought David was being a bit vague when it came to telling me about his friendship with Lang. He seemed to be concealing something, almost as if he didn't want to hurt me by telling me the truth . . . or was it merely my imagination?

By this time it was quite late in the morning, and I had an appointment to see the lawyer who handled my contract for *The Happy Hooker*. David and I got dressed and he dropped me off at the lawyer's office. We agreed to see each other again that night at about eleven.

I returned to my apartment several hours later and my answering service told me that Bob Lang had been calling and that I'd better return his call right away. Before returning his call, I was reminded of something from the night before. During dinner, Polly had said that Bob was giving an enormous party the following Wednesday, and he had the *chutzpah* to be charging ten dollars per person. This covered the entrance fee, booze, and food. Bob Lang, what a first-class creep! I couldn't stand him. He's a tall, fair-haired, homely jerk with mean blue eyes and a malicious gossiping tongue. Then I thought, "What the hell? I can ignore that creep and there'll be people there I'd like to see. So screw him and his ten dollars. I can afford his bloody entrance fee!" So without realizing it, I'd talked myself into going to his party. In fact, I'd go with David.

I picked up the phone, dialed the number I'd been given, and there was Bob in his best nasty-nice voice, inviting me to his party.

"Hi, Xaviera, how are you? Did you hear I'm giving a super party next Wednesday with all kinds of famous people, straight as well as gay? Listen, I want you to come, especially now that you're going to be a superstar when your book comes out. Oh, by the way, am I in your book? I hope you didn't use my real name. You didn't, did you?"

"No, darling, you're not in the book. You might be freaky, but not freaky enough to be mentioned. Thanks for inviting me to your party. I'll see if I can make it . . . I think I might. What time does it start, anyway?"

"Heaven's sake, didn't I tell you? It starts at five o'clock and the admission fee is ten dollars a head. Do you mind?"

"No, why should I? I just hope you don't get raided, because, officially, you're not allowed to charge admission to a party, unless you're a charity organization of some kind . . . Maybe it's a party for the Prevention of Cruelty to Animals? It isn't that, is it?"

"For God's sake, Xaviera, don't be such a bitch, will you? I've got to make a living, too, don't I?"

"How about your stud service and your superdogs? Don't they supply you with enough business? How is business anyway?"

"Yeah, man, it's tough. Nobody's got any money nowadays and I have to feed my two Great Danes steak every day."

"But, Bob, your rent costs you almost nothing. What do you pay for that crummy little pad of yours?"

"Would you believe it? This dump costs $280 a month!"

"So, a few tricks a week, and you've got your rent money. Mine costs $550 for three bedrooms and I have another one that costs $230. Believe me, that's a lot of bread. Besides, don't you have a roommate?"

"Sure, babe, but you're a rich lady with all the dough you got as an advance. Somebody told me it was one hundred thousand dollars. You've gotten all of it, haven't you?"

"No. I only got a percentage, which isn't too bad, but sure as hell Uncle Sam is going to take a good hunk of it. Besides, my business is dead."

He didn't say anything to this, so I added, "Oh, by the way, Bob, I met a friend of yours, a kid called David. I met him yesterday at Polly's . . ."

His response was a series of staccato questions.

"Yeah, what about him? He and I come from the same hometown. What do you know about him? Did you make it with him? Man, he's a faggot like all the rest of us!"

When he spat out these words at me, I actually felt myself shudder and, for a minute, I didn't say anything. Then I heard Bob yelling in my ear.

"Hey, babe, are you still there? What's the matter?"

"Nothing, nothing at all," I answered as coolly as I could manage. "I was just wondering. You mean to say that David is a fairy . . . he's a stud like all the boys I meet at Polly's? We're talking about the same David, aren't we? From Tennessee?"

"Yeah, man, he and I were weekend roomies for a while. He didn't know a soul here and when he got a furlough, he worked for me a couple of times, and besides . . . I liked the kid an awful lot myself."

Wow, was that some kind of insinuation—that he, that ugly bastard, and my gorgeous David were *lovers!* All of a sudden, I felt like puking at the thought that David made it with Bob and stuck that beautiful cock up Bob's . . . No, that couldn't be true, not after we'd made love so beautifully. David couldn't sleep with a bitch like Bob.

"Well, thanks for the information, Bob. I would have sworn the kid was straight . . ." I couldn't bring myself to tell him whether I'd made it with David or not. I just left it to his vivid imagination to figure out.

"Anyway, I'll see you at the party, if I can make it. Thanks again for inviting me."

I put the receiver back in the cradle of the phone and

at that moment, I didn't know what I was doing or why. I knew I had to settle this once and for all with David when I saw him later that night.

That afternoon Larry was up at the apartment, as usual, to take me out for an early dinner. Somehow, no matter what fights we have or little affairs I have on the side or how busy I once was with my clients, Larry has always been there in the late afternoon to take me out for a quick dinner. He's also done most of the food shopping for the apartment, which was really wonderful of him since I'm hardly the domestic type, and on Sunday mornings he would get up before me and make the best breakfast in the world. Well, we were just about ready to go out for dinner when the phone rang and it was Polly calling me. She began to yell and scream at me, something she'd never done before, and I thought to myself, "For crying out loud, what the hell does everybody want from me today?" I hadn't done anything wrong as far as I could see. All I did was ask Bob about David.

From what I could gather from Polly's ranting at me, Bob had completely reversed the conversation I'd had with him and was telling half of New York City that *I* said David was a faggot—that it's true, David *is* a faggot— but that I'd also told him other stories that were complete lies. Bob's garbage mouth had spewed out all kinds of stupid, malicious gossip, and Polly, who'd calmed down some by now (I'd given her straight answers to anything she asked me), warned me that Bob might try to take revenge on me because when David found out who'd been really spreading stories about him around the city, he'd be coming after Bob. Or else, he'd be coming after me with a vengeance.

It all sounded unreal to me, a vicious faggot circle-jerk, but I thought I understood what was really going on. Bob more than suspected that David and I had made it and he was bitchily jealous, so he was doing his best—which would be any other human being's worst behavior—to make David upset with me. He obviously was dying to sleep with David, and had been turned down.

Well, I told Polly I was "going to help stick Bob's plan up his rotten ass." David had to know the truth and he was going to be done with Bob for good now, hometown buddies or not. I was so concerned with Bob's ugly behavior that it really didn't occur to me that I was more or less admitting my affair with David to Polly, but she didn't pick up on it. Instead, she warned me again that I'd better watch out for Bob. She believed he was hoping somehow to get me in trouble with the police, and if that weren't enough, he might visit me at my place with his ugly fucking dogs. Polly also said she thought the guy was off his rocker and it would be in my best interest to stay far away from him. I agreed. Certainly going to his party would be a big "no-no." I didn't want to even be in the same city as that vicious schmuck!

About ten minutes after I'd spoken to Polly, the answering service rang and said that a gentleman had called while I was on the phone. The man said that it was urgent he speak to me. Well, despite my retirement, the service was under instruction never to give out my number—which was now strictly for friends—and of course, I knew who that "gentleman" was. It could be none other than the man of the hour, dear old Bob Lang. Who else?

Meanwhile Larry was wondering what the hell was going on since he had only followed one side of the conversation between Polly and myself. He had no idea of what had happened since yesterday when we all had dinner at the Adam's Apple. He didn't know I'd slept with David, or about all the intrigue that had come about as a result of my one-night "affair."

Before attempting to explain anything to Larry, I decided to return Bob's call. Why not? I had nothing to hide. Besides, I wanted to tell him to shut his filthy mouth. I couldn't let the matter rest there and wait until everything just blew over by itself. I called Bob at his apartment and before I even had a chance to say anything, he began to attack me with foul language.

"You bitch, you bull dike, you lousy, rotten chick! You've got a lot of balls to spread rumors around that David is a faggot and had an affair with me. You know I can make plenty of trouble for that kid, don't you? You fucking bitch!"

"What the hell are you talking about, Bob? All I know

is that Polly called me up, excited and angry because I was supposed to be spreading stories around that David is queer. Man, you don't know what you're talking about. The only person I talked to was *you* and if you recall, *you're* the one who called me. I returned your call, because you invited me to your lousy party. Remember? I haven't talked to anyone but you about David."

He tried to interrupt me, but I wasn't having any more of his crap.

"You've nothing better to do than put your slimy malice into other people's mouths and spread your disgusting lies all over town," I continued socking it to him. "I bet you told ten people who don't even know me, or anything about me, the story of how *I* called David a faggot.

"Mister, you're sick! I always thought you were a screwball, but now I know how sick you really are. Believe me, I don't want to have anything more to do with you and I hope you understand that you'd better shut your goddamn mouth."

He tried once again to interrupt what was rapidly becoming my tirade, but I stopped him by merely talking louder than he. I could play word games, too!

"Do you know that David is very upset? The only consolation is that he knows you said it, and not I. And I don't believe he was ever your lover. It's just your sick, lousy fantasy. You wish you could make it with David . . . You should be so lucky. Now you'll probably go back to Polly and tell her I said you and he were lovers. But I'll beat you to the draw, and call her myself. I'm not losing my friends because of you.

"And by the way, for your information, I *did* fuck David and it was really great. I don't usually discuss my private life with people like you, but I just wanted you to know. Believe me, that kid is no queer. You dig me?"

(Very brightly, I was saying all this in front of Larry.)

"You cunt, how dare you talk to me that way! You're a bigger bull dike than any chick I've ever met. You, you, you . . . You're a pervert, that's what you are!"

I asked him, "What the hell has that got to do with David being a faggot or not?"

"Everything!" he screamed in a shrill voice. "It means

that *you're* the one who's sick. You'll fuck anything, anything that walks, crawls or moves."

"So what?"

"So, plenty. Maybe David likes a piece of pussy once in a while, but he still prefers cock, baby, and he ain't gonna get it from me. He's not gonna get any business from me any more, thanks to you. Baby, believe me, you're gonna get yourself in a hell of a lot of trouble if you don't watch out. I know the kid's parents and I also know he's about to get an honorable discharge from the service. I will personally see to it that that discharge is not honorable. All I have to do is let the U.S. army know that David is gay, and I might as well let his parents know, too. So, girlie, it's *you* who better keep your big mouth shut." With these words, he slammed the phone down.

By this time, I was terribly upset and, to make matters worse, Larry started yelling at me about how stupid I was to get involved with a bunch of fairies, and how sick and cruel they were and more vicious than even the cops. I shut my mind off. I stopped listening to Larry and tried to think only of the wonderful moments I had had with David. I knew that David would choose me over that ugly bastard, Bob Lang.

I finally asked Larry to go. I loathe arguing. I felt sick and had a headache and without any further argument, Larry did leave. I could tell he was very hurt because I'd cheated on him and with a kid, at that. He knew he couldn't compete with a twenty-one-year-old boy, strong as a horse. The consolation he had was that David was probably a faggot, so my affair with him couldn't last very long. Oh, if he only knew how wrong he was to think this. The night I'd spent with David proved that he was no fairy, at least not where I was concerned!

At eleven that night, David called about our date. I told him to come right over and within fifteen minutes he was ringing my bell.

He looked so young and boyish and clean cut. He was carrying a gift for me—a record. He actually blushed as he handed it to me. His first present to me. It meant so much to him, and to me, too. It was his favorite record, he said, and I remember he'd played it several times when

we were dining at the Adam's Apple. A new album by
The Association. I realized how wrong I'd been when I
thought he was indifferent to me that night, because he
told me he'd wanted me the moment he'd met me at Polly's
apartment. He said he didn't want to hurt Larry or Polly
by showing how much he cared. After all, it wasn't very
often that Polly had a chance to seduce a boy who wasn't
completely gay. I kissed and hugged him. I'd missed him
so much this whole day. He made me forget all the aggra-
vation and terrible things which had happened to me. And
apparently he'd heard none of the garbage that was being
thrown around New York this day. Well, I wasn't about
to bring it up.

David walked over to the hi fi, removed all the records,
and put his on. We switched off the lights in the living
room, cuddled together in my large leather reclining chair,
listening to the words which enveloped us. He held my hand
and stroked my hair. After the day I'd had, it was so peaceful and lovely just to be close together. I remember the
words of one song so well. They gave us both a feeling
that they were written just about us—those lovely words
being sung in the darkness. We listened to them over and
over again, until they were inscribed on my heart.

Cherish is the word I use to describe
All the feeling that I have hiding here for you inside.
You don't know how many times I've wished that I
    had told you,
You don't know how many times I've wished that I
    could hold you,
You don't know how many times I've wished that I
    could mold you,
Into someone who could cherish me as I cherish you.

I began once more to feel how sensitive this boy was,
far more so than I'd realized. He might be only twenty-one,
but he seemed to have more depth and maturity than many
men twice his age. He really touched me.

We spent the night together and it was just as wonderful and satisfying as our first night. Just before we were
ready to doze off to sleep, I felt I needed that final reas-

surance, and I hesitatingly brought up the subject of studs and Bob Lang. I finally asked David outright whether he'd ever slept with Lang, or even worse, was he still having an affair with him? He gently laughed at me and pointed out what seemed obvious—if that were true, would he be here with me? He reminded me that he'd already told me that he'd been Bob's guest when he came to New York on weekend passes. He admitted that he knew Bob was crazy about him but he'd never let Bob touch him.

David had to leave the next day to get his discharge— his furlough would expire the next day—but he promised me he'd immediately return to New York and me. And he kept his promise.

The next weeks David and I were together almost every weekday night. He even had some clothes hidden in my second bedroom closet, underneath some winter coats so Larry, jealous as ever, wouldn't find out. It was so good to have David with me, although he always came in around midnight. He was, so he told me, working as a bartender in a gay bar—mostly because of his looks. But that didn't bother me because I certainly knew where he was spending his nights after work. In my arms. Between my thighs. Inside of me.

One day I took David shopping. I bought him a warm winter coat and made him throw his beloved army jacket away. After all, it was now winter and that thin coat didn't give him much protection against the weather. I also bought him a suit. He didn't have any clothes except for a pair of jeans and some old woolen trousers.

The next day, I told him to come out with me again, and we'd buy him a nice pair of boots. The ones he was wearing were five years old and were shabby and worn out. He was proud as a peacock as he skipped along beside me like a kid out for a treat. Finally he saw some great boots in the window of a store on Lexington Avenue in the Fifties.

It was a popular shoe store where—David couldn't have known this—they basically supply footwear for pimps. Most of their boots have high heels and come in wild, loud colors. But David was, after all, a kid from the sticks when it came to fashion, and he chose a pair of high brown boots, quite plain, with a medium-sized heel. He wore them proudly and looked very manly as he walked tall and swaggered out of the store. "Well," I said to myself, "there goes fifty dollars on plain old cowboy boots." Still, I enjoyed spending money on someone I cared for. What the hell, the kid didn't have any money. And anyway, why shouldn't I be nice to him? I was going to be seen with him, and I wanted him to look presentable. To be perfectly honest, it wasn't only for his sake I was doing all this but partly for my own ego.

The next day, I went down to Barney's—New York's largest clothing store for men—with Larry to buy him a Pierre Cardin suit. I'd promised to buy this present for him as soon as the book came out, but since I'd received some of the advance money several weeks before, I was going to keep my word in advance. The book wouldn't be out for some weeks yet. So while Larry picked out his suit, I went downstairs and bought some nice sport shirts for David. I knew he'd be pleased as well.

Larry didn't say anything, but I could see he was surprised when I came back later carrying a big paper bag under my arm. I'm sure he knew I'd bought something for someone else. Who, he wasn't sure. But I didn't care. After all, it was Christmas time, so why not make everybody happy? I don't ordinarily go on shopping sprees. By nature, I'm terribly thrifty and watch my money as though it's going out of style!

Despite the emotional complications with Larry, and I preferred not to think about them, I was really having fun living with David. We'd sleep late in the mornings, wake up and make marvelous love, then have breakfast. Later we'd go shopping or do errands. Whenever I had some personal or business matter to take care of, he'd become my private chauffeur and drive me around town in his magnificent Ford—at least the muffler had been fixed and he no longer drove the Ford as though it were the lead car at Le Mans—and take me to the doctor or dentist or my lawyer's or wherever. He'd find a parking place and sit downstairs and wait for me—faithful like a doggy—no matter how long it took.

Around four o'clock every afternoon, he would say

goodbye and go his own way. Where? I really never asked. Maybe intuitively I didn't want to be reminded of the fact that he might actually be hustling, although he still claimed to be a bartender. In that sense, I was adopting an ostrich mentality, hiding my head in the sand.

By this time, I had pretty well adjusted myself to the idea that David might be selling his body every now and then, but his extra activities didn't seem to prevent him from keeping it up up up with me, so I couldn't really complain.

Finally one night, David, as soon as he came home, blurted out that he hated all this deception, but he felt he had to earn his own money and not just live off my generosity. He was, he admitted, not only tending bar but was also doing some stud service, but certainly not through Bob Lang. It mostly happened through the bar and he tried to be selective but was performing other services than just being a joint to be copped.

He could see that this news didn't exactly make my evening, so he tried to cheer me up by telling me what he regarded as an amusing story. That evening he'd agreed to go off with a rather unattractive middle-aged gentleman and no matter what that gentleman did for him, David just couldn't get an erection. He should have walked away from this almost silly scene, he knew, but he hoped to earn enough money to buy me a really nifty present and he wasn't about to blow—pun intended—the arrangement he'd made.

I still wasn't being terribly amused by this tale of cocks at half-mast, but I did know that many homosexuals who hire boys through a male stud service absolutely insist on masculine-looking males and frequently the hired young men are really heterosexual. They service homosexuals to supplement their incomes—and I genuinely believed this to be so in David's case, although that didn't make me any happier with his chosen line of work.

I said as much at this point in David's story, and he tried to appease me by telling me that he usually asked his clients to have some girlie magazines in their apartments so he could get aroused by looking at them, instead of at the client.

Well, this particular session, the man had no helpful girlie magazines around, so David told him to mind his own business—*that* had been hard for some time now—while David got something he needed.

The "something" he needed was a small group of nude Polaroid pictures of me he'd taken a few days earlier, and he went over to his coat pocket and took them out. The client was still on his hands and knees—as David had ordered him to be—and he told him to really bend forward, so he couldn't see what David was doing. And what David was doing was to use my pictures to get an erection. (It's not the greatest compliment I've ever had, but it did strike me as pretty funny.) Thus, with an erection finally in hand and with his eyes closed, he fantasized that he was balling me instead of buggering some old fart with his ass sticking up in the air, and finally was able to do what he'd been hired to do.

I still wasn't about to cheer David for his ingenuity at achieving erections, but I really couldn't get angry with him either, so I ordered him into the shower because of the idea of sleeping with him after he'd gone the Hershey Bar route hardly turned me on. And this night was the first time I didn't take a shower with David, although we'd showered together almost every single night he'd stayed with me.

We made love that night, but I refused to do it from the rear because of David's earlier activities that day. I guess I was also refusing to take David at face value any longer.

The next day, David said he wanted to revisit his hometown to try and make up with his parents and could I lend him a hundred dollars so he could buy some decent presents for them? I really didn't know if he was lying again, but I preferred to believe in his honesty at least this one last time and gave him the money. He promised to return all the money I'd loaned him and I said I was sure he would. It was beginning to snow, and since his decrepit old Ford was hardly a snowmobile, I suggested he get an early start to beat the storm. After all, it was a long way to go. He said he'd be back in a month. I said I'd look forward to his being back. And of course I never saw him again.

Some time later, Polly told me that David had never been a bartender. My innocent David turned out to have been one of Manhattan's most sought-after male studs, who certainly didn't need any financial support from me. I received this news without any great rancor—and without too much surprise, either. Life plays funny tricks, to be sure, and there were so many good times with David to remember.

Another experience richer, I could look back at the whole affair with a smile on my face, remembering the irony of the Happy Hooker getting hooked on a gorgeous young man who was both more—and far less—than he seemed to be.

THE GIRLS IN MY LIFE

I guess there's many a famous retired stage actress or perhaps a former femme fatale of the silver screen who has included somewhere in her memoirs a chapter devoted to "The Men in My Life." This thought occurred to me while reading a fairly recent biography of the original sweater girl herself, Lana Turner. In this case, the inspiration may have been the fact that Ms. Turner—at this writing—has shed at least six husbands, and was once married to Robert Eaton, a young author I happen to know quite well.

Quite candidly, I sometimes identify with these women because I, too, am a retired celebrity of some kind. Being a glamorous—and notorious, if that's your bag—madam surely made me as famous as many a movie actress, but I, unfortunately, was not retired from my profession because of my wish to do so or because of outdated fashions or fading looks. My enforced retirement came about because of corrupt police actions and because America has antiquated moral codes which also happen to be law.

Also, being foreign certainly didn't help me any, although my "differentness" did help me tremendously when I was working my way up to the pinnacle of my profession.

I'd tried to be an Old World Charmer, and I flatter myself I succeeded somewhat in that regard.

However, to return to our retired actresses and their memoirs, whereas they might commemorate the menfolk in their lives, I'd like to pay homage to "The Girls in My Life." Rereading my first book the other day—it's awful of me, but I keep rereading it and liking it; I'm just like the Alka Seltzer commercial (!)—I became acutely aware that little attention had been paid to the girls I'd known best who usually had done their fucking best to help me become successful. And I'm ashamed of this omission amongst all the emisions.

So, I've decided that in this book I must devote some space to the provocative topic of the girls in my (former) life. Each girl will get a short section devoted to her—a sub-chapter, if you like—and each section, with perhaps one obvious exception, is a very special "thank you" note from me.

MU8 ---8

This story is about a telephone number that had been the hottest telephone line in New York City. It's the number men called when they wanted to get laid! It is, of course, the so-called "hot line" I bought from Madeleine when I first became a madam.

Readers of my first book may recall my description of a police bust. The police usually grabbed all the phones and cut the lines. Then I'd have to use connections within the phone company to get new phones installed.

In July, 1971, my most important phone line, MU8 ---8, was busted. This number had been in Madeleine's possession for eight years. She must have had good connections with the phone company!

Some months after the bust, I decided to call that number to see who'd inherited it. I dialed it and a high-pitched voice answered, "Hellooooo." At first I wasn't sure whether it was a male or a female at the other end, but the voice became more masculine as we talked and it was obvious to him that the caller was female.

"I'm sorry to disturb you," I said, "but my name is Miss Hollander and I'm the previous owner of your telephone number. I hope having it hasn't caused you any inconvenience."

"Oh, I *know* what you mean!" he said, giddily.

"I realize you must have had a lot of calls meant for me."

"Oh, you ain't kidding, lady. Up until all hours of the night I'm getting calls like crazy—and almost always from men!"

"Sir, let me explain. I don't know whether you've read the book that's been out since February 1st called *The Happy Hooker?* Anyhow, I'm the author and maybe you'll recognize my name—Xaviera Hollander. And you now have my old phone number."

"Oh, yes, *Hollander*. I've seen your name and picture in the papers. Oh, my, I never dreamed I had *your* old number!"

"Well, anyway, you know by now the kind of business I was involved in."

"Oh, yeah, I figured out—*whoever* it was the number had belonged to—well, all, or mostly all, the calls were between eleven at night and three in the morning. You see, you're lucky I'm a night owl."

For the next few minutes we discussed what a "flourishing trade" I must have had, and I felt a little hesitant about asking him my next question. Which was going to be, would he mind referring certain people—mostly people who'd become good friends through our business dealings —to me? I wanted to keep in touch with them and the phone company wasn't about to give them my new number.

"Sir," I said, "I'm afraid I didn't catch your first name."

"It's James, and if youre going to ask me what I think you're going to ask me, the answer is yes."

"Is this going to be hard on you? You know, until I've told everyone who should have it my new number, you may still get calls in the middle of the night. I'd hate for you to be awakened one night and become so aggravated that you feel like slamming the phone down. I wouldn't blame you, of course, but I just don't want it to happen. I've been out of touch with some of these people for a while and they may not realize the number's not mine anymore. . . ."

"Well, don't worry, Miss Hollander, I happen to be 'night people' and I'm always up late, late, late—usually to three or four in the morning—and that's the latest your friends call. Occasionally it's been inconvenient, but I manage to spring up and pick up the phone . . . in any case, I'll never slam the phone down. Don't worry about it. Honestly. . . ."

So we talked a bit more, and I told him to pretend that he was my butler, or even Madeleine's butler if for some strange reason the call should be for her. Actually Madeleine had had a butler, which was what gave me the idea, and I didn't think anyone would be startled to hear a man's voice answering what was supposed to be my number.

"Forget it," James said. "Most of them hang up the second they hear a man's voice."

I felt he was being terribly nice, to say the least, and I wanted to do something to repay him for the inconvenience I'd caused him, so I awkwardly posed this question.

"James, as you know I'm out of the business, but I still keep in touch with a few of my girls, and could I—as a token of my appreciation—send you some gorgeous creature to . . . well, you two kids could work it out . . . but I just want you to know it's for free—my 'Dutch treat'— because it'd be like a gift for all the inconvenience you must've gone through. . . ?"

There was silence on the other end and I knew I'd pressed the wrong button. Of course I hadn't seen him, and voices can be deceiving, but suddenly I felt I'd offended him by even mentioning a girl.

"Oh, I'm really sorry, Miss Hollander," he finally said, "but you couldn't have known that I'm with the ballet and, well, really, I'm doing a great deal of exercise and . . . well, I'm *really* not in the mood to see any girls. But, *honestly*, thanks so much for the offer!"

"Well, I just thought. . . ."

"Oh, listen, I don't know *how* to refuse decently . . . It might sound like an insult, but really, I don't mean it that way . . . well, I'm just not into *that* right now. I'm—oh, geez, I'm really not interested in girls . . ."

Ahem. The moment he said "I'm with the ballet" I got the message . . . Still, he'd sounded like such a cute guy! I was tempted to say, "Don't worry about it, baby, I'll send you a boy," but there'd be no point in that. After all, he had been kind and his sexuality was his own business.

So I said, "Well, some day if you feel like it, stop by and have a drink. And if you like, I'll give you an autographed copy of the book." He seemed grateful to have the conversation over, and we left it that way—I'd hear from him when he had time to come by and say hello and have a drink.

A month went by and I more or less forgot about this phone call. True, some phone calls came through after being referred by James, but it didn't seem so unusual that casual friends were reaching me.

Then one day the phone rang in the afternoon and it was James. I didn't recognize his voice at first because it was very "gay"—almost distorted—and finally I had to ask him, "What's the matter? What's your problem?"

He seemed hesitant to continue, and then it all spilled out. "You know, Miss Hollander, the ballet business has been awfully bad and I haven't had any chance to do any theatrical ballet. I've been going to school and doing my exercises and to make ends meet, I've been driving a cab. And I'm so sick of it. I've been driving twelve hours a day but I don't make more than fifteen or twenty dollars and I'm starving. I have a very expensive apartment to keep up, you know . . . well, Miss Hollander, can I come by and see you for a few secs. . . ?"

"Of course, come right over and we'll talk." It was obvious that whatever he wanted, he wasn't going to talk about it over the phone.

Around half an hour later James arrived and I immediately knew I'd been right about his sexual preferences. He was blonde and feminine-looking, with brown eyes and light silky hair draped over his forehead. His face had a frightened look on it, made more evident by his very pale, almost bluish complexion. He looked slightly ill and I wanted to put him at ease.

"James, come on, take off your coat and relax. Make yourself comfortable. Do you want a drink? Some coffee? A cigarette?"

"Oh, no," he replied, "I don't want anything, really. I'm very happy to meet you."

Just then Larry came in from one of the other rooms, along with Rod, an old friend who is a real estate broker, among other things. (He's produced films and rock festivals, among his various enterprises.) Larry gave James a bone-crunching handshake—the poor kid almost fell through the floor—and Rod just sort of acknowledged him with a good-natured grin. Rod is a very swinging, good-looking guy in his early thirties and as soon as James' gaze fully took in Rod's good looks and physique, some color came into his face and he seemed more relaxed. If I can judge these things correctly, he immediately started flirting with Rod, who is about as heterosexual as you can get and who ignored all James' innuendoes.

We were all seated in my living room, having something to drink, but you could feel the tension in the air. I decided to let it all hang out.

"James," I said, "tell me—are you gay?"

Larry almost choked into the Coke he was drinking and Rod felt an overwhelming need to be in another room so he wouldn't fall apart with laughter. I suppose I might have been more subtle, but this was getting us nowhere. Before James could answer, Larry also excused himself, saying he had some phone calls to make.

It was just the two of us now—James and me—in the living room, and James shyly looked at me and answered, in a soft voice, "Yes, I am gay. . . ."

"James, I didn't feel I could ask you over the phone if you wanted me to send you a boy instead of a girl, but the offer still stands."

"Yeah, well, you know, that's the whole problem. I'm twenty-three years old and very emotional and I'm working at the dance, but I don't know—I seem to be a failure. I'd like to do something where I could make some money. . . ."

"Why are you looking at me? I'm a retired madam—I'm not running a house anymore—and so I can't help you on that score. I'd like to help you out but what can I do for you?"

"You know all those men who've been calling up? Some of them sounded so groovy. Isn't there something for me with some of those men?"

I didn't mean to be cross with him, but I blurted out,

"Listen to me—those guys are calling up with hard-ons in their pants for chicks! They're not about to go fuck guys or be fucked by guys."

James seemed stunned by my outburst, so I said, more calmly, "Look, wait a minute. Let me think about what I can really do for you . . . What do you really want to do? You seem like such a loner."

"That's it, you know. I'm such a romantic and I'd love to have a real boyfriend one day. Maybe some day some guy'll even keep me—because I hate driving those cabs. I never know my way around. I get lost and people get angry at me and tell me to shut off the meter and once I even got hit. Aw, it's such a shitty situation."

His eyes got misty and I genuinely felt sorry for him. The times that homosexuals really get to me is when they're being so sensitive and adorable and always getting themselves into trouble. Poor James—what a loser he was!

"Tell me honestly, James," I said, "what do you have in mind? Do you want to become a male prostitute, or what?"

James erupted with enthusiasm. "Uh . . . *yeah,* right on! Right on—that's it. You hit it right on the nose."

"Look, when you showed interest in the size of my business, you were obviously interested in the amount of money I was making. What are you looking for—love or money?"

"Yeah, well, I'd rather fuck somebody I really like, but since I need money so badly I'm willing to be a hustler. I think I can get it up twice or three times a day, providing it makes me a few more bucks than hacking a cab for twelve hours."

Okay, if that was what James wanted, I'd help him all I could without getting at all personally involved. I would, I told him, refer him to a couple of male madams I knew from the old days—not Bob Lang!—and the rest would be up to him. I would give him two numbers to call and my best wishes, but that was all.

"Go see them tomorrow. Look nice. Maybe even take a picture of yourself because that's what they like to have. Just introduce yourself and say you're a newcomer, and a friend of mine."

James seemed elated at this turn of events, which gave

me an idea. I knew a radio reporter—a good-looking black man named Matt—who is very "AC-DC." He can make it with a chick if he digs her, but he *loves* boys. Matt had been a "tester" for my gay boys. If I knew a guy wanted to become a stud, I'd call Matt and say, "Look, will you check him out. Is he big enough, is he strong enough? Is he nice enough?" Matt loved these "test sessions," and would give me the kind of knowledge I could never have from just looking at the guy in my living room.

So I suggested to James that he contact Matt first and see how he got along with him, and James said he would. He didn't waste any time in doing so because Matt called me the next day and said he'd "really balled" James, but that he was "very, very green and needed lessons." (*Consumer Report* couldn't have given me better service!) However, said Matt, he liked James and would take care of his new career.

Before I left the country I learned that James was thriving in his new profession—that he'd become a green young stud in whom older men were taking a particular interest.

Maybe he'll find one to keep him.

I hope so, for James' sake, since that's what he seemed to want most.

I wonder if he still gets calls for me.

I wonder if he's truly glad we met. After all, my phone number changed his life.

And so ballet's loss is buggery's gain. . . .

The Girls in My Life

SANDY: A Little Gypsy Blood
Never Hurts or, Mona Lisa Is
Alive and Well in Argentina!

I guess if I had to vote for one girl as the resident sexpot in my former organization, I'd give my vote to Sandy. Only nineteen, Sandy was a natural beauty from Argentina who didn't need make-up because she had it all. Long, luminous black hair. Great big brown eyes with natural long black lashes. High cheekbones. A youthful face which, with her childlike smile, made her seem the epitome of innocence. And a stunning figure. In my address book, I used a code system to describe the girls, and next to Sandy's name there was the notation "BB," meaning big boobs. The only girl who really topped Sandy in the breastworks department was a watermelon-sized creature who earned the notation "DDD," meaning three-dimensional, but Sandy's breasts were far more beautiful and she was a crowd-teaser—and a crowd-stopper—whenever she wore a low-cut dress.

But Sandy's great sexual appeal can't be explained merely by mentioning her beauty and great body. Much of it had to do with her manner—calm and serene. Any man going to bed with Sandy might believe he was seducing a vestal virgin. Some virgin! Sandy had a passionate interest in sex —typical of so many South American girls—and was a holy terror in bed. Men couldn't seduce Sandy—they were too busy keeping up with her! Her popularity was such that my other girls sometimes had to ask me to tell Sandy to leave the room so a regular customer would choose one of them.

Rather than being a vestal virgin, Sandy was more of a wholly-roller. Another explanation of her popularity is that she had a much less professional attitude towards our customers than most American girls. Sandy, quite simply adored, loved, enjoyed, dug, liked, was entirely compatible with the act of fucking.

While Sandy was all in favor of straight sex, she specialized in bi-sexual love, and many men were quite willing to spend double the usual amount in order to partake of a threesome. Sandy preferred playing the "butch" role and if the other girl wasn't turned on by a lesbian scene, all she had to do was lie back and let Sandy work her over with her snakelike tongue. Sandy was sure to turn the girl on and make her climax, and what began as a fake scene usually turned out a genuine little orgy. Our Sandy was a perfect combination of apparent innocence and obvious know-how, and most Johns got so excited watching the girls make out that they'd want to take part and finish the job. As soon as Sandy saw this, she would turn her full attention to the John and suck his erect penis with her ever-ready mouth. She would then throw her big, voluptuous body on top of his stiff cock and rock back and forth on it, going faster and faster, and when it was orgasm time, the bed itself made noises. This passionate girl was a real-live love goddess—the image of raw ecstasy with her long, black hair wet with perspiration, her face moist with exertion, her magnificent bouncing boobs. The male partner in her sex act, no matter how drunk or tired he might be, couldn't help but come from the force of her savage love-making.

Sandy had a boyfriend, Raoul, who was an attractive Argentinian boy of seventeen with pale features and dark wet eyes. Raoul looked almost as innocent as Sandy, yet wanted to work for me as a stud. I decided to "try him out" to see if he met the qualifications. I usually didn't do this, but he really was a yummy-looking boy and appealed to me tremendously. Sandy not only was willing to cooperate in Raoul's audition but she insisted on a three-way audition.

It turned out to be an unexpected combination of business and pleasure. A customer friend of mine, Jerry, had often expressed the desire to participate in a swing where he could suck a young boy's cock. He agreed to pay well for the scene if, at the same time, he could screw a pretty girl—in this case, Sandy. All Raoul had to do was let the man go down on him. This was a perfect situation for all of us.

Jerry liked Raoul and could not stop sucking and jerking off his cock, while Sandy was going down on me. I was not accustomed to a girl going down on me—it was usually the reverse—but, in this case, since she was so divine, I made an exception. We later reversed the roles, and I made her come.

All the while I'd been admiring Raoul's magnificent young torso, and every so often his sweet limpid eyes looked at me, as if to ask: "What is happening next?" So while Sandy was driving Jerry wild by feeding him her right tit and playing with his hard cock, I moved Raoul's head down below my navel and had him lick my stomach while his fingers caressed my shoulder, neck, and breasts. He gave me head in a delicious way. When I looked down at him, I could see his long, shoulder-length dark hair covering my pubic area, and this, combined with watching the scene next to me and feeling Raoul's rapid, warm tongue inside me, really set me aflame. I couldn't stop coming, I was so aroused. Then, I pulled his face up and we began kissing. We seemingly couldn't stop kissing and this, together with the madly screwing couple beside us and the pungent odor of sex and sperm and sweating bodies, just about overpowered us. It was a wild, wild orgy, and went on throughout the night. Raoul not only got his audition—he got the job.

A few months later, when I had to close up shop, Raoul and Sandy decided to return to their native land. Argentina, I have to believe, will never be the same.

ON CUPID'S SHAFT

The few times I frequented a hairdresser in New York last fall, I usually went to see Cupid, who worked in one of New York's newest hotels—a high-rise monster on Avenue of the Americas. Cupid was the nickname I'd given him because he really looked like an angel with his dark brown hair, curly over his forehead and long in the neck, his big brown limpid eyes, and his full lovely mouth.

Cupid had a slightly effeminate manner about him, but it wasn't irritating, not to me at least. He indeed *was* gay all the way, but he did tell me that on one occasion, some years before in Mexico City, he had liked a girl very much. Why tell me this? Well . . . not only was she the only female to whom he'd ever made love, but according to Cupid, she looked exactly like me. (I gather this was meant as a compliment.) Not only that, said Cupid, but she was as "cuckoo" as me—bi-sexual and fun-loving and unpredictable.

Cupid was of Cuban descent and spoke fluent Spanish as well as English. No woman in his salon escaped the stories of his amorous adventures, and they generally adored him. Indeed, after hearing his stories they would spill out their own life tales in full, lascivious detail. Furthermore, he was asked for advice by these women on many occasions, and this was another reason I had decided to call him Cupid.

Cupid was really intrigued by my life-style, and when the book came out he became my biggest fan. Every woman who sat in his chair received a promotional spiel from Cupid —"buy *The Happy Hooker* and straighten out your sex life" seemed to be the gist of it—but Cupid had also memorized vast sections of the book and would quote them at length. I never learned if this helped increase his tips or not.

Cupid, by my guess, was in his mid-thirties but with his boyish face and slim body could easily pass for several years younger. However, he complained to me that despite his youthful appearance he was getting too old to be kept and that he most probably would have to forget about ever having enough money to open up his own hairdressing salon, which would have been uni-sex, Cupid said.

Cupid wasn't much given to complaining, though, and soon enough he was telling me about his new lover, an exciting young man called Tony, just nineteen years old and *muy bonito!* So here was Cupid, worried about money and spending everything he made on this young lover of his. He not only paid for all their dates together, but was sending the kid through college!

Since Cupid and I got along so well, he invited me to do the town one night with him and his young lover—a gay tour of the city, from one joint to another, if you will. Larry was out of town on a rare business trip, so I figured—why not?

Later that night we met at a bar and Cupid introduced me to Tony. He was certainly a very attractive young man— he reminded me of Tony Perkins, the movie actor, at first glance, but had more bulk to him—and wherever we went that night, homosexual heads turned in our direction. Truth to tell, I was more than a little attracted to him myself— the more I looked at him and got to know him, the better he looked to me—and I asked him, finally, how he'd become a homosexual.

Tony had had sexual experiences with girls in his mid-teens, he said, but when he was seventeen he was seduced by a man and somehow that had been the deciding factor in his sexual make-up. He could still enjoy girls, he said, but he was more aroused by male lovers.

That night I decided it might be a lark to get Tony and
Cupid into a sexual swing. The three of us. Tony and I had
been dancing—we were in a bar that tolerated men and
women dancing together instead of just men—and the erection he had told me he wouldn't be adverse to the idea. But
Cupid certainly vetoed it. I'd forgotten how jealous homosexuals can be, and I immediately felt sorry that I might have
caused Cupid some pain. After all, I was only playing a
little game and he obviously cared a great deal for this young
man. I tried to make amends when Cupid dropped me off
at my apartment, but Cupid was very moody and unwilling
to accept my apologies. I felt bad about this and made an
appointment with his salon the first thing the next morning
for later that same day.

"Cupid," I said when I saw him, "don't be mad. It was
just an idea. No harm done."

"It's allright, Xaviera, he does that to me all the time.
But with you it really had me worried."

"How can I make it up to you? Shall I buy us dinner?
Or what?"

"No, nothing really . . . I'll probably break it off with
him fairly soon anyway. I can't afford to keep that boy
in college. . . ."

"I'll tell you what—I do have a good idea for a swing
for us . . ." I went on to tell Cupid that I thought I could
arrange a threesome between him, me, and my friend Walter,
an art dealer. Cupid had been very interested in Walter before he'd met Tony, and this struck him as a just ducky
idea.

Okay, the idea was fine with Cupid. Now for Walter.
This was an aristocratic man who had no homosexual tend-
encies, so far as I knew. Because of his intimate involvement
in the art world, he of course knew a great many homosexuals and through friends of friends he'd heard of Cupid
and in fact had sent me to Cupid. They'd met at a gallery
opening or two, and Walter had recommended him by saying,
"He's actually quite droll for a hairdresser. I'm sure he does
good work." Poor Walter—what strange connections of
logic he made.

Walter lived in his own little world, a sophisticated one,
to be sure, yet terribly limited. Still and all, Walter, in his

early forties, was a very charming and attractive gentleman and no wonder my horny Cupid was turned on to him. Walter had a beautiful head of thick, auburn hair, a rugged, yet sensitive, face, and a very good body. He was tall and physically impressive and was known for his kindly attitude towards people and his witty remarks as well.

So one night, while Walter and I were having dinner, I said, nonchalantly as hell, "Hey, Walter, one of these nights, I think we should invite Cupid—you remember that handsome little darling, don't you?—to come over to my house and have a three-way scene. How about that?"

I held my breath.

Walter seemed shocked at first, then seemed to be considering my perverse proposal. Actually I'd excepted him to spill something over my head because so far as I knew, he'd never even slept in the same bed with a man.

"Xaviera," he said, after a few moments' thought, "you do have a way of coming up with unusual ideas. . . ."

"Are you offended?" I didn't want to lose him as a friend, not even to pay back Cupid for my little flirtation with Tony.

"No, no," he said. "Actually I hear some of my professional associates discuss these things, and occasionally it all makes me somewhat curious. But, I must say, I don't think I could bring myself to be buggered by some fellow . . . really, now, that's a bit much, don't you think?"

He was asking me! I answered that no one should do anything with anyone unless they wanted to, and the other person agreed, but if this conversation was in any way offending him, then let's talk about something else. Art. Mayor Lindsay. The price of cabs. Anything.

No, he answered, the whole thing was intriguing—so long as I'd be there "to conduct the orchestra."

Well, with some misgivings—mostly on my part—we decided to go ahead and see what would happen. My guess, for what it's worth, is that every man, no matter how square, has a hidden yen for something "different" in sex. Or else Walter had a whole secret sex life I knew nothing about . . . at least the few times we'd been to bed he'd been quite conventional and not at all inclined to experiment.

The following week I arranged the big event with Cupid, who by now was calling me day after day, asking, "When can I come over, when do you expect me?". I told him it was all arranged and he was ecstatic. On a Friday night around ten o'clock Cupid rang the bell. Walter and I had just come back from a light supper. Despite his enthusiasm for the event, Cupid seemed nervous, and an hour went by before anybody made any move. Finally it was me, suggesting that we all freshen up. I directed Cupid to one bathroom and made him take a shower while Walter and I took a hot bath together in the other bathroom.

Walter was more than a little uptight and nervous himself when I guided him into the bedroom, and so I tried to reassure him by saying, "Don't worry, I'll be with you. You'll have nothing to be afraid of." Then Cupid came dashing in with an orange bath towel around his waist, carrying on like a virginal little teenage girl on her first date. But I never saw Cupid so cute-looking as he looked that night precisely because I'd never seen him without his clothes. He really had a slim, divine body. I got turned on myself. If only he hadn't been gay, I'd have loved to fuck him right there and then.

The action began. Walter lay on his back and I was lying over his upper torso, with one breast under his arm and the other almost in his mouth. While I was sort of embracing him and kissing his face and ears so he couldn't really see what was happening, I looked over my shoulder and saw that Cupid was sitting right on top of him, facing away from us. Then I took a closer look and saw that Walter had a big hard-on and that his hard-on had been stuck into Cupid's ass.

This was amazing to see. Cupid riding him like a horse. Despite all my experiences in bed, this was a new one, this male horse and rider act! It was exactly like a girl fucking a man, except that Cupid was a man.

So Walter was fucking Cupid and Cupid was jerking himself off, making excited moaning noises. After a few moments, Cupid grabbed my shoulder, softly, and motioned me to leave the two of them alone. I tried to cooperate, but the moment Cupid swung himself around and tried to lean down into Walter's face to kiss him, Walter started screaming and yelling, "No, no, I don't want to kiss a man! Stay here, Xaviera, please, please."

Jesus, what a fiasco I'd started. Cupid was insulted and went off into the living room to sulk. Walter looked mortified. I was embarrassed. I figured it was time to call The Big Event off and went into the bathroom to get a washcloth so that Walter could clean himself up. I apologized to him, then excused myself so I could go into the bathroom and take a shower. I didn't need a shower, I needed a few minutes to figure this one out. . . .

When I emerged from the bathroom I'd about decided to pour a drink for Cupid and Walter and then send everyone home. So imagine my surprise at the scene that greeted me: Walter was still on the bed, his arms thrown over his face so he couldn't see what was going on, and Cupid was sucking his cock with considerable pleasure. After watching them for a minute or so, I found that the scene was making me want to participate, so I joined them and we had a real old-fashioned daisy-chain going. Cupid sucked Walter and I sucked Cupid. At one point Cupid became so excited by this that he actually tried making it with me, neglecting Walter entirely, and I must say he really tried! But he went limp and groaned that he just couldn't make it with chicks, and I certainly wasn't insulted by his failure. Not even by the fact that the moment he started sucking Walter's big cock again, his own became rigid once more. This mad scene was beginning to strike me as terribly funny—I went out of the room so I wouldn't be giggily right there.

I regained control of myself in the living room and then returned to see what had transpired in my absence. Incredible. Cupid was back on Walter's cock, riding him face to face now, but Walter's face was hidden under a pillow he was hugging. I'd heard him moaning with pleasure just before I came back in, so evidently the pillow acted not only as a blindfold, but also as a silencer or gag.

Still and all, no matter what Cupid did to him, Walter didn't have an orgasm and Cupid was getting discouraged. I left them alone for a few minutes more, hoping that Walter would at least have some pleasure out of this—a good climax or two—but when I returned, Cupid was sitting on the bed, looking sadly at Walter and his pillow. I went over to Walter and pulled the pillow off his face, saying, "Okay, let's call it quits—I guess this wasn't such a good idea, after all."

Walter, very hot and sweaty from his torrid love affair with the pillow, looked at Cupid's morose face and said, weakly, "Well, I won't say I didn't enjoy any of it, but. . . ."

I could see that Cupid was ready to take this as an invitation to start sucking Walter's cock again, but I put a hand on Cupid's shoulder and said, "Enough, Cupid . . . I hope you had some fun, but the adventure is over."

"It wasn't bad," he began to say, a trifle bitchily, "but I've had—"

"*Bastante*," I said. "We tried, we all tried, but it wasn't meant to be."

A few minutes later Cupid had left and Walter was still lying there, looking rather morose himself. "Xaviera," he finally said, "do you think . . . eh, I could . . . well, somehow redeem myself in your eyes?"

"Oh, Walter," I said, "what a sweet pussycat you really are! What's to redeem—it was just a wild idea that didn't work. Nobody's been hurt, if you aren't, and we'll just forget it."

"Yes, well, I wished I'd at least have had an orgasm— even a small one—for Cupid's sake."

I laughed. "Walter, go take a shower and I'll change the sheets and meet you in bed when you come out. We'll see if we can't make you have an orgasm—even if it's 'a small one'!"

Walter came three times that night, once between my breasts and twice deep inside me. And we did everything under the sexual sun. The best was making love 69 style, and I sucked on his big balls for what seemed like hours, feeling them get hard in my mouth, one by one, and then playing with his penis, which is shaped extremely well, until he was ready to come, and then we'd quickly merge our bodies so he could explode inside me. And he was giving as well, eating me with great gentleness, yet making sure I had a powerful orgasm. What had started out as a three-way scene ended up with two players, but both knew their parts very well, and the scene played very well indeed, after all. At least I was satisfied by the last three acts.

"Walter," I said, just before we both fell asleep, "I hope I didn't shaft you with Cupid. I—"

"My dear," he said, softly cutting me off, "it's as the Englishman Sir John Harrington once said: 'It is better to love two too many than one too few.'"

I thought his arithmetic was off, but it was a sweet thought, so I kissed him and said goodnight.

I dreamed that night about cupids, but the traditional kind—not those who work in beauty salons.

The Girls in My Life

KATHY: The Wrong Calling

Kathy is a pretty twenty-year-old brunette with hazel eyes, a fine straight nose, and a full, made-to-kiss mouth. She is not "stacked," as they say, but has a shapely body. Her breasts are attractive, firm, and fairly big, but the part of her body that really gets to men are her legs, which are long with beautifully tapered thighs. Kathy loves to show off her legs by wearing the shortest of miniskirts. But she's in no way as much an exhibitionist as so many other of my girls were.

Kathy and I met when we were both starting out as call girls, but then we drifted apart and I never expected to see her again since we hadn't bothered to exchange addresses or telephone numbers and we had no friends in common. So I regarded it as sheer good fortune when I met her at Madeleine's the very first night I worked there. We were very pleased to see each other and our friendship renewed itself right then and there.

For the next few months Kathy and I both worked for Madeleine and therefore saw a great deal of each other. Then I decided to join forces with Georgette Harcourt, while Kathy remained with Madeleine. Kathy had been living at Madeleine's for some time when she suddenly moved out, taking a room in a not-so-nice hotel for which she paid outrageously high rent. I wasn't able to learn exactly why she'd moved out of Madeleine's nice place into a fleabag hotel—Kathy was vague about it—but I'd grown accustomed to her slightly mysterious ways. In a way I felt I knew her rather well, but actually I knew very little about her family or background. I guess we talked about me most of the time—Kathy, a quiet, well-mannered girl from the Boston area, was a good listener and at that time I was glad for someone to confide in. And while I pride myself that I, too, can provide a friendly ear in time of need, I do so love to talk!

We fell out of touch for a bit—I had taken over Madeleine's business and spent my days reorganizing her black books to conform with my own listing system (and my nights helping my customers spend a little money in order to become happily spent)—but one day I received a call from Kathy, who told me she'd now moved in with Georgette. She was rapidly becoming the most-traveled prostitute in town.

Still, it sounded like a good move to me. Georgette's establishment did not have the class or ambience that Madeleine's had had, but certainly it was better than living in a crummy hotel room. But Kathy was not at all happy with her new arrangement.

Despite the fact she was bringing in a lot of business, and was kicking in fifty percent to Georgette, she was being charged a hundred dollars a week for rent and, worse yet, had to pay for her food and drinks. Poor Kathy couldn't even sneak in a little free Vitamin C in the mornings, since Georgette would measure the orange juice container each time it was put back into the refrigerator. I'd known Georgette wasn't in Madeleine's league as a lady of breeding, but I hadn't realized she belonged at the head of the class when it came to stinginess.

But the stinginess, Kathy said, miserably, was only part of it. She and Georgette had fights over how much food had been consumed and how many drinks were consumed. And over money—Georgette was constantly owing Kathy her share of the money received by Georgette from Kathy's customers. Moreover, a night seldom went by without Georgette having a screaming, violent argument with her boyfriend, who was considerably younger than she and who was not one of Nature's great gentlemen. These ugly brawls, Kathy said, were making her nervous and fearful that something really violent would happen one night—and she didn't want to be there to see it.

Thus I wasn't at all surprised to receive a call from Kathy a few days later asking if she please couldn't move in with me. At first I didn't know how to respond. I was very fond of Kathy, but there was a part of her which remained inaccessible to other people. It wasn't merely that she was quiet and passive, there was something strange about her, something I couldn't fathom. Then, too, I am so very concerned with women's appearances and Kathy, the few times I'd seen her of late, just wasn't paying much attention to how she looked. It was because Kathy obviously did not care about her grooming and make-up that she was no longer the very attractive fresh-looking girl I'd met.

Still, how could I not be sympathetic to her plight? The poor kid needed some civilized surroundings, that's all—after that hotel and Georgette's prison-farm atmosphere—so I told her to pack her bags and join Xaviera's happy little household.

Kathy moved in just before Christmas with nothing but a toothbrush and a small pocketbook. I asked her where her luggage was, and she replied, "This is it." So I assumed she planned to buy some new clothes, since the familiar brown dress she had on was the same one I'd seen her wear a number of times recently.

How wrong I was. Kathy instantly became part of the furniture and showed no interest in anything, even going out socially. Her excuse was that she had no clothes. And no shoes. She had only one pair of shoes, and they had holes in them, so she couldn't go out to buy either shoes or some new clothes. Finally I gave her a pair of my sandals—which happened to be a size too small—so she could go out and buy some shoes. Which is about all she did buy. A dress or two and one pair of shoes.

What was wrong with this girl? She'd become so phlegmatic, lazy even, about herself and everything else. Even my other girls, who also liked Kathy, were concerned about her but they couldn't figure her out any better than I could.

Why should such an attractive girl not give a damn about anything, most especially herself?

If only Kathy liked to screw! That would have brought something warm and exciting and rewarding into her life, but she now seemed to loathe being a call girl. She evidently found sex—at best—no fun, and obviously hated going out on appointments. I was rapidly heading toward my wit's end as to how to deal with her. With my storehouse of nervous energy and stamina and my lust for life and all it holds in store for adventuresome people, I was finding Kathy an impossible drag to be living with. She'd sleep half the day away, spend another two or three hours waking up, and then never really be with it.

Having none of the right answers, I decided to try asking some of the right questions. And the right one was: "Kathy, what are all those bottles of pills you have?"

Yes, our quiet Kathy, who had a year of college, was already eligible for a doctorate in pill-popping. Her handbag was a walking drugstore of "uppers" and "downers"—Dexedrines, Dexamyls, Seconals, Tuinals, "Black Beauties." You name a pill and Kathy had it, either in her handbag or her drawer. No wonder she was so groggy and passive, barely able to acknowldege that she was in the same room with anyone else. Several times I'd seen her in the bathroom, standing before the wash basin, washing her hands slowly and methodically, rinsing them and then washing them again, then repeating this process until half the bar of soap was gone and her hands were red and blotched from all that rubbing.

Kathy took her "ups" to stay awake and her "downs" to go to sleep, and that was the entire rhythm of her life. Up and down, and going nowhere. She took on enough customers to pay her bills and afford her pills—which is why sex was meaningless to her.

I begged Kathy to stop the pills, or at least cut down, and for a while she seemed to be better. At least she would become animated and much more of her old self when a certain handsome and amiable Italian-American customer visited the house. Bud was his name, and he was wealthy and great fun to be with. All my girls responded to him—he was a first-class flirt—but the best thing, so far as I was concerned, was that he paid attention to Kathy and she thrived on it. Not that he singled her out for special attention, but he treated her kindly and obviously made her feel more of a person as well as more of a woman. Bud managed to be cool and reserved and friendly at one and the same time, and gradually he stopped being a customer and became a friend and part-time protector of my house.

Given her new mood, Kathy would go out on dates, but when she returned, at whatever hour, she would call up Bud. I happened to know that a lot of the time Bud was in the sack with a model or stewardess or some other gorgeous creature, but Kathy would ignore what was obvious and chatter away for as long as she could keep him on the phone. What often happened, Bud told me, was that Kathy's nocturnal calls proved to be a considerable turn-off for his companion of the moment, but he didn't seem to mind too much.

Once in a while Bud would bring over some of his "tough" friends and treat them to some girls, but Kathy would refuse to go to bed with any of them, or even Bud. In fact, her new principle seemed to be that she wouldn't sleep with Bud in the house at all. Only at his place. And if he displayed any affection for one of the other girls, she'd sit in a corner and chain-smoke and pop some more pills. She may have been writhing with anger on the inside, but outwardly she remained calm and seemingly unperturbed.

One day, about four in the afternoon, Kathy was still sound asleep and I needed her bedroom because I was expecting three or four men for fun 'n games. I tried waking her up by shaking her and talking to her, but I couldn't budge her from her deep sleep. So I decided I'd have to apply what I called my "Gestapo Method." This involved turning on the stereo full blast and lifting the blinds in her room so the sunlight streamed down right into her eyes (which, like most addicts' eyes, were light-sensitive).

A bit later, I looked into the room and there was Kathy standing nude beside the bed. She was crying and her hands were placed over her breasts and pubic area. Her legs were crossed as though to shield part of her nudity and she seemed terribly vulnerable and distressed. So my "Method" had worked—too well!

During the next few weeks Kathy avoided me as much as possible, seeming to try and fade out of sight whenever I was around. She had stopped working and began to owe all her friends money. There was also increased friction over her increasing use of drugs, Kathy regarding all my efforts to help her get off the pills as a personal insult.

Finally she moved back to Georgette's friendly little hostel —no small insult to me, I thought, although I realized she obviously wanted to hide from me. But I was able to keep informed on Kathy's life. And Kathy's life, it turned out, had taken a strange turn via Georgette, who'd given birth to a daughter, the illegitimate child of her young lover. Since that "pimpstick" was still married to a rich young woman, whom he wasn't about to leave for Georgette, and was already the father of two children by this woman, the baby was strictly Georgette's responsibility—and Kathy's. For Kathy was devoting most of her time to taking care of the baby and, Georgette said, seemed to love her new work. From being a call girl who wouldn't go out, she'd become a baby-sitter who loved to live in.

It's now the next spring, 1972, and I've been involved with the Knapp Commission, and I'm officially in retirement. Coming in one afternoon, I checked with my answering service and was told that Kathy had called from a public phone and would be back at that number at a certain hour. When I called, she was there. She had read about my various troubles and was very concerned for me, and how I was and what I was doing. My God, this sounded like a different Kathy from the poor, sad creature who'd fled my apartment some months back. Acting on an impulse, I asked her if she wanted to move back in with me. Her answer was an immediate and eager "Yes!" She said she'd be over as soon as she could pack.

"Pack?" I wondered what her luggage would be this time.

However, when Kathy arrived at the apartment I was amazed at the change in the girl. She was completely off drugs: fresh, energetic and charming. She'd left Georgette's house a while back, she said—but not before Georgette got someone to take care of the baby—and had knocked around the city. This accounted for her wardrobe still being modest, since she hadn't been working and owed money to various loansharks, including her Bud.

Still, scant wardrobe or not, here was Kathy, happy and smiling, interested in books and music and, perhaps most wondrous to relate, very anxious to help me in any way in my new career as a writer and lecturer. So she was appointed on the spot as my Press Secretary-in-Residence and was to become invaluable to me, answering the phones, handling the mail, arranging appointments, and actually helping me organize the material that was to go into this book.

Even more gratifying, she displayed an absolute trust in me and opened up to another human being for perhaps the first time in her life. She told me she never received any love from her parents and that she grew up in an emotionally poisonous atmosphere. Both parents were drunkards and her father would beat his wife and the children mercilessly. Her family situation was so sick that it was almost a classic Freudian case study and Kathy grew up hating not only her parents but herself as well. She ran away from home when she was eighteen, after that first year in college, and had never seen her parents since. She didn't know if she wanted ever to see them again, but at least she could talk about it now.

Therefore, there should be a modestly happy ending to this story. But I can't offer you one. Kathy, without my realizing it, became a "secret drinker," and began to act as she had on drugs. One day I came home to find she'd run off with some underworld type and I was never to see her again. Through Bud, who always seemed to know her whereabouts, I was able to learn that she was "all right," but that's about all I learned.

I hope she's really all right. I thought she'd done a wonderful job of coming up from the depths, especially with me, but I can see I didn't quite know her as well as I thought I did. Or as well as I should have.

If I ever get back to New York, I'm going to find out how she is, and I truly hope I like what I find.

GETTING MARRIED

Saul was his name. He was twenty-eight, of Russian-Jewish descent, and he worked as a postman. Or, as he preferred to be known, as a letter carrier.

Saul, I must say, was easy to sum up. His financial situation: a salary of $120 per week. Living conditions: he shared a small flat in Queens with an unemployed roommate. His ambition: to become a rich man.

I don't intend to be mean-minded, but Saul reminded me of a walrus with his big, brown doggy eyes. He had long dark hair, kind of greasy-looking, a pallid complexion, yellowish teeth, and a large black mustache. His feet were flat. His hands were usually sweaty.

Although Saul wasn't terribly bright, he did have a bit of a sense of humor—a redeeming factor, to be sure, but it wasn't enough to make him very attractive to women. He'd never been married and generally dated young Jewish girls who were still living at home. Momma knows best—these were all professional virgins, and they stayed that way.

So Saul married me instead.

I met Saul while I was running a brothel. He was introduced to me by a lesbian girl friend of mine named Jacky, whom I had once met at a gay beach in Riis Park in Brooklyn. She knew about my profession and that I sometimes needed boys to be studs for those special occasions where I provided male prostitute service. At that time Saul was not yet employed by the Post Office, but was working at a menial clerk's job in a publishing company, pushing tons of paper around for a low salary. Jacky told him about me, and Saul, anxious to make an extra buck but not ambitious enough to look for a better job, was ready and eager to offer his stud services to me.

When Saul came over to the apartment, he was obviously very nervous and was stuttering very badly. I was tempted to ask him to show me his endowment—the size of his penis—but that would have been too much for the poor boy. From the way he was behaving, I should have ended the interview even before it started, but I thought I'd give him a chance.

Under my questioning, which I kept very low key, he admitted that he'd never made love to a man in any way, nor had he been sucked off by a man. The boy had no qualifications to be a good stud and I was beginning to wonder how adept he was in bed with women, but that was none of my business. I told him as nicely as I could that I didn't think he'd enjoy being a stud and that one day I could use him for something else maybe. I did feel sorry for him.

He thanked me and told me that even though he wasn't married, he needed money badly—he needed a car, he said—and that he'd always be available for anything I wanted. He seemed very intrigued by the bevy of good-looking females that decorated my house—one sexier than the other—and I promised to keep his address and telephone number in "my files."

During the following months, I did not hear any more of Saul. Jacky told me he had changed jobs and had become a postman, that he was dying to buy a car but still didn't have any money. He again conveyed the message to Jacky that any time I needed his help, I could call on him.

When I got that message, I was in the midst of immigration problems. I was facing expiration of my visa, and it was hard for me to get an American sponsor. I'd been arrested several times while running the bordello and knew I couldn't change my status unless I married an American. This, I was told, was the only sure solution to my deportation problems, and the thought occurred to me that perhaps I should give Saul a call and ask him if he'd care to get "married." It would be strictly platonic and would be arranged on a business basis.

Of course the man I most logically should've been thinking of marrying was my boyfriend Larry. We were great friends and lovers, but Larry would never agree to a marriage of convenience. I wasn't ready to marry Larry and live with him seven days and nights a week, and that was the only kind of marriage to me he'd consider. As for me, I greatly enjoyed our dinners and weekends together, but wanted my freedom during the week.

There was another candidate, a man named Lester. He was forty-two, attractive, and reminded me of Larry because of his silver-grey hair. Although Lester was a good athlete— he taught tennis for a living—I liked to call him my "Jewish peasant" because he always dressed like a peasant, in bulky shoes and trousers which seemed at least one size too large. However, underneath his ill-fitting clothing, Lester had a good body and he was quite a proficient lover. He also cared for me a great deal, and he was desperate to get married.

So why didn't I marry Lester?

Well, Lester had never been married and he was basically a terribly lonely person. He'd been under psychiatric care for years because of his deep depression and both his psychiatrist and lawyer told him that I would be the type of woman who'd sue him for divorce and alimony as soon as I had my papers.

Lester was ready to marry me in a second, no money involved, and yet he chickened out at the last minute—on the advice of his psychiatrist and lawyer! It's really kind of ludicrous—Lester barely eked out a living as a tennis instructor, and I had far more money than he did, yet I'd want alimony from him! As for immediately suing him for divorce, I was very aware of Lester's deep feelings for me, and for my part I was very fond of him so I'd hardly do anything that would hurt him.

Here I was, stuck—Lester, who loved me but was scared to marry me; and Larry, who loved me, but wouldn't agree to my conditions for marriage. I began to panic because time was running out and I didn't want to be deported. My own lawyer wanted no part in my husband-hunt—although there are lawyers who specialize in just this sort of legal work—because he felt I should only marry for the right reason—a four-letter word spelling L-O-V-E. Since I wasn't ready for that, I decided, I was ready to speak to Saul.

That didn't take long. I called him and he appeared at the apartment almost as rapidly as Superman himself might have made the trip. He was intrigued by the business of the bordello and flattered by the idea of being the husband of New York's Number-One Madam. So he accepted my "proposal" on the spot.

After seeing a lawyer, Saul's conditions for marriage were that I pay him a thousand dollars out front; that I write him an ante-nuptial agreement saying that I would not stay married to him longer than a year; that I pay all the legal fees for the divorce; that I not sue him for alimony—this nonsense again—and that neither he nor I require any money from each other.

We also had a verbal agreement that I wouldn't sleep with him or have any sexual relations with him. However, seeing the horny look in his eyes the two times he'd been at the apartment, I, kidding around, promised him one of the girls every week. He could take his choice and I, Madam X, would treat him to a girl and pay her myself.

I made this promise as a joke, but Saul was to hold me to it and came around every week for a girl during the small remaining time I was a madam. Thus my little joke turned out to be an expensive one.

The Big Event of 1971—my marriage—was arranged for April 2, by coincidence the day after April Fool's Day. The witness on my side was Kathy, who was then one of my roommates; and for Saul, his roommate, Dick. Also present were Saul's twenty-one-year-old brother, Jack, and "my old man," Larry, who wasn't particularly entranced by his role as "father of the bride." He was to give me away and I was to give a thousand dollars to Saul as his wedding present.

It was a lovely, bright spring day. I was dressed in an

expensive yellow Pucci dress with a matching coat and Saul and his kid brother wore tuxedos. There were red roses for the ladies and carnations for the mens' lapels. That morning, Freddy, an arty young photographer friend of mine came over to photograph the wedding party—although we hardly expected to make the society page of the New York *Times*.

Oh, yes, despite our splendid attire, it wasn't to be a church wedding.

We were going down to City Hall for a ceremony as efficiently short and sweet as possible.

Saul and I had taken our blood tests, gotten our marriage license, and I'd bought some inexpensive wedding bands. We'd planned for everything, except the honeymoon!

Actually Saul looked the best I'd ever seen him look. The few meetings we had at my apartment prior to our wedding, Saul had arrived in his mailman's uniform and was usually sweaty and unshaven and unkempt-looking. On one occasion he scared the heebie-jeebies out of one of my girls who didn't know him and took him for a policeman. Even I had to agree, while laughing my head off at this outrageous case of mistaken identity, that Saul, with his visored cap, could be mistaken for a cop. A badly dressed cop, but a cop nonetheless. But today, I really had to admit, Saul looked pretty respectable. He was clean-shaven and had washed his hair and combed it neatly and, all in all, looked every inch the Handsome Husband.

To tell the truth, though, his kid brother, Jack, was a cute little devil and a lot groovier than Saul would ever be. He'd been over to the apartment, and both boys, coming from a simple, hard-working Jewish family, admitted they'd never had it so good as when they visited the apartment and were treated like kings. They were served snacks and drinks and had had the opportunity of meeting some of the most beautiful girls of New York.

When we arrived down at City Hall, we were told to wait in a large room until the clerk came out to perform the ceremony. With some time to kill, I did my usual thing—which is to observe what's going on about me and see what I can learn from it. Our little wedding party was relaxed and having some fun, but some of the other groups looked as though they were about to attend a funeral rather than a wedding.

In particular there was one Puerto Rican couple sitting quietly there with depressed expressions on their faces. It was obviously a "shot-gun wedding." I looked from her pretty face to her very distended belly and I guessed she was a lot closer to having a baby than she was to conceiving one. Studying this couple put me into a quiet rage: with birth control and, if necessary, abortion services so readily available, no one should have to get married because of a pregnancy. It's unfair to the couple, and could be fatal to their ability to be good parents.

On the other hand, it wasn't all gloom. There was also a black couple, very wildly dressed—for instance, both were wearing white, high-heeled boots then very much in fashion. The bride was a chubby young lady who'd somehow managed to stuff herself into a short white wedding gown that had to be at least one size too small for her. It was sexy in its way, and in wonderful contrast to her giant Afro hair style. As for the groom, he couldn't have been hipper—as colorfully mod as could be imagined. However, it wasn't their manner of dress but their manner which drew my attention to them. Unless I was crazy, they and their group of friends were whacked out of their heads. Not that they were obtrusive in any way. Quite the contrary—they were the happiest, friendliest group in the huge room and the groom later confessed to me that they'd smoked some grass before coming downtown and were feeling no pain. I seldom use drugs, not even grass, but I have to admit they added a lot of cheer to this huge room that was supposed to be the daily site of so many happy events.

Toward the back of the room there was a young hippie couple and since we didn't seem to be getting any closer to the Big Event, I wandered over there and struck up a conversation. Truth to tell, it was hard to tell the prospective groom from the bride because they each had shoulder-length hair, but the future bride was wearing a faded denim miniskirt and had, I presume, prettier legs than the groom.

She was anxious to get married, this young woman told me, because she wanted so much to get away from her family. She'd just turned eighteen—she looked fifteen—and he was nineteen, and marriage was the only way out for her, she kept insisting. It was "a bad scene at home," she told me, because her father had been a drunkard for years and was constantly beating up her mother. Her mother had had several nervous breakdowns and whenever she wasn't around, her father would beat up on his daughter. It reminded me of Kathy's background, but at least Kathy wasn't getting married to escape from home.

I asked her if she loved her husband-to-be, and she answered she "sort of dug" him—all the while giggling shyly as though the question embarrassed her.

As though to change the subject, she pointed out the sign on the wall regarding the proper dress in which to get married at City Hall.

(1) The man should wear a jacket and tie and the woman a dress or skirt.

(2) No slacks or hot pants should be worn by the woman.

"Would you believe it," said my young friend, "I had to borrow a dress to get married in because I never wear anything but blue jeans." Then she added, again with the shy giggle, "I'm surprised they let us wear miniskirts."

The room kept filling up, and there was a certain grumbling about how long everything was taking. People had celebration plans and now they were going to be late.

I wished the young couple luck and moved around the room some more, as much to keep from getting bored as anything else. In a far corner I noticed an elderly couple who seemed fairly oblivious to the general tumult of the now-quite-crowded room. They were patiently waiting their turn without any seeming notice of how long it was taking. They seemed very much in love and were holding hands like a pair of starry-eyed teenagers.

To me, at least, their little tableau was very, very touching. This was a couple who had found one another late in life. Maybe they each had a broken marriage behind them, or had lost their spouses to death. For all I knew, it could be the first marriage for each in the autumn of their lives. And there they sat, relaxed and really "together" as they were preparing to build a new life together. Of all the people in the room, I most especially wished for their marriage to blossom and for them to live to a happy old age.

Filled with sentiment, I returned to my own little marriage tableau and learned that our turn was "not too far off." Ahead of us, Larry said, was a youngish couple a few seats away. She was a "Wasp"-looking type with reddish hair and freckles, wearing a very pretty full-length white lace dress that I bet had belonged to her mother, who was there, to be sure, if one may judge by the resemblance between mother and daughter. And Dad was there, too, looking fairly pleased about the whole thing. But not as pleased as the future groom, a big Irish fellow who'd already had more than a few belts under his belt—judging by his ruddy glow and expansive manner. He was talking it up with his friends, but kept throwing a loving look at his fiancée, who caught each look and returned it with equal affection. There was also a little girl, around five, who picked at her own pink lace dress and seemed not quite aware of what was going on. Aha, I surmised, it's a second marriage for her—that's her little daughter. So if my guesses were correct, there were three generations of women at this ceremony . . .

My romantic speculations were interrupted by the clerk who came out of the small room in which the actual weddings were performed and called this group in. I saw Saul consult his watch, just as I was doing, to determine how long the ceremony was going to take.

About fifteen minutes later the couple emerged with wide, happy grins on their faces. They were holding hands and kissing each other and all their friends were milling around them in a joyous little crowd. All was ecstacy. Then —a bureaucratic bomb fell in their midst.

The clerk in the cage-like office who actually hands out the marriage certificate had suddenly announced from within his shielded office, that he was sorry to have to tell them that they "were not officially married under the laws of the State of New York!" The bride turned as pale as her dress and the groom turned kind of purple.

"Why not?" she cried out. "What happened? We just went inside and the whole ceremony took place. Aren't we man and wife now?"

The clerk responded that they were *not* man and wife

now because the Marriage Bureau had made a mistake. They had taken their blood tests less than eight full days earlier—as required by New York State law—and according to New York State law, therefore, they were not legally married. Since this was a Friday afternoon, he suggested they come back Monday and get married again then.

The scene then became a comic opera scene as played in an Italian B-movie. The bride began weeping and crumbled into her fiancé's arms—he was still her fiancé at this stage—and he, both angry and confused, kept asking his friends how "anything so stupid" could be allowed! The girl's mother was very upset—she sat silently weeping in a corner of the waiting room—and the father of the bride was protesting about how they'd planned a big wedding party that afternoon in an exclusive hotel and about how the newlyweds were to fly to Acapulco after the party for the honeymoon, and all the arrangements had been made . . . !

At this rate I figured the bride and groom would end up fighting with each other by day's end and the wedding would be called off over the weekend. What they should be doing, I told them silently, was to tell the schmucky bureaucrats to go screw themselves and since they *were* married in their heads and hearts, just go ahead with their plans. They could always go through the formality of another ceremony at some future date.

However, instead of some rational—and liberated—thinking taking over, the groom and the bride's father and the groom's friends were getting angrier and angrier and seemed about ready to tear down City Hall, and some guards appeared—obviously called by the license clerk—and ushered the whole group out of the building with strong warnings not to "disturb the peace."

While all this bloody fiasco was going on, the black couple I'd noticed earlier were told it was finally their turn to become man and wife. As the groom walked past me, he laughingly said to me, with a stoned look in his eyes, "That's what happens when you don't have it all together. That's why I got my head so freakin' high. I don't want to have to listen to all this bullshit—I just wanna get married to my baby here. I ain't takin' no chance of gettin' kicked out of here without that lousy piece of paper. Man, either

I get married to this baby right *now,* or *forget* it. It's now or
never!" And with these tender loving words, he slapped his
plump bride-to-be on her prominent ass.

She smiled demurely and whispered to him to keep quiet.
But one of his friends, obviously questioning the wisdom of
his friend's outburst in City Hall, half-whispered to me,
"God, if they find out they're stoned, maybe they won't
marry them, either. That man thinks he's a smart-ass, but
he better just shut up."

Well, the black couple walked into the room to get married and more or less flew out—very much married. Stoned
or not, they'd followed the rules of the house and were re-
warded with a marriage certificate.

It took another half-hour before Saul and I could officially
become man and wife, and when it happened it was some
turn-off. Perhaps I wasn't there for the right reasons, but
it was hard to believe that loving couples in any kind of
romantic mood could be—by choice—getting married in
crummy rooms like this one in city halls all over the world
by men monotonously droning out a blah-blah-blah series
of sentences which stopped having any meaning to them
long, long ago. Maybe I'd been naive—it sure as hell
wouldn't have been the first time—but I'd believed that
the marriage ceremony was always at least a friendly, per-
sonalized procedure, not this cold, impersonal, almost
computerized drone.

Saul and I were officially declared man and wife at two
o'clock in the afternoon. What started out as a kind of lark
had turned into a chore. Because it was later than we'd
expected, Larry had to go back to his office, and so he gave
me money to take everyone out to a wedding lunch. I also
knew he'd not relished a moment of the entire charade
and didn't blame him for wanting to cut out. I said I'd see
him for dinner that night. "We'll have a honeymoon party,"
I whispered to him.

We all squeezed into Dick's car and Saul insisted on
doing the driving. I sat in the front seat between Saul and
his kid brother, Jack, and Kathy and Dick were in the back.
In a very few minutes Kathy and Dick were kidding around
in the back, really smooching it up.

Watching them go at it, I felt a sudden urge to do a little kidding around myself, but not with my new husband. In any case, he was thoroughly occupied with the task of maneuvering the car through the midtown congestion.

Yes, since I'd given Saul a nice wedding present, I should give one to his cute kid brother as well. I knew the kid'd had eyes for me since he'd first met me, and so while Saul carefully steered the car, I carefully steered myself in the direction of Brother Jack and gave him a friendly little hug. He seemed a little embarrassed by this sudden attention from me, and he couldn't have dreamed what was coming. *(Him.)* I leaned way over to the right and unbuttoned his shirt so I could reach his navel with my tongue. This made my short Pucci dress hike up my thighs quite a bit and little Jack now had a big bulge in his pants.

Since I couldn't imagine, for the life of me, what this could be, I decided to probe further in my research into the true nature of kid brothers. I delicately unzipped Jack's trousers and reached in to see what had caused this sudden expansion of his personality. My goodness gracious, there was this large throbbing cock peeking out at me!

Since I do have some experience in these matters, I applied a firm grip to this new member of the wedding party and gave him a kiss hello. "Come on and join the party," I whispered to my new friend, and with a firm handshake, I fully removed him from the confines of Jack's underwear and trousers. He was a fine, big fellow, all right, but he seemed to have a problem he wanted me to help him with. Well, of course, that's what I was there for! I'd helped him come out, hadn't I? Now it was time to help him come off.

For the next five minutes or so, I used artificial respiration —the "kiss of life"—on my friend and applied massage as well. Jack was squirming all over the seat and so was Saul, as he tried to keep one eye on traffic and the other on his bride and kid brother. Evidentally he took that one eye off traffic for he suddenly slammed on the brakes in order to stop at a red light. And just as he did so, Jack exploded in my mouth and all over my face.

My scientific analysis of the event is as follows: my friend was able to produce a gusher of sperm because of three factors. These were: (1) my mouth on his cock, (2) my firm grip on his balls, and (3) the sudden braking of the car. I believe all these factors were important, but not in that order. If pressed to select the key factor, I would say my sucking expertise was dominant. In any case my friend had a magnificent coming-out party and I had a facial I hadn't expected.

Slightly astonished at the roaring outcome of my friendly gesture, I looked in the mirror and there was this new cream —Jack's Juice—over half my face and everyone in the car broke up at the sight. Except Saul, who was probably not amused at his virgin status. Actually I wasn't totally amused at how sticky my face felt, but it *had* been a funny climax to my honeymoon trip—and in the most romantic of spots, a crowded car in heavy New York City traffic.

We finally made it crosstown to a West Side restaurant and after cleaning up, we had a fast, but definitely good-natured, lunch. Then Saul had to return to the Post Office for his afternoon shift and his brother went home to their parents' house in Queens. Dick dropped Kathy and me off at my apartment, where I resumed my normal business day. To tell the truth, I didn't feel very married.

Every Wednesday afternoon, there would be a visit from Saul to collect on my promise of a girl for him. This was better than having to go to bed with him myself, but the schnook—as though to pay me back for the case of "blue balls" I must have given him on our honeymon excursion across Manhattan Island—kept insisting on a different girl each week. So long as business was good, I managed to provide him with variety, but later on, we had to change the rules.

What bothered me most about Saul was not the girl per week he required, but the change in his personality. I found I'd liked him better when he was a shy little fellow wanting to become a professional stud. Now he was sometimes almost overbearing, acting like the house despot. Not only did one of the girls have to screw him, but he made the rest of us listen to his boring adventures as a mailman and his under-sexed dates with stupid little girls who never fucked.

None of my girls liked him very much, and the only

compensation they received—outside of the twenty-five dollars I gave them each time—was that Saul had the fastest gun in town when it came to ejaculating. He kept promising he'd last longer—as though the girls wanted him to be their long-lasting lover—but his performance seldom changed in terms of stamina. Even if he meant well, he didn't make love well.

One of the things that intrigued me about Saul's being in our midst each week is how Larry not only tolerated him but tried to be nice to him. One day Larry gave him some shirts he'd bought for Saul on sale, and instead of being grateful my twirp of a husband complained that he'd prefer wilder colors next time! It's as though to make up for being so short on lovemaking abilities, he'd decided to be long on *chutzpah*. Oh, well, I didn't marry him for his good looks . . . or his good manners. . . .

One Sunday Larry and I decided to take some of my clothes and things over to Saul's place just in case Immigration checked there to see if I was really living with my husband or not. When I saw what Saul's neighborhood was like, I was sure glad I wasn't living there with him. All the men seemed to be walking around in their undershirts, either working on their cars or tending their gardens, and half the women were hanging out the windows, curlers in their hair, discussing food prices and the weather and the latest gossip. It was clearly a neighborhood in decline: So was Saul's apartment—although what helped make it neat was a combination of very little furniture and no carpeting. When we came in, Dick, Saul's roommate, looked up from reading comic books only long enough to say "Hi" and continue the argument he was having with Saul.

I looked around the place—I didn't want to get into their argument—and the only reading material was comic books or girlie magazines. After hanging up my clothes in Saul's closet and putting some costume jewelry and cosmetics on top of his bureau, I went back out into the living room to find the argument still going on, with Larry as official arbiter. Dick was out of a job and his parents had stopped helping him with his share of the rent. Since Saul had gotten a thousand dollars from me—which made him a "rich man" by Dick's standards—he expected Saul to pay the rent until he could get another job. Then he'd pay Saul back, of course. He'd do the same for Saul, Dick said, if he were in Saul's position.

Larry looked at me and said, "It's going to take the wisdom of Solomon to settle this dispute," which meant to me, "Let's bug out of here." But Saul then mentioned he was going to make his usual Sunday visit to his parents and would I like to come along and meet them?

Meeting my in-laws! What a treat it would be to be a secret daughter-in-law . . . I looked at Larry and asked him if he'd mind driving us over to "my in-laws," and he looked at me as though I must be in need of instant institutionalization. However, he sighed and said, "Okay, go meet Saul's parents." Knowing me, he knew I was determined to do it once I'd given in to the impulse.

Fortunately Saul's parents didn't live too far away, and on the way over I noticed he was still wearing his wedding band. I'd removed mine the moment we left City Hall, so I asked him why he'd kept wearing his ring and he answered he was "kind of proud" of it. How did he explain it to his parents, I asked him. He told them it was a friendship ring he'd gotten from one of his girlfriends. Aha, I thought to myself, at last he's gotten *something* from one of his dates!

We arrived at Saul's parents' apartment building in a few minutes and, as I'd expected from Saul's conversations about them, it was an old apartment building which had seen better days. When Saul rang the bell, his mother answered. She seemed a typical Yiddishe Momma in her late forties, short and faded-looking, with brown hair turning a nondescript color that wasn't yet grey but wasn't brown any longer. I knew right away that any female coming home with her Saul would have to pass muster all the way.

The apartment was modestly furnished but obviously clean and well-cared-for. Most of all, the place had a lived-in look but the feeling I got was not so much "comfortable" as "worn-out." Saul insisted on giving me a guided tour of the place, and on the way to his old room, we met his father, who was just emerging from the bathrom, zipping up his pants. He was older than Saul's mother, mostly bald, with little tired eyes. He walked with a stoop, and my immediate impression was of a good man who worked hard all his life to make ends meet and now was really weary—of working, and perhaps of life. When Saul introduced us, he responded politely with a very heavy Yiddish or Lithuanian accent, but after a moment or so of conversation he seemed to perk up a bit. His eyes took on a sparkle as he looked up at me and he became more animated. When Saul said he wanted to show me his old room, his father nodded, straightened his back a little, and went out into the living room.

Saul's room held no surprises. He had shared it with his brother, who still lived there, and it was a typical boys' room, with toy cars and airplanes all over the place. There was an American flag on the wall, some pin-ups above his brother's bed, and some comic books lying around. I noticed a pair of roller skates under one of the beds and a fishing rod standing in the corner. Nothing exciting, but kind of sweet. In some ways, Saul had never left this room. . . .

When we returned to the living room, Saul's mother had made tea. We chatted—the father had already dozed off in front of the television set—and I felt rather self-conscious about the difference in our clothes. Men don't sense these things right away, but women do. She had on a tired old *schmattah* and I was wearing an expensive green knitted pants suit. The way she was examining me, I couldn't escape the feeling that she envied me for my taste in clothes and the fact I owned the kind of fashionable clothing she had never been able to afford. Yet at the same time I felt this, she was being friendlier, asking me all about myself.

To make her feel comfortable with me, I began speaking Yiddish to her and—*l'chaim!*—the ice was broken immediately. She came over on the couch with me and gave me a little hug, saying, "Oh, how nice. You speak Yiddish. You don't *look* Jewish . . . How come a high-class girl like you, who looks like a *schicksha,* speaks Yiddish?"

This was really all one question so I carefully explained that I was from Holland, that my father was Jewish, and so on. Now she asked me—I could have predicted it—what I did for a living.

"I'm a successful interior decorator," I answered, avoiding Saul's eyes.

"That's *nice,*" she more or less gurgled. "What do you decorate?"

"Interiors . . . apartments . . . offices." I was lying like crazy, but what was I going to say, "Oh, hi there, I'm Madam X and I have a nice little house decorated by beautiful girls who fuck for a living."

Nothing subtle about this lady: now she asked me if I'd ever been married and I managed to answer the question without answering it. I mentioned something about having been engaged and she assumed I was speaking of Holland. So we talked about Holland and I explained that my father was a very sick man.

She inquired further about his health and I explained that he had suffered a stroke after a career as a very successful doctor.

Oy gevalt! I was suddenly living in a Jewish mother joke—at the mention of the word "doctor" Saul's mother gave out a happy little yelp and pulled on her husband's sleeve to awaken him. "You hear, Abie, you hear. A doctor . . . her father is a doctor." Saul's father didn't seem to grasp the great significance of this information and, still half-asleep, he muttered, "Wha . . . what, what happened?" The house might have been on fire for all he knew.

"Abie, her father's a doctor, would you believe it! Such a nice girl and from Holland—a *Yiddishe maedel* from Holland." Saul's father gave me a sleepy little smile, although I don't really think he was awake yet.

Meanwhile the mother had turned on her son and begun a cross-examination in which he could only manage to get in "Ma . . . uh . . ." before she went on. "Why didn't you bring a girl home like this before? You ought to marry her if she'll have you. She is from a good family, after all . . ." It went on like this until Saul was squirming like I hadn't seen him squirm since our post-marital game of penis envy in his brother's car. If only he could find himself a nice, respectable wife instead of all those silly young girls he took out! Didn't he want to make his mother happy? Halfway dreaming about a *chupa* (Jewish wedding ceremony) she kept saying, "What a nice girl, not even a *schicksha,* a nice girl from Holland!"

Now she turned back to me—I half-expected her to ask me to produce my bank book and credit references—and shifted gears in my direction. Now that we were friends (and I really did like her despite her tyranny over Saul!) she could come right out and ask me about my green pant-suit. Admiring the material at close hand—she started to feel the material, then evidently thought better of it—she asked, almost maternally, where I had got my "lovely suit" and did I mind if she asked how much it had cost.

I told her I bought it in Saks Fifth Avenue. It was an Yves St. Laurent suit—and I'd really forgotten the price.

Another key word: "price." She turned on Saul again: "If only you made more money. You couldn't afford a girl like this—her clothes alone would keep you broke."

All this while I was torn between feeling sorry for Saul and an almost insane desire to roll on the floor with laughter. His mother was magnificent! The Ultimate Jewish Mother! I might feel badly about having visited Saul's parents later on, but right now I wouldn't have missed it for the world.

It was my turn again. "Didn't you say you are an interior decorator?" she asked me.

"Yes, that's what I said."

"Well," she continued, "you must make a bundle of money."

"I make a fairly good living, and I am pretty independent," I said.

Over to Saul: she yelled at him, "Do you hear that, Saul, you should have become an interior decorator!"

Uh uh, no fair. I had to defend Saul! "Everyone should do what he or she wants to do. After all, don't we need letter carriers as well as interior decorators? Which work is more important?"

Feeling I'd done a little right by Saul, I also felt this was a good time for my exit. I really had to go, I said, because I had an appointment for five o'clock (which was true). I went over to Saul, gave him a little hug—our first real body contact!—and kissed him on the cheek. I then thanked his mother for all her hospitality, said I'd enjoyed the visit very much (again true), and hoped I'd see her again. She tried to wake Saul's father up, but he was quietly snoring away again—I suspect he slept in self-defense—and I said not to bother him. My last thought, upon leaving that apart-ment, was that I hoped the old man, in the middle of these mother-and-son dramas, was able to dream about the good times he had when he was young.

As Saul and I left I heard her whisper to him that I was the type of girl he should marry. If only she'd known!

Some time later I got a phone call from Saul. He seemed pretty upset. He told me his roommate had gotten himself into a lot of hot water. Dick had gotten a job but only for a short while. and now he was broke again. And Saul said, "Now something very bad has happened."

I asked him what it was.

"Dick has knocked up his girlfriend. They've been seeing each other on and off for a year now. She's an Italian chick and Dick, you know, is Jewish. Now it turns out the broad is about three months pregnant and her father is threatening to kill Dick. The chick's father is a real tough guy, you know, connected with the Mafia . . . They want revenge, both her dad and her brother."

I was listening but didn't quite know what Saul was getting at. What the hell did I have to do with his roommate's troubles?

"Why are you telling me all this?" I asked him.

"Wait a minute," Saul said, "let me finish the story . . . If Dick pays the father five thousand dollars, he'll consider not killing him and forgive him for what he's done to his daughter."

"Saul, why didn't Dick take the girl to an abortion clinic? Abortion is legal nowadays, or why didn't he take the girl to a good doctor and have the baby aborted there?"

"Are you crazy?" Saul yelled in my ear. "You know how those Guineas are! Their girls have to be virgins when they get married. and Italians look on abortion and the Pill as a sin. Xaviera, you should know better than that."

I told him not to talk nonsense. After all, they weren't a bunch of kids, so why didn't he marry her? They'd been seeing each other for a year, hadn't they?

"But he's got no job to support her."

I repeated that if Dick was fucking around with this girl for over a year, obviously it was no rape scene. She most probably loved to get fucked.

Saul said, "Look, Xaviera, Dick really needs that bread.

Jesus, he needs at least four thousand dollars and he can't borrow anything from his father. He has no bread and his poor mother goes out scrubbing floors in an office building until late each night. If he doesn't get that money in the next two or three days, he'll get a bullet through his head. And I'd hate to be in the same house with him when that happens."

"Listen," I said, "I'm beginning not to believe a word of this. The whole story is just a lot of bullshit and this whole conversation is ridiculous. And, what, for Christ's sake, do *I* have to do with this whole thing anyway? Listen, baby, you and I might be married, but I am not going to deal with Dick's problems and certainly I don't expect him to deal with mine."

I was about to hang up the phone when Saul started stuttering, "Listen, Xaviera, all I ask you for my roommate is to lend him four thousand dollars so we all can breathe again and don't have to fear for our lives . . . he says he'll definitely pay you back. He said he'd get a job next week or sooner."

Saul then went on to point out that for me, "four thousand dollars wasn't a lot of money. "For you," he said, "it's only a matter of a couple of weeks' work and you'll save my roommate from being killed. You don't want him to get killed, or me by accident, do you?"

"To tell you the truth, Saul, at this moment I couldn't care less whether he drops dead from fright, if your story is true. But it looks to me like you guys are trying to blackmail me to the tune of four thousand dollars. I've given you girls and I've given you one thousand dollars for doing absolutely nothing and you still haven't filled out any immigration forms for me. Saul, as far as I am concerned, you have a nice little arrangement going for you. Don't spoil it now and don't get me involved with your roommate's problems in any way, shape, or form. Let him try and blackmail someone else."

Larry had just walked into the apartment and saw by looking at me that I was pretty aggravated with the person I was talking to on the phone. He asked me who it was. I held my hand over the mouthpiece and said it was Saul. I quickly explained the story and suggested to Saul that he should talk to my "old man." For the next ten minutes they carried on a very heated conversation. Then Larry hung up, with a few choice curse words for Saul.

Saul, my dear husband, didn't show up for the next three weeks, not even to get his regular Dutch Treat. Then he finally called to ask for a girl. At least he didn't ask me to make up for the "scores" that he'd missed. And I never heard another word about Dick and his labors of love.

Up until July, 1971, everything went well. Then I got arrested, and I decided not to have Saul fill out any immigration papers. I was too hot to fool around with a marriage deal, yet I wanted to stay married for a while, in case I might need him later on that year.

In September, Saul showed up unexpectedly, accompanied by a young woman. She was a twenty-four-year-old school teacher from Brooklyn, whom, Saul said, he'd been dating for a couple of months. She was hardly the innocent virgin type, still living with her parents, that most of his previous girlfriends had been, but rather a bitchy young woman who'd already been married, divorced, and left with two kids.

She and Saul obviously hit it off quite well, and now the lady was pushing him to get a divorce. She, not Saul, suddenly slapped a subpoena into my hand and told me that Saul wanted to sue for divorce on grounds of adultery.

"Adultery?" I asked, absolutely incredulous. "You know our whole marriage was a fake. But do you know that Saul got one thousand dollars out of it and some extra gratuities. I'm sure he hasn't told you about that yet. Isn't that right, Saul?"

Saul turned beet red and managed to stutter that his lawyer had suggested he seek a divorce on grounds of adultery because that supposedly would go through quicker.

"What's your rush?" I asked him.

"Saul wants to get out of this and as soon as possible," she answered for him. "He's afraid he'll get himself in trouble now that you've been all over the newspapers . . . well, maybe you'll drop his name, and his reputation, you know, his parents and all that . . . even if I wasn't pushing him, you'd only stay married for another half year or so, right?"

"Allright, allright," I said, "if you're in that much of a rush, I'll contact my lawyer, but please change that adultery bit, because you know as well as I that that's considered to be a crime morally. All I need on top of prostitution charges is an adultery charge in a divorce case."

Since the grounds Saul wanted to use for the divorce would be disastrous for my immigration case, I engaged a smart—and, of course, expensive—attorney and the two lawyers (I agreed to pay both of their fees) arranged to obtain an annulment. We would state that the marriage was never consummated, so that while the marriage had been a lie, the annulment was the honest-to-God truth.

Working out the papers for the annulment took, altogether, about two months. Around Christmas of 1971, we finally pursued the annulment action. Saul and I weren't speaking to each other as a result of his new girlfriend's presence, just like a real husband and wife getting a divorce. Saul had resisted the lack of consummation idea—I guess he was protecting his image as a terrific stud—and finally we had to use Kathy as a witness to ensure the granting of the annulment.

Kathy and I, my lawyer and Saul's lawyer, and Saul went into the judge's chambers. The annulment took place in the Queens Court House. Kathy went in to see the judge beforehand. Later on, the judge asked, "Saul, did you have any intentions of raising a family when you married Xaviera?"

Saul: "Yes, I had every intention of raising a family when I married Xaviera."

Judge: "Xaviera, did you have intentions of raising a family when you married Saul?"

Xaviera: "Yes, I had seriously wanted to have his children."

Judge: "Kathy, did you see either Saul or Xaviera discussing this matter before their marriage?"

Kathy: "Yes, about two weeks before they were married, I saw them together on the couch, snuggling, holding hands, and kissing. They were both talking about how great it would be to get married and have a couple of kids."

Judge: "Is this true, Saul and Xaviera?"

Both of us: "Yes, this is true."

Judge: "So what happened after the both of you got married?"

Xaviera: "My husband deserted me. He never spent a night with me, and we never consummated the marriage."

Judge: "Is this true, Saul? Did you desert your wife on the night of your marriage."

Saul: "Yes, I did."

Judge: "So, in other words, you never really consummated your marriage? Do I understand you correctly? Kathy, did you ever hear anything about this?"

Kathy: "Yes, I saw them quarrel shortly after the marriage. I never saw Saul stay overnight. I saw him come and go during the day, and one night, I saw him get into a bad fight with Xaviera. He almost hit her in the face, but she ducked in time. The marriage was on the rocks almost immediately."

Judge: "This is reason enough for me to annul your marriage, since it was never consummated. Herewith, your marriage is annulled. You, Saul Brodsky, and you, Xaviera Hollander, are no longer to be considered husband and wife. The formal papers will be forwarded to your attorney's offices within the next month. Thank you very much for your presence. Goodbye."

So this was the official end of my marriage to Saul, the letter carrier from Queens!

The Girls in My Life

ELFIE: The House Clown

Made In Germany: tall, long-legged, blonde, bright-eyed, effervescent Elfie. She gave my house *das Gewissene etwas* (that certain spice), a lot of color, warmth—her own special atmosphere, as it were. Elfie was unique.

An appearance in the living room by Elfie was an event. She didn't enter a room, she conquered it. The Parade of the Conquering Heroine might describe her more casual entrances, with her huge handbag part of her uniform or else an unbrella raised in salute to herself.

Elfie's "uniform"? Well, the only thing uniform about Elfie was her love for the color white. White hot pants. White sweaters so tight her breathing should have been impeded. Long white gloves. White wigs so platinum they matched any of her whiter-than-white Ivory Snow outfits. Was Elfie trying to project an almost-virginal image? I honestly, to this day, haven't figured her out. If any of the other girls had worn those outrageous platinum wigs, they'd have looked silly. But Elfie—well, dear Elfie was right in uniform. But underneath the uniform, the woman—the real person—was hard to locate.

I guess Elfie wanted it that way. We did know she'd had a kind of tough life back in Germany as a barmaid but *that* Elfie—we never got to meet her. *Our* Elfie was a dynamite

lady with a large grin and a larger repertoire of outrageous
lines, all delivered with a crazy (to both the Johns and the
rest of us) Kraut accent (she really was the only German
person I've known with a grand sense of humor, which is
probably unfair of me to say) that made her not only a
show-stopper but a business stopper. When Elfie was "on,"
no one went into the bedrooms to get "off." I'm sorry I
can't describe any of these "happenings"—they really defy
description. You would have had to be there (and I'm sorry
you weren't!).

Well, not only did everybody seem to dig her when she
was dressed, living it up in the living room, but men absolutely adored her in the bedroom because she was (un-
beknownst to them) the greatest faker of orgasms in Creation and really knew how to turn those men on. Sometimes,
purely for amusement, I'd manage to get involved in a
three-way scene with her and some quiet, boring customer
who really was no fun to be with and when she got into that
crazy clowning mood of hers, I often had a hard time keeping
a straight face. We'd both be working over our friend in the
bed, and she'd turn to me when he wasn't looking and make
faces like a *paljasso* (clown), all the time convincing her
customer that she was absolutely enraptured by his love-
making.

While he was on top of her, almost pushing his shoulders
through her chin, she would, her clowning face towards me,
carry on like gangbusters, screaming and moaning in a
wildly vocal parody of fine lovemaking. "Oh, Daaaaarling,
fuck me, hold me tight. Put that cock deeper inside me, all
the way . . . yes, *wunderbar*. Oh, *schatzel*, it is so beautiful,
I am waiting for you, uhhhhh, give it to me, ahhhhh, by
God, you do have the biggest cock in town, don't you?"
(Meanwhile winking at me like a naughty schoolchild.)
Then she would carry on and moan: "Oh, darling, I can feel
that prick of yours, all the way up my warm cunt. Come
on *schatzie,* give it to Elfie, she wants you so badly, fuck me,
fuck me!"

When she carried on like that, I had to stuff the edge of
the pillow or part of the sheets in my mouth to keep from
bursting out in loud laughter. And of course I was very helpful. While she was carrying on, I'd occasionally pinch her

on her boobs or blow kisses in her ears to distract her. In-between her carrying-on, she'd whisper a different version of her comedy scene in my ears: how lousy he was, how heavy he weighed, what a bad breath he had, etc., etc. Luckily I always had some background music on and between all the panting and sighing he never understood a word of her kidding, which was generally in German, anyway.

If her guy was still not ready to come, I'd crawl next to him or right behind him and assist Elfie in her appointed tasks by fondling and massaging his balls and cock or helping him put it back into her cunt or if it seemed slippery, keep him from getting off the road. With a few more screams and hot talk from Elfie and me the guy would eventually explode in a glorious climax, believing that all three of us had achieved utter satisfaction from his panting and pumping. If only he knew that Elfie and I had both sore jaws from the laughter that took place while he was seriously working on his climax . . . Remember—the customer always comes first.

However, if the customer happened to be an attractive young man, then Elfie would honestly enjoy her work and she definitely did not have to fake orgasms. She loved sex. The room would really reverberate with genuine love sounds that could be heard all the way to dear old Deutschland. Elfie never claimed to be anything like demure. She could come with the noisiest of them.

Talking about white, her favorite color, one day she purchased a puppy, a white toy poodle not yet housebroken, and brought the little bastard over to my house in her pocketbook. Every night the little stinker used to shit all over the place, in the kitchen, behind the couch, in the hallway, and Elfie would run after him to clean up his droppings. One day, when I picked him up and held him up high above me, genuinely admiring the cute little bugger, he crapped all over my shoulder and clean sheets. Love me, love my dog . . . No thanks, Elfie!

Despite her apparently jolly nature and generous personality, Elfie had had and still was having an unhappy personal life. She had been disillusioned by lots of men. These guys most probably took her goodness for granted and simply took over from there. And Elfie also faced deportation because of her soon-to-expire visitor's visa.

She didn't want to go back to Germany, where obviously she had earned some very bad memories. As she'd confessed only to me, when she'd been a barmaid, in a horrid, sordid section of Hamburg, some of her guys had roughed her up and one of her ex-boyfriends had virtually knocked her into the hospital on several occasions. Worse yet, he was the father of her ten-year-old daughter. (I was the only one among her friends in America to know about the child.) Finally she managed to run away from him, leaving the child with her parents. They had no money so now she was responsible for not only supporting her child but also her parents. Life was hardly a comedy for Elfie and, as you might well expect, her great good humor was something of a facade. As I got to know her better, I realized how much she relied on alcohol and pills to keep her spirits up.

Then, instead of being genuinely funny and fun to be with, she got out of control and would ofttimes be merely vulgar and unpleasant. After one of my arrest cases, in which she had been involved, she developed an immense fear about getting arrested again, because that would have meant immediate deportation for her.

Finally, and so sadly, the combination of more and more booze, the pills, and her psychological problems made her impossible to live with and I had to sever our business relationship, but not our dear friendship. I wanted desperately to help her but she resented anyone's advice, regarding it as criticism instead of affectionate help.

Several months after Elfie and I stopped working together, I learned she'd been hospitalized and had almost died of liver and kidney ailments. When she recuperated she decided to pack her bags and go off with a good-looking guy with whom she was in love—all news to me!—to Reno, Nevada, where incidentally prostitution is quite legal. If nothing else, should she consider getting back to her profession, she wouldn't have to worry about the law chasing her.

However, the last I'd heard, her new boyfriend—an aspiring photographer whom I'd met once and who struck me as a decent man, a bit simple but an okay guy—does not want her to work as a hooker anymore. So, dear Elfie has maybe stopped being the paranoid prostitute and is having a real chance at happiness.

Auf wiedersehen, Elfie; it was so good knowing you.

I wish you well with all my heart.

JIMMY, DON'T JUMP AGAIN!

I'll remember David, my hustling friend, yes, but of all the men I've met over the last year—and there have been, I confess, quite a few—the one who most elicited my sympathy and who perhaps was the most remarkable of all was Jimmy.

I met Jimmy through rather strange circumstances, shortly after my last arrest case. I had gone to a charity dinner party with an Italian count named Fabrizzio—a nice quiet banker in his mid-thirties who had taken me to several society events as his companion for the night. And the night ended at my door, which was fine with me. Fabrizzio wanted to have an attractive woman companion at these affairs, and I was curious about the people who went to such events. I found the women cold and competitive, each anxious to top the other in latest fashions, number of gallery openings attended, newest restaurants visited earliest—you name it. The men were a more familiar breed. In fact some of them had been clients of mine, but at these parties they would stare right through me and coolly say hello as though we'd never seen each other before. That was all right with me, too, as you soon find out who the real human beings are in the business I'd most recently been a part of. I could understand their not greeting me as an old friend, but these guys went overboard to be as unfriendly as possible.

As we say in the old country, fuck 'em. I had, but I sure wouldn't anymore!

So what I learned from these parties is that the women are a good model on which not to base yourself, and the men are either snobs or phonies. I'm generalizing, sure, but the parties did tend to become a bore, and certainly less fun than parties thrown by my friends who weren't in the Social Register.

I shared these sentiments with Fabrizzio, and he said he mostly agreed. However, he said, there was a good friend of his I'd really like if I met him. And the reason he hadn't been at any of these parties was the same reason that I hadn't yet met him.

Fabrizzio was being unusually mysterious, but he'd always been straight with me and he'd made me curious about this friend of his, whose name was Jimmy. He suggested that I give Jimmy a call and see how I liked him. Fabrizzio assured me I'd be glad I did so.

So one day not too long after my last date with Fabrizzio, I did make the call and Jimmy and I hit it off over the phone right from the start. He sounded very upper class but also very friendly and funny. And after talking with him for a while, he even sounded less upper class—Etonian or something British—to me.

After about a twenty-minute conversation, Jimmy said, "Hey, this is silly—why don't you pop over here. I'm on Seventy-second Street, right off Madison."

I hesitated a moment, and he continued, "Listen, I'd come to see you, but I really can't just now. You'll see what I mean when you get here."

"Okay," I said. "I'll take a cab and see you soon."

To my surprise, I found myself actually hurrying to get ready to go out and meet this mysterious Jimmy. I got a cab without any trouble—always a good omen in New York City—and in a very few minutes I arrived at Jimmy's place. It was a handsome townhouse, but there was no elevator and I found myself walking up several flights of stairs. When I got to his floor, out of breath—not realizing the depth of each stairwell, I'd charged up the stairs like a racehorse—

Jimmy let me into a lovely old apartment with a fire going in the living room.

I thanked him and sat down, and when I finally recovered my breath, the first thing I realized about Jimmy was that he most resembled a walking skeleton hanging in between two wooden crutches. He was standing there—hanging there, really—grinning at me, and I was happy to see that his face, while thin, was quite attractive. He had long shoulder-length blonde hair and haunting blue eyes, kind of sad and melancholic yet something wild and cynical, perhaps, there as well. The grin remained on his face, which accented its strong lines, mostly because he was so terribly gaunt. His hands, I noticed, were large and strong-looking, yet the nails were manicured and I guessed on the spot that he'd never done any manual work in his life, no more so than any of his other society chums.

Jimmy couldn't help but feel himself being scrutinized—he'd have to have been blind in addition to crippled to do so—and he said, still smiling, "Sorry, he should have told you about my situation, that sly, secretive Fabrizzio, but I guess he meant well . . . You're looking at my hands, huh, big hands but hands like a baby, never worked a day in my life . . . I guess your thoughts pretty good, huh?"

"Very good. You should take up mind-reading." He was very intense, but somehow it didn't bother me.

"Let's see . . . what else? Oh, you're wondering about this fucking manicure. That one's easier—at least easier than why I never worked a day in my life. As you can see, I can't very well make it out of the house, so some friends sent a chick up to take care of my nails . . . yeah, and since it's a bit hard for me to get down and bite my toenails off, she did those, too." He had stopped smiling and was looking a little pathetic.

"Jimmy, stop it already—who cares about your toes and nails? How did you get yourself into this horrible condition?" I said, indicating the crutches.

He hobbled over to me and extended his hand. "Hope you don't mind if we shake hands?" he said, the grin back on his face. "I'm Jimmy. . . ."

I took his hand. "Delighted to meet you. My name is Lady Du Barry."

"Yes." he said, kidding with me, "I know the family well. Did your father go to the University of Hamburg with my uncle?"

"Perhaps. I can't say for sure, because Father left home when I was in finishing school, studying embroidery."

"Hey, Xaviera." Jimmy said suddenly, as though to interrupt our little game, "let's go into the other room. There's a chair there I can sit in without hearing my bones creak." With that he swung himself around on his crutches and led me into a second room, a cozy study with a desk and walls of bookshelves. There was a fire going here as well.

Jimmy lowered himself into a large, old-fashioned leather easy chair and indicated a matching chair, across from him, for me to sit in. He pointed one crutch toward the fire, saying, "I know it's weird, having a fire going at this time of year, but in my present condition I get the chills, easily, so a guy comes up and keeps the home fires burning . . . Oh, *I'm* not very polite—can I get you something to drink?" He started to help himself up from the chair, and I could see that it was painful for him.

"No, no, I'm perfectly fine. Just sit back and tell me what happened."

"Well, I could use a little something," he said. and pulled himself up and onto his crutches. As he went by me, I could see how the clothes just hung on his frame—Jimmy must have been at least six feet tall, and because he was so thin looked even taller—and I could almost count his ribs underneath the knit shirt he was wearing.

He yelled from the kitchen, "Are you sure I can't get you something? Fabrizzio says you don't drink—you some kind of Puritan or something?"

"Yes, an orange juice," I yelled back from behind my chair. "And, yes, I am a Puritan. I have no vices . . . to speak of."

I got up and went into the small kitchen to bring back the two glasses for Jimmy while he hobbled on his crutches behind me. I sat his drink on the lamp table alongside his chair and then sat down myself with my orange juice. Friends have asked me how I can manage to drink so much orange juice, and I always reply that I've tried wine and liquor and don't care for the taste. Orange juice is my favorite drink, bar none!

"We were speaking," Jimmy began, the wide grin back again, "of the Puritan life. *I've* been living it, God knows, but you, too. . . ?"

"Yes, I flunked my exams for the nunnery but have been practicing without a license."

"Hey, Xaviera, no shit now, I really was sorry to hear about your 'busts' by the police."

"Well, maybe it's all for the good. Running a house was only fun when it *was* fun—with no harassment, but I'm happy to be out of that life. It wasn't any fun—just nerve-wracking—at the end."

"Anyhow," Jimmy said, "I want you to know that I really dig hookers, if they're 'real people,' 'cause when they are they're the greatest chicks in the world."

"On behalf of my friends and former associates, I thank you . . . but, really, Jimmy, are we ever going to talk about *you*—and those crutches? Fabrizzio didn't tell me a single thing. I don't mean to pry, but I'd really like to hear what happened."

"Well, it's a long boring story, but here goes . . . I'm twenty-six and I've lived an absolutely worthless life. I was born with a silver spoon in my mouth—you know the expression?—because my grand-daddy was the founder of a large banking and trust company here in the city. I never have to lift a finger to take care of my material needs. It's all there, all the loot I'll ever need for the rest of my life."

"That doesn't sound so tough to take. It's a lot harder to be bored without money than it is with it."

"Yeah, I know—I really shouldn't complain because if I *had* to earn a living, I don't know what I'd do . . . but to continue the Great Saga, I was brought up by nurses and nannies and tutors and I went to the right prep schools—including Oxbridge, don't you know—and the right Ivy League schools and then I became a professional playboy. On the town every night, dating a series of stupid little cunts with nothing on their minds except weekends in the Hamptons and evenings at Le Club and Raffles and P.J.'s and black-tie dinner parties and all the rest. The eternal small talk, the eternal drivel—all the bullshit and intrigue and behind their small minds, one thought: to get the right catch and live at the right address and then to buy the right house in the right suburb and—"

"Whoa there, Jimmy," I said, "no one *made* you go out with those chicks. The city is full of interesting women. The *world* is full of interesting women, and nobody was forcing you to stay in the New York party-party scene."

"I know, I know," he replied, softly, "but I was a victim of too much breeding, I guess. I went out with these broads out of habit, and I went to hookers out of need. At least I had some real fun with them."

"Didn't you ever go to bed with the girls you went out with?"

"Sure, they all screw—everyone screws, haven't you heard! We've been sexually liberated and every date—every good time—ends with a screw. But I was generally so bored by the end of the evening that I preferred to go to a good house and get my rocks off without any pretense, without pretending that the time in bed with a woman meant any more than a good roll in the hay."

"Well, it's not the first time I've heard that line of thought. . . ."

"Look, I have no right to complain—I had my jollies, one way or another—but you've got to be pretty stupid not to know when you're leading a meaningless existence, that there's a real world out there and you've no part in it!"

"Is that . . . why the crutches? Did you try to do something to yourself?"

"Several things. The first was to enlist to go to Vietnam. I didn't believe in the 'threat from Communism in Southeast Asia'—the Viet Cong swimming across the Pacific to infiltrate San Diego and Palm Springs—or any of that crap, but Vietnam was the burning issue in America and I wanted to know what it was all about. I'd beaten the draft in college, and now I was going to be like the other poor slobs who had to serve in 'Nam. I was going to prove that I wasn't better than them—that I was *one* of them. . . ."

"Did you? What did you prove?"

"Nothing, really. First of all, I was an officer, so it wasn't the same, except when we were out in the jungle. There was real democracy out there, I'll tell you! We had more money and better equipment than the Cong, but the fight for life and death was pretty equal . . . so in a way, I guess being there was the only real thing that *has* happened to me. The people were for real, and so was the suffering."

"Were you wounded there?" I asked, wondering if I'd *ever* hear the explanation for the crutches. It wasn't that I was impatient with his story—on the contrary, I was fascinated—but I felt he kept holding something back.

"No, I was—ah, 'wounded' here. But that's a ways off in the story. You got the time and energy to hear the rest of it?"

"Yes. I have the time if you have the energy." He was looking weary and drawn, and I didn't know if this was from the effort it took to tell the story I seemed to have asked for—actually I'd expected a brief explanation, not this whole painful experience of his—or his physical condition. I thought maybe I should leave and hear the rest when he was feeling better, and I suggested as much.

"No, no, please don't—I really groove on the company. But maybe it'd be better if I lie down. You mind? There are a couple comfortable chairs in the bedroom. . . ."

"No, of course not. Can I help you?"

"Yes . . . just follow your leader." He hoisted himself up with the aid of one crutch, and I came over to help support him on the other side. Together we shuffled past the kitchen and down a hall into a darkened room which was the bedroom. The curtains were still drawn, and Jimmy asked for his other crutch, which I'd been carrying for him, and hobbled over to the bed and after some fumbling, lit two candles standing in plates on the bookshelf behind the bed.

It was some room. Easily as big as the living room, with a fireplace and a tall window on either side. The bed was a waterbed, the biggest I'd ever seen. There were books all over, in bookcases and in piles on chairs and on the bed and on the floor, and ashtrays filled with cigarette butts and empty glasses and several Scotch bottles—all Chivas Regal, no less—and I couldn't help but wonder if Jimmy didn't do all his living in this room rather than in the rest of the comfortable apartment.

On the walls, in addition to the built-in bookcases, were a series of paintings of horses, all by the same artist, and on one side of the room there was a large closet, the doors open to reveal a huge wardrobe of suits and sport jackets. And over the fireplace were some framed family photographs, and I went over to examine them while Jimmy got into bed. There was one of Jimmy as a young boy with very light curly hair down to his shoulders—just like now! —and a rebellious expression on his face. The other portraits were of his family—of his two brothers, he told me, and his parents. Maybe I'm reverse-prejudiced or something, but I thought the snottiness virtually dripped off *their* faces, and I said to Jimmy, jokingly, "You're a real 'Wasp,' aren't you, Jimmy?"

"No," came his answer, "but *they* are." He indicated his parents' photo.

I turned my attention back to Jimmy. He was still getting out of his clothes, with considerable difficulty, it seemed. I made a move to help him, but he motioned me not to. "Got to know where the really weak parts are," he said, pointing a finger toward his back.

"Is a waterbed good for a weak back?" I asked him while he was still struggling to get out of his shirt.

"For mine it is. I can't stand a regular bed. At least not yet."

He had his shirt off, finally, and was now undoing his pants. I offered to help again, and he nodded, easing himself to a sitting position on the low bed and putting his arms behind him on the bed, for support. With a gentle tug I was able to slide his pants down his long legs and couldn't help but notice that his legs were more muscular than his upper torso, which was the proverbial skin-and-bones.

"Yeh," he said, reading my thoughts again, "the doctor says to exercise as much as I can, so I bounce around the apartment all I can stand. It has helped rebuild my legs at least . . ." With that, he eased himself back on the bed, pulled a sheet up to his waist, and lit a cigarette from a pack on the shelf behind him. "Pull up a chair," he said, after a long inhale, "and we can kibbitz some more."

Instead of pulling up a chair, I kicked off my shoes and pulled my dress over my head. This was done strictly on impulse, because I wanted to be on that waterbed, beside him. I didn't know where sympathy ended and genuine affection began, but I really felt close to him—as though we were already old, old friends—and I wanted to be close. Not sexually close, because I'd be afraid even to caress him, much less make love to him, but at least physically close.

So with just my panties on, I carefully snuggled under the sheet close to him, not really touching except for my head, which I carefully lowered into the crook of his arm, sharing the pillow with him. I think he must have been as surprised to find me there, alongside of him, as *I* was to be there, and he said, kiddingly, "Ahem. Ahem there, Miss Hollander, I'm not aware that you were invited to bed with me. . . ."

"I wasn't. Should I leave?"

"No, please be my guest," he said quietly, and for a time-less period we just lay there, barely touching, his arm around my shoulder. Every few minutes he would shift around to get another cigarette, but otherwise we just lay there motion-less, Jimmy chain-smoking and blowing the smoke in the air and the two of us watching the smoke rise into the danc-ing candlelight. Jimmy seemed millions of miles away—such a strange bird he was—and I really wished I could learn what had happened to him, what was really bothering him so much.

After an interlude of silence—it could have been fifteen minutes, it could have been more—he finally spoke. "The only good friends I have—they all live down in the Village on Carmine Street. Two of them are Iranian boys from very wealthy families, who have completely rebelled against their backgrounds. They live like hippies most of the time, con-stantly stoned, and now and then they try and make a buck as stock brokers or bank trainees or something. Because of their family connections, they can manage this, and at least they work *some* of the time.

"There's another guy, a tall good-looking cat from Madrid whose family is filthy rich. He's thirty, travels a lot, but whenever he's in town he falls in there. Then there's the other of my real good friends, a black kid from the Bahamas. No bread whatsoever but the grooviest guy you can imagine —helpful, intelligent, a lot of laughs. He just happens to be too damn lazy to work—I'm independently wealthy and he's independently lazy—so the others let him live there without charging him for rent or food. His contribution is to supply drugs for them—they pay for the stuff and he does the scoring. Anyhow, they basically all think along the same lines I do, and I damn well have intentions, when I can walk without those freaking crutches, to move out of here and in with them!"

"Jimmy, do you consider *that* 'real life'—just hanging around, getting stoned all the time? What's so great about that?"

"Hell, I don't know—don't ask too much, Xaviera, I am desperately trying to straighten out my head, but I just don't know where to start. . . ."

"Jimmy, you've been avoiding one question ever since I got here," I said. I had turned toward him, with my body propped on my elbow. "What exactly did happen to you?"

"Okay, here we go, ready or not. It's really not very exciting . . . I merely fell off a roof a couple of months ago."

"Fell off a roof! For chrissakes, what were you doing on that roof in the first place?"

"Oh, it was just one of those crazy early spring nights, kind of hot, and I had nothing better to do. Mind you, I wasn't even stoned—what I *was* was fed up with the world and living in it. I was fed up with New York and I was fed up with America—and I got this crazy idea to go up on the roof and watch the moon and the stars and the whole fucking universe and pretend that someday I would wake up to find myself on another planet. So there I was, standing on the edge of the roof, and all of a sudden I felt this mad, crazy urge to go off the roof and do some flying. I would jump off, fly around a little, and then cruise down to a landing."

"You're putting me on—you must have been zonked out of your mind."

"No, I was totally convinced I could fly. I would fly and then safely land down on the street."

I didn't say anything. What could I say?

"So . . . off I flew, Jimmy the Birdman, and the next thing I recall was waking up in a hospital weeks later— they told me I'd completely lost my memory for the first few weeks—with my entire body in traction, bandaged from stem to stern. I'd survived my little 'flight,' but don't ask me how . . . I often think I would have been better off dead.

My agony before had been mental and spiritual, and I had to go add this broken body to my problems."

"Jimmy, weren't you really trying to commit suicide? If not consciously, then subconsciously?"

"Baby, I told you, I was in one of those shitty moods where I don't know *what* was in my mind. Besides, haven't you ever wanted to fly?"

"No, but I've been on the balcony of a nineteenth-floor apartment and thought of jumping off—and there was no doubt about what was in my mind that night. Suicide. But I thought better of it. What if it wasn't a sudden death? What if I were crippled the rest of my life?"

Now it was Jimmy's turn to say nothing.

"But I *do* know what you mean about the sky and the stars," I said, anxious to make the conversation less morbid. "Some nights, looking out over Manhattan, with the moon and the stars in the distance, the sky seems to be beckoning to you, like the mother of us all, saying, 'Come to me, come to me. . . .' "

"Yeah, I can dig that," Jimmy said.

"Listen, Jimmy, I have got to ask—will you be better? What do the doctors say?"

"The doctors give me a seventy-five percent chance to recover completely, but I will have to be a model patient, exercising on schedule and getting plenty of rest. I broke nearly every bone in my body, you see, and I was in the hospital almost four months."

"It must have been awful. And you're so thin. . . ."

"Well, I wasn't always this way. I used to weigh a hundred and eighty." Then he quipped, "Lost sixty pounds, but not my life!"

"What about your parents and friends—did they visit you a lot?"

"My parents came to see their invalid son faithfully, once a week, like clockwork, but I think I was some embarrassment to them—after all, a son who thinks he can fly, what kind of son is that? Actually we haven't gotten along for a long while, and now they're convinced I'm some kind of nut . . . Who knows, maybe I am."

"What about your friends?"

"My Village buddies came by, although half the time

they were stoned, but they meant well. As for my 'uptown' friends—well, a few of them managed to fit me into their busy social schedules, but I think I was an embarrassment to them, too. As for the chicks, well, what good was I to them if I couldn't take them to all the right places. A couple of them fell by here when I got home, but when they saw I couldn't entertain them—that they had to play a little nursemaid for me, in fact—they made themselves scarce."

"Shouldn't you have a regular nurse here—to help you getting dressed and eating and all the little things?"

"Yeah, I should—I can afford it, certainly, and the hospital recommended it—but I'm a loner by nature and probably always will be. Actually I'm in too much pain a lot of the time to want anyone around. I just drink a lot and then sleep it off. Sometimes Anselmo, the black friend I told you about, comes by and we smoke a little, or pop something, and that helps a lot."

"Boy, that's some recovery plan you have!" I said, laughing but really disturbed by what he was telling me about his days and nights.

"Say, Xaviera, you wouldn't care to apply for the position of day nurse, would you?"

"Do I look like a nurse to you, day or otherwise?"

"Frankly, you look delicious to me—you look like a lady with *nibbly* boobs and a nice full sweeping inviting ass, the kind I could hold on to and bite into. I really dig your ass, you know that?"

"Oh, oh, sounds like you're not so sick after all. How long has it been since you've had sex?"

"*Groan*—that's the sound of my cock groaning! It's been since before the Great Flight of 1971 took off. Those nurses, even the ugly ones, wouldn't come close to me. Not even a blow job in the middle of the night to help a poor patient sleep. There was this one young redhead, and I was *sooo* horny, that I came right out and asked her to give some head, and she snickered. She knew what it meant, all right, but she wasn't having any. Yeah, she actually snickered and said, 'Jimmy, you be a good boy, now. You've lost a lot of weight and you aren't even strong enough to move your hands, much less your sexual organ.'"

"So why didn't she move your 'sexual organ' for you?"

"To tell the truth, she was kind of a prick-teaser. When she straightened out my bed, she'd wiggle her ass and lean over and let me see down her nurse's uniform—you know, shit like that."

"Just a minute, Jimmy, I want to hear the rest of your story, but let me get you another drink and me some more juice. I'm all dried up from what you've told me so far."

I returned in a couple of minutes with a Scotch on the rocks for Jimmy and "the usual" for me. I gave Jimmy his drink and then carefully got back under the sheets from the other side so I wouldn't spill any juice. All this while I was bare-breasted, of course, but I'd never given it any thought, so engrossed was I with his story. And Jimmy, until the last few minutes, had been so engrossed in telling it, that I don't think he was really aware of my physical presence— my body, the "sex object" Women's Lib talks about—next to him. I felt toward him as a dear sweet, admittedly crazy, younger brother, and in any case, now that I was aware of his multitude of broken bones, I wasn't about to fool around with him. Some other time, perhaps, because I was already crazily fond of him, but the idea of making love with some-one so fragile was simply something beyond my experience, and I'd be much too concerned about hurting him to enjoy it, even for a minute.

"So what else about this nurse, Jimmy?" I asked.

"Nothing much," Jimmy said. "When I got a little better, I said to her one day, 'You know, you are not a very nice person. Every time I see you—unless it's my imagination— you do your best to turn me on. And then you don't even acknowledge the sexual electricity between us. That's just not fair.' And since I could now move my arms, I tried to lift off the sheet and show her the place my big cock was hiding. . . ." He looked at me wistfully.

"Quick! Don't stop—what happened?"

"Nothing. She actually tapped me gently in that area, said, 'Now, now, we mustn't excite ourselves until we're well again,' wiggled her ass about four times as provocatively as before, and left me lying there with a painful—a fucking *physically* painful—erection. I could have killed her if I could only have gotten off the bed! I don't remember ever having been so angry and so weak—both at the same time.

Being horny physically drained me, without my ever having gotten 'drained' the right way."

"Poor Jimmy . . . didn't you ever get your rocks off during those months?"

"Sure, I have a rich fantasy life, and so I had some terrific wet dreams—in Cinemascope, Metrocolor, and Panavision all at once. Hey, don't ever knock wet dreams—they can be life-savers. I've had some really first-rate wet dreams in recent months—worthy of an Oscar, cast of thousands, tons of 'tits 'n ass,' as Lenny Bruce used to say."

"Jimmy," I said, emotionally, I guess, "when you get well—I promise, we'll—"

He interrupted me by taking my hand and placing it on that part of the sheet covering his groin.

"Xaviera," he said, in a loud, kidding voice, "I josh you not—He is risen!"

And he was.

Hmmm, what to do? I really would loved to have given Jimmy some pleasure, but I was so afraid of even embracing him.

"Jimmy," I said, "look, I'll give you head, since that cockteasing nurse didn't, but nothing more—you're not well enough, and don't fool around and pretend you are. It's painful for you even to move."

"Yes, Teacher, anything you say, Teacher," and he moved the sheet away from him to reveal a truly magnificent cock, standing up for all the world to see. Fortunately for Jimmy, the World, which probably would have been disapproving, wasn't there—but I was, and I . . . well, I approved.

"Jimmy, that's no little boy you have there," I said, first planting a light kiss on his mouth, then moving down on the waterbed until I could raise myself over his mid-section. Beneath me was one of the finest cocks I had ever seen. It was handsome. Awesome. A Gentleman's cock, to be sure! Without touching Jimmy's body, my arms supporting me on either side of his thighs, I bent down to give his fine cock a proper greeting, but my light kiss seemed to encourage a considerable springing back and forth on the part of Jimmy's obviously most healthy part.

"*Hey* there, Jimmy," I said merrily, "here's one spot on your body which hasn't lost weight. Am I right or not?"

"Believe it or not, Xaviera," Jimmy replied, not a little the proud peacock, "but I swear it's smaller since the accident. You should see me when I'm at my normal weight. It's really bigger then—or at least thicker."

"Poor thing," I mumbled, bringing my mouth down over his entire penis, "it needs some exercise. Just like the doctor said . . ." I was now *so* horny, it had happened *so* subtly, I was *so* intent on giving Jimmy some pleasure after all these months, that I almost bit into his swollen cock, so eager was I to make love to him.

"Hey, Xaviera, easy as she goes," he said, torn, probably, between the pleasure my mouth around his cock was affording him and the fear I'd somehow bite it off.

"Sorry," I mumbled—after all, my mouth was full—"but you've really turned me on and this is the only thing I can think of for us to do."

"I can think of other things," Jimmy said, grinning a crazy grin at me, "but you go ahead with what you're doing—it's greeaatt! . . . really . . . just . . . great . . . oh Jesus, so great!!!"

By now, being careful not to jar poor Jimmy's body, I was hovering above his eager cock, sucking the head, running my tongue down the entire shaft until I reached his balls and then gently kneading and kissing those, then returning to his penis, moving back up to the head and settling there for a while, nibbling and sucking and tonguing him.

I don't know how long a normal healthy man, who'd had sex with regularity, could have withstood this loving onslaught of mine, but Jimmy, to his considerable credit, held out for three or four minutes and then erupted with a thick white gusher of love, despair, frustration, confusion—you name it, all that Jimmy had stored up in him. His emaciated body actually shook, and for a moment I was afraid I'd done a terrible, dumb thing to him, but then he settled back on the bed, grinned at me, and said, so gratefully it could have broken my heart, "Oh wow . . . oh, oh, oh, *wow!*"

I moved up against him, body to body, but gingerly, careful not to have any of my weight on him. He turned to me and began kissing me, not at all gingerly, and I returned his lovemaking but always with the gentlest of touches, the most reticent of embraces, the most "polite" of squeezes. Truth to tell, everywhere I touched him I felt bones, and it just made me more cautious than aroused. But I *was* aroused, and when Jimmy said, "Let's fuck," I really wanted to, but for once in my life, I was really afraid to pull a man onto me, or to climb over him and begin riding him.

But Jimmy placed my hand on what had become a stupendous hard-on again, and all doubts went out the window when he whispered, kissing my ear at the same time, "Please . . . let's try . . . I'll let you know if it's too tough for me. . . ."

I had made love on a waterbed a few times before, but it's not exactly familiar ground to me, and so, very, very calculatingly, I moved my body over Jimmy's and lowered myself onto the wonderful-looking cock of his.

To put it bluntly, Jimmy and I fucked our brains out, though I was constantly expecting to hear some bones cracking and, in those moments when I *knew* I was in control, did my best to put as little weight as possible on any part of his body. I tried to do the whole thing—like a man—on elbows and knees. Jimmy just lay there—of course the waterbed made things interesting—and all that moved from him was inside me, but, oh my!—there was lots of strength there, and we made beautiful, beautiful love that day.

I learned to take advantage of the waterbed and by my movements above him, could rock the mattress into gentle ripples of movement and by slightly moving my knees on either side of his body, I moved us both into a lovely simultaneous orgasm.

"Yeeeow," shouted Jimmy, "whoopee, I'm coming, I'm coming, *am* I coming!"

While not as vocal as Jimmy, I had a pretty good orgasm myself, and what I wanted to do, at that point, was to enfold Jimmy in my arms, to clutch him and embrace him and hug him and roughly kiss his face all over. But ever mindful of those brittle bones, I eased myself off him and settled my body on the bed next to him, where I gave him an affectionate squeeze or two and then lay back to relax. I'm sure he got the idea—like two kids, we lay there holding hands.

After a half-hour or so, Jimmy was horny again, and this time we assumed side positions, and whatever we lacked in motion, the waterbed made up for. I could feel Jimmy's cock moving to and fro inside me, right to left, left to right, as we jiggled our bodies on the bed and achieved a sweet rhythm between our bodies and the bed. Jimmy played with my breasts during the entire time and I ran my fingers gently over his buttocks and the backs of his thighs and again we had a fine time. When we'd both come, I pulled him close to me and we lay that way for a while. If it weren't for the delicious tingling in the back of my thighs, and the nice wet feeling inside my vagina, I'd say my feelings for Jimmy at this point were almost maternal. Or was I just doing the job of a good nurse. . . ?

I balled Jimmy once more that day and evening—I thought he had it (ahem!) coming to him—and when it was done, and I could see that he really was slipping into blissful sleep, I quietly left the bed and got dressed and went home.

It had been a very surprising day and, in many ways, the most fulfilling few hours I'd spent in a long time. I wasn't in love with Jimmy, but I certainly did adore him in a very special way.

I saw Jimmy several times after the first wonderful day we spent together—and "spent" is certainly the right description for that day—and then not at all for months. I'd left him my number but, not hearing from him, I just assumed he was busy with his recovery program or else was feeling a lot better and was back into his old routine of chasing around with the jet-set birds again. I hoped he wasn't as bored as before, but in our time together he had seemed a lot healthier mentally, as well as physically, so I didn't worry about him.

Also this was the period of my police harassment and the moving and the start of my sessions with the D.A.'s office, so I had little time for social life. I tried to call Jimmy once or twice, but getting no answer I realized that he must be able to get out now, and that was gratifying to know. I told myself it would be better if I stayed out of his life and gave him a chance to find himself on his own. In any case, I was sure he knew that my door was open to him any time of the day or night.

It was early December when I finally heard from Jimmy. He called up, sounding very stoned, and invited me to come down and meet his friends on Carmine Street. He had moved in with them, he said, having said farewell to his former phoney friends.

As it happened, he caught me on an evening when I had no plans, so I said I'd grab a cab and come see him. I was really very pleased to hear from him, but it bothered me to hear him sounding so stoned.

I arrived at Carmine Street around forty minutes later, and Jimmy met me at the door with a big hug. At least he'd put on some weight—he certainly seeemed to be feeling a lot stronger—but he still didn't look well. There was a sickly color to his face and he looked very pale and tired. I knew he needed my help again and immediately I was sorry we'd been out of touch. However, feeling guilty wasn't going to do either of us any good.

Jimmy introduced me to his friends, and they all seemed nice enough—that is, if you can tell much about people when they're stoned out of their minds. But we sat around and had some laughs, and a lot of hash was passed around. To be a good sport, I tried to smoke some, but since I don't smoke cigarettes at all I was very bad at inhaling and I coughed all the smoke out. Everyone laughed at me but it was all good-natured—not the kind of put-down some "heads" do to anyone who isn't into the drug culture.

Everyone was being silly now, and while much of the laughter was being caused by the most ordinary things, it was kind of contagious and I found myself very relaxed and comfortable with these people. They accepted me as a friend of Jimmy's, and therefore their friend, and there were absolutely no personality games or status games going on in the room. I was glad I'd come.

We were all sitting in a circle, passing the hash around—except for me—and Jimmy was sitting across from me, in an old chair. He smiled at me most of the time, and finally he got up and came over to sit down alongside me. "Hey," he said, whispering in my ear, "I hope you like my friends?"

I nodded yes.

"Hey, I hope you can spend the night?"

I nodded yes again.

"Want to go upstairs now?"

Yes—a third time.

Jimmy and I quietly got up from the group but I got the impression from some remarks being passed back and forth by his Iranian friends that they thought this was going to be an evening of group sex—with me being the "groupie."

"Jimmy," I said, "I like your friends well enough, but not well enough to sleep with them. Tell them not to bother us, will you."

"Don't worry," he said, "that's just talk. They're too spaced-out to concentrate on something as important as sex."

"I hope so," I said, "because I'd like this to be a good evening for us."

"Me, too," said Jimmy. "It's okay—don't worry."

Still, as we went up the stairs one of the Iranian boys started to follow us. Jimmy turned around and, without raising his voice, said, "Hey, man, cool it, will you . . . Xaviera and I really want to be alone."

"Sure, Jimmy, sure," his friend said, "I was only kidding. May Allah smile on your lovemaking."

This was making me feel a little self-conscious, but Jimmy correctly interpreted this and reassured me. "He was just kidding around, Xaviera, really . . . we may live together, but it's not *that* kind of scene. I mean, if we shared girls, there'd be enough to go around, not any gang-on number."

"I believe you," I said. "I guess I'm just not used to the drug thing. We just don't turn on in my usual crowd. Ha, you know what—I guess that makes us very square in your eyes and those of your friends. . . ?"

"No," Jimmy said, pulling me close to him, "you look nice and round in my eyes and—I'm sure—in the eyes of my friends. That is, if they can still see straight."

We both laughed, and after climbing another flight of stairs, we were up in the attic of this old Carmine Street house. Jimmy had given up his posh East Side apartment—actually he owned the apartment and was subletting it to a friend, he told me—for this attic! It had a huge antique fourposter bed, without the top; a bureau; some beaten-up easy chairs; a table with a portable phonograph on it; and a couple of lamps. And, naturally, books all over the place. But no empty bottles of booze.

Actually, as Jimmy and I got into bed with each other, and I looked up at the wooden beams leading to the roof, the place seemed kind of cozy and special. Jimmy asked me if I wanted to snort some 'coke,' and I automatically said no.

"Are you sure?" He said. "It's easy to do and will make you feel really groovy."

"Oh, all right," I said, feeling there were a whole lot of experiences I didn't know anything about, and I might as well try them once.

"Jimmy fed me the 'coke' in a little spoon he'd had hanging around his neck and showed me how to "snort" it. I did so, and my nose felt terribly ticklish. But not much else.

"Nothing's happening," I told him.

"It will. Just relax."

My head began to feel a little light, and there was a kind of cold feeling behind my forehead, but I certainly didn't feel whatever being stoned was supposed to feel like.

Jimmy got up and put some records on the phonograph and now it was beginning to get to me. The music seemed to have texture and to be coming from every corner of the room, going through my brain and making me part of it. The room itself, especially the roof, seemed to be breathing and the beamed ceiling looked so inviting I felt like flying up to it and sitting there, laughing down at Jimmy and really grooving with the music from on high.

Jimmy pulled me to him and our bodies seemed to be electric—his skin felt so sensuous and his hands and mouth on me seemed to feel almost velvety. And his cock—oh, his cock!—it seemed four times its normal size and when he put it in me, I felt as though his body had literally moved inside me. And the sensations, everything felt so g-o-o-o-d and each sensation was more prolonged, more intense than the one before it. His mouth and tongue made my breasts feel more and more sensitive and I felt as though I had the largest, sexiest boobs in the world and my nipples must be four inches long and then it became his hand playing with the crack of my ass that felt so good I didn't know if I could stand it. And always that giant cock inside me, filling me, driving tendrils of overwhelming sensation throughout my body until my cunt was my mind and my mind my cunt and I was inside myself and inside Jimmy's cock and I wasn't even sure if we were on the bed or floating a foot or so above it or maybe we had become part of the bed and the bed was fucking both of us . . .

My head felt so light and occasionally there was dizziness and then I would seem to rise out of it, out of my body, and be able to look down at Jimmy and me fucking our brains out on the bed. And I'd laugh to myself at how good we were fucking and how good it was feeling and my body would seem as light as a feather and then there'd be nothing but my body—I was all body and there was a giant penis completely growing inside me and filling my entire being.

Oh, oh, I thought in a suddenly lucid moment, if it could *only* be this way forever, and for the first time I understood why Jimmy liked to get stoned and then there was Jimmy's voice inside my mind, taking over my mind, saying, "Far out . . . far out, far out . . . Xaviera, you really are a fantastic chick . . . every time I see you, I know something great is going to happen. . . ."

And then I couldn't hear him anymore—his voice sounded faint and far away—and I was nothing but sensation. I had become my orgasm and I felt I was the entire universe and my body shook and quivered and it seemed it would go on forever and I didn't know if I could stand such intense waves of pleasure, pulling me inside my body, never to let me go.

Then Jimmy's voice again, reaching me into my brain and making me sane, Jimmy's voice soothing and caressing my brain. "No other girl does this to me . . . what is it about you . . . you love to love and be loved, that's what it is . . . yeah, yeah, that's what it is . . . hey, don't you feel how strong I am again, I can spear you on my cock and I can spear you and carry you around the room, through the house, around the world . . . God how I dig fucking you, screwing every part of your body—"

And, as he said that, he suddenly pulled out his cock and turned me around and started sucking on my big toe and kissing the sensitive bottoms of my feet and then moving his mouth up my ankle and calf and thighs until I was screaming for him to eat my cunt and he was and it all began again, except now Jimmy was part of my insides and his tongue was driving me wild and I had to pull his body to me and take his great cock inside my mouth where I sucked on it and licked it and kissed it for what seemed like hours. Jimmy's body and my body were the same body now and his cock was part of my body and together we shared an orgasm that seemed to shake the bed and the house and the world itself.

Some time later—I have no idea how much time had passed—I said, utterly exhausted, "So . . . that's what making love on 'coke' is like. . . ?"

"No," said Jimmy, "it's always great, but never like that before. That was absolutely, absolutely, absolutely . . . far fucking-out. . . ."

We fell asleep holding hands and did not wake until morning. I will have to see a lot more of Jimmy, I told myself when I left the Carmine Street house the next morning, but I was not to see him again for quite some time.

For Jimmy's world, I had to learn, there is no timetable. And so you saw him—when you saw him.

II. TSURIS*

*Yiddish term meaning "troubles"

COPS 'N' ROAMERS

It should have been a tranquil period in my life. I was concentrating on finishing up my book. My personal life was fairly settled—for a change—although it wasn't exactly the usual boy-girl arrangement.

Although I still had some furniture in my old apartment, and the lease there hadn't yet expired, I was now living in the Twenty-fifth Street penthouse apartment, and Takis, my gorgeous Greek lover, had moved in with me. He was between jobs and it was nice to have him around the house all day. We'd sleep late, have a leisurely breakfast, and make love whenever we felt like it.

At the same time Larry was still my "steady" boyfriend. The relationship between Larry and myself was still good—a bit frustrating for Larry maybe—but the three of us were relatively happy together.

Of course it wasn't all bliss. Because of the sessions I'd been having with lawyers and the forthcoming interrogations at the district attorney's office, I was sometimes irritable and tense. Also, although I'd moved my clothing and personal effects and some furniture into the new apartment, there was still a lot of unpacking to do plus the business of moving the furniture I'd left behind. So we'd sometimes have arguments—mostly over stupid things—and would end

up on little battlefields. The funny thing was that the battle-
field line-up usually consisted of Larry and Takis on one
side and me opposing them. But because we were friends
as well as lovers, the battle usually got settled after a few
harsh words had shot out of our mouths. That was the
worst of it.

One day, about a week before the movers were supposed
to come and remove all my furniture from the old apartment, I went uptown to the apartment to make sure everything was packed and ready to be moved. Things were fine
there so I got ready to go back downtown. I took the
elevator down to the lobby and was half-way out the building when I realized that the man talking to the super in the
entrance of the building was the same police officer who'd
arrested me the last time. Since the lobby was T-shaped,
with elevators at each end, I was able to stand right where
I was, without being observed, and partly hear their conversation. From what I could overhear, the officer was asking the super if I still lived there and that dope was telling
him that I *did* still live there and was going to move out
officially the next week!

What a *stupido!* I'd told the super numerous times never
to reveal anything to anyone about me, and here he was
setting me up so the cops would watch the building and tail
me. Obviously they'd follow the moving van to the very
door of my new apartment. I'd have to move as soon as
possible and cancel the other movers.

This was managed rather easily—the new movers did the
job the next morning—and so far as I knew no cops had
come along for the ride. A few weeks passed without incident until one Sunday when the doorbell rang at three in
the morning. Takis was fast asleep next to me—we'd already
been asleep for a few hours—and I dragged myself out of
bed and groggily went out into the hall to the intercom. I
asked the doorman who was downstairs and a strange voice
—not the doorman's—answered that it was Michael. I told
whoever it was that I didn't know any Michael and, anyhow,
what did he want at such an ungodly hour?

"I'm a friend of Ed's," he answered.

"Ed who?" I shouted back through the intercom.

"Ed MacNammara, the super."

This was odd because I wasn't that friendly with my new super and certainly had never told him about my former business. And he sure as hell had never sent anyone up to see me, especially at this time of night! The man downstairs kept insisting on seeing me, and I simply insisted that he go away. I hung up the intercom phone and went back into the bedroom and tried to fall back asleep.

About five minutes later, the doorbell to the apartment rang. I looked through the viewer and saw a big, husky guy with a fat face standing outside. "What do you want?" I asked him, without opening the door, and he said he was Michael.

"Get lost, I don't want to talk to you . . . just get the hell out of here."

"What is your name?" he asked, without leaving my door.

"None of your goddamn business. If Ed sent you, you should know who I am. Right?" So the creep finally left.

I didn't feel right about what happened and I woke up Takis. Takis quickly got dressed and went downstairs and, sure enough, there were three men standing outside the building. They looked like cops to him, and he quickly took the elevator back to the eighteenth floor and walked up one flight. Not quite sure who the guys were, Takis and I finally went back to sleep and for the rest of the night we weren't disturbed.

But three nights later, again at about two in the morning— this time I had a girlfriend staying over—the doorbell rang again. I went to the door, looked through the peephole, and asked who it was. The answer was: "Police—open up the door. We've got the superintendent with us. Open up."

"Forget it," I replied through the door. "I have no intention of opening up the door to any policemen. I'm not doing anything wrong, and I am *not* going to open this door."

"If you don't open up, we'll have the super open your door with *his* key."

Since the chain lock was on, they'd have to break the door down to get in—super's key or not—but this speech did shake me up because I already had one court case coming up and I certainly didn't welcome any more trouble with the law. But while I was thinking about this, the cops seemed to go away. At least I heard the elevator come up and they weren't out in the hall anymore.

They'd left, all right, but only to go downstairs and actually get the super. This time I opened the door a little, leaving on the chain, and asked them just what the hell they wanted. I was feeling virtuous, in addition to angry, because there was no one in the apartment besides Takis and my friend, and anything we'd done that evening had been for fun, not finance. The cops—there were three of them, plus my super—said that they now had the super with them, which was pretty obvious—the poor man was standing there in his pajamas and bathrobe looking perfectly miserable at having to be there at all—and they wanted to come in.

I told them that, super out there or not, they'd better get themselves a nice little search warrant. I also asked the super to have them formally identify themselves, and this seemed to inspire in them a strong desire to be elsewhere.

"We'll be back," they more or less snarled at me and left, taking the super with them, I surmised, so I couldn't speak with him and learn if he knew who they were. Or if they really were cops. Anyone can rent a uniform.

That poor super! In the weeks to come, he would be awakened at all hours of the night and not once would a cop identify himself properly. At most they'd flash a badge at him and avoid answering his questions. So without their names or badge numbers, I couldn't report their harassment to the authorities.

Still and all, I was pretty sure of the game they were playing. They told the super one night, after waking him at 4:00 A.M. and literally lifting him out of his apartment, a cop under each arm, that this harassment was designed to get me out of their precinct. As for poor Mr. MacNammara, he'd be happy to see me leave so he could get some sleep!

But I'm getting ahead of my story. Two days after that second visit by the cops, I came back to the apartment after having done some shopping and when I took the elevator to my floor, there was an Irish-looking guy with a crew cut, wearing a loud checkered jacket, snooping around the hall. I got out of the elevator and he rushed in, as though I'd caught him doing something he shouldn't be doing. I immediately smelled "cop," but he took the elevator down before I could take a closer look at him. This was getting me good and pissed off—nighttime, daytime, was I to have no privacy at all!

I went into the apartment and double-locked the door. Then I told Takis what had happened and we agreed that sooner or later the police were going to try and pick me up on some charge or other. I buzzed down to the doorman and asked him if he'd seen anyone around who resembled a cop and he answered, "Yes, quite a few." So Takis and I decided it might be best to leave the apartment for a while— I'd go stay with a friend and he'd move into a hotel room.

I packed some clothes and put my big address books into an airline bag, since I didn't want the police to break in and find the books there. I was out of the business, to be sure, but the books were far too valuable to simply throw away. There were lots of personal friends listed in those books and I'd never gotten around to transferring their addresses and phone numbers to a new book.

We were ready to leave. I put on a wig and donned a huge pair of sunglasses that covered half my face. I also changed coats. Takis and I took the elevator down to the basement and were able to leave the building from the garage exit. Peeking around the corner of the building, we saw two police cars and three plainclothes men talking in front of the building. To me, they looked all set to raid the place, even though I could've told them there was nobody upstairs. Now I was sure they were after my books. They'd probably discovered that I'd stolen the books back after the last raid.

Takis and I decided to make tracks and I called Larry from the bar on the corner to tell him what we were doing— fleeing the police. I told Larry who I was going to stay with and asked him to pick me up there in the evening.

Larry came by that evening and we had a long, unhurried dinner and I felt a little better. For the next three days I stayed in my friend's apartment during the daylight hours, watching television or else catching up on my reading, and I came out only at night, to have dinner with Larry. By the end of this time I felt I should be able to go back to the apartment. Either the police had raided it, or they hadn't— and I was planning to put the black books away for safe keeping, after copying down phone numbers of some close friends.

When Takis and I made the move back, there were no policemen hanging around the building, and so far as I could tell, the apartment had not been touched. For that matter, it seemed as though the police had gone away, hopefully for good. I was feeling fairly chipper about things, but Takis remained moody and restless because he was afraid of being busted again. His lawyer had told him that since he'd only been picked up once, the court would probably dismiss his case, but it was still pending and we decided that it might be best for him to move out until things were really settled between him and the law. He couldn't afford another arrest, even if it was on a phoney charge.

I thought it might be pleasant to live alone for a while, but in case the police harassment started up again, it would be good to have company. So I asked around, and a friend suggested I speak to Marsha, a Canadian girl I'd been introduced to at a party. Marsha, my friend knew, wanted to give up her present studio apartment because it was too small—and not at all worth the high rent she had to pay. I called Marsha and we made a lunch date and by the time lunch was over, I had a new roommate.

Marsha, while a Canadian national, was half black and half Jewish—how I'd love to read her family history!—and looked Indian (that's Asian Indian, not North American Indian). I thought she was absolutely stunning—she helped support herself by doing some modeling for a well-known photographer—and admired her extraordinary breasts. However, in contrast to her beautiful, sexy appearance, she was really very quiet and polite, most reserved, and a refreshing change for me after all the mad ladies I'd known over the past couple of years. I was sure we'd get along fine, and we did.

One night, a few weeks after Marsha had moved in, Linda, a very good friend of mine who'd remained loyal and helpful to me during all my troubles and arrest cases, came over for drinks. She brought along a darling young stockbroker she'd been dating, a tall dreamboat named Stu, and we had a pleasant evening drinking—me armed with my perennial orange juice—and talking. I told them about the police visits and by now we could even find some humor in what had happened, particularly the situation of poor Mr. MacNammara—who probably would have donated a month's salary to me to move to another building!

It was getting a bit late and Linda and her date were about ready to leave when the doorbell rang. I looked through the peephole and there were three Chinamen outside, one of whom I recognized—he was the manager of a restaurant near my former apartment. How had they gotten up unannounced? I opened the door and asked them what they wanted—although I was pretty damn sure of the reason for this nocturnal visit—and the manager of the Chinese restaurant mumbled something about "paying you a visit. We've missed you."

Well, if he'd been alone, I might have invited him in for a drink since he'd always been nice to me and my girls, but I didn't want this group visit—he and his friends always arrived in groups, and stayed for hours—so as diplomatically as I could, I declined the pleasure of their company. "You see," I said, "I have some friends over and, anyway, I'm not in that business anymore."

They seemed reluctant to leave and I was about to tell them to scram in no uncertain terms when, as though cued by the word "business," five plainclothes cops, all big as bulls, came marching down the corridor, this time accompanied by the doorman. Rather than stand my ground, I reacted by instinct and pulled the three Chinese men inside the apartment, slammed the door, bolted it, and put the chain lock on.

It's remarkable how you can feel guilty when you have nothing to be guilty about. Here we were, all being made nervous wrecks by those cops pounding on the door and up to the moment the three Chinamen had come to my door it'd been as social an evening as could be imagined. I didn't know what arrangement Linda had with her stockbroker, but I sure as hell wasn't selling anything these days, so why did I have to hide behind locked doors! I was as angry as I was scared, but then I decided "to hell with it" and made everyone drinks. If the cops wanted me, they'd have to break down that steel door and then I'd have something to complain about to their superior officers. We sat in the living room and tried to be relaxed, and I think the most nervous one in the room was Stu, the stockbroker. I told him if he left, we'd all be in trouble, and his response was to gulp down his drink and then get up to make himself another. As for the three Chinese gentlemen, they seemed to be okay. They were chattering away in Chinese, so I couldn't really tell how they were taking this. I let them help themselves to generous portions of Scotch—and the more they consumed of my spirits, the better their own spirits seemed to become.

By now it had gotten quiet outside but I wasn't ready even to go out in the hall and have a look. Stu offered to take a look through the peephole and when he hadn't returned after a few minutes, I suddenly realized he must have sneaked out on us. This put me into a panic because it meant the door wasn't double-locked anymore and I still had my black books in the apartment—I'd been too complacent and hadn't put them away for safekeeping yet. I rushed to relock the door, grateful that there was no one outside in the hall. So I took advantage of this lull in the evening to stash my black books back into my always-ready airline bag.

Well, there we were—three girls stranded with three Chinamen who still had their overcoats on. And the fun was just about to begin.

The police were back, noisier and more violent than ever. They pounded at the door for a straight half-hour, this time using their shoes and gun handles—or at least that's the way it sounded from inside—and I couldn't understand why one of my neighbors didn't call the police about these guys. If they were using the heels of their shoes they must have looked pretty funny out there in their stockinged feet and I was reminded of Premier Khrushchev banging on the table at the United Nations some years ago.

Our friends, the Chinese legation, were now pretty unsettled by all the commotion outside and it was obvious that they wanted desperately to leave. But I made them stay put, reminding them that this is what they got for coming up as uninvited guests. If the cops got hold of them, I pointed out, they'd be accused of patronizing the house of a prostitute, even though this wasn't true. And since two of them spoke and understood very little English, we'd all be in hot water,

if only because they couldn't explain themselves properly
to the cops' satisfaction. The cops, I told them, would probably believe they'd gone to bed with us with their overcoats
on!

I don't know if I really calmed them down or not, but at
least they sat down. I poured them another drink. I made
everyone another drink. I poured myself yet another orange
juice and went into the bedroom to think. It was getting
worse outside and there had to be some way to lead my
little flock out of danger. I threw some clothing into the
airline bag and took what money I had in the house and
stuffed it inside my panties. Then I took the flight bag and
went out into the living room, prepared to do something or
other.

The action outside my door had taken a new turn. The
cops were still pounding on the door and threatening me if
I didn't open it up, but the doorbell was now silent—they'd
probably broken it—and now I heard the super's voice yelling through the door that he'd have me evicted if I didn't
open the goddamn door! If it'd have been a little quieter
out there I might have felt sorry for him, having been
dragged out of bed still another night, but suddenly I heard
a sound that struck terror in my heart.

It was the key being slid into the door—the cops must
have ordered him to unlock the door—and the door jam-
ming up against the police chain. (It must have been named
that way to keep the police out.) The girls and I rushed
out into the hall, dragging the Chinamen with us, and while
the police were pushing against the door from the outside,
all of us were pushing back from the inside. It could have
been a scene from a Charlie Chaplin movie because the
more the cops pushed and yelled and slammed against the
door, the more we leaned and pushed against our side of the
door. They were screaming at us and the Chinamen were
muttering in Chinese and I was cursing them in Dutch and
it's just lucky for us that the chain held. We were also lucky
those cops outside were such big louts because that meant
that not all of them could get their bodies against the door
at any one time. Finally one combined push by all of us
inside got the door shut long enough for me to throw the
lock again.

There was a momentary pause in the commotion out-side—perhaps they were debating what to do about that chain lock—and I decided right then and there that there was only one way to get out of the apartment and that was out the window. I could have tied sheets together to make a kind of rope, but there wasn't time. I didn't have a terrace but the apartment immediately below did, and there was a large awning over their terrace. The trick would be to sit on my window ledge, lower ourselves onto their awning, and go down the side of the awning—because the front of it went past the edge of the terrace and to slip off that way meant a parachute drop without the parachute.

The Chinamen went out first, then Linda. I dropped my flight bag to her, telling her to hide it inside one of the giant flower pots lining the terrace. I figured if the police got into the apartment, they weren't about to drop out the window like we desperados were doing and wouldn't inspect the terrace. Now it was time for Marsha to make her exit—which she did successfully—and then me. I took a last look around the apartment to make sure I wasn't leaving any-thing very valuable behind for the cops to swipe in their frustration. I didn't have a handbag, or a coat—so I put the apartment keys in my panties as well, and—Geronimo!

It was almost my last act in this world. What happened was that the Chinamen had helped Linda down, and then Marsha, and then fear overcame whatever gallantry they felt and they were bugging out. Linda and Marsha were trying to stop them, but I wasn't about to wait for anyone's help. I let myself down on the awning and, because my hands were slippery, I couldn't stop myself from sliding down the front of the thing, and I just barely managed to land inside the terrace. I more or less bounced inside the front of the terrace, rather than outside, or else I'd have fallen nineteen stories to the street. I'd twisted my ankle, my hands were bleeding, my dress badly torn, but all that mat-tered at that moment was that I was on the right side of that ledge.

It had been dark in the apartment below but now a black maid was standing in one of the bedroom doors, flabber-gasted at all the people running through the apartment. She was, I later learned, staying there as a caretaker for the apartment while the middle-aged homosexual couple who lived there were off on a cruise. (They later moved out because they were unsettled by all the "crime"—drugs and wild orgies—they were sure was taking place right over their heads.) I tried to explain to the maid that there was no reason to be frightened—"Don't worry, we're not robbers. We're just passing through . . . uhh, just a little argument with my jealous fiancé." I tried to reassure her but I wanted to get out of there before she called the police, who were just a yell or a scream away.

By now the Chinamen had disappeared into the night, and Linda was on her way, too, though I warned her there'd be policemen downstairs and to try the basement level exits, and Marsha and I needed someplace to go and hide. The only person I actually knew well enough to ask for help in the building was George, a nice guy in the real estate business who knew something of my situation and who lived with his wife on the tenth floor. It was way after midnight, but we had no choice and went tip-toe, as fast as we could manage with my ankle hurting, down eight flights of stairs to his floor.

Fortunately they were up. His wife, a young brunette who did cancer research for a nearby hospital, was a little startled to find two mad women outside her door at 1:30 in the morning, but let us in when she heard the trouble we were having. George, who had been watching TV, told us to go into the bedroom and try to calm down while he'd go "out for cigarettes" to see what was going on downstairs.

When he returned, he said the police were holding a good-looking young guy—this was undoubtedly Stu—and three Orientals down in the lobby. Stu and the Chinamen were sheepishly sitting on the bench in the lobby, while the cops hovered over them, firing questions to beat the band. A few days later, when I called Stu, he told me the police had detained him until 4:00 in the morning, but he simply told them the truth and stuck to it. When the police caught up with me, they told Stu and the Chinamen, they'd serve subpoenas on them forcing them to testify that they'd paid me money for illicit services. Ha! The only illicit service I performed that night was to dispense a lot of liquor without having a liquor license. And without getting paid for it, either.

Stu also said that the police were expecting me to try and leave the building by the lobby, since they had the basement exits covered. Linda had discovered this and had simply left by the lobby, nonchalantly walking past the cops, her boyfriend, and the Chinamen. The police, since they were looking strictly for me, or for men who might have been visiting me, weren't interested in Linda, since they probably didn't know she'd even been in the apartment.

George was saying we'd be perfectly safe here unless the police searched the building, apartment by apartment, which was highly unlikely because of the hour and the absurd situation. Marsha and I were hardly dangerous criminals with a price on our heads. So he suggested that we share the pull-out bed in the living room while he and his wife would go to sleep in their bedroom. She fixed a compress for my ankle, which by now was badly swollen, and then taped it. The night was half over by the time we all finally got to sleep, but I felt secure and was so grateful for their help that I was able to drop right off to sleep.

The next morning I got up early because I wanted to get back into my apartment for some clothes and things, and then move out for a while. The building was sure to be under surveillance at least part of the time and sooner or later I'd be arrested on some fictitious charge. There was just no point in staying there after the events of last night.

Marsha and I went upstairs, tried the door, and found that the chain lock was still on. Either the police had given up trying to break in, or else the lock had held. Jesus, now what? There was only one solution—someone had to go back the way we'd escaped. It couldn't be me, with my ankle throbbing away, and Marsha wasn't up to any acrobatics, so we decided to ask one of the maintenance men to help us get into the apartment. Marsha went downstairs and returned with a young Puerto Rican lad, and without explaining the circumstances of why we were locked out of the apartment, we told him what he'd have to do. To help translate the instructions, I handed him a ten-dollar bill.

We all went downstairs, me still using Marsha as a kind of crutch, and rang the bell of the apartment below. You can imagine the look on the face of the elderly black woman when she came to the door and opened it to find us there . . . again. Before she could get too frightened or excited, I said we were locked out of our apartment and had to use her terrace again. I pressed some money into her hand, patted it, and thanked her for all her help. The young maintenance man went out on the terrace, picked up my flight bag from inside a large planter, and then nimbly used the awning to reach the window above.

"It's really all right," I told the maid. "See, *he* works for the building and he's just helping us out." She looked absolutely perplexed by all this, but not frightened like the night before, and Marsha and I said thanks and goodbye to her and went back upstairs. The maintenance man had opened the door and I gave him another tip, asking him not to say anything to anyone about this. He still seemed nervous. *"Mi querido amigo tu tienes mucho miedo,"* I said, "but don't worry—if anyone asks about this, I'll say it all has to do with a lover's quarrel."

Marsha and I grabbed two suitcases and began throwing clothes into them, enough clothing for at least a couple of weeks—after all, we wouldn't be going out on the town at night—and I called Larry and told him what'd happened. He said he'd be over as soon as he could to pick us up and would carefully check the building for police. He arrived about a half-hour later, having made sure there were no cars or cops parked downstairs.

"Let's go while the going's good," he said.

We used the basement exit again, Marsha and I staying inside until Larry brought the car around.

It took us quite a while to find a decent, not too expensive, hotel, and the place we picked, not far from the Hilton, turned out to be less respectable than it looked. Pimps and Times Square prostitutes used the hotel and, on a few occasions, thieves tried to get into our room. I knew the owner of the hotel since he was one of my former customers, so I thought he might agree to a *prix d'amis*. However, I suspect he was charging me an even higher price since he'd read in the papers that Madam X was hiding from the police.

Larry came by to take me to dinner every night, and sometimes we took Marsha along, but it was no way to live.

I knew that Marsha wanted to return to Canada, eventually, and the events of the past month would certainly prompt her to go back a lot sooner than she'd planned. She was much too quiet and reserved a girl to be hopping out of penthouse windows in the middle of the night. So was I, for *that* matter.

Larry and I started hunting for a small place for me, someplace to stay until the heat was finally off the penthouse apartment. We finally found a nice, cozy studio apartment that I liked not too far from the Twenty-fifth Street place. It was a third-story walk-up in a small apartment building, with no doorman, but the rent was fairly reasonable and I enjoyed fixing it up. I bought a few pieces of furniture and turned it into a real doll's house. Larry would take me over to the old place from time to time and I'd sneak up and get some clothing.

Things remained quiet and calm, and there were no more Keystone comedies starring the police and myself.

The Girls in My Life

CASSANDRA: *Carissima!*

I don't think she spoke more than twenty words of English, but she and I communicated very well indeed.

Cassandra was thirty, divorced—with two children, a girl of seven and a boy of twelve under the care of her parents back in Caracas—and she came to New York with the same illusions of many another foreign woman. To find the right man. In Cassandra's case, to find the right man, marry him, and then bring her children to New York. But her pursuit of *Señor* Right was somewhat limited by her almost nonexistent English. Because she did have Spanish-speaking friends in town, Cassandra did not get to practice on her English as she should have. In fact she was more than a little stubborn in this area. On the other hand, if there was an English expression addressed to her which she did not understand, and she thought it was something harsh or an insult, she would burst into tears.

Cassandra had beautiful big almond-shaped eyes, with an Oriental expression of mystery in them, that turned me on from the first moment I met her. Her skin was light brownish, and she had coal black hair, worn shoulder-length, and a full, sensuous mouth.

Still, when I say she was lovely I refer more to her personality than I do to her looks—which were certainly strik-

ing. She had never been a prostitute until she came here and
when I met her, she was just beginning to work here and
there on cheap dates for several Spanish madams, particularly one big, gross, Columbian madam. She made very
little money and was very disillusioned, and I was pleased
to take her under my wing. Needless to say, she moved into
my apartment, and apart from being a wonderful person,
she turned out to be a great, great cook!

I worked on teaching Cassandra how to dress—now she
could afford some better clothes—and she really blossomed
in this department because, with her particular skin hue,
almost any color suited her. Her body wasn't all that great,
but her eyes and dark hair and pearly white teeth more than
made up for any figure deficiencies. What had happened
was that she never got her waistline back after the birth of
her second child, and this really bothered her.

I don't know if it was because she missed her children,
but Cassandra adored young men, especially if they looked
on the innocent side and in need of a motherly type. As a
prostitute she was very friendly and warm-hearted, but occasionally she got hurt because of her lack of fluency in English.

One night a customer called and asked for a girl to be
sent over to his place. No specifications or particular requests. So I sent over dear Cassandra, glamorously dressed
in a red suit and yellow scarf. She left with a happy smile
on her face only to return a half-hour later, tearful and
genuinely upset. I asked her in Spanish what had happened
and she told me the man had sent her home, rudely as hell,
because he "wanted a white girl and not a Negro chick!"

The following week the phone rings and a customer speci-
fies he wants a black girl. "Have I got a girl for you!" I tell
him in my best Jewish madam voice. He arrives, I introduce
him to Cassandra, but he refuses to go with her. "I asked
you for a black girl," he argues, "and this one is white."
So here was a man, obviously bigoted, who was also color-
blind!

Poor Cassandra! Too dark for one man and too light for
another!

Each time I soothed Cassandra's sorrow and one day I
decided to go one step further to let her know how high I
held her in my esteem. She had never made love with a

woman and I decided it was time to take her cherry in that respect.

No one around, no customers, no curious boyfriends. I wanted her all for my own, but I still had to first persuade her that it wasn't dirty or bad for her. Compared to most prostitutes, Cassandra was still rather gullible and naive, and she was convinced that once she tried it with me, she wouldn't enjoy sex with men as before. I told her this was nonsense, that the two sensations were entirely different.

Unlike some of my other female flings, I simply liked Cassandra and wanted to add something to our friendship. I knew she didn't have a particular boyfriend at this time, and I assured her I'd do all the work—completely assume the male role.

One afternoon, after having carefully prepared her mentally, I led her into the bedroom and just made love to her. Gently and tenderly. It took me what seemed like an hour to get her turned on—to kiss her, caress her breasts, go back to her face and suck her tongue deep inside my mouth, then kiss her body from top to toe. Cassandra's navel region was somewhat less than beautiful because giving birth had left visible stretchmarks on her belly, but they really weren't too bad and down below was a truly gorgeous cunt, pinkish-purple with big protruding outer, as well as inner, lips.

In times of loneliness or frustration, Cassandra loved to masturbate and this was clearly visible to anyone with a sharp eye for studying cunts. From all her hours of self-love her lips had grown bigger and thicker and, surrounded by a small forest of thick black kinky hair, the whole flower combination looked absolutely divine to me. She was clean as a new-born babe, and her juices tasted just fantastic.

The moment I put my mouth on her vaginal lips, a shudder went through her body. She spread her legs farther apart and soon, over her embarrassment, she even assisted in feeding me her cunt, pulling apart the purple outer lips to reveal a lovely bright pink clitoris. A bit of a masochist, she begged me to chew on it, move it around as fast as possible, and pull and push it.

With my other hand I was finger-fucking her as though there were no tomorrow, and Spanish expressions were pouring out of her mouth. As she came I buried my nose and lips inside her and slurped away as though nectar of the gods were being served up. She was screaming for pleasure and almost pulled half the hair out of my head.

Did I convert her to bi-sexual love? Not really. She remained my private property and so far as I know, no other woman has been able to go to bed with her. In fact, at the first sign of a female advance, she retreats back into her prudish shell. The vibrations she had with me, I guess, haven't been matched by anyone else, and even if men will pay for a three-way scene, Cassandra will pass.

Since I really did care for Cassandra as a person, I directed her to a highly esteemed plastic surgeon and she had her stretchmarks removed and work done on her waistline, believe it or not. She suffered a lot of discomfort for months, but emerged a more confident woman—confident that her body now was as much a cause of pride as her face.

This proved to be a wise move because Cassandra is basically not a hooker at heart, and the last I heard of her she had gotten married to a young American for security and was having a hot affair with a cute young German lad for passion's sake.

A good-hearted woman—and a mixed-up kid. I liked her a lot.

Adios, mi Vida.

ROOMIES: DEBBIE AND THE WELCOME WAGON

Because of the continuous police harassment, I had been forced to hide out temporarily in a small studio apartment, but still maintained the three-bedroom penthouse on Twenty-fifth Street. After Marcia moved out, Debbie moved in, keeping me company.

I'd met Debbie through a mutual friend. She was a cute little blonde Jewish girl from Brooklyn who looked a bit like Sylvie Vartan, the French singing star who is married to Johnny Haliday—himself a great vocal artist. Debbie's only bad feature was a mouthful of bad teeth, but when she had her mouth closed, she looked like an innocent teenager.

Appearances are deceptive, as you know. Debbie was only nineteen, but she'd been in the business since fifteen. She also had a tremendous number of names and addresses, and while she didn't seem to use her lists of Johnny-Come-Lately (or sooner) very much, she did call her Johns from time to time and offer her services. These were mostly twenty- or twenty-five-dollar Johns, but being her own boss, she didn't have to pay anyone a cut. In any case, it was all done outside our little studio apartment, at their places, and I couldn't have cared less about it.

Debbie slept a lot during the days, but when she was awake, she was a regular Jewish Momma to me and she cleaned up our small flat as though cleanliness was going out of style. I really liked her—she was full of cozy sweetness and seemed to have a good word for everyone.

The only fault in her character, it seemed to me, was her taste in boyfriends. She was going with a nice Jewish creep from Brooklyn named Arnie Malberg. Now Arnie had the same last name as a certain disreputable real estate broker who'd once cheated me very badly, but I saw no reason to make a connection between the two. Although, when I spoke to Arnie over the phone, I heard a nasal Brooklyn accent which did remind me of the ratfinkswine who'd cheated me.

If Debbie had any other flaw, apart from her rotten taste in boyfriends, it was her "pill habit." She was forever asking me either for sleeping pills or Dexedrine. I couldn't help her out with barbiturates since I never used them, but I occasionally did take diet pills and sometimes I'd give her a few. I later discovered that Debbie was an "up and downer" freak. She was used to stronger stuff than my mild diet pills which accounted for her going to sleep at 6:00 A.M. until 3:00 P.M. in the afternoon. Then she'd get up and start rushing around cleaning the house. In other words, she'd take a "down" to put her to sleep and then she'd take an "up" to wake her up and give her pep, like Kathy.

Still, Debbie didn't cause me any trouble, but along comes trouble, called Arnie. Arnie of the shifty eyes and slick ways who was perfectly content to let Debbie support him. I didn't care about that—it was Debbie's right to be a masochist if that was her scene—but I certainly didn't want him in my company. But she began insisting that she wanted to be able to see Arnie at our place a few times a week—which was, for me, a few times too many. So I said to her, "Look, I'll go and live up at the big place and if you want, you can have Arnie stay with you here. At those times, you can consider the place yours. But whenever I tell you to have Arnie leave so I can stay here, you'll have to make him go."

She agreed with pleasure, happy as a little hummingbird.

Anyhow, on weekends, Debbie would go out to her little Brooklyn apartment, clean it up spic and span, and fuck Arnie's brains out, away from the phones and any outside monkey business.

I was back in the big apartment, and Larry was staying with me, on and off, but usually just over the weekends. I loved my new-found freedom, and much of the time I loved just being alone. In fact, I sort of concentrated on being on my own, reading, writing, or just watching television, and sometimes seeing some of my old friends.

One night, I told Debbie I'd like to switch pads for the night because I wanted to be absolutely sure of being alone so I could concentrate on reading the galleys of the book— which had just come in. Around eleven, I had to go back to the big apartment to deposit a check from a Dutch television show in the cashbox in the bedroom, and quite a scene greeted me. There was Mr. Arnie, acting very much like the Lord of the Manor. Sure, I'd asked Debbie to watch over the place, but I didn't expect to find Arnie there in all his naked glory. In my bed, this scrawny little pasha was drinking my booze—three-fourths of Johnny Walker Black had gone down his bony gullet and cigar ashes were strewn all over the place.

The television in the bedroom and the stereo in the living room were both blasting away loud enough to be heard nine apartments away while good reliable Debbie was trying vainly to clean up Arnie's mess faster than he could make it.

Without saying anything to Arnie, I immediately went to the closet where I kept the cashbox and put the check away. When I returned to the living room, Debbie immediately whispered to me, "If I were you, I wouldn't leave the cashbox in the bedroom. Why don't you hide it away somewhere? You know, Xaviera, even though Arnie's my boyfriend, I don't trust him when it comes to money. Better hide it. Put it in a drawer or something."

So, I took her advice about being careful and went back to the bedroom, got the box, felt Arnie's foxy eyes pierce through my back, closed the bedroom door behind me, and put the cashbox in a drawer in the living room under a sweater.

I thanked Debbie for her advice and because I felt sorry for her, I didn't chase them out. I said I'd go back to the studio apartment and continue my reading the galleys, but I begged her, in the future, not to have Arnie over there because he always made a mess out of the place. She assured me she was cleaning up after him and asked whether I couldn't see how hard she was working to keep the place up to snuff. She said she didn't want to fuck or suck Arnie anyway because she had a sore mouth and her teeth were killing her, but he was comfortable to have around the house. She'd been to the dentist twice that week. The dentist had pulled out most of her teeth and she looked like a little old lady with just a few choppers in her mouth. I felt sorry for her, because I could imagine how painful things had been for her.

That next morning, I had to go down to the district attorney's office. Then I had lunch with a friend, and Larry picked me up at my lawyer's office around four o'clock. Afterwards, we went home to the big apartment on Twenty-fifth Street because I certainly didn't feel like going back to the studio. I should mention at this point that Debbie never had a key to the Twenty-fifth Street apartment and, as per my instructions, had always been let in by the doorman.

I unlocked the apartment door, and as I walked in, I knew something was very wrong. When I checked out the apartment, I saw all the closets were open and then when I looked to the left, I noticed every drawer in the chest I had in the living room had been pulled out. There were sweaters lying on the floor and stuff was scattered all over the place. No clothing was missing, but when I checked the chest of drawers, I saw my money box was gone. I was almost afraid to look in the bedroom where I kept some carefully selected pieces of jewelry, cameras, a movie camera put away in the drawers. When I walked in the bedroom, I saw that my king-size bed, where Arnie had been residing the night before, was not only rumpled but the mattress was torn open and the pillows were thrown all over the floor. My closet doors were open and all my clothes were pulled off the racks. Yet, none of the clothes were missing, and so I wondered why the robbers had pulled them off the hangers. Then I checked the other bedroom where my fur coat—my mink —had been hanging. It was still there, to my great surprise.

Larry immediately began yelling and screaming that this rip-off must have been done by Arnie and Debbie. I argued that I didn't think this was so, because Debbie had been really cleaning up the place and had even told me to hide the cashbox. Someone else must have done it while they were out.

Still, the fact that Debbie wasn't there angered me. I told Larry that if she called or, better still, came back that night, then of course, they couldn't have done it. They'd have just taken all the money and run. Anyway, if she had done it with Arnie, why didn't they take the fur coat? Larry said he didn't trust either of them—especially not that little motherfucker, Arnie. I told him I didn't trust them, either, but if they wanted to steal, why would they mess up the place this way?

Larry didn't buy my argument. I'm pretty gullible and I hate to mistrust anyone and I couldn't believe Debbie would do such a thing. We'd been really good friends and she'd treated me like a little "Mommala" and even had me chat with her mother one day on the telephone. How could I think badly of her? When Larry and I started figuring out how much money was gone, it turned out to be about a thousand dollars cash and six hundred in checks.

One of the checks, which was payment for a Dutch television show I'd done, was stupidly made out to cash, instead of in my name. Upon checking out the apartment further, we discovered a carton of perfume missing we had bought tax-free in the Islands. Since it was around Christmas, whoever had stolen the perfume could easily sell it to people who wanted to give some very good, yet inexpensive, presents. All the cameras were gone as well, including the projector. You can well imagine how furious I was.

Almost mechanically, I started putting all the clothes back in the drawers and on the hangers. We now knew that the things stolen were the money, the cameras, the perfume, and some rings. Even my address books were still there. None of my expensive coats were missing. I couldn't understand it. The only thing I could think of was that they didn't have enough room to put all the stuff in, because they had to walk out of the building with the doorman watching. But they could just put the money and cameras and perfume in a shopping bag and stroll out.

Debbie did finally call me the night of the robbery around seven o'clock. I calmly told her to come over because I wanted to talk to her. She gave me a sob story about just having gone to the dentist and that he'd pulled out more of her teeth and how she was dying of pain. Angrier than ever, I said, "Bullshit! Come on over here right away. And give me the number of your dentist." Debbie refused to give me the number. But she promised me, "Okay, I'll be right over with Arnie."

"No, I don't want that motherfucker Arnie in my house anymore." But then Larry whispered in my ear that I should let her bring Arnie along, so we could find out what really had happened.

Two hours went by and—surprise—no Debbie or Arnie showed up. Meanwhile, I remembered that Arnie had left his phone number with my answering service a few weeks before along with a message for Debbie. My intuition told me then to make a note of that number since I might need it some day. So I called the number, which turned out to be his parents' house. His mother answered the phone. I told her I was a friend of Arnie and wanted to know how I could reach him. She seemed suspicious—a real worried Jewish mother. Poor woman, to be blessed with a creepy son like Arnie. She kept asking me all kinds of questions. What did I want from her son? What he had done wrong now? She was, indeed, very worried and started crying on the phone. I felt genuinely sorry for her, figuring the old lady already had enough *tsuris* from this marvelous young man, so I didn't ask any more questions. I certainly wasn't going to tell her what I suspected her son of. She kept asking, but I told her everything would be all right and not to worry.

Just as I hung up the phone—at ten o'clock—the doorbell rang, and Arnie and Debbie walked in. I was relieved because I felt that if they came over, they could have never robbed the place. When I told them what happened, Arnie went into the bedroom and started looking under the mattress on the bed. I asked him what he was looking for and he started yelling that the night before they'd hidden about four hundred dollars under the mattress, money that she, Debbie, had saved to pay for the dentist. He started screaming that he'd hidden it and now it was gone. I said he had a nerve to ask me where *her* money was. I'd thought he was the one who'd robbed me.

Arnie then began to put on a tremendous act. He said

to Debbie, "Where's your fur coat? Go and see if it's still here." For the last few weeks, I'd seen Debbie wear a chic black and white mink, which was, I suspected, a hot fur coat. She'd gotten the coat from a former boyfriend. This particular day, however, it was very cold outside and when Debbie came in, she was wearing an old, camel-colored cloth coat. To tell the truth, she looked pretty drab in that faded coat and her blonde hair pulled back with a rubber band.

They went through all the closets with Arnie yelling, "Goddamn, fuck it. Deb, your fur coat is gone!" He continued to yell about the bloody robbers and crooks who'd stolen Debbie's coat and how poor Debbie had to work so hard to put some money together. He accused me of making money much easier than Debbie. He then started sobbing about poor little Debbie having to pay her dentist and what were they gonna do and was I sure I didn't take her fur coat? Of course, I had taken it—and eaten it!

Then I told Arnie I'd found his number and called his mother, and then he really got upset. He told me his mother would have a stroke if she found out about the robbery. She had high blood pressure and a bad heart and that would be all she needed. And why had I called there in the first place? His mother was a nervous wreck. So Arnie and Larry and I got into a fight. Finally, I said, "GET the hell out of my house. I don't want to see either of you again."

I was all set to forget about the whole episode, when, the next Saturday, a girl called me up.

"Hi, there, are you Xaviera Hollander? My name is Welcome, Welcome Friend. Debbie had given me this number. I was supposed to get together with her during the weekend and we were supposed to go to some discotheque or just see what is happening in town. You know, I am from Los Angeles, California, and just arrived here a few weeks ago and I don't know too many people yet. So you must be Xaviera, eh? Debbie has talked very highly about you. I would love to meet you."

"Welcome is your name? How pretty. I've never heard such a sweet name for a girl. You must be a love child with a name like that. Anyway, Welcome, welcome to New York. By the way, where are you staying? Can I take your number down and give the message to Debbie maybe? You see, she is not here right now and I have no idea where she spends the weekend. All I know is that she might be with Arnie. Do you know him?"

Welcome, probably sneering, said on the other end, "Hum, yes, certainly, I have met that little jerk. Debbie is far too nice for a kid like that. I happen to like Debbie; but Arnie, I can't stand him. There is something so dishonest about him. I just don't know what exactly it is. By the way, Xaviera, can I come over and meet with you, since Debbie has told me such nice things about you. You seem to be a very warm and understanding human being. Oh, and as far as my phone number is concerned, I am actually getting kicked out of my hotel this afternoon because I can't afford the rent and have no place to stay. It was a horrible dump anyway. That is what I wanted to discuss with Debbie as well. Maybe she knows someone I can move in with for a while."

Since I liked her voice and manner, I decided to invite Welcome to come right over and if I found I got along with her, she might even move in later on that day. But I had to see her first. So far, she seemed okay.

Half an hour later, Welcome rang the doorbell three times as if there was a fire in the building. She was a lovely girl, exactly as I had expected her to be. We had good vibrations from the first moment we met. She was not exactly beautiful but had a very pretty face and lovely hazel eyes, surrounded by tinted eye glasses. And vivacious! Her hair was auburn and shoulder-length and it waved around as she kept moving her head and talking with her hands, and almost her feet. Indeed, not a quiet, passive girl, I thought to myself. Certainly will bring some life in the brewery, as they say in Holland.

I finally asked her, when I managed to get a word in, "So what are you doing in New York? Are you working in an office or are you like Debbie, hooking on the side? What is your story and why did you come all the way to New York from sunny Los Angeles?"

"Well, I had all kinds of troubles back there. I have a lovely three-year-old boy, who is with my mother at present and she threatened to take the child away; says I 'neglected' him. I think she envies me for having such a beautiful baby."

With this, Welcome pulled out of her tremendous pocket-book a huge photograph of a lovely baby boy, with twinkling eyes and goldish-blonde curly hair. Indeed, a kid to envy. If only all babies could be so beautiful! Even I felt jealous; my maternal instinct was awakened. I was interested in Welcome's life story and wanted to know more.

"Yes, his father was the most gorgeous man you can dream of. He was what you might call my dream prince, and a prince he was! He was a Russian prince, who came to L.A. for a few weeks. We had a wild romance for only one week and I wanted his child so badly that I conceived after having slept with him just that week. He was so beautiful, as a person, as well as sexually. Superintelligent and a real gentleman."

"So what happened to your dream prince?" I asked her.

"He left me and I never heard from him. He doesn't even know I carried his child or ever gave birth to a dream baby. I do miss my little boy. Can you imagine? But . . . at home, my mother was a horror and after all, I had no money to support the child. I somehow always lose my jobs. I don't have *"sitzfleisch,"* you know what I mean? Can't stay in one place long enough. I am half-Jewish and Debbie told me you were Jewish, too, so pardon my Yiddish in between.

"Anyway, here I am in New York," she went on. "I'm indeed working, but not as a hooker. Never have tried that, I have always given it away. I love men too much to sell my body."

It was rapidly becoming obvious that Welcome was off in her own little world—she was the ultimate "love child" or something like that. One story she told me really illustrated how good she was—good almost to the point of absurdity.

One night Welcome was strolling through Central Park, during early evening, a time when the park is beginning to be deserted and no place for pretty young ladies—or ugly young ladies, for that matter—to be alone. She was walking down a path in a wooded area when she suddenly felt herself seized from behind. A man had come out from behind a tree and had one arm around her neck and with the other was trying to tear off her blouse.

By all logical deductive powers, Welcome should have concluded that he was trying to rape her.

But what does Welcome do?

She doesn't scream. Doesn't yell for help. Instead she gently takes ahold of the man's hand inside her blouse and says, soothingly, "Sweetheart, if you really want to fuck me so badly, why do it here in the park, where it's so cold? Come along with me, come to my house where we can make love in a nice warm bed. . . ."

Hearing this, the man released her, staring at her in astonishment, and ran away as though she'd been the mad person in the encounter. He'd come to the park for a nice violent rape, and instead he'd come up against tenderness and affection. Who could blame him for thinking it a crazy world!

I asked Welcome where she'd been working and she replied, "I'm working during the daytime at a real estate office as a secretary. I work for Richie Malberg and his partner, Sandy, groovy guy, but a bit of a toughie. They know a lot of bad boys, you know. I would rather stay loose and just listen to things happening without interfering. To each his own."

When I heard that name, I felt like I'd been jabbed by a needle. Maybe Welcome could shed some light on the mysterious robbery that had occurred the previous week? I wouldn't tell her beforehand what had happened, but I would just fish as to what exactly she knew about Arnie, Debbie *and* Richie.

I thought that if Arnie had done something wrong, Richie, who was probably his brother, would certainly know about it and even though Welcome came on like a bit of a cuckoo —nervous and fluttering—I could see she was extremely intelligent and I trusted her. If only this time I would not be let down. Someone once gave me a new definition of a friend: a friend is somebody who you *think* you can trust. It's certainly the way I've always regarded people.

I decided to let the subject go for a while so as not to arouse Welcome's suspicions. It was getting late already and Larry and I were supposed to go to the theatre. So I told Welcome to quickly go over to her West Side hotel and check out her stuff. She seemed very pleased at this.

"Oh, by the way, thanks a lot, Xaviera, for letting me move in here. I just have one big bag with me and if you don't mind, can you maybe lend me a little suitcase or a big handbag, so I can drop some more stuff in it? I really don't have too much with me. I'll be back in a jiffy."

Welcome left with a big suitcase of mine, and her "jiffy" turned out to be three hours long. Larry and I had to give up our theatre reservations and wait for Welcome to return. Finally, at ten o'clock the doorbell rang, and as I opened the door, a young, good-looking taxi driver was carrying her suitcases up to the apartment. By God, I thought, all she had was one suitcase, but this . . . this was a whole house getting carried into my apartment. Boxes and boxes full of records and books— a lot of poetry books and records of Bob Dylan, Dory Previn, Carole King and Elton John— an electric typewriter, a record player, boxes with shoes and hats and boots, and finally, about four suitcases with clothes, coats, etc. She really had moved out of California forever, it seemed. The cab driver was awfully nice and, as it turned out, his name was Nicolai, a Greek. No wonder he reminded me a bit of my Greek lover, Takis. They had just met and before Nicolai left, Welcome quickly jotted down my telephone number and took his. The next night, he came over again and fucked her all night long. Welcome, as it would turn out later, was a real love child, who would pick up any good-looking young boy from the street or taxi and take him home and fuck him. No money—all love. She needed love so badly.

Anyhow, this first day, after Welcome was settled in, Larry and I had ordered up some Chinese food for all of us. Later, well-fed and feeling relaxed with Welcome as a member of the household, I decided to see if I could learn some more about Richard and Arnie. "Welcome, tell me how close are you to Debbie? Are you really good friends, or what?"

"Oh no, I just met her a few times at the office and she seemed nice and was concerned about me."

"When did you last see Debbie?"

"Actually, I last saw her on Thursday, the day before yesterday," she said, beginning a long ramble. "She had just been to the dentist who pulled out most of her teeth. Poor kid. She must have suffered and it'll cost her a fortune to get that mouth fixed. Am I happy I have such good teeth! I hardly ever eat sweet things, anyway. But her teeth must have been that bad because she takes all those drugs all the time . . . at least that's what Richie told me. You know Richie and I sit down sometimes and talk quite a lot. Richie just got this job and he was damn lucky, because he had a lot of trouble in his previous real estate office. Fooled some people out of money and they tried to sue him. He just moved out in time. He has a wife, you know, with a baby and a second one on the way. She is all right, but the Malbergs are not up to much good.

"What do you mean 'not up to much good'? By the way, what kind of coat was Debbie wearing last Thursday?" I asked her as nonchalantly as possible.

"Oh, as usual, the black and white fur coat. She says it's mink, and it reached down over the knee with her black boots. Her hair was pulled backwards with a rubber band. Arnie was there, too, and they seemed very nervous and were whispering in Richie's office. Arnie had come in with a carton of perfumes and asked whether any of the girls wanted some perfume for Christmas— to buy, of course. Actually, there were some other things they'd brought in and locked up in the closet, and I heard Richie say that it would be more difficult to get rid of the cameras than of the perfume. I heard Richie and Arnie make plans to make a big hit or "score" some day, about a few weeks ago. Arnie asked Richie's advice as to how to do the job. He had the place, but where would they hide the stolen stuff? So, Richie offered his office, of course, since nobody would suspect him."

"Ah ha," I said, relieved in a way.

Finally, I knew the true story and again, it was Larry who'd been right from the first moment on when he'd said Arnie and Debbie had stolen my things.

"Tell me, Welcome, did you hear them discuss any money, by the way?"

"Yes, as a matter of fact, now that you're mentioning it. But why do you want to know all this?"

I then explained about the robbery and how Debbie and Arnie had pretended they had been robbed themselves. However, now that I knew that Debbie still had her fur coat, I realized that it had all been a fake scene and it was dear Debbie and dear, dear Arnie who had pulled out all the drawers trying to make it look like a real robbery. Welcome was really upset to hear this and she promised to find out more details on Monday. I asked her what else she remembered. "Did they mention any money or checks. You know they ran away with my money box as well."

"Were there any checks in the money box?"

"About six hundred dollars in checks."

"Oh God!"

Then she proceeded to tell me that there was a girl in the office named Angelica. A nice, young square kid who had a bank account and a check-cashing card. She'd been asked by Arnie and Debbie if they could use her card as identification, because they had to cash some checks. Oh well, I thought to myself, I may as well forget about getting those checks stopped because by this time those creeps have probably cashed them, gotten the money and, who knows, spent it all! Also, I didn't want to get Angelica into trouble. She was a nice, innocent girl who didn't know beans about what happened. But I did call her to tell her the story. She seemed scared when she told me it was too late—the card *had* been used by them and it wasn't until later that she realized what was probably going on and how she'd been used. When she thought about the perfume and the cameras they were selling, she figured out they must be "hot" merchandise, especially since it was around Christmas.

Was I going to have any revenge on this loving couple? Well, I called Debbie's mother—I had her number—and told her exactly what had happened and to say that at the very least I was angry with Debbie. I asked her to see if she could get Debbie to return at least some of the things she'd taken. I told her I wanted the rings back and the cameras. They could keep the money. I knew they would anyway.

A few days later, a very timid Debbie called me up. The Queen of *Chutzpah:* she didn't say "sorry" or apologize. She didn't say she was going to bring back some of the stuff. What she did say was could she please pick up her suitcases, which she still had at the studio apartment? Not exactly amused, I told her she had a hell of a nerve to ask me to let her get her cheap, shitty clothes. I told her she had a lot of balls to call me at all, and I asked why she didn't return the stuff she'd stolen from me. Now she finally said she was sorry, but she seemed more bothered by how I'd found out about it.

Perhaps I should have let her steam in her own curiosity, but instead I let her know that her own friend, Welcome, had told me.

"But Welcome isn't really a friend of mine," she said with surprise. "I met her at Richie's office just once. She wanted to have a drink with me, sometime, so I gave her your phone number since I was with you most of the time . . . Oh gee," she moaned in her first sincere moment of this disgusting conversation, "If I *hadn't* given her your number, *you'd* never have found out about Arnie and me."

This was like adding insult to the injury of being ripped off by one of your best friends. "Look, I may be a bit gullible," I lashed back at her, "but I'm not a complete idiot! Eventually I'd have found out. I suspected Arnie, that prick of yours, first of all, way back in the beginning."

After a lot more of this depressing conversation, I finally convinced Debbie to return my rings and cameras and leave the package with the doorman. She agreed, I realized, because she wanted to make up with me and so I told her if she'd give me back what she'd taken, I'd be her friend again. On the other hand I told Larry and Welcome that once I got my stuff back, I'd never let her crooked face inside my door again. She could go whistle for her clothes and, in fact, I burned everything in the incinerator. I felt that was one small way I could take revenge against her. And when I checked up on Arnie, I found out that he was a professional sneak thief and that Debbie was his accomplice. He specialized, it seems, in stealing from his friends and those of Debbie. And so did his little fuck-mate. I learned that Debbie had made photostats of my address books and she was going to be calling people I used to know.

But in about two weeks she began calling me day after day. She told me that Arnie had deserted her, taking all the money, and she'd changed all the locks and finally gotten an unlisted phone number. She was broke and she couldn't pay her dentist. She was walking around without most of her teeth and she didn't have any money to buy food. Her business was not working out at all. I told her it was her own fault, and she deserved everything she got.

Luckily, I didn't weaken as usual and let her come back. Normally, even if somebody does something bad to me, I usually end up feeling sorry for them, relent, and let bygones be bygones—until it happens all over again. But this time— *basta, finit!* If I'm going to be robbed, I prefer it be done by perfect strangers.

The Girls in My Life

CORRINE: THE HOUSE INTELLECTUAL *(Intellectual House Calls)*

Corrine is something else again.

Super bright and super built.

Big-hearted. Not to speak of being very big-boobed.

Pretty. Not gorgeous. But really attractive. And the only such lady of my acquaintance—the professor turned pro.

Corrine is now twenty-five, ridiculously voluptuous, and her pert face—last time I feasted on it—was topped by a short haircut that made her hair almost boyish in length. But surely that is the only boyish thing about her, by any length of description.

I would love to attend a lecture at one of Corrine's classes—she teaches art at a famous New York City university and I imagine that half her students have their own artistic notions (that's erotic art we're now talking about, folks) about Teacher. But, so far as I know, Corrine doesn't indulge in that kind of extracurricular activity or give after-hour seminars.

I was introduced to Corrine by Mike, a mutual friend who had met her at Le Directoire, one of Manhattan's "in" discotheques. Mike is what used to be called a playboy. He is in his early thirties, quite personable, and possesses the kind of sparkling wit that makes him the confidante of many a single girl. And, once confidence has been established in Mike, he manages to establish something else in these lovely young ladies he meets in discotheques.

But it's funny about Mike. After he's balled them a few times—given them a dry run, as it were—he then introduces them to me as potential call girls.

By the time I met them, he's heard their life stories and knows all their problems—which might include a generally sexless sex life or a bad job or a job which pays badly or whatever—and he brought them to Madam X for a possible solution to their problems.

Corrine, though, did not fit the above pattern. She had a fine position and she supplanted her income with some weekly support from her "old man." When she told me this, she meant it literally because the gentleman in question was in his mid-sixties. She saw him three times a week, did his cooking, and occasionally they screwed. Her weekly retainer for this was the large sum of fifty dollars a week.

It's funny. When we began talking, Corrine, Mike and I, we discussed student unrest, politics, modern art, and music, and in a very few moments, I realized that Corrine was one of the brightest persons I'd ever met. In other matters, she wasn't so wise.

"Corrine," I said, "you're really not being compensated for what you do for him."

"Oh," she replied, "so far as I'm concerned, he's merely 'tipping' me for being good to him. I don't do it for the money."

"Why not do it for the money if you enjoy sex?" I asked her.

"Look, I'm not being superior or anything but I've got one career and I don't think I could manage a second one."

Mike then entered the conversation again. "It's not a matter of a second career, Corrine. What could be groovy for you is that Xaviera knows a lot of attractive young guys with lots of money who'd be only too happy to pay you to lay you. You'd have the best of both worlds—fucking for fun *and* for profit. Your own little mutual fund."

I watched Corrine very carefully. I was sure she seemed more interested. But it wasn't the word "pay" that made her eyes light up; it was the word "lay" and the words "a lot."

She was obviously a very sex-loving girl and her hot feelings
made her big brown eyes glisten.

"Corrine," Mike continued what was really a kind of
intellectual argument, "you'd be *much* better off spending
a few nights at Xaviera's than cruising around the discotheques looking for guys. Here you have a choice of good-
looking, horny guys while at the discotheques you never
know what kind of creep the guy might really be. Besides,
why fool around with an old man—no matter how nice he
may be—when you can have more fun and money here?"

"I think you're getting through to me," Corrine smiled.

"Oh yeah," Mike added, a little slyly, I thought, "did I
mention that Xaviera really digs girls?"

Corrine looked at me a little wonderingly, so I smiled
at her.

"Am I right, X?" Mike laughed at the two of us with our
silent looks.

"Corrine," I said, "I'm very happy to have met you and
you've impressed me as an extremely smart girl. I also get
the impression that you really dig sex. So I'll ask you:
Have you ever had sex with a woman?"

She was blushing like crazy at the question and unless
I was greatly mistaken, the idea of having a woman make
love to her was really turning her on. "No," she finally
answered after some hesitation, "but I've often dreamed
about having a beautiful woman make love to me." She
paused for a bit and then charged right into it. "Okay, I
want to know more. Tell me all about it . . . but please
remember, I'm new at all this. I regard myself as pretty
sophisticated and I adore sex with men—I'm a big girl and
I like my men big—but in all honesty I'd like to try swinging
the other way, too."

"Corrine," I replied as seriously as possible, because I
knew how seriously *she* was taking all this, "you really have
come to the right person. I *do* love girls, but actually I simply
love people—I think that explains it all. So if a woman is
interesting and pretty and seems to like me in return, why
shouldn't I go to bed with her?"

"It certainly seems logical enough," she said. "I guess
I've just never thought of it that way."

"Look," I said, "I'm much much more selective in my

choice of women partners than I am with men. I've got to be really emotionally turned on by a woman, while with a man I can just dig him as a good fuck—just as you do. But in my time here, I've fancied certain girls more than others and we usually ended up having an affair. And I can assure that that particular girl, my lover, would get more business and make more money than any of the others. Maybe this isn't quite fair to the other girls, but someone has usually been my favorite racehorse, so I played favorites. Anyhow these affairs come to an end sooner or later, and . . . well, then on to the *next* filly in my stable!"

Corrine laughed at my "horsie" analogy, which pleased me as I was not anxious to offend her in any way: I, too, was getting turned on by this talk.

"I hope the great debate is over," Mike said, cheerfully, and before she could object. he was leading the two of us into the bedroom, and while he sat, more or less cuddled up in the armchair next to the bed, I gave the professor her first lessons in lovemaking with a woman. Happily for both of us, she proved an apt pupil. I'd pleased her—so I was pleased.

The next day, Corrine rang the doorbell unannounced. At that particular moment, I was rather busy on the phone, and I really couldn't pay much attention to her. I said something like "Hello, take a seat. I'll be with you as soon as I finish a few phone calls," and returned to the bedroom.

Later, when I came back into the living room, I found, much to my astonishment, that she was undressed and lying on the floor, hugging one of my fluffy pillows against her body and obviously getting all worked up. I quietly tiptoed over to her—she hadn't heard me enter the room— and kissed her neck. I felt a shiver go through her body. She reached up and pulled me down on the floor with her. In a few seconds, I was nude as well, kissing her sweet mouth, then working my way down. As I reached her bushy triangle, her pubic hair was all wet and curly. Her tremendous breasts were hard and her nipples erect with excitement. Corrine really needed me and we made love, losing all sense of time and place. Her breathing became faster and faster and finally she reached a climax with both her legs wrapped around my neck, almost stopping my breathing with her passionate grip.

From that time on, I could count on Corrine for assistance as a call girl. But what she actually became was my lover. On a rare, quiet evening, she and I would retire to the bedroom and make love while the other girls were in the living room.

One day, a few months after we'd met, she brought over a cute puppy, a lovely black cocker spaniel and, in a funny mood, I tried to teach the dog to go down on its mistress. But the dog was either inhibited or square and ran away to another room.

Despite our wild good times together, Corrine still enjoyed men, and when one of the other girls had trouble with a John who was outrageously big, they'd ask me to send Corrine as a substitute ballplayer and she'd finish the job.

But as the months went by, it did become increasingly clear that Corrine had acquired an enormous fondness for pussy and she was becoming somewhat of a "butch." She told me she sized up women on the street and paid more attention to women than to men. A few visits later, she confessed to having gone down on approximately two dozen women and that she'd seduced one of her best friend's girlfriends. Then she became a genuine swinger and attended numerous orgies where she surely got to satisfy her taste for pussy, not to speak of an occasional cock for dessert.

So Corrine, the professor turned pro, evidently learned to enjoy life a lot more vigorously than she had when she spent those quite evenings with her "old man."

I'm glad to have had the opportunity to play pedagogue to her professor.

THE D.A.'S INTERROGATION

Over a space of many weeks I spent more time in the office of Assistant District Attorney Kenneth Conboy than any place except my apartment. Mr. Conboy, of course, is on the staff of New York City District Attorney Frank Hogan, and he was assigned to work with me regarding the police corruption scandal I had helped bring to light in mid-summer of 1971.

I had previously been involved with Knapp Commission investigations, although I had avoided actually appearing in person before the Commission. This was the period when Teddy Ratnoff—known as "Abe the Bugger" in my first book—was coming over to the Fifty-fifth Street apartment in which I'd been living in addition to operating my brothel. Knapp Commission agents had tried to subpoena me four or five times, but each time Teddy got them off my back. These agents even went so far as to go to my lawyer's office and hand him a subpoena to try and force me to testify. For reasons of personal safety, I wasn't at all anxious to testify before the Commission about certain persons, be they policemen or politicians, who might have had something to do with me in my recent career as a madam. I wanted to live to see my twenty-ninth and thirtieth birthdays. . . .

However, now, as a result of my July arrest case, I was more or less forced by Assistant D. A. Conboy to cooperate with him in that office's investigation regarding police corruption. The options were these: either appear at his office whenever he wanted me there to identify certain tapes the D. A.'s office had confiscated from Ted, and thereby earn immunity from the various charges facing me, or else face certain court conviction and a prison sentence of several years for running a house of ill repute.

Since I'd been in court a depressing number of times already, with nothing being resolved—each time the case was postponed—and had spent thousands of dollars in legal fees (I'd assumed responsibility for bail money and legal costs of the girls who'd been arrested with me), I desperately wanted the entire business to be over. I also hoped my cooperation would help me in the deportation proceedings against me.

Of course if I were convicted, we could always appeal the case, but my lawyer advised me to cooperate with the district attorney's office because immunity meant my case would be dismissed. I called Mr. Conboy's office and agreed to cooperate, but pointed out as well that I was facing possible deportation and might not be available to him for very long. He advised me not to worry about this, that his office would help me as much as possible. He said a letter from his office to the Immigration Department would ensure my being able to stay in the United States for quite some time. I guess he more or less kept his promise (although I will have more to say about this later on): this whole business started in August 1971 and I remained in America through the following April.

So week after week I took a cab downtown to Assistant D. A. Conboy's Centre Street office—usually four or five days a week—and listened to tapes and tried to identify the voices on Teddy's illegal wire-taps and explain the situations where I'd been forced to make pay-offs to crooked cops. Mr. Conboy was also quite interested in the amounts of money I turned over to these minions of the law.

I still had my big black book—the famous one—in my possession and when it came to revealing its contents to the district attorney's office I had to balk at this line of questioning. Again I was reminded that my immunity was based on giving the D. A.'s office my complete cooperation, or else my case wouldn't be dismissed and I'd be in further trouble for lying under oath. I told him that I *was* cooperating, but that our agreement was that I'd deal with the tapes, not the Johns who'd been my clients.

We were able to drop this subject because Mr. Conboy's chief interest was now Patrolman William Phillips, known as "Nick" in *The Happy Hooker,* who'd made national headlines by testifying to his own graft before the Knapp Commission. I'd liked "Nick" as a person far more than Teddy Ratnoff and while I was sure he was one of the biggest "bagmen" in the city, there wasn't anything else I really knew about him.

Mr. Conboy wasn't at all convinced of this and the more we discussed Phillips, the more I felt I was being coerced into lying about the man. I don't mean to imply that Mr. Conboy wanted me to lie—but he wasn't getting the answers he wanted and he believed they were there, all right.

He kept asking me, "Are you sure you only met him this past April?"

"Yes," I kept answering, "I'm sure I met him late in March or early in April of 1971. I'd never seen Mr. Phillips before and I'd never paid off any other cop." I told him that when I did make the pay-offs to Phillips, it was handled through Ted Ratnoff. Teddy and Phillips and I had gotten together at my apartment one night and the two of them arranged the whole thing without my having a word to say about it. I was told by Teddy I had to cooperate or else be deported. And the fee for police protection, set by the two of them, was $1,100 a month. For all I knew, Phillips himself took a lot of this—but I was telling all I knew.

I kept having to assure Conboy and his staff that I wasn't lying. I repeated the circumstances of my meeting Phillips and all I knew about him—which wasn't much, and most of it stuff Teddy had told me—which certainly couldn't be trusted.

They kept prodding me to tell them the names of other

madams and call girls paying money or dealing in any way with Phillips, but I told them that so far as I personally could say with any certainty, I seemed to be the only nut crazy enough to pay off a cop. Most madams were obviously more discreet in their work than I'd been, I told them, and it was my misfortune to have become sort of a nationally known charity organization for poor cops. Conboy and his staff weren't amused by my attempt at levity, but I hoped they believed I was telling the truth.

All this while I'd been wondering why the D. A.'s office was pushing me so hard about knowing Phillips, and finally, some months later, the dawn broke. There had been a double murder three years earlier—a man by the name of Jimmy Smith had been murdered, along with a call girl named Sharon Stango. Both had lived on Fifty-seventh Street. I also lived in that neighborhood, not too far away, at the time of the murder but I was then living with my fiancé, Carl, and was very much a straight girl. I was engaged, all right, but not in prostitution. In fact, all I knew about prostitution in those days was what I'd read in the papers, and about all I could recall on that score was the raid on a famous house in the East Nineties where a lot of prominent people were suddenly running out into the street, to escape arrest, in the briefest of clothing. This townhouse, which contained a swimming pool, was later bought by socialite-politician Carter Burden.

Well, this obviously wasn't much help to them and I was beginning to realize that they were attempting to build a case against Phillips as the murderer—and this is why they wanted me to have known him, not just before last April but three years ago.

I was asked if Phillips had threatened me at any time, or had he tried to do me any physical injury? I said, "Certainly not." To me, Bill Phillips—or "Nick" as I knew him—seemed to be an "honest" cop, "honest" in the sense that although he took bribes, he delivered what he promised. For three months I'd paid him to avoid police busts, and there were none.

The only time I saw him angry, I told them, was the night he'd found out that Teddy was recording all their conversations together, especially after pay-off money had been exchanged, on behalf of the Knapp Commission. Phillips wanted to know if I'd known about this—and of course, I hadn't—but he certainly didn't threaten me. His anger was directed at Teddy—and probably at himself for being taken in by Teddy—but this was the only time he'd ever raised his voice in my presence.

Conboy and his staff kept on relentlessly with the same questions: had Phillips made any physical threats to me? I kept giving them the same answers: *No.* I told them they could not put words in my mouth. If what they were after was the truth, they were getting it, and I hoped at some point it would be to their liking.

The next thing they wanted to know was if Phillips had ever gone with any of my girls or brought any of his friends up to the apartment. I answered that Phillips had introduced Teddy to some police officers but that no policeman associated with Phillips had been up to the apartment. On the night we made a deal, I'd treated Phillips to a girl, but otherwise he seemed a "nice, decent man" in his personal behavior. He never asked me for a girl or paid to sleep with a girl. The first night—that was the only time. I wasn't going to invent any other girls, or threats of violence, for them. It never happened.

Eventually I was to read in the papers that Phillips had been indicted for the double murder. It seems that after he'd appeared on television as a Knapp Commission witness, some of the people who lived in the building in which the murders had taken place recognized him as someone who came there and had put the finger on him as the murderer. While I was in Europe his case came up, and after a sensational trial, the jury ended up hopelessly deadlocked. Despite the hung jury, a new trial had been ordered.

I don't know whether Bill Phillips is guilty of those murders. I've heard people who've followed the case say the police are out to "get" Phillips, discredit all his testimony for the Knapp Commission that allegedly exposed so much police corruption. I just don't know. Privately I hope he is proven innocent and acquitted on this charge. It certainly wasn't up to me to involve Phillips in additional difficulties, because so far as I was concerned, he acted like a gentleman and, what's more important, he has already confessed to any crimes I knew about.

The visits to Conboy's office went on for months and when the questioning wasn't being so fierce and relentless, I sometimes enjoyed myself. Conboy could be a charmer when he wanted to be, an elegant bachelor who apparently couldn't be seduced. In contrast to him, his two associates reminded me of dwarfs, and they could be quite funny when they weren't asking the same question 1,001 times. The more they nagged, the more I tried to be the Complete Lady, but there were more than a few times I almost lost my cool. Still, my immigration case kept getting postponed, as they'd promised it would be, and by dint of some wishful thinking I began to hope I'd eventually get my green card, which would allow me to be able to stay in America as a permanent resident. For that matter, if it hadn't been for those crazy immigration laws, maybe I'd still be a Manhattan secretary looking for Mister Right to come along and change my life.

It was now late January, 1971, and my book was soon to be published. I felt I'd been as cooperative as possible and didn't anticipate any trouble from the district attorney's office with regard to the book. But, as has happened too often before, I was once again being naive.

In the earlier version of *The Happy Hooker,* there was nothing about the Knapp Commission. But one of my co-authors, novelist Robin Moore, kept insisting that we'd be crazy not to capitalize on the publicity I'd received as a result of my involvement with the Knapp Commission hearings. Robin said, and the publisher agreed with him, that the Knapp Commission material was—insomuch as I could use it at all—"powerful stuff" and would be the important final chapter in the book. So we produced this last chapter—all of it subject to the editorial decisions of my editor, Bob Abel, and legal decisions of the Dell lawyers as to what could be printed without inviting legal action—and the book was at long last ready for the printers!

What I hadn't counted on was a surprising prohibition from Mr. Conboy's office. He insisted on seeing the galley proofs of the book when they were ready, and I showed them to him—over the objections, I must add, of my publishers, who weren't the least bit amused by what they regarded as a threat to freedom of speech—namely, my right to tell what had happened to me.

Well, if I was understanding him correctly, Mr. Conboy wanted to prevent the book from being released. He wanted to stop me from appearing on radio or television to discuss the book or anything connected with it, and he seemed to be putting a kind of embargo or restrictive order on my movements. In other words, he didn't want me to do any talking anywhere if I wasn't talking to *him* or the Knapp Commission. He stressed the immunity he'd granted me and the dismissal of my case and strongly cautioned me not to speak to anyone about my almost-daily visits to his Centre Street offices.

Frankly, to me this seemed intolerable. I'd cooperated fully and no one in his office had said my public appearances would in any way jeopardize indictments they were then hoping for. Yet, I was being given a series of dictums —"Thou shalt not do this, or that, or this, or. . . ."—that made no sense at all to me or to any of the professional people who were consulted on the matter.

It all became academic when the book was finally published because I was suddenly a "hot" author—for once the word was being used differently—and it was impossible, not to speak of silly, to keep me away from the media.

Conboy's office called up and said I'd have to "be forced into silence," because this publicity was ruining my effectiveness as a witness, but I countered by pointing out that my testimony was a matter of sworn-to-record and I wasn't about to deny any of it on my publicity tour. I'd do my best to avoid the subject but when it came up, I wanted to be honest. Well, *diplomatic,* and honest. Couldn't the New York City Police Department understand this? I would avoid, as best I could, questions about any and all political issues the book raised, but I wasn't about to be censored about the book. It had happened to me, much of it was painful to recount, but it was all true—and how dare they tell me I couldn't tell the public what experiences I'd had! Yes, it had happened to *me* and although a lot of it was far from flattering, I wanted to have my life

story known for whatever insights it might provide to
people everywhere. This may have been a totally optimistic,
or totally arrogant, attitude before the book was published,
but the remarkable numbers of letters I've gotten have
proven it to be an entirely realistic one.

There was another factor, which I kept no secret from
the district attorney's office. I knew I was being followed
a lot of the time, whether by the police or the press or
some unknown, or slightly known, set of former admirers,
I couldn't say. By now the press knew of my many visits
downtown with Mr. Conboy and his staff, and certainly
the police knew of my activities. But, more significant, I'd
been informed by certain nameless individuals that the
mention of their names would result in my taking a submarine ride in the Hudson, sans submarine. This should
have frightened me, but it didn't—maybe all those weeks
of being with Conboy and his legal beagles made me believe, for a change, in the protection of the law for lawful
purposes—and I didn't panic when certain individuals
tried to put the heat on me. Yet I had no intention of
living under any kind of police protection anymore—I was
going to live *my* way, whatever that happened to be.

When the first lecture or media appearances occurred,
I usually tried to forewarn the audience that there were
certain topics from the book I still couldn't discuss in
public because they were being studied by grand juries.
As it happened, however, these weren't the subjects of
enormous interest to audiences—perhaps they'd become
inured to the idea of police corruption—and the D. A.'s
office no longer tried to interfere with my right to speak
out, as a human being, on something about which I had
unique knowledge and, maybe, some very valuable insights.
After all, I was paying my own rent, buying my own food,
and these public appearances were to be my only source
of income until book royalties would come in—more than
a year off. So the D. A.'s office had no right to interfere
with my making a legitimate living, particularly since it
had taken such exception to other ways I had of making
a living. . . .

Still, as I've indicated before, it wasn't brimstone and fire downtown on Centre Street. One day, right after the galleys had been submitted and we'd agreed to disagree, I arrived at Mr. Conboy's office to find everyone sitting around and laughing, waving their hands zanily in the air and generally behaving like a bunch of schoolboys. By checking what they'd been reading, I realized they were reacting to my statements to the effect that I usually can tell, by looking at the size of a man's hands and nose, how well he is endowed.

It was bad enough that the testimony I'd given had been challenged so often by these men . . . but to have my sexual expertise put up to ridicule—well, I took matters in hand, as I've done so many times before! I went around to each man, grabbed one of his hands, examined it, and then issued a verdict on the size of his organ.

"You're long and skinny," I said to one of the smaller men.

"Oh, you're kind of short and fleshy . . ." to another.

And for Mr. Conboy himself, who was by now prepared to be a good sport and subject himself to *my* cross-examination for a change, I had this prognosis: "Mr. Conboy, you're big and strong . . . wow, such big hands—you must be a real lady-killer in bed. Look at those *firm* hands!"

He didn't blush, but I can tell you he wasn't offended, either.

Yet a relatively few moments later he was telling me he thought my book was pure pornography, written for commercial purposes only. He also informed me that most of it could never be true and that if I sold more than a few thousand copies, it would "be a miracle." (When the book goes into its umpteenth printing and there are five or six million copies in print, I may just send him an autographed copy as a compliment to his vast knowledge of book publishing and people in general!)

There were a few minor changes he wanted in the chapter about "Abe" and "Nick" and the Knapp Commission, but he personally seemed prepared to wash his hands of the whole business. He also gave me a final caution about not saying a word to the press, but I simply told him to forget it—I had been a most "cooperative" witness and had spent months at it, with the only guarantee that I'd remain in America for as long as my testimony was needed, and now my publishers were arranging a huge publicity tour for me and I wasn't about to miss it! I was going to talk my fool head off about the things I knew so much about, but police corruption wouldn't be one of my topics nor would the income a top madam can make. In addition to my Immigration Department troubles, I would soon be having Internal Revenue Service problems, so my discretion in these areas could be assured.

The only postscript I can add to this chapter is that the D. A.'s office did, after all, finally afford me some police protection. It happened one night after all those months of *schlepping* downtown to Centre Street—always at my own expense, I might add. I still had two apartments at the time—one to seclude myself away from police harassment—but this particular night I thought it'd be safe to return to the Twenty-Fifth Street penthouse and stretch out a bit. Living quietly in a studio apartment had been pleasant in its way, but I was feeling mildly claustrophobic. I was alone in the apartment, at three in the morning, trying to finish reading a book before I fell asleep, and there was suddenly loud knocking on my door.

My immediate reaction, based on past experience, was that I'd have to hole up again in the small apartment, but I also realized that there was no reason I *had* to do so. At last the black books were in safekeeping, and I really had done my duty by the police.

I suddenly felt an anger, almost a moral anger, really, and I went to the door and shouted: "Why don't you contact Mr. Conboy, the assistant district attorney of New York, and tell him how you've been harassing me! I've been going downtown at least two or three and sometimes five times a week, and if there's some information you need why don't you call him up, or District Attorney Hogan, maybe! I've done everything asked of me for months now, and tonight some stupid cops are standing out there trying to bust my chops! Well, you'd better just do a disappearing act because if I open this door and you try and arrest me on some charge, there's going to be some big embarrassment in your precinct headquarters, because I'm going to turn the D. A.'s office on to you! You're bothering me without cause, and I'm going to seek an injunction against you because you're breaking laws right and left. . . !"

Henceforth I didn't get any late-night visitations, as described in the previous chapter. My civil liberties speech had apparently done the trick. Or some calls downtown had. . . .

The Girls in My Life

BRITT: She Voted Herself
"Most Likely to Succeed"

If I had to select one of my girls as a classic physical type, I'd have to choose Britt. Anyone meeting Britt for the first time would receive the impression of a classic tall blonde beauty from Scandinavia. Britt is Scandinavian—she grew up in Stockholm—and she certainly is a tall leggy blonde. In fact Britt's luscious legs are really her outstanding feature and she loves to flaunt them in the shortest, tightest pair of hot pants she can manage to wiggle into.

Britt grew up in Sweden, but she has lived in a number of places and it's hard to determine her age. She could be anywhere between twenty-seven and thirty-five—I know she'd gone through several skin peelings to give her face youthful contours, and it's seldom one sees Britt without false eyelashes and her face carefully made up. She also wears a long blonde wig over her own, much shorter hair.

I must say that Britt projects one hell of an image of that classic blonde. But actually she was attractive rather than being a raving beauty. Her eyes were on the smallish side and her nose was definitely a bit too petite for her face. Then, too, though her manner was pleasantly cool—even blasé at times—on occasions when she was feeling aggravated there'd sometimes be a nervous tic around her eyes.

Britt speaks at least four languages fluently, and little wonder. When I first met her, she'd just arrived in New York from Mexico City, where she had been a call girl for several years. She'd been deported from Mexico when the police raided her house and found a supply of drugs there. Britt claimed that the drugs had been planted there by the police, acting on a tip-off from a competitor of hers. Because of the drug charge, her operation was immediately closed down by the police and she was forced to leave the country posthaste.

When we first met and she was telling me about herself, she said she'd had to leave without collecting the money she had in various bank vaults and safe deposit boxes, but later on—when we had become good friends—she confessed she had probably spent most of her money on her various boyfriends, guys who were generally some years younger than she was. These handsome young studs weren't pimps but not too far from it, since they either beat or talked her out of her cash.

Before Mexico City, Britt had lived in Paris, London, and various German cities. She'd also lived in South America, in Caracas, and all this globe-trotting had added to her sophistication and worldliness. But it wasn't her woman-of-the-world charm that attracted men so much as those Scandinavian features. A first look at Britt was like a sexual fantasy come true!

When Britt came to work for me, everything seemed to be fine between us. Then I learned that she was regularly breaking a house rule—she was giving her name and telephone number to the clients. I always did some spot-checking on my girls to see if they were being as square with me as I was with them, and only Britt, it turned out, was giving clients her own business card. When I asked some of the men who'd slept with Britt to tell me the truth about her, they showed me her cards, which had campy pseudonyms on them—for example, the name of a month, like May or June.

I considered letting her go, but something compelled me to keep her on my staff. I knew she was a smart cookie, a lot smarter, in a business sense, than most of the other girls and in a way I admired her ambition. In any case, all the time she was preparing to run her own operation she was making a lot of money for me. We needed each other—she was one of my most popular girls and she needed to work for me to build up her own clientele.

After a period of months Britt began showing up less and less at my house, and when she did she'd only go out on the important calls which meant a nice fat fee. Then she stopped showing up entirely and I learned through the grapevine that she had set herself up in a magnificent duplex apartment that she and her current boyfriend had had renovated and redecorated at quite a lot of expense.

I also noticed that some of my regular customers had become strangers. But this only proved bothersome for a few weeks because they began reappearing at my house, where there was not only plenty of choice with a Dutch flavor but the assurance of a few laughs in addition to loads of tender loving care. Britt, I learned, was complaining about her business, which only goes to show that it takes a lot more than a book of telephone numbers to become a successful madam. Also, if there is such a thing as old school ties, there is also such a thing as being loyal to the madam, who is, after all, something of a "schoolmarm" herself.

When I got out of the business I reestablished contact with Britt who—in search of eternal youth—had turned to plastic surgery to improve the merchandise. This doctor gentleman lifted everything but her skirt, but his work turned out to be something of a fire sale—you know, damaged merchandise. He'd operated on her nose to remove a small bump that had actually given character to her face, gave her a partial face lift round the forehead and eyes, and even did work on her breasts. However, he neglected to insert silicone implants and when Britt examined herself after the surgery, she discovered that her nipples were higher but her breasts were still slightly drooping.

When I visited her in the hospital, she was in considerable physical distress and her face looked as though she'd walked into a brick wall. Later on, sad to say, it was obvious that the operation had been pretty much a waste of time and money. Maybe she looked a bit younger but her little nervous tic had worsened, and I think she simply should have left well enough alone.

Not too long after the operation she left the country to try her luck in Japan, but she found Japanese men very un-screwable and the Orient very, very inscrutable for the kind of business she had in mind. In short, the big hop across the Pacific proved an even bigger fiasco.

Britt moved back to New York about the same time I was leaving the country. It's strange, but of all the girls I've known she is one of the few who still keeps in touch with me on a regular basis. She called me before I left to say she was back in business in Manhattan, still maintaining that expensive duplex and a new (probably equally expensive) boyfriend.

We fell out of touch while I was in Europe, but when I returned to Canada late last summer, I gave her a call and she sounded very chipper over the phone. But when I asked her how business was, I got her standard answer: "Bad, bad, bad." Still, someone was paying for that expensive pad of hers, and I'm sure it's not her boyfriend of the moment. I think Britt just believes it's wise politics to cry poverty in order not to inspire hostility in her girls or a competitive streak in other madams. In fact I think Britt has all the goods to become a rising star in the New York galaxy if she ever sets her mind to it.

So when I try to analyze why Britt and I have become fairly good friends, I suspect it is because I have recognized something of myself in her. I admire her ambition and her tenacity in trying to achieve her goals. She is also a very bright person, and the times we went out on dinner dates together were almost always merry evenings to remember. Our art was to *be* a hooker, not to act like one.

Happily, we were able to get together recently. When I was in the Bahamas, she took a short vacation and came to visit me there on her way to Europe. I hardly recognized her. Her hair was short and straight, and completely gone was the glamorous blonde. Now she was a redhead—even her pussy hair was reddish.

She also had new breasts, which she proudly revealed.

The byproduct of a three-thousand-dollar breast job all the way from Brazil. This time she'd had her breasts completely lifted, and despite the scars, then still very red, that are supposed to take half a year to clear up, she was very pleased with her remodeled chest. Now her breasts really look super under any type of dress.

Oh, yes, Britt is no longer a madam—at least for now. She was going to Europe to meet a rich male friend in Paris, and beyond, that, she said, who knows? Life is short, but the world is big. . . .

Wouldn't she eventually go back to New York? I asked. Yes, probably, Britt said, but not as a madam, since the "Latin Quarter"—as she calls our mutual South American friends—represents too much competition, all living in various apartments in one building.

So I don't know where I'll bump into Britt again. But I know I will see her again, because that's the kind of relationship we have.

ON THE MIAMI TRAIL . . .

Toward the end of my sessions with the district attorney's office I felt I had to take a break or else suffer a nervous breakdown. Three months of constant interrogation had really frayed my nerves.

I spoke to Assistant District Attorney Conboy about this and he agreed it would be a good idea for me to get away for a while. In fact he actually seemed sympathetic to my plight. Some sun would do me a world of good, he said, adding that he envied me my little vacation. The only condition he placed on my going away was to let him know where I could be reached in case of an emergency.

Upon my return, Mr. Conboy said, he'd still want to see me but not on the intensive basis of the past three months. There were other people being called in to testify and so there'd be less need of me. So Larry arranged for a week's stay at the Eden Roc Hotel in Miami and, apart from the district attorney's office, no one knew where we were going.

What a relief to get away from the grind of the question sessions and chilly New York! Actually the beach itself was a bit cold for swimming, because of the wind, so Larry and I decided to stick to the pool area. But almost

immediately the bright Florida sun and pleasant weather
made me cheer up.

After a couple of quiet days of sticking close to the hotel,
we decided we were ready for some social activity, so I
called up an old friend, Vernon, who lives in Dinner Keys.
Vernon was a friend from my bachelor gal days, and I
would see him whenever I went to Florida. Since Vernon
hates New York, these were the only times I'd seen him
in recent years. But, being good friends, we kept in touch
via telephone calls and post cards.

In his early fifties, Vernon has made it in the business
world, but basically he's still the hillbilly from Tennessee
he once was. He can be difficult at times, but if he likes
you his heart of gold takes over and he's great fun to be
with. Physically he reminds me of a chubby little teddy
bear, though I'm sure he doesn't think of himself in those
terms.

When he got my call, Vernon was extremely happy to
hear from me. I hadn't told him we were coming south,
so it was really a surprise. Vernon had heard me speak
about Larry, but had never met him, so he immediately
invited us to join him for a cruise on a luxurious yacht
belonging to one of his friends. Vernon has his own boat,
but it was modest compared to this 56-foot yacht, he said.
His friend, whose name was Roger, owned a house on
Palm Island that had once belonged to Al Capone, and
we'd see that, too. It sounded great.

The house, as it turned out, was old and delapidated,
although workmen were busy restoring it. Roger's young
son gave us a guided tour through the place, pointing
out the work being done and describing how the house
would look when all the work on it and the gardens was
complete. One day, he said, the place would be turned into
a museum. This surprised me somewhat—why spend all
that money to fix up the place and then not live in it?—
but the boy explained that they were living mainly on
board the yacht anyway, at least until the work was
completed. And when I saw the yacht docked at Roger's
marina, I could understand why—it really was beautiful
to behold.

It seems we were to be the newest additions to a little

yachting party. There was Roger and his wife, Jacky. They were an attractive couple, Roger in his early forties and his blonde wife a few years younger. There was another couple, Pim and Pat, around the same ages. Pim was a pilot, Vernon told me. His wife, who intrigued me more, looked very good for her age, possessing a nice, trim figure. And rounding out the crowd was Vernon and his twenty-three-year-old girlfriend Candy, who was really quite a beauty.

Candy was from Cuba—her mother, who was Cuban, and her German father had fled the island when Castro took over—and had the same fierce innate pride that I have found in other Cuban friends. She had large big brown eyes and curly pitch-black hair, which she wore pinned up, and she made a very slim and elegant appearance. Candy did some part-time hooking in Miami, I learned soon enough, but a lot of time she was living with Vernon, with pretty much the same relationship that I had with Larry on weekends.

There was plenty of food and liquor on board and it was, as I'd expected, a very relaxed atmosphere. So much so, in fact, that what I hadn't expected—some sexual by-play—began to take place after we'd been out for a while. Maybe it was just the sun warming everyone up . . .

Pat, the pilot's wife, obviously had eyes for Roger, our host and captain. Jacky, Roger's wife, was sniffing after Pim, who in turn seemed rather attracted to me—especially after I took off my bikini top while sunbathing. Vernon, for his part, was a true democrat—he was after everything female on board, but in particular Jacky. Larry and I weren't flirting with anyone, nor was Candy, who got along fine with me but not so well with the two older women.

Roger anchored the yacht and while the men went to the stern to do some fishing, Candy and I went swimming. Then it was time for lunch.

So far there hadn't been any real swinging or swapping, although there had been some huggy-kissy games up on the bridge. Jacky kept after Pim, who wasn't having any, and then she made a small pass at Larry, who gracefully indicated he was already with a friend for the afternoon. The sun was making me feel all warm and buttery, but so long as Larry didn't show any interest in the other women on board, I wasn't going to do anything to make him jealous. I'd come to Florida to relax and that was just what I was going to do.

It was now after six and we were headed back. We'd probably reach Palm Island just as the sun finally set and it was a lovely ride over the shimmering waves. I'd been admiring the water and the sky when, turning my head toward the stern of the ship, I noticed Pim and Jacky in the shadows of the early evening, together in one corner. He was sitting in a deck chair, wearing nothing but a towel around his waist, and she was on her knees, before him, her head bobbing up and down under the towel. She was obviously giving him a spectacular blow job, but he didn't seem to be reacting. He just sat back passively, not even touching her body or shoulders or hair. She was just a warm mouth to him, evidently.

(By the way, ladies, doctors say that sperm is good for your skin because it contains lots of proteins. I mean to swallow, not rub in!)

Larry and I watched this amusing little scene for a few moments and then decided we'd join the folks up on the bridge. Roger was up there steering the yacht, unaware of what magnificent head work his wife was displaying on the deck below. Or perhaps he didn't care, since Pat was standing behind him, her body against his back, caressing his shoulder blades with her mouth and fingertips. Another intimate little scene. . . .

Well, perhaps we should try the bow of the ship for company. There, Vernon, having given up on his other shipmates, was lying on the deck, his head on Candy's lap. We joined them, and everything was peaceful and harmonious as we watched the Miami coastline and the lights from land dancing across the waves at us.

Every so often we'd hear some sound from a part of the boat—a sigh or, once, a groan which was definitely sexually inspired—and in a subtle way this made for a very erotic atmosphere. I didn't know about the others, but I was finding the contrast between the beauty of the water and the changing light and the sounds of hanky-panky going on elsewhere on the ship to be something of an aphrodisiac.

"Take it, easy, Xaviera," I told myself. "Surely you can survive one yacht ride without getting horny."

Larry was stretched out, his arms behind his head, watching the sky and seemingly very content. I was beside him, in much the same position, and in order to be even more comfortable, I took off my bikini top again. It goes without saying that I'm not shy about such things, but Larry was between me and the others and, besides, the light was rapidly fading and we'd soon be in semi-darkness. But I didn't count on Vernon's sexual radar. It took him about ten seconds to notice I was topless for the second time that day. And another second to make a comment.

"Look at your nipples, Xaviera. Don't try to kid me—you're getting horny."

He was right about my nipples having gotten hard and rigid, however it wasn't horniness but the breeze coming off the bow of the ship that had done it. So I said, clucking, "Ah, poor Vernon . . . can't appreciate nature on a beautiful night. Take off your shirt—the breeze will make your nipples stand out, too."

"Aw, g'won, Xaviera, you're thinking that everyone else on the boat is doin' it, and it's gettin' the ole blood heated up."

Before I could reply, Candy answered for me. She said, in a dignified voice, that any women's nipples would stiffen if they were bared to a cool breeze.

"Oh yeah," said Vernon, "go on 'n prove it. Expose your titties to the cooling breezes. . . !"

"Okay, dumb-dumb, I will." And with that she flipped off her own bikini bra and stood there, brazenly, offering her breasts to the evening breezes. As though we were judges at a beauty contest, the three of us—Larry, Vernon, and I—circled Candy, keeping her large soft nipples under close observation. And sure enough, out they came, stiff and pointed, like two dark pencil erasers in the middle of a pliant brown circle.

I stood beside Candy, sisters before the breezes, and the two men now circled the two of us, making comparisons, and testing—not with just their eyes but with their fingers and mouths as well—to see whose nipples were the stiffest.

"I guess I got to vote for Xaviera," said Vernon. "Those are regular bullets she has out there."

"I don't know," said Larry, now very chipper, "those are pretty good little beehives on Candy's chest."

Naturally after watching all the intrigue on the ship all day long, this nipple-twirling and nipple-nuzzling was having its effect on us, and it was Candy who really launched the best part of the evening.

"Okay, Larry," she said. "We've proved our—ahem—points. Now how about you? What would the breeze do to a man's cock? Will it make it go stiff and erect?"

We all knew what this dare was all about, but what Candy didn't know is that Larry's penis can get large and hard under conditions like this. It happens to him sometimes in a cold shower. Still, I didn't know how he'd respond to Candy's teasing. So I was a bit surprised when he did quickly slip down his swimming trunks, and Candy got *her* surprise when she found herself gazing upon a very, very erect penis. As a matter of fact, I looked at Larry's face and I more than suspected he was feeling rather proud of his giant hard-on and big balls cooling themselves in the night air.

Candy turned to me and said, almost as though she were a small girl and had just seen a toy she wanted very much, "Xaviera, I'm very sorry and I hope you don't mind, but I think it would be a terrible waste if I turned down a chance to enjoy a cock as beautiful as Larry's." I took a quick glance at Larry, just to be sure he felt the same way, because Larry is not kinky, and lots of times the prospects of a swing puts him off. But I could tell from the little look he gave me that he was saying, "Not this time, Xaviera, baby. This time I am definitely ready to participate."

So I smiled and shrugged and said, "Then let's get to it! All of us! Come on, Vernon, I get you!"

So I pulled Vernon's pants down. He was wearing beige jeans—the kind that are supposed to look sloppy but cost fifty dollars a pair—and I had to tug a bit to get them off him. But while I was tugging with one hand I was busy with little flicky scratches of my free hand all around the inside of his thighs, and when I finally threw those jeans aside, believe me, Vernon was ready, too.

And that's how our "fun at sea" finally got started, on the bow of Roger's yacht heading into Miami, with the four of us fucking away for all we were worth on two air mattresses. Candy in particular was going crazy, her legs wrapped around Larry's waist, then flailing around in the air, then twisted in some odd way which found one leg tangled in a roll of rope and the other jammed between Vernon's legs. Each time he would pull back in an up-stroke from me, Candy's leg would lift him right into the air. Then his weight was too much, her leg would collapse, and he would come crashing back into me like a piledriver. I was laughing so hard my sides hurt, but it felt also so good that I came very quickly, and so did Vernon. Along-side us, Larry and Candy weren't far behind, with Candy shouting marvelously pungent Spanish expressions of pas-sion to the skies. Larry and she had switched positions, and she was on top and having the time of her life, bounc-ing up and down on him and, finally, driving herself down on him for one last ride down his cock and shrieking in such ecstasy that they must have heard her on shore.

If not, they at least had heard her—and us, the com-bination sound of lust and laughter—all over the yacht, and suddenly a light from the bridge was shining down on us, and voices were saying: "Hey, look at those sly ones—quiet all day and as soon as the sun goes down, they swing like crazy." (This sounded like Pim, and not a little jealous, maybe.)

"Oh, my . . . that one's well-endowed, *isn't* he?" (This from Jacky, Roger's wife.)

"Too bad we're so close to shore . . . I could use a little more satisfaction myself . . ." (Since it was another female voice, it must have belonged to Pat.)

"Good show, folks, but make ready to disembark." (Ah yes, the Skipper speaks . . . the final authority.)

In a very few minutes we did dock, and since it was late we said good-bye to everyone—I gathered from the ex-

pressions in the crowd that the swing might have become
an all-ship affair had we been able to stay—and, after
thanking Roger for a grand day, drove off with Vernon
and Candy. We'd originally planned to have dinner together but we all agreed it would be more fun to get dressed
up and go out the next evening, when we weren't so tired.
So they dropped us off at our hotel, and Larry and I
went upstairs and went right to bed. I mean we went right
to sleep. *That's* how tired we were.

The next morning I woke up before Larry did, and after
getting up and washing my face, came back to bed, prepared to wake him up as well. There was a bulge in the
sheets, and upon investigation I discovered that my friend,
who wasn't yet awake, was nonetheless sporting an enormous hard-on. Hmmm, could he be dreaming about the
wild Candy, who rode him into Miami harbor? Or who
was he dreaming about? I diddled with his erection a bit,
gently tapping it and blowing kisses on the head, but
Larry didn't awake. So I carefully pealed the sheet off him
and, without actually touching his body, leaned over and
took his dreamy cock in my mouth. I nibbled at the spot
beneath the head, the little circumcision area that is so
sensitive, and then I actually took his penis in hand and
swallowed as much of it as I could contain in my mouth.
Better than any alarm clock, this woke Larry up!

"Wha-at?" he mumbled, trying to rise, but I put my
hands on his chest and, without much resistance on his
part, pushed him back on the pillow. I realized I was still
horny from last night, and I held Larry's cock with both
hands, near the base, and did my best to gobble up the
whole thing, in long strokes, down as far as I could swallow, then up to the head, nipping and licking and kissing
and laving the entire head with my tongue, then down again
as far as I could go, then back, never taking my lips away
from the shaft of his penis. Finally I settled on making love
to the head, tonguing the small hole and licking underneath,
that sensitive area, until I felt his body tremble, ready to
come, and I really went down on him, taking the whole
large thing in my mouth again!

Minutes later, when Larry was revived, he asked, "What
was that all about?"

"There was no orange juice in the room, and I needed my vitamins."

He laughed, pulled me into his arms, and we made love for the next hour. Sex can be a great sleeping pill when you're tired but not tired enough to fall off to sleep, but I have nothing against starting off each day with a bang, either!

After showering and having breakfast, we went out on a shopping spree. That is, Larry went crazy and bought me a complete new wardrobe. I won't ever accuse my "silver fox" of being less than generous when he likes a person.

One of my new dresses was intended for that night, because we were taking Vernon and Candy out for dinner to reciprocate for the nice time we'd had the day before. Candy looked stunning that night and I must say we turned a few heads as we went through the hotel lobby toward the dining room. The place was full of conventioneers, and they really don't mind goggling. Then, to our surprise, we suddenly had the hotel photographer in our midst asking if we'd like to pose for some publicity pictures. He meant publicity for the hotel, but since I had a book coming out I could use the pictures for my own publicity needs. Or just to send home to my parents, to show off my tan.

For the next ten minutes he took pictures of Candy and me, the two of us, and others with Vernon and Larry. We created something of a stir and I heard people wondering if I was a model or celebrity or what. I wonder what they would have said if I told them I was a retired madam. Or if I'd smiled and said, "Hi, there, I'm 'The Happy Hooker'!" But instead I just smiled at the onlookers and let them enjoy the scenery.

After our surprise photo session we had dinner and then Vernon took us on a tour of some of the local discotheques, and we finally headed back to the hotel around two in the morning. It had been a fine evening and we'd really enjoyed Vernon and Candy's company.

The next morning, while I was sunning myself by the pool, I was paged to come to the telephone. It was Vernon, calling to thank us for the dinner. Then he told me that something "strange" had happened to him on the way home. He hadn't been driving too fast, he said, but two state troopers had ordered his car to pull over to the side of the road. They asked to see his license and in general acted as though he must be driving a stolen car. Vernon's hillbilly streak came out and he wanted to punch them both out, but Candy calmed him down. He had to answer questions for almost half an hour, he said, and he was allowed to get back into his car and drive home only after giving them his name, address, and all his phone numbers, including the number of the phone on his boat. They also took down his license number. Nothing like this had ever happened to him before, Vernon said, but I reassured him by saying that that kind of thing can happen anywhere and they were probably just making a spot check in the hope of turning up stolen cars.

Larry and I spent a quiet day but when he checked with his office in late afternoon, he learned he was needed back in New York on some urgent business matter. Larry felt bad about it, but he really had to cut his vacation short. But he insisted that I stay in Miami since I was so enjoying my time away from New York.

I had been a good girl all this time and now that Larry had to go, I thought I'd stir up some excitement. I was a mite weary of "people-watching" at the pool. So many of the guests were rather ancient—about five years younger than God—and some of the womenfolk had more make-up on them than they had skin. They tried hard, but I suspect Avis is more successful . . .

I thought of calling Vernon, but then I remembered I had another old pal in Miami, a great guy called—would you believe it!—Larry. He was a big husky stud whom I'd met in Puerto Rico. We'd dug each other instantly and had a marvelous time in bed, and when we returned to New York we'd kept in touch.

Larry owned some discount record stores down in Greenwich Village and did a dynamite business because of his bargain prices. Sometimes Larry would steer some of his friends in the entertainment field over to my little house of entertainment and these were always fun nights—his buddies were mostly young, good-looking, and big spenders. No hassling with prices, all the money up-front, and generous to the girls—what more could a hard-working madam hope for. . . ? Well, it didn't hurt that they brought their own liquor along and would welcome newcomers with a drink and a funny story.

As for Larry and myself, we had an arrangement which pleased us both. I didn't charge him for sleeping with me, and I wouldn't touch any of his friends if he didn't touch any of my girls. It worked out fine. Larry really became a good friend—a kind of diamond in the rough—although he sometimes was moody because he was worried about his business and the people who were after him. If nothing else, I knew our Larry had been a bad boy somewhere along the line.

As indeed he had. As I got to know him better, Larry confided more and more in me, and he had quite a past. As a kid he'd gotten in with a gang of street toughs whose speciality was stealing coins from telephone booths. When the police were close to catching them, they moved on to another state and another telephone company. Then Larry moved on to forging checks, hot credit cards, and other youthful games. I know this sounds sordid, but Larry would tell these stories of his youthful enterprise with enormous gusto, one hand going through his thick black wavy hair, and what made them such great stories was that Larry could look back at himself and laugh at what he did— which made it funny for everyone else as well. He could even kid about his arrests.

Finally Larry went "straight" and got into the retail record business. Well, not exactly "straight"—because the honest way somehow was not Larry's way, and one reason he could sell records at lower prices than his competitors was that he hadn't paid anything for some of them. Larry, as I've said, is a big rugged man so he didn't cause any suspicion when he walked into a record store wearing pants that were rather loose, held up by extra-strong suspenders. In any case he always had a raincoat on, and his routine would be to lift about twenty records out of the rack, stretch his suspenders apart, and drop the records down the front of his baggy pants. He also wore specially designed undershorts to help keep the records in place and protect the family jewels. If things were going smoothly, he'd move to another rack and add some more records to the load in his pants. Then he'd either button his raincoat or hold it closer and nonchalantly stroll out of the store. When he was "full," Larry said, he knew how a pregnant woman feels.

One day his record business career almost came to a hasty end when a store detective and a store manager both realized what he was doing. Larry tried to run for the door but the records were threatening to emasculate him so he pulled all of them out of his trousers—he claims this time he had about forty albums in his private "wearhouse"!—and threw them all over the place. This enabled him to run the hell out of the store and into the car he had waiting outside. A pal of his was the driver, and the motor had been kept running in anticipation of just such an event. Also the car had phoney license plates from another state, so even if the detective took down the license number it couldn't be traced to Larry.

Another way Larry had of offering discount records was to dub existing records and tapes, and this got him into trouble, he said, with the FBI. When he told me this, I decided I'd better cool our relationship. We did go out once or twice more, but Larry was suspicious of everything and everybody these days and not such great fun to be with. When we went to a restaurant or bar he'd insist on facing the entrance so he could check everyone coming into the place.

Then Larry seemed to disappear off the face of the earth and I didn't hear anything about him for some time. Eventually I heard that Larry had been arrested and his warehouse of bootleg and stolen records was under federal lock and key. Larry had served some time in jail but now was out on bail. He'd moved to Miami, where a friend had started a record store. But Larry had to go back to Manhattan periodically to appear in court. He still had heavy charges facing him and his partner was also under indictment there. I heard all this second-hand, although one day a postcard arrived from Larry, saying he'd settled in Miami to start a new life and was alive and kicking.

Thinking back on all this, I was of two minds whether

to call Larry. On the one hand, it might not be smart to be seen with him if he was still in trouble. On the other hand, he may really have gone straight this time and I really would like to see him. Some dinner, and, who knows, maybe a little sex afterward . . . mmmm, I couldn't think of a better dessert. Our sexual relationship had always been fantastic. Ummm, I remembered his strong hands and sensuous mouth . . . ummm, I was going to call him.

To my surprise he was listed in the Miami directory and I didn't have to call Information. Larry was pleased to hear my voice and I told him I was surprised it'd been so easy to find him. "I have nobody to hide from," he said, "and if someone wants me badly enough, they can easily find me, so why make things complicated. . . ?" He did add, however, that his office number wasn't listed, although he didn't explain this.

We made a date for eight that night and I was to meet him in front of the hotel. I wore a long white evening gown, cut very low in front, and while waiting for Larry to come I collected some admiring glances from the men passing by, particularly the older gents. The usual routine would be for the old man to check me out and his wife to check him out by pulling him away. I didn't mind—it doesn't cost anything to look.

Larry pulled up and I got into his car and gave him a kiss hello. He looked well—he had a great tan—but there wasn't even a trace of a smile on his face. He suggested we go out to his new apartment for a drink before going to dinner, which would be about a twenty-minute ride, and almost from the start he seemed tense and nervous. Larry kept looking in his rear-view mirror and at first I attributed this to the heavy traffic; then I realized that something must be bothering him. But he didn't offer any explanations and I didn't ask for any.

Then Larry turned off the main highway and started going down narrow side roads and I wanted to know what in hell was going on. I took a look for myself in his rearview mirror and saw not one, but two cars following us. Damn Larry and his strong hands and sensuous mouth— why hadn't I followed my first instincts and not called him! At least if I'd gone out with Vernon and Candy I'd be sitting in some nice restaurant instead of driving down a dark side road with a black car and a brown car tailing me and my date.

Now I *had* to know what was going on, so I asked Larry who did he think was following us and why the two cars? He said he didn't know. Well, couldn't he give them the shake by speeding up?

"No," he said, "all I need is a speeding ticket—I've got to stay clean down here . . . I don't know who the hell is following us. The whole thing is pretty strange—I've been living in Miami now for a few months, and I've stayed out of trouble with the police as well as the FBI."

I asked him if he thought it was the FBI following us.

"There's no reason for them to be following me. My case is still pending back in New York and I show up whenever they want me there . . . I'm clean as a whistle down here."

By now I had my doubts about that, but I didn't say anything. Larry went on, "I wonder who the hell those guys are! If there was only one car, I might be able to shake it off, but two . . . it's too difficult."

Meanwhile we were still driving all over the Florida landscape and it began to seem an eternity had passed since we'd left the hotel. I started to ask Larry how much further we had to go to his apartment, but before I could finish the sentence he interrupted me, saying, "Hey, look, before we get to my place I've got something I have to get rid of! And I don't want them to see where I throw it out of the car, either." He sounded pretty worried about something, which certainly didn't make me feel any better about being along on this joy(less) ride, so I decided to ask some questions in the hope of getting some honest answers for a change.

"I don't know what you're talking about," I said. "Aren't you supposedly one hundred percent clean! If they're not following you for any good reason, why should you be scared?"

Larry turned his face toward me, his face hard. "Look, Xaviera, you're the one who has been in the news constantly over the past few months, and *you* are the chick who's the black sheep—the 'wanted' person in New York now. I've read in the papers that you're still under investigation by the Knapp Commission *and* the D. A.'s office . . ."

I replied in a cold voice that I had been in fact a great help to the D. A.'s office and that I had their permission to come to Miami for a week's vacation, so why in hell would anyone bother to follow me! Then, feeling a bit spiteful because of this misadventure, I said, "Larry, I am not a known criminal and I certainly could never match your impressive list of convictions."

That set off a little argument, with Larry finally sneering at me, "C'mon, baby, don't act like a child. They *must* be after you . . . and I sure as shit don't want to be tailed by anyone, whoever the hell they might be, and particularly not by two cars at the same time."

Very uptight now, he rapidly went on: "I do have to get rid of something in the car, an address book with some very important names in it. It's in there." He was pointing to the glove compartment, and I leaned over and opened it. Inside were quite a few tape cassettes, the car's registration papers, and some loose papers, all piled together in a disorderly way. I didn't see any address book. In the rear of the compartment was a brown paper bag and I asked Larry if it were in there.

"Nah," he said, "there's some goodies in there."

"What kind of 'goodies'?"

"Aw, you know—gum and candy bars." He'd hesitated when he said this, and I thought Larry would want to look in the compartment himself, but instead he pointed to a large supermarket and parking lot coming up on the right, and said, "Look, Xaviera, I can't shake those bastards loose and I don't want to be followed for the rest of the night. I'm going to make a sudden turn into there—don't be frightened, but it's going to be an abrupt turn—and you get out and get into that phone booth and pretend to call someone. That may bother them. They'll think you're calling the police or someone for help. Meanwhile, I'll go in the supermarket and buy a couple of Cokes or something. Then we'll just take it easy and see what gives . . ."

He did as he said and pulled into the parking lot full speed, so fast that the brakes shrieked. I "nonchalantly" got out of the car and with shaking knees strolled over to

the phone booth and pretended to be making a call. I
wished I had somebody to really call! Larry went inside
and picked up two Cokes. This all took no more than five
minutes. When I saw him return I left the telephone booth,
and as we were ready to get back into his car, from out
of nowhere a police car zoomed up right next to our car.
There were state troopers, two of them, and built like
orangutans.

I'm sure Larry hadn't expected this to happen. The
troopers came up to him, their flashlight on his face, and
asked what he was doing there. It seemed a rather stupid
question, and he treated it that way. "I'm about to have
a Coke with my girl," he said.

Their response was to make a few nasty remarks I won't
repeat here because they were so crass and stupid. Which
got Larry good and angry. "What's wrong with that, huh?
What the hell do you guys want from us? Did I exceed
the speed limit—the hell I did!"

Larry was angry, all right, but I suspected he was really
quite under control because it wouldn't pay for him to
blow his stack at these two guys. He looked around to see
what had happened to our two faithful followers, but
neither car was anywhere to be seen.

Now the two troopers were yelling at Larry because he
had not produced his driver's license for their inspection,
and he was telling them to "take it easy . . . I'm not hard
of hearing." He took an agonizingly long time in getting
his license out of his wallet and I knew he was doing it
deliberately. When he finally handed it over, the two
troopers, reading by flashlight, seemed to be memorizing
Larry's driver's license instead of checking it out, and
finally Larry asked them if it was in order or not.

One of the two ugly square-heads said, "Yeh, I guess
so, but what about your car? Is that registered in your
name as well?"

"No," Larry said.

Boy, they were sure they really had him! "Hey," said
one, "how come it's not registered in your name if it's your
car?"

"The car is registered in my company's name," Larry explained, as though talking to two children. "That's a fairly

common practice these days, when you mostly use a car for business purposes."

They then asked him the name of his company, its address, and finally did what most highway patrolmen would have done twenty minutes earlier—asked for the car's registration papers. Obviously these were all in order, because the two inspected them as though reading the fine print. I must say, if you'll forgive the sexual innuendo in the midst of all this law and order adventure, that they seemed to be inspecting me as much as they were inspecting Larry's license and registration papers. Most times this is flattering, but not with these two apes.

Since the paperwork period was over, our two upholders of the law felt it necessary to inspect the car, but they really didn't have their hearts in it. They just poked around a bit and flashed their lights in each corner of the vehicle. But they kept coming on strong. "Hey, man," said one of them, perhaps the more stupid in a contest of illiterates, "is there something inside this car you don't want us to find out about, maybe? Some grass . . . or hash . . . or who knows what?"

Larry looked at them and answered, as haughtily as possible—and I hoped *I* was the only one to pick up the actual tremble in his voice—"No, not to my knowledge."

Apparently "bored" by the entire proceedings, he invited them to go ahead and search the car. "I assure you," he said, "that this car is not stolen and that it belongs to my company."

Larry obviously meant this as a put-off device, but it didn't take. They were going to do their job, no matter how many wasted hours it would take.

One of the troopers checked out the front seat again with his flashlight and finally remembered to include the glove compartment in his inspection. There were lots of tape cassettes jammed in there, and the trooper grabbed several and produced them for all to see. "Hey, yah like music, huh; what kinda music yah like?"

Larry replied he liked "all kinds of music" and that, after all, it was his business to like music, and some more bullshit, and then he applied the coup de grace. "Hey, fellas," he enthused, "there's some real good sounds here—hell,

take them all, if you like, and bring them home to your
wives and families as presents!" With this, he went over to
the car, gently brushed aside the trooper who was still
flashing his light around inside the car, and took all the
tapes out of the glove compartment. He laid the tapes down
on the front seat, then closed the glove compartment and
loaded the tapes into the arms of the nearest trooper, the
one who'd still been inspecting the car. "Here," said Larry,
"you guys decide on how to divide these—who gets what."

The trooper with his arms full of tape cassettes said,
"Thank you, sir. My wife will certainly enjoy these, and
so will my youngest daughter."

"I hope that's all for tonight, then?" said Larry.

"Yes, sir, thank you, sir," said the other trooper, the
one more clearly resembling an orangutan. "By the way,
sir," he added, "where did you say your shop is located
again?"

Larry named a street, but the trooper didn't bother to
write it down so I guess he was just testing Larry to make
sure the tapes were his to give away. But there'd never been
a moment's hesitation in accepting them from Larry.

They drove away, giving us a final wave, and we both
breathed a sigh of relief at being rid of them. We got under
way ourselves, and within a few minutes our two friends
were back on our tails. Larry offered the theory that the
state troopers had been sent to question us by whoever was
in the two cars because they wanted to keep their identity
unknown to us.

"Why?" I asked him.

"To find out who I am and what I do and also to look
you over. I don't know 'why,' but they're after one or the
other of us. Soon enough we'll probably find out. . . ."

I didn't say anything, and he went on. "Meanwhile I still
have something I have to get rid of, and I might as well
tell you what it is. If you'd known about it, you'd probably
have wet your pants when those troopers were searching
the car.

"You know what else is in there?" he said, indicating the
glove compartment.

"No, I don't have a clue. Some kind of 'goodies'?"

"A gun, baby, an honest-to-God gun."

"A gun?" I said, slightly startled by his revelation. "How come I didn't see it?"

"It was in that paper bag. No 'goodies' in there, kiddo . . . I just invented the address book to have you poke around in there and maybe find the gun . . . you know, some kicks! And it was the gun they overlooked, thank God."

"So that's why you were so generous with your tapes," I said.

"Xaviera, do you realize how many years in jail it would have meant for both of us if those stupid cops had spotted the gun? At least two years, since I don't have a license to carry a gun . . . neither of us needs that kind of hassle."

With every passing second I was wondering why I wasn't back in my hotel room, watching television, but I didn't say anything. I wanted him to get rid of that gun before doing anything else. Larry continued talking, telling me that the Miami police are usually very smart and tough cops, and we'd been lucky these two were gullible and happy as little children to receive those tapes. "And now," he said, "I really want to get rid of that gun before we get stopped by our friends behind us."

I silently seconded the motion but didn't say anything because by now the whole evening had me pretty scared. Larry had said we were now near his house, so my anxiety wasn't helped any when he suddenly speeded up, turned into a series of dark streets, then zipped into a little alleyway. He'd lost the two cars behind us, at least for a minute or so.

As we passed a Chinese restaurant with a bushy garden in front of it, Larry grabbed the paper bag, leaned out the window with his left arm, and tossed the bag over the fence separating the bushes from the parking lot, all the while driving at a fast clip. There was no sign of our two friends.

"Are you just going to leave it there?" I asked, referring to the bag with the gun.

"Don't worry. I know the restaurant owner pretty well. That little Chinaman is a good fellow and a pal of mine, who owes me a few favors, as it happens. I'll come back when the coast is clear and pick up the gun and put it into safekeeping."

About now two sets of headlights were turning up in the car's rear-view mirror, so we knew our friends were back with us again. But they didn't interfere with us in any way and in a few moments we were finally pulling into the entranceway to Larry's apartment building. It was, he'd explained, one of the best-protected buildings in the city. You have to get by a guard who sits in a booth at a gate about two hundred feet in front of the building—it was like entering a private club, Larry said—and there were also a doorman and lots of building personnel.

Sure enough, there was a guard in his little gatehouse and he greeted us with a friendly "Good evening sir, good evening, madam" and waved us in. Larry pulled up in front of the building and a doorman hurried out from the lobby to greet us and hold the door open for us. Larry asked him to take care of the car and also whispered something to him I couldn't hear. I assumed it had to do with keeping an eye out for those two cars.

The lobby to Larry's apartment house was very posh—spacious and immaculately clean, with white marble floors and modern art on the walls—and the apartment itself was very well done. Very contemporary, very expensive, but good taste. I excused myself to freshen up, while Larry was making himself a drink and getting me my usual portion of Vitamin C. When I returned to the living room, I told Larry I thought the place was very nice indeed.

"Thanks," he said, taking a long tug on his drink. "I only moved in about a month ago. It took me a long time to find just what I need—I need safety first and foremost—and once I saw this building I liked the way it's run and the service they give their tenants."

"You sure as hell are liked—or at least respected—by those guys downstairs. They're almost obsequious to you," I said.

"You ought to know me well enough to know that they're good to me because I grease their palms better than anyone else in the building. After all, my life may depend on them some day. I have always spent money on the right people. Money buys you power and don't let anyone bullshit you any differently. Without money you're lost in this world, and particularly in the ole U.S.A. Money may not buy happiness here but it sure can provide a little comfort."

He paused for a moment to have some more of his drink, then continued, "Just to show you how sharp they are, I'll bet you anything that within the next five minutes the telephone will ring to let me know that the guys driving the two cars following us have been told to wait outside the gate. The guard in the booth won't let them come inside under any circumstances, unless he gets my permission to do so."

"You must be kidding me," I said. "You mean we can't even relax here, in your apartment?"

Larry said this might be one way of finding out who they were and which of us they wanted. (He was still insisting this might have something to do with me, which made no sense whatsoever.) If they did show up at the gate, Larry said, we should get right out of there because he didn't want to give them any opportunity to become suspicious about our relationship. I didn't really understand what he meant by this, but I didn't get a chance to ask him because just then, as he'd predicted, the phone did ring and it was the guard at the gate. Larry told me to get on the other phone and listen.

The guard told Larry that "two gentlemen had just arrived in two separate cars," flashed some kind of identification, including badges, and wanted to know who Larry was and in what apartment he lived. They also wanted to know "who the lady was who had accompanied him since early evening." The guard declined to give out any information until he had spoken to Larry. He was calling for instructions, he said.

Larry angrily snarled into the phone, "Tell 'em to fuck off, I don't want anything to do with them!" Then, a moment later, more calm, he said, "No, try and get their real names and where they're from."

The guard answered, politely as always, that once they'd flashed their badges they'd avoided providing any further identification. Larry, back in control now, apologized to the guard for having blown up at him and instructed him to tell the men that he and I had returned to his apartment for just a few minutes and then departed again. But not to give them any other information.

Then Larry, ignoring the fact the two cars were surely downstairs waiting for us, dragged me out of the apartment and into the elevator. We took it down to the basement garage, got into his car, and roared out of there. As we got outside, we spotted the two cars double-parked, lights dimmed, just outside the guard's entrance to the building, so we started the same little game of "Follow the leader" again.

But this time Larry drove straight back to my hotel, with no detours along the way. The cars followed us but didn't bother us, and within fifteen minutes we were back at the Eden Roc. We hadn't had dinner, we certainly hadn't had any sex, and what we had had was a perfectly awful evening.

Larry said he was sorry it had gone so badly but that he thought I should go straight up to my room. He would really like to come up with me—we could have some food and drinks sent up, he said—but he wanted to see if he could find out "who the bastards are who've been following us all evening."

His talking, and the strange excitement of the evening, were making me horny as well as hungry, but he seemed determined not to come into the hotel with me. "Darling," he told me, "please don't use the phones in your room except for room service, and if you have to make a personal call, do it from a phone booth, or another hotel, because I'm sure they have your phone tapped. I'm sure it's you they're after because why else would they ask my guard about the woman with me?"

I still didn't see the logic of this, but Larry just kept talking.

"The moment I have more news on this, I'll let you know, but not by phone. And I'll be up in New York in a few weeks because I have to be in court then." He moved over closer to me—we were parked under a palm tree and it was really kind of intimate, in its way—and we embraced and kissed, preparing to say goodbye.

"Now you stay loose, baby," Larry whispered into my ear, "because I really am sorry we didn't have a decent chance to be together. I really dig you all the way—you are one hell of a nice kid, and they shouldn't chase you around like some kind of animal. Next time we meet, it should be on a deserted island, so we can make love all day without being spied on and interrupted. I would love to eat you up alive. . . ."

Our close embrace and his talk had turned me on so much that I found myself taking his hand and pushing it up under my gown—I wasn't wearing panties—and virtually into my warm moist cunt. I was sure our two friends were parked somewhere near us, but it was dark in the car and, anyway, I just didn't care.

With one hand Larry was fingering me while with the other he was pulling my suntanned breasts out of the gown and caressing them. He leaned over and his mouth paid loving attention to my nipples and neck and mouth. While enjoying all his attentions I'd also had the presence of mind to zip open his fly to reveal a lovely, hard prick and I wanted so much to have it inside of me. But that would simply have been too dangerous to do in the parking lot.

We both moved around some in that front seat so I could get my mouth onto that delicious-looking cock, and while he was playing with me and fondling me I was taking as much of his cock into my mouth as I could and still breathe. Within seconds it seemed to grow inside my mouth, become longer and thicker, and his balls were large and hard. I had to smile, for a second, remembering all the record albums they'd helped to support. I had already come once and was ready for an encore, and within twenty or thirty sucking motions Larry was coming also. My dinner thus far that night was a Coke, a glass of orange juice, and Larry's sperm, and it was certainly good in its way.

When we'd both recovered from the tension of our orgasms, we sat up and straightened up our clothes, a little embarrassed, perhaps, at what wild animals we'd become in the space of a very few minutes. Perspired and thirsty, we said our good-byes and I went up to my room, cleaned up, and ordered some food from room service. It had turned out that sex with Larry wasn't dessert, after all, but an appetizer, and I was hungry as a wolf, devouring a big steak, a salad, plus two large fruit juices.

I felt pretty good as I got ready to go to bed, but that night I was to have a horrible night's sleep, full of nightmares. I kept dreaming about police and FBI men walking around the hallway, peeping underneath my door, putting hidden devices in my room and, at one point, even breaking down the door and threatening me with a revolver to "talk, talk, talk."

When I woke up, after my fitful night's sleep, I decided to take the first flight I could get on back to New York. Whatever was going on, I wanted no part of it and despite the fine weather, I'd had more than enough of Miami. I managed to share a cab out to the airport with a nice hotel guest, and on the way out there I asked the driver if we weren't being followed and he agreed we were. This time the car following us was a green Ford, and the driver was wearing a hat and dark glasses. Whether he was one of my "friends" from the night before, I had no idea. I just sat back and counted the minutes until I could get on that plane.

The fare, with tip, was six dollars and my companion and I split it down the middle.

Back in New York I was immediately in touch with my old reliable Larry to tell him what had happened, and he said he'd been followed as well, but he hadn't wanted to upset me. He wasn't sure, he said, whether the phone was being bugged, but he wouldn't be surprised if it had been. And he, too, was tailed right out to the airport. His driver had noticed it, Larry said, but they had no way of figuring out who it might be.

I took it easy the rest of the day, had dinner with Larry, and got a good night's sleep. The next day I called Mr. Conboy and made an appointment to see him. I went down to his office later in the day and told him I was very upset by what had happened and did he know anything about it?

He said it was all news to him. Maybe some unknown enemies were after me? Or was it all my "vivid imagination"—or maybe I was "just plain scared"? None of this was the least bit amusing to me, but he honestly didn't seem to know anything about Miami.

About a week later, this time down there at his request, I was approached by his two "lilliput" associates. They pulled chairs over to mine, sat down, and began their nasty little act.

"Hey, X, tell us honestly, why did you have so many pictures taken of yourself while in Miami?" said one of the gnomes sarcastically. "You really must love yourself, don't you?"

"How the heck do you guys know what I did in Miami? What business is that of yours?"

"Oh, don't worry, we know every move you made," said the other one with a big grin. "We also know every penny you and Larry spent in the hotel drug store, for instance, and in the hotel's boutique and every item you bought the following day with Larry in the shopping center . . . Hey, that fellow must have a lot of bread! What he spent in those three days on you, we don't even spend in four months on our wives. You must be lucky or was that *your* own sinfully earned money, maybe?"

I didn't say anything. I just glowered at them.

"C'mon, you must have been paying that guy some bread while you were running a brothel," said the first one. "Who's kidding who?"

Now I really got pissed at them, blasting out: "What do you want from me! Larry is not my pimp and never has been. I have never paid him a penny from the monies I made. It has always been he who has paid our expenses, the air trips, the hotel expenses, the clothes he has bought for me." I didn't know if they were believing me, and what's more, I didn't care. I just wanted to hit back for a change. "You think I am crazy enough to pay him? Yes, if he were maybe eighteen years old, I might have considered it. That I've done at times when a kid has been very low on bread, but not with a man who has a good position in the business world. . . !"

I paused in my tirade and then thought, "What the hell, why let them get on my nerves." So I changed tact with them.

"By the way," I said, "what else do you guys know? Tell me something more original for a change."

Dwarf Number One continued showing off his knowledge: "How about the boat ride you had and your visit to Al Capone's old house, interesting, eh, the dead Mafia boss's stomping grounds? Hey, furthermore, we *are* sorry about those two naughty fellows giving you and your friend in the record business such a hard time. That cat was bad news anyway, has too many convictions on his list. We know his face pretty well in court. Rough guy. Yeah, you need someone like Larry, your own 'silver fox,' who has never been in trouble, a clean guy. What are you futzing around with crooks for?"

"The only fellow who seemed like fun company," the other went on, "was that guy, Vernon, or whatever his name was. Seemed he really liked you very much. . . ."

Well, I gathered they hadn't been watching us on the yacht, via a U-2 plane, but the amount of information they did have was absolutely astounding and they weren't through yet with showing off their little espionage system.

"And last but not least, why couldn't you get your own cab to the airport? Why did you have to share with a guy? Trying to make a quick fifty bucks in the cab, maybe? You paid the cabdriver three bucks—and he paid the other half. You see, baby, we are very well informed."

By now I was absolutely flabbergasted but also very upset that the district attorney's office had arranged all this harassment. It was clear to me that they didn't trust me one bit and had gone to extraordinary lengths to follow my movements.

This was later confirmed by Vernon. Both the FBI and the State Crime Committee had been dogging my footsteps. Vernon had been interrogated by two FBI agents shortly after I left Miami. They came to visit him on his boat and asked him all kinds of ridiculous questions. Was I involved in any drug scene? Did I have any intentions of leaving the country permanently via Miami? And, most hilarious of all, did I have any plans to start something like a floating brothel, maybe on Vernon's boat?

Hmmm, this was not such a bad idea! I could see myself and my girls and customers floating and fucking in international waters. No police to bother us. I might consider it next time I get to Miami!

Larry from Miami, when he came to New York, told me he'd been questioned as to how well and how long he had known me, and whether he had ever given me any money, or supplied me with customers. Larry told them that we were now just good friends, that he'd never been an actual customer of mine—which was true—and that he'd never had any kind of money dealings with me, which was also true.

They hadn't pursued the customer's business, he said, for which both of us were grateful. At this point it couldn't have hurt me, but it wouldn't have done his situation any good to have supplied me with customers, even as a favor.

Needless to say, all this was very dismaying. True, in society's eyes I had been guilty of the crime of operating an illegal business, but prostitution as I was involved in it was not only a victimless crime but a "complaint-less crime." No one had done any harm, and no one was hurt. I'd been cooperating with the district attorney's office for months now, and my reward was a lot of double-dealing. It seems I had to be treated like some heavy criminal, an Al Capone himself, and this was just absurd. The money spent on shadowing me all over Florida could have been far better spent on trying to deal with gangsters and robbers and sky-jackers and murderers. The crime rates keep rising, the FBI tells us, so what is it they're doing besides following Xaviera around Miami!

The Girls in My Life

IRENE: Our Top Banana

Irene is a short girl, just under five feet tall, with well-developed breastworks and a firm, but certainly prominent, backside. She is from South America—half-Indian and half-Spanish—and has sharp, marvelously chiseled Indian features. Her complexion is dark olive, which makes her look as though she has a permanent suntan. Her dark looks are also accented by short, raven-black hair.

Irene came to New York from Ecuador, where her father owns a horse ranch. Believe me, when he bred Irene, he bred a wild filly—she lent something wonderful to the atmosphere of my house, having the kind of great disposition that turns on everyone, male or female. It wasn't only her vibrant personality but also her deep, almost mannish, voice, colored always by a heavy Spanish accent. Irene could be terribly funny even when she wasn't trying to be—which wasn't too often, folks—but whenever we laughed, it was with her, not at her, and she would laugh, too.

In addition to her outrageous sense of humor, Irene was a great asset to me because she simply adored fucking. She had a deep, abiding passion for cock. She also had a very square fiancé, a South American lawyer, whom she intended to marry and go to bed with some day. (They'd only been going together for a year, so there was no rush!)

In his eyes, she was the precious little virgin flower—Spanish tradition is very "heavy" on virginity—he was one day going to deflower. In my eyes, Irene was this great little chick who came over to the house every time she felt in need of a hot pants holiday!

Like Corrine—whom you'll meet a bit later on—she coveted men who were more than amply endowed. But Karen is a large, voluptuous dish, and Irene, despite having more than a little something to hold onto, is a little peanut. Obviously it's not only what's up front that counts—it's also what's inside.

Irene held a day job in Brooklyn as an accountant for a Spanish-language employment agency, and if she didn't have a date with her *amor,* she'd go home to Queens and change into her other "working clothes." I can't say I always agreed with her choice of "night-work outfits," since she leaned toward micro-mini skirts which accentuated her short stature and made her look squat because of her sizable ass and boobs. I preferred her to dress in decollete dresses with long skirts because this is how she looked sexiest, but it took a while to educate her to this point of view.

Before Irene worked for me, she'd never earned more than $150 a week. Now she had extra spending money and how she loved to spend it! She'd go to every big department store sale and buy three copies of the same dress in different colors. When it came to clothing, Irene was like a kid in a candy store.

She was also that way when it came to sex—continually horny, and even a little over-demanding at times. But even when she was being sexually "greedy," Irene couldn't help being funny.

Just one example should suffice to give you the idea.

One night—I remember it was kind of quiet, being early in the week—Irene was sitting in my black swivel chair, turning herself around and around out of boredom. There were several other girls sitting around in my living room. Come to think of it, it was almost surely a Monday night because that was traditionally the night when customers were either too tired or too broke to pay for play. Tom Jones was singing on the radio, and that was about the only cheerful sound in the house. In fact, instead of complaining about the money they weren't making, the girls were complaining about the money they'd spent over the weekend.

Suddenly there was Irene's voice, a blithe spirit in our midst! She was talking to herself to beat the band. It was all in Spanish and too rapid to follow. So we asked her to translate. She was still sitting in the swivel chair but was hidden from us because the high-backed chair was facing a corner of the room, and from behind the chair came her translation: "Emilio is hungry, *pobrecito* Emilio, you do not have anything to eat for the last three days."

What the hell was she talking about! There was not a single man, much less an "Emilio," in the room.

Irene spun around in her chair, her legs spread apart, her colorful *Emilio* Pucci underwear showing. "Emilio," she explained, laughing all the while, "he no have too much money for an expensive meal, so he is eating [here she indicated her crotch] at the 'Y'!"

Then, switching stories, she said, "Actually Emilio [now her crotch itself was being dubbed 'Emilio'] he not a hungry little animal. He in fact a vegetarian. He be happy with just one *beeg* banana!"

Her jokes broke the gloom, and then two of the phones rang, and then all of them, and as if by command, the night became a complete ball. (Yes, yes, *yes,* pun intended!) Within half an hour the place was pleasantly filled with laughter and customers, and Irene was happily stuffing her furry little animal with a "beeg banana."

Irene was easy to please. And she was very, very pleasing.

III. QUIETUDE BEFORE THE BIG EGO TRIP

PRESS PARTY

At last! My book was now officially published and I was throwing an enormous party to celebrate the event.

Invited were Dell editors, publicity people, sales executives, a small army of my friends, and what seemed like the entire press corps of New York City and environs.

By the time the first twenty-five or so people had arrived, there was only one "important luminary" missing—me, the guest of honor. I was still in my bedroom struggling with some lousy new false eyelashes I'd purchased for the occasion. I usually wear very little make-up but I knew there'd be TV cameras at the party, and press photographers, and I wanted to look good for the press. But the layers of different color pancake make-up and eyeshadow weren't getting along together, so I had to do the whole job all over again. And the harder I worked on it, the later I was becoming for my own party. Haste makes waste, the old saying goes, but in this instance haste was making a mess!

Every so often Larry would knock gently on the door to tell me more people had arrived, and who they were, and when was I joining the crowd?! I'd reply, "Soon, soon, make them drinks, will you, I'll be right out," and then go back to putting this new face of mine on right. Now the main battle was with the new eyelashes, which kept falling down.

Finally I made my belated appearance and it was already wall-to-wall people. We'd removed chairs to make more room—my next-door neighbor, Sascha, had been kind enough to take my big green leather recliner into her apartment and over a two-day span her cat fell in love with it and more or less destroyed it—and pushed tables against the walls, but already it didn't look as though many more people could comfortably fit into the apartment.

A large Dell contingent arrived and one of the editors said, "My God, Xaviera, you've got the wildest assortment of press people I've ever seen here! How did you do it?"

As it happened, I'd hired myself an expensive publicist, but that couldn't explain this huge gathering at 6:30 P.M. Apparently this was the "in" party in New York this evening.

Some people I knew showed up, had a drink, paid their respects to me, and left because the crush was too much for them. I can't really say I blamed them. With the press alone it would have been a big crowd, since there were people from the Sunday New York *Times*, and *Women's Wear Daily* and *New York* magazine and *Esquire* and the foreign press and, of course, all the local TV and radio stations. I made my way around the room being introduced to people whose names I'd only known as bylines in newspapers and magazines or else TV "names," and everyone seemed quite optimistic about the book's chances to become a big best-seller. It had already made the New York *Post's* best-seller list four days before the official publication date, but little did I dream that it'd be Number One exactly one week later!

I was introduced to Gay Talese, the best-selling author, and near him was my old pal, Robert Eaton, whose book based on Howard Hughes' life story was just out. That night Bob left me an autographed copy of his new book, but I never got to read it because someone swiped it during the party.

I'm sorry to say there was quite a lot of this sort of thing during the course of the evening. Huntington Hartford showed up, as usual with four tall gorgeous young blondes on his arm, and this was fine with me because he'd been invited. But in his entourage and following in his wake were the parasites of the jet set society—the party-crashers and leeches who would rather show up at a party where they know there's going to be plenty of free food and drinks than take a girl out for a decent dinner.

I wasn't going to let these party-crashers spoil my evening—truth to tell, it wasn't the first party of mine at which they'd arrived uninvited, and it always seemed more energy than it was worth to ask them to leave. Tonight, I hoped, they'd find the crowd too large for their liking and find another "in" party to innundate.

I was talking to Robin Moore, my co-author, and his date when I noticed some of these people were not only *not* leaving the party, they weren't leaving the bar, and it annoyed me that they were getting lavishly drunk at my expense. They'd also, I learned from Larry, gone through the food as though they'd just gotten off the boat after ten days in steerage class.

All this could have been tolerated, but besides being supergenerous to themselves with my food and liquor, now they were ripping off my book. Dell had installed two complete book racks of *Happy Hookers* in the apartment to display the book and, later on, to ensure that each press representative received a copy of it. Half the invited guests were yet to arrive and one rack was already close to being empty. These crashers were stuffing copies of my book into any pocket which would hold a copy, and their girlfriends were filling up their handbags with copies. That did it! Where these people were concerned, I was no longer a genial host. Just for them, I would become a regular party-pooper!

I went over and asked them what they thought they were doing—opening their own bookstore? The books, I said, were intended for press people, not rip-off artists, and I'd appreciate their returning the copies they'd taken. Instead, one of the guys laughingly asked me if he could have another copy to take home to his roommate. I told him to get his ass out of my apartment as fast as possible and to take his assortment of friends along with him. If he wanted another copy of the book, he could pay $1.50 for it—since he sure hadn't spent any money on anything else this evening.

I don't know if it was my anger which made them leave or the possibility that some of my male friends at the party might have them thrown out the door, but at last they left.

I felt better immediately—tossing those people out that evening somehow made up for the other occasions I'd wanted to do it, and hadn't—and my spirits were buoyed even more when the doorbell rang and a well-known female columnist, who writes under the name of "Holly," made her entrance, accompanied by two very attractive young men, one of whom turned out to be her younger brother. Carey, henceforth this young man, who had the reddest hair and the bluest of eyes, also had as much of my attention as I could spare for most of the evening—for upon first sighting this handsome young man I'd chosen him to be my next victim!

However, first things first. I wanted first to get friendly with his sister, the columnist. The few times "Holly" had mentioned me previous to this, they'd been snide, uncomplimentary little items. However this evening, when the party thinned out somewhat—by nine the place was no longer roaring although there were still loads of people, and since liquor was in strong supply and I'd had more food sent up, the party really was at its most pleasant—we got to have a good talk and I was most flattered when she said she'd read the book and liked it, but that meeting me had introduced her to a more intelligent and sensitive person than she'd found portrayed in my book. I was hardly so jaded a celebrity at this point that this kind of flattery didn't turn my head at first, but the real evidence of her new opinion of me appeared the next day with a nice big item about me, plus a picture, in her column.

The party was now getting smaller and more intimate and I got a chance to spend some time with Carey. I know it wasn't the liquor—since I don't drink—so maybe it was the headiness of the evening. In any case, I found him so cute! He was so youthful-looking with his long red hair almost covering his eyes. His hands in particular were really very beautiful, long and slim and, to use a cliché, the hands of an artist. Quite unlike his sister, he had a cultured English accent, and when I finally got a chance to ask him what he did, he said he was a fledgling actor but that he also contributed items to his sister's column. Yum, yum, if I didn't devour this young man tonight, I'd surely do it tomorrow night. But tonight . . . who'd it be? I knew Larry had to leave before midnight, and I knew the room was full of attractive men.

Amongst the crowd of media people—in fact he was one of the first television celebrities I'd met—was one of my favorite people—Jacques. And I wouldn't at all mind ending up the evening with him. But we had an understanding that we wouldn't let our wonderful little lark of some months earlier get out of our control. Which it could easily have done, at least on my part.

Since we'd met, as a result of the Knapp Commission investigations, Jacques and I had been unusually good friends. He was able to give me valuable information about my case, and of course it wasn't long before we were lovers, at least for a few brief weeks. But Jacques' marriage is too important to him to risk an involving relationship outside it, and in the tenderest of fashions we agreed to stay friends but separate as lovers.

I cherish my relationship with Jacques. He will always be my dear friend and the warm glow between us will rekindle whenever we meet—the German saying, which translates "In your eyes I can find your soul," perfectly describes the deep human electricity between us—but I had to respect his feelings because they sprang from within the same deep wellspring of emotion that made the man behave so kindly to me.

Jacques had met me at a low point in my life. I'd come to America to marry the man I loved. I lived with him and worshiped him for way over a year until he changed and got so kinky I had to be rid of him. Then I tried to make my way in America, but my emotional state translated itself into a promiscuous way of life. But it was just by accident, as readers of my first book know, that I ever received a dime for having made love to someone I liked, and from then on it was like the Greek "Wheel of Fire." I had no intention of becoming a hooker, but it seemed a way out of my financial problems—I'd come here with no money at all —and it was only ambition and my sense of adventure that landed me as New York's leading madam in so short a space of time.

But at no time had I expected, much less wanted, to have

an encounter with the law. All that is humiliating to me, and sometimes it's hard to say what I feel about the whole thing. How do you measure great new friends, marvelous times, wild times, funny times, financial security for the first time in your life, against the ugliness of messing with the law? Without the first, the second would never have happened. I have to be realistic and wonder whether I made a great mistake, or whether I somehow took one of those risky "Dares!" which life occasionally provides . . . and I should be capable of having savoured the good things and endured the rest of it.

In any case, Jacques, handsome, mature, and intelligent, was someone I could look up to. He made me feel like a teenaged girl when I talked to him, and there was no mood I could hide from him. Although I loved just looking at him because he is such a fine-looking man—high forehead, dark wavy hair, brown velvety eyes—his real importance to me was an authority figure, a kind of father image, if you will, which I needed when things were going so badly.

And what exactly did Jacques do to inspire such admiration and affection? Well, when I was tense or had a headache, he would massage the back of my neck and my head, and when I was depressed, he read me French poetry and sang me medieval French love songs which might never have appealed to me if someone else were doing it. When he talked about sexual love to me, he could make me blush—again feel like a teenaged girl full of joy and lust and sadness and confusion—but when we made love, I was all woman.

Still, the most important thing Jacques provided for me was a totally objective ear—sympathetic, but ruthless in his honesty. If I tried to twist the reasons for my having done something, he would force me to examine them so I'd have to admit I'd been rash or unwise or overemotional. He would comment on what I'd just told him with wit and sharp observation, and while sometimes it was painful to live with what he was telling me, I always knew he was doing it out of friendship and not to have any advantage over me.

We came through our intense—yet tender—times together better friends than ever, and I was really pleased to see him here tonight. As the party ran down and he was still there, I was in the hope he might be able to stay over, but he gently chided me for trying to suspend the rules of our little agreement for even one night.

"I'd love to," he said, a smile on his handsome face, "but you know I can't."

"Home to the wife, huh?" I said, pouting a bit.

"No, back to the office—then home to the wife," he responded, giving my face a little caress with the palm of his hand. And with that fond gesture, he said goodnight.

Oh, well, I thought to myself, there's still Carey and some good-looking lads at the party. No need to panic. But when I looked around for Carey, he, too, was about to leave.

"Must you leave so early? The party's just becoming really intimate . . ." I said to him, a considerable amount of invitation in my voice.

"Oh, gee, I have to," he said—I'm pretty sure my invitation had escaped him—"we [indicating "Holly"] have to go to another party. She *promised* . . ."

"Well, I hope we meet again," I said, ever the friendly host, but really thinking to myself, "I hope he takes the hint and makes a date. 'Tomorrow?' Why, yes, Carey, I'm free tomorrow. I'll see you then. Call me in late afternoon."

But all he said, the naive little schnook, was: "Yes, I hope so, too."

Oh, well, time to see what's still available in the Under-30-Tall-Dark (or Light)-Good-Looking-With-Bedroom-Eyes Department. Hmmmm, the party really had cleared out and there wasn't much to choose from. . . .

At ten the remaining survivors of the party drifted into my bedroom to watch the "Ten O'Clock News" on Channel 5. I had been interviewed by Channel 5 newsmen earlier in the evening—in my living room, as a matter of fact—and they'd said they hoped to get it on that evening's "Ten O'Clock News." So there we were—a few hardy souls—sitting on my big bed or curled up on the carpet waiting to see Xaviera on the telly. The program was two-thirds over before I came on, and I must admit I got a little thrill watching me at my own press party. Someone gave a small cheer, and I seconded the motion.

By midnight, the party was completely over. My wonderful maid, Bette, had done a remarkable job of cleaning up during the party itself, doing more as the party wound down, and now the place looked as good as ever. She deserved a medal, but since I didn't have any medals handy, I gave her a large tip instead. I think she appreciated that more than any medal.

There are two things I remember from the last hours of that evening. One: Among the last persons to leave was a girl who'd worked for me, and her leaving reminded me of how well those of my former girls who were there had blended into the party. How many people at that party would have been startled if I'd gathered the girls together and introduced them as a group of call girls, each and every one! They were some of the most stunning women at that party, and their presence demonstrated once again that a call girl can be as attractive and ladylike as any so-called straight date that a man likes to take to dinner and the theatre.

Two: There *had* been some bad planning at my party— how else would I have ended up going to bed alone!

The Girls in My Life

PATTY: I Pay the Price for Pleasure

Whenever I talk about lesbianism and my being fond of girls, I'm reminded of a girl-crazy night in early June of 1971. I was then still in business, but mostly on a "take-out" basis. This particular night two very attractive young bankers from Philadelphia were in town, staying at a sumptuous brownstone in the mid-Sixties. One of the two men, whom I'd known for some time, had called up asking for a couple of good-looking girls—they were paying a hundred dollars for starters for each girl, and while I knew they'd pay by check, I also knew their checks were good and their budget unlimited.

Well, instead of sending over two girls I sent over four—so they could have their pick—and I decided to go over myself to collect the check and make sure everything went well. I didn't usually do this, but I had my reasons for doing so this evening. And one of these reasons was named Patty.

Patty was one of the four girls I was sending over, a tall and truly lovely Argentine girl. A natural redhead, with freckles and a milky white skin, Patty had a knock-out body—breasts that weren't too big, but very firm and erect, and a pink pussy surrounded by wonderful red hair, trimmed very short. She and I had more or less been lovers for a while a few months earlier—she was working for me in my house

219

and I really dug her, although the only times we'd made love had been in "scenes" where men paid for a threesome. But since Patty was my favorite girl at the time, she knew she'd make more money than anyone else.

When I arrived at the townhouse, Patty was sitting in the living room waiting for one of the guys to finish up with her girlfriend Barbara. The guy and Barbara were in an adjoining bedroom, with the door wide open, and I was getting turned on watching them go at it. Patty didn't know where my other banker friend was—probably in one of the other bedrooms—and since there seemed to be some "leisure" time between sessions, I decided to do Patty myself. Couldn't let this gorgeous creature go to waste, could I?

Two months earlier, Patty had gone back to South America for a vacation and I'd really missed her, so now that she'd returned I was dying to be with her again and let her know she was my favorite girl of the hour. But I hadn't let her know just *how* much I liked her, since I didn't want her to become conceited about her charms. These things can get complicated because when the affair is over, and the flame for a particular girl has been extinguished, we still had to work together.

Still, this night I was in the mood to really do a job on Patty. I gently removed all her clothing while only taking off my dress. I wasn't wearing a bra, so all I had on was a bikini slip and panties. Patty and I settled down on the posh living room couch, as luxurious as any bed, and I spread her legs, without any resistance from her, to be sure, and put myself in between them. On my knees, my face on her pubic triangle, I began kissing and caressing my oh-so-pretty (!) Patty. Her beauty exposed, her skin was smooth like that of a virgin—a lovely, young virgin.

Patty's eyes were closed and I could see her eyelids tremble as I slowly, teasingly, reached her vagina with my tongue. Her mouth was half-way open and her lips were moist. Her nipples became hard the moment I touched her clitoris with the tip of my tongue, flicking it left to right. Patty's uniqueness was that she had this fantastically big clitoris. It was almost the size of a little penis, when aroused. I'd never in my life encountered anyone with a clit like hers. This night it was easy to find, although nicely hidden away in her foreskin. The moment I sucked it, it began to grow bigger and bigger in my mouth. It was like sucking on a man's cock. She grew hard, and her outer labia got wet immediately. She reached a climax in about five minutes. Her juices were all over my face, and I could feel her clit contract and still pulsate.

I was so happy that I had satisfied this beautiful red-headed baby. I didn't expect anything from her. I was content merely to rest my head on her belly and relax for a while; then I softly massaged her back and shoulders.

When we caught our breath and glanced into the bedroom again, we could see that Barbara was still screwing and working on the Philadelphia banker. I was still so turned on to Patty that I took off my slip and panties and climbed on top of her. Again I could feel her clitoris starting to grow bigger and bigger. It was rubbing against mine and stimulated me very much. While I did most of the work, she lay flat on her back as I squeezed her legs around mine, holding them tight while I rubbed my cunt against hers.

I interspersed our passionate caresses with soft kisses on her eyes, forehead, and mouth, especially her mouth because those beautiful wet lips were so inviting. I plunged my hungry tongue into her mouth, around and around, and I closed my eyes. Meanwhile from the bedroom, we could hear moaning and heavy breathing. The lovers were reaching their orgasms, or at least were very close to it.

That turned me on even more, and Patty, by this time, had become fantastically excited. That is why men and women should learn, when they make love together, how to stimulate each other by making certain noises. Even if they don't do it naturally in the beginning, after a while they'll discover how exciting it can be for real. You become more and more turned on to your bed-partner. There is nothing duller than a quiet bedroom. Never mind what the neighbors think. Maybe you'll set a good example and they'll learn something, or follow in your footsteps, or whatever.

Patty and I were really charged up from the noises of Barbara and her client and we almost reached a climax by just rubbing together. Wild out of my mind by now, I quickly climbed off her and started sucking her delicious pussy again, playing around with my rapid long tongue. Then

I squeezed my legs around her again and kept my cunt pushed against her leg, squeezing her hard. We climaxed simultaneously.

It had been a tremendous session and I didn't care if Patty made love with anyone else that evening. But my banker friend finally emerged from the upstairs bedroom, or wherever he'd been, and took Patty off with him. Which was fine with me—the pleasure principle will never be spoiled by a little profit being thrown in. If I hadn't already made such delicious love to Patty, I would have gone with Patty and the banker upstairs, but there was no need to be greedy. I dressed, made myself comfortable and began reading a magazine.

About half an hour later, Patty came downstairs and I was all set to give her fifty dollars in cash—her half-share of the hundred dollars the banker had paid for her. So imagine my shock when she said, without a trace of a smile, "You owe me another hundred dollars."

"Are you kidding?" No, she was dead serious.

"I don't know what you're talking about," I told her, adding a few choice swear words in Spanish.

"Xaviera, you made me come twice. You've used my body twice and you came once yourself. It's a hundred dollars for each time you made love to me; but since half of it is yours to keep, you only owe the hundred dollars . . . because we're such good friends." Now she smiled at me.

I wasn't amused. "My God, Patty, when I got here you were sitting around doing nothing, so I thought I'd excite you a little, warm you up for your John. We've been lovers before, haven't we . . . and I missed you a lot when you were gone!"

Yes, Patty admitted, we had been great lovers and great friends, but as far as she was concerned Johns always paid for sex and I'd used her just like any John. Besides, she said, she really needed the money because her trip home had cost so much.

By now I was furious with her, so I said, "Okay, you bitch, if that's the way you want it to be, I *will* take my cut and I'll give you fifty dollars instead of a hundred . . . that is, if you don't mind! I am not about to pay you a hundred-dollar rate—you get the usual fifty-dollar rate!"

So Patty went home, having gained one-hundred dollars for her evening's work—fifty dollars from the banker and fifty dollars from me—but she lost me as a friend. I hope the loss was worth fifty dollars to her.

That Patty certainly taught me a lesson. Not that I shouldn't pay anyone to have sex, but it taught me how tough-minded business partners can be. I had given this girl a lot of work because I was very fond of her. I also felt a little sorry for her because her English wasn't the best. But she blew it all. Patty could be damn sure I'd never call her to help me out any more.

It was cheap of her to do something like that to me—just as it would be cheap on my part to take advantage of my customers. Something I've learned in life is how and when to use tact and diplomacy, and the moment I feel anyone is taking advantage of me, I tell him or her to get lost. But if I like a guy, or a girl, and feel like treating him or her nicely—well, that's a different story and a lot more pleasant one to tell. And, happily, there've been lots of those.

THE CRAZY EVENING

One night I was at home, answering some letters from friends in Holland. My roommate Kathy was frying herself a grilled ham and cheese sandwich in the kitchen and she asked me if I wanted one, but I said no, I wasn't hungry. Between lines of the letters I had to keep a watchful eye out for Bagel, my one-month-old beagle, who was scampering around, terrorizing the place and shitting in every possible corner of the apartment.

The phone rang and I got up to answer it. The man on the other end identified himself as Justin, a good friend of friends of mine from Philadelphia, and he said he'd heard about the book and if I was planning on visiting his city to publicize the book, he could probably be of some help.

Well, this was a pleasant turn of events on a dull evening. "That would be very nice," I said. "How can we get together?"

He asked if I would like to meet him for dinner. "We could have a bite, and then plan your trip there," he said.

I replied that I was dressed very casually and feeling lazy this evening, so if he didn't mind my attire, why not come over for a drink? If he was hungry, we could always send out for something. "That's one of the advantages of

living in New York," I quipped. "What you want, call up
for it!"

"Maybe that's the only advantage," he kidded, and said
he'd be right over. He sounded quite nice over the phone.

It was almost an hour before the doorbell rang. Justin
was a fairly attractive man in his late 30s, blond and blue-
eyed, and unless I miss my guess, he'd had a few refueling
stops on his way over here.

Justin made himself comfortable and when I asked
him if he'd like a drink, he specified the best Scotch I had
—he must have memorized my liquor supply as he walked
into the apartment. Justin, armed with a large Johnny
Walker Black on the rocks, began the conversation by telling me—Kathy was more or less wandering through, not
really with us at any one time—that he works for one
of the networks in Philadelphia and knows all the media
people.

To test him, I asked what programs he thought I might
have a chance of being invited on, and he displayed a daz-
zling knowledge of the Philadelphia TV and radio scene,
citing which personalities were "drinking buddies" of his
and which just "professional acquaintances." Then he discussed the newspaper situation and *Philadelphia* magazine,
which, he said, is one of the best—if not the best—of the
nation's city magazines.

"Would *Philadelphia* do something on me, do you
think?" I asked.

"Well . . . I don't know . . . usually has to be a local
angle, but then if the book gets really big . . . well, we'd
have to play it by ear, I guess. But I know the editor real
well. So don't worry."

In the meantime, by getting up and going over to the
bar to help himself to large measures of my best Scotch,
Justin had more or less assumed the host role and I was
beginning to wonder if I shouldn't have accepted his dinner invitation, after all. But I was wearing an old housecoat and really didn't have the ambition to get dressed and
go out.

Justin kept pouring and talking, but now he was announcing in a loud and arrogant manner that he was the
type of man who is always able to find himself a woman

who wants to go to bed with him wherever he goes—and always "for nothing."

Kathy had sat down with us a moment or so earlier and we both looked at each other in a slight state of shock. One minute Justin had been talking about publicity for me, the next about his being God's gift to women! Oh, oh, I wondered—did Justin expect some advance gratitude for the favors he'd promised me. . . ?

Justin then started telling us about the unending stream of beautiful women who had gone to bed with him and about those who had even offered to pay for his charms— though of course he never accepted.

Ho-hum, I said to myself, the only woman who would offer this lush any money would be paying just to get rid of him.

Ah, now Sir Justin—much taken with the spirits—was telling us how he has spent quite a small fortune on the fair sex in his time and never goes anywhere empty-handed. At that point he took a look at his hand, which wasn't empty—having a glass in it, *as usual,* which was, *as usual,* quite empty—and he lumbered over to the bar again.

I took this opportunity to whisper to Kathy, "Pssst, call up Mario—he said he would call some evening this week —and ask him if he can't be sure to come up for a drink *this* evening, and as early as possible. We may need his help in saying goodnight to this clod."

Justin was back and once more regaling me with stories of what a big spender he was. Now, I had invited him over, to be sure, but if he was going to come on this way, he deserved to be put on by me.

"Justin," I said, "since this is a strictly social visit, don't you think you should have brought along a little present for the hostess?"

This was meant to be playful, but at least it served the purpose of making Justin, for the first time that night, grope to find the right words.

"Ah . . . where is the telephone directory? Give me the number of the nearest flower shop and I will call for flowers."

"Darling, don't worry about flowers; it's the gesture that counts. Anyway all the flower shops are closed after nine o'clock in New York, but . . . well, the liquor stores are certainly still open. They stay open for hours yet, and since you've polished off an entire bottle of Johnnie Walker Black, I don't mind if you insist on calling the liquor store and ordering up two bottles, one to replace the one you just finished so rapidly and one simply as a nice little present. . . ."

Juiced or not, Justin was able to change the subject quickly enough and we were now back to Philadelphia and his work. So I reminded him that I hoped to visit Philadelphia on my publicity tour. Instead of getting back on the right track, Justin now loosened his tie and placed his arm tightly around my shoulders. I could hardly move from his grip. Justin, dear Justin, was getting horny.

"Dear old boy," I said to him, half-jokingly, "are you having trouble inside your pants? Booze does not seem to affect that part of your body, maybe your mind slightly, but not your penis, which seems to be trying to tell us something."

I was kidding, but Justin wasn't. He took my hand and pushed it toward his pants and toward the bulge in the material. "Ah, Justin," I said, still joking with him, "I see that you are right-handed because left-handed men usually wear their penises on the right side. At least this is something I have observed as a connoisseur of flies and contents therein. . . ."

Justin was not exactly put off by my kidding. He was talking about Philadelphia and the visit I was going to make there. Poor Xaviera, alone in a strange city, alone and miserable in a cold, forlorn hotel—no, this mustn't happen. Justin the Good will get me on all the top TV shows, any TV show I want, just so long as I let Justin the Big Spender show me the town and then share his luxurious digs for the night. Well, I had to thank Justin the Good and Justin the Big Spender for his kind thoughts, but I kind of suspected that my publisher would not leave me stranded in Philadelphia.

The game was becoming tedious now, and I removed Justin's hand from my shoulder and turned away from him so that he had to release my other hand as well. I wasn't being coy—his tight grip was giving me a backache, and

I needed to stretch and feel loose. What I hadn't counted on, however, was that in stretching, I pulled my thin housecoat closer to me in some places and moved it away from my body in others. This was having an effect on Justin the Schmuck that I hadn't intended, so I decided I was going to play some games with him he wouldn't forget—that is, if he remembered anything of the night after dipping into a second bottle of my Scotch.

"Darling, would you mind giving me a backrub . . . come on into the bedroom and, please, I hope you won't mind when I take this off, so you can give me a thorough backrub . . . I've got some great Jean Naté body lotion, smells delicious, and really turns me on." All this delivered with a sexy voice. I sort of sashayed into the bedroom, with Justin hot on the trail.

I hadn't really planned out this scene, but Justin was on the bed before I got there, his shirt already opened all the way. "Uh uh, Justin," I told him, "tie off is enough for now. First priority is to give Xaviera a wonderful backrub . . ." With that I slipped out of my housecoat without making a production out of it and, nude except for my bikini panties, lay face down on the bed.

Justin took the oil and began massaging my spine—not too bad, actually, for an amateur. But as he moved his hands over my lower back, Justin was getting more and more horny, and when I felt only one hand on my back rubbing oil into my skin, I was pretty sure what Justin was trying to do. I sneaked a peek at him from under my folded arms and he was quietly trying to unzip his fly. He had just managed the feat when I suddenly rolled away from his hand and stepped off the bed.

Justin more or less lurched across the bed and tried to pull me down. He grabbed my right breast and began to kiss it. Just then—my God, what divine intervention!—there was a knock on the door and Kathy's voice saying, "Xaviera, Mario is here . . . I'll make him a drink."

"Wonderful, darling, tell him I'll be out in two shakes!" Then, turning to Justin, I said, "Thank you for the backrub, Justin, you have some real talent in that area."

I put my robe back on and went into the bathroom to freshen up. Justin followed me in, standing there with his fly open, a hard-on pressing against his shorts, pleading with me. "But, Xaviera, I promised you, didn't I, that I'd get you on any TV show you want . . . Just let me stay with you for an hour or so. Don't you see what's happening—I'm all hot and bothered for you, baby, you really turn me on so tremendously . . . I . . . I haven't had this feeling for so long, please let me fuck you, baby, and I guarantee I'll do anything you want me to do, provided . . . of course that I like the book myself. . . ."

Zing! That last sentence did it. I was almost feeling sorry for Justin—he was finally being a little human—and then came that zinger.

"Justin," I said in a cold voice, "frankly I don't care if you like the book or not. Lots of people already do . . . but what's more important, Justin, is your contempt for me as a person."

"Why's that, you think—because you love money and hate men, right?" he said, snarling in a semi-drunken voice.

"No, *wrong*. I've only hated men at those moments when I realized that I was doing all the giving and they the taking. At least when I was a prostitute, it was all honest and up-front. No illusions and no lies about the relationships, which made it easier for both parties and made it possible for both parties to have a lot of fun—when they both liked what they were doing. And if a girl didn't enjoy sex, then she didn't work for me. It made no sense to have her around."

"Aw, you're all the same," Justin slurred at me.

"No, Justin, baby, we're *not* all the same—we're just more honest than such Great Lovers as yourself, who will trade promises galore for some sex you just *think* you haven't paid for. You can spend a whole night wining and dining a woman you may not even especially like because you'd like to go to bed with her at the end of the evening. You pay for your sex, all right, but indirectly. With you it's a bribe. . . !"

"Hey, listen, now . . . I don't have to take this—"

"No, Justin, baby, *you* listen for a change, and see if you can follow *this* logic. If *you* don't want to pay for sex, why should *I* give it away to someone I don't care for? I didn't ask you for any favors—you offered—and if you *want* to

do me some favors, don't ask for my body in return. That's
no 'favor'—that's another bribe. Or that's simply asking me
to pay you back for the favor. . . ."

"Well, I really was gonna do what I said. I really know—"

"I'm sure you do, Justin, but that's not the point. I didn't
like your attitude from the moment you walked in. If you
can get any broad you want for free, how come you can't
get me or my roommate! You know, Justin, you're an attractive guy and if you'd been more human, more sympathetic, I'd have considered going to bed with you even if
you'd never heard of Philadelphia and its TV stations."

Justin just stood there, slowly zipping up his fly and
putting his shirt back into his pants and buttoning it. You
can bet his hard-on was gone.

"Look, Justin, I have someone out there I want to see.
Go out and introduce yourself to Mario and have another
drink."

Justin looked at me—actually did a little boy pout—
and went out. At that moment I actually felt sorry for the
schmuck—he didn't understand anything about himself.
But, no, Xaviera the old softie wasn't going to try to educate Justin. Better she should educate the handsome young
man waiting for her outside. Educate Mario.

Ahhhh me, to educate Mario would be a pleasure. He
looked like a young Vittorio Gassman. Yummm, those
dreamy black eyes and wavy black hair. To look at Mario,
you would think he must be one of Rome's leading young
rakes, but actually he was—or seemed to be—a shy young
man. He is the son of a leading Italian exporter, and his
father had sent him to New York to learn the workings of
the New York office. Mario apparently had few friends in
the city, although his English was rather good, and he was
rather uncertain of himself in New York. That's why, I told
him in the elevator—he had only lived in my building for
the past month or so—he must come by for a drink. And
his timing had been perfect—he appeared just when he
was most valuable to me, as a turn-off for Justin. But Mario
would not have to wait to go to Heaven for his reward.
If things went well this evening, he would get his reward
right here on Earth. . . .

Instead of the old housecoat, I now put on a slinky

negligee and, after a few final brush strokes to my hair, went out into the living room to greet Mario.

Mario was sitting on one end of the couch, Kathy on the other—staring morosely into her drink—with Justin facing them from a big chair. Poor Mario. The strange girl on the couch with him seemed to be in another world. The big blonde man was sitting there with a confused look on his face, not knowing whether to leave or stay. And here was Miss Hollander, greeting him in a sexy negligee. A typical Manhattan evening. . . ?

"Mario," I said warmly, "how nice of you to come to see us. May I make you another drink?" At the mention of the word "drink," Justin looked more alert but I had decided to ignore him, if possible, in the hope he'd take the hint and go away. But no, as Mario and I proceeded to the bar, Justin got up and went over to where Kathy was sitting, zombielike, and tried to start a conversation with her. Poor Kathy—she was drinking heavily those days—and Justin would do as well to try and start up a conversation with the Sphinx.

Mario and I took seats at the bar, making small talk. He was giving me his early impressions of New York and where possible, I was offering concrete advice on where to shop for clothing, what the good restaurants are, where the good values are. It is going very well, I told myself, and we are going to get along just fine. I thought I heard a warning buzzer go off in my head—"Don't count your victims, heh, heh, Lady Dracula, until you've actually bitten them on the cock"—but it was really the doorbell from downstairs. It was Suzanne, a former girl of mine, who is usually good fun, and even though I wanted to be alone with Mario, I figured that maybe Suzanne could do something about Justin.

Suzanne had gotten hooked on drugs when she was thirteen and stayed an addict until she was eighteen, when she kicked the habit. This isn't strictly accurate because she is now in a methadone program and is heavily reliant on that drug, but at least she functions—has a hearty appetite for food in addition to her sound sexual appetites—and is grateful to be off the needle. Since leaving me, she had been working in a posh midtown massage parlor and didn't seem to mind it. "It's clean work," she kidded, "and sometimes the tips are big."

Suzanne saw a kind of "Big Mamma" in me, and came to me when she was down in the dumps or else needed some advice. I wished she had picked another night, but I certainly couldn't turn her away. When she came in, I whispered to her, "See if you can get Justin over there—the one on the couch—to take you out for dinner. He has been my guest long enough."

After being introduced to Mario, Suzanne sauntered over to Kathy, who was brightening up a bit, and Justin, who looked approvingly at her through glassy eyes. Suzanne has a trim figure, almost boyish except for a very pert ass, but her face—cute as hell, with a pixie nose, large hazel eyes, and lovely long blonde hair—will make any man turn around. Justin, for example, was obviously trying to pull himself together to make an impression on her. At the same time that I was billing and cooing with Mario at the bar, I was watching Justin and Suzanne—Kathy had excused herself and had probably gone to bed—talking on the couch.

Truth to tell, Justin seemed to be doing all the talking—between refills of his favorite food, Johnny Walker's best beverage—and Suzanne was trying very hard to look interested in what he was saying. Finally, from what I could observe, she must have told him he was boring her—after her experiences, Suzanne is a no-bullshit chick—because he got up from the couch, charged over to the bar, poured himself a stiff drink, downed it in two heroic swallows, and then marched over to Mario and me. "Xaviera," he said, trying to articulate each word, "I would like a moment with you." He turned to Mario, did a funny little bow from the waist and said, "If you will excuse us, sir."

"But of course," said Mario, probably wondering what this inane charade was all about.

Justin and I went off into the hallway, where he turned to me and said, with as much dignity as he could muster, "I think perhaps I should return to my hotel now. It seems my presence here is not wanted. However, I am sorry I neglected to bring you a present. . . ."

"That's quite all right, Justin. I was only joking." My God, does the clod have some manners, after all?

"On the other hand, I would be grateful if you would permit me a little present."

He was confusing me. "What's that? I don't quite understand."

"I would like to be presented with a copy of your book," he said, stiffly.

Well, sure, that seemed a small price to pay for getting rid of him.

"I would like to take it with me back to the hotel and read it there tonight."

"All right, Justin, I'll get you a copy—I'll also autograph it, if you want."

"No, that won't be necessary," Justin said, a mean little smile coming over his face. "You see, I only want the book to jerk off with."

"What—?"

"Yes, with your little book I will be able to get my rocks off without paying for it."

"Justin, why don't you go fuck yourself—that'd be even cheaper." He had me in a cold fury, but I wasn't going to let the louse get the better of me in this exchange. It was his same old arrogance oozing through again—even sobering him up.

"Yes, my dear," he continued, the smile now set on his face, "with that dirty little book of yours, I can have a most pleasant little jerk-off, you see, and I won't have any need for any ladies this evening."

"Justin, dear heart, it's not a 'little' book—it's 311 pages for those who are sober enough to read. And I would like you to have the book, but since I have to write for money, I will have to ask you to pay for it. Only a dollar fifty to get your rocks off—that's not so bad, is it? And just think, you're saving the tax by buying the book directly from the author—isn't that nice?"

The smile left his face and we stared at each other. For a moment I thought he might hit me, and I began to hope young Mario would be as gallant as he is handsome, but Justin finally grinned at me, sheepishly at that, and said, "Touché, baby, you're a good in-fighter . . ." Then, pulling out his wallet, he handed me a ten-dollar bill and said, "Keep the change. It's been a real entertaining evening."

"No, Justin, I will give you your change. I am *tempted* to keep the change, all right—it is not really enough to replace even one of the nearly two bottles of Scotch you've knocked off tonight—but, no, this is a straight business deal and you are offering a dollar fifty—and no more—for some sex, so you deserve your change. Coming up—one dollar and fifty cents' worth of sex."

I took Justin's bill and went into the bedroom, where there was a carton of the books. Then I checked my wallet for change of Justin's ten-dollar bill, and I was happy that I had the right change. I would have hated to have short-changed dear poor Justin. Life had already short-changed him enough.

I handed the book to Justin and opened the door for him. He gave me a little wave, and then—to my surprise—a kind of shy grin played over his face. "Goodnight, Xaviera," he said, offering to shake my hand, "it wasn't what I expected, but in its own way it's been kind of fun."

I accepted his handshake, thinking to myself that the word "fun" was certainly open to many interpretations. Justin left and I told myself the evening thus far had been worth at least a dollar fifty in experience alone. But not an experience I'd especially ever care to repeat.

I returned to the living room and to my visions of ravishing my dark young Italian prince and—oh, oh, me-o, my-o, what's this?—Suzanne was now curled up on a bar-stool next to Mario giving him the complete "Gosh,-you're-a-good-looking son-of-a-bitch!" treatment she does so well (and usually even means it).

Well, I certainly hoped Mario would be able to make the distinction between a sexy, mature woman of the world and a cute young thing with only a darling ass and glori-ously large eyes and beautiful blonde hair down to her ass, almost—only these modest things to recommend her. I hoped Mario could make these distinctions, I certainly did, because otherwise I would have to whisper sweetly into Suzanne's sweet little ear that she had better find some other fun thing to do tonight than to make off with Mario, or else I would ever-so-sweetly toss her out the door on her sweet ass.

I was thinking all these ever-so-feminine thoughts when the goddamn doorbell rang again! All I wanted was a quiet evening with Mario and suddenly I'm playing station master at Grand Central Station. "Who is it?!" I hissed into the intercom. Oh, damn, and damn again, it was Jimmy, my dear, dear Jimmy—probably the only man in New York I couldn't say "Stay downstairs!" to tonight. I sighed, said, "Come on up, Jimmy," and prepared myself for an evening certainly different than the one I'd hoped for.

The greeting between Jimmy and me was more than just a handshake. It was a warm embrace. The tall blonde young man with his hair now cut shorter and the piercing blue eyes was wearing a grin from one side of his face to the other. I knew right away that he was slightly "high," to say the least, and so was his friend, Edwin, a short chubby Irish guy, who, as it turned out later, was completely coked up. Jimmy certainly looked a lot better than when I had last seen him several months before in the Village. And I recalled how he'd looked when I first met him—little more than a skeleton with blue eyes.

The Jimmy of tonight looked a lot stronger and healthier and yet there was a strange almost weird look on his face. He still seemed pretty fucked up, not only because he was stoned. I really wanted to get into his head tonight and had all but forgotten about my plans for Mario, who was now sitting in the living room talking with Jimmy's friend, Edwin, and Suzanne. Edwin had found himself a comfortable spot on the rug, laying flat on his back, grooving on the conversation but not quite with it.

I led Jimmy into my bedroom so we could talk privately, but almost right away Jimmy began pushing me down on the bed, gently, yet firmly.

"Jimmy, please stop that . . . I really would like to make it with you, but knowing you, you will be content to make it with Suzanne. She is cute and young and All-American—just the way you like 'em!" I was teasing Jimmy because he had once told me I was the exception to his usual run of Anglo Saxon blonde types who looked as though they had just stepped out of the society pages of *Harper's Bazaar.*

"Xaviera, listen to me—I'm sorry I haven't called you for so long, but you know how things are in my crazy life. I've moved back uptown—the Village scene was just too much—and I'm doing the same dumb things again. Sure, I'm in great demand by the ladies, but they're the same ladies as before and I'm running around the same way as before and . . . shiiiiit! already I'm fed up with the little Waspie girls who don't turn me on anyway!

"So here we go again—the bored-with-life routine!—and tonight I said to old Edwin inside, I said, 'I want you to meet a real honest-to-God groovy chick' . . . and by that I meant *you* baby, you hear me! I might have neglected you but sure as hell have not forgotten you—*no way!*"

The words had poured out of his mouth almost faster than he could say them, and his face was so intense it frightened me—he seemed to be near some kind of snapping point, and I didn't really know how to deal with him. "Jimmy," I said, "I want you to calm down and think about things. Now why are you so miserable?"

"Come to think of it," he grinned, his face now more relaxed, "I *do* have to cheer up one of these days . . . except I'm feeling more and more depressed."

"Are you always on drugs these days?"

"No, I do my share of boozing, too. But when I'm really high, I feel *that's* where everything's at—like that time we snorted 'coke' together, that was sensational, and afterward I felt great for a day or two. Hell, I don't know—right now this is 'reality' to me and I can dig it." He was touching ever so softly, my cheek and my breast and my thigh. "Honey," he said, "maybe this is all the 'reality' there is in the whole fucking world. . . ."

"Hey, there, Jimmy, do cheer up. *I'm* with *you,* Jimmy-Boy, and that's what counts—*carpe diem,* take the day as it comes. And maybe one day you will really meet the right woman for you and there will be meaning in that."

"Not me, darling; *not* for me. I want to float around and stay loose . . . but right now, I . . . am . . . horny. I want you so badly, really missed you. But . . . I bet you

have got that good-looking Italian kid inside waiting for
you. . . ?"

I nodded. After all, I *had* invited Mario up for drinks.

"Tell you what . . . you do your thing and I'll do mine.
Dig it. Tonight no more sad faces . . . By God, you turn
me on, babe, but you take care of that kid inside, he looks
like he needs straightening out . . . I'm not gay, but he
really is gorgeous . . . Hey, promise me that when you're
making it with him, you'll think about me. If I end up
in the other bedroom, I'll do the same."

Jimmy and I went back into the living room, where
Mario was sitting with a little boy lost look in his eyes.
I walked over to him and apologized for not having paid
much attention to him. Then I took his hand and led him
over to the bar, where we could speak more intimately.
"Look, Mario, as you may have gathered, this can be a
kind of crazy place, and tonight it's really that way. When
I asked you up for a drink, I'd hoped to have a nice, quiet
evening with you that would end up in bed. But it's not
going that way at all, is it? So why don't we be honest
and skip the formalities and just go inside and slip beneath the covers and see what we can find out about
each other . . . I know that sounds forward of me, but
the only way we may have any privacy at all is to grab
some right now, before the place really begins flying."
I could see that Jimmy had produced a box of amyl nitrates
and was passing them around. It was now or never to
get Mario inside with me, while things were relatively
normal.

He nodded, shyly, and, eager as a little kid, followed
me into the bedroom.

I closed my bedroom door behind us and we both
quickly undressed. Mario revealed a truly darling body,
with only a few fuzzy hairs on his still suntanned chest.
His cock was still hidden in his navy blue bikini underpants, however, and there was clearly no bulge there. I
guessed I would have to warm him up thoroughly before
we would go into action.

Mario, really *very* shy, dove under the sheets, covering
himself up almost to his chin. I joined him under the

sheets. It was cozy there, kind of protective like a tent, and yet cool. We began kissing and I cuddled up in his arms, having decided to take things slowly. But after about ten minutes of cuddling, I was slowly kissing his earlobe, caressing his face, and moving my fingers through his pitch-black hair. I could feel little shudders up and down his spine.

Mario still didn't seem to quite know what to do with his own hands and I gently guided them around my shoulders and then downwards towards my nipples. Now I pulled his face lower so his mouth could cup my breast, assisted by his slim long fingers. At least he showed himself to be quite capable of breast-feeding and so I decided it was time for the finishing touch.

However . . . when I moved my mouth below his navel and pulled down his underpants, finally, I could hardly find his toy.

Mon Dieu, what a disappointment. I had been so eager to make it with him. His fingers were slim, but long, so I figured that if his penis might not be thick, it at least would be lengthy. But no . . . none of that.

To make matters worse, the phone rang twice during this period—one wrong number and one dumb unimportant call—and this disturbed Mario even more. At one point he got kind of aggressive and said, *"Fa'n cullo,* can't you let that damn phone ring or else take it off the receiver. . . ?" Little did he know that I cannot let a phone call go unanswered, still a hangover from my working days.

Time after time I started to try and work up Mario's cock, but no luck. Then it dawned on me that maybe the kid was psychologically troubled because of all the people in the house, and that's when I crawled back into his arms to reassure him. We chatted for at least half an hour about all kinds of things, important and trivial, and it turned out that the trouble indeed was in Mario's head. What had bothered him was the fact that Jimmy and I seemed to be very intimate friends and we had disappeared for a while.

Then he very timidly said, "Xaviera, I might not have been in this country very long, but I obviously have read your book and know all about you, you know, gossips in the building. I have been very anxious to know you better, since I first bumped into you, but . . . you know what . . . I think the anticipation has made me, you know, no good at love tonight."

"Don't worry, we'll fix that," I said.

"Not only the anticipation," he went on, "but then a horrible thought entered my mind."

"What's that?" I asked him laughingly.

"Xaviera, let me ask you, *prego,* with how many men have you slept before? Must have been thousands?"

"Ha, ha ha!" I really laughed out loud this time. So *that* was his problem. "You mean tonight, darling, or before you met me, or what? During my life . . .?"

"Uh, you know what I mean—while you were . . . the hooker, of course."

"Sweetheart, I have long since lost track of that, but so what . . . tonight it is only you and me and there has been nobody else before you and even if this is not so, forget about that—it is *you* who count and *you* who I want to please and to please me. Remember, cut out all the other horrible thoughts."

"Yes . . . but . . . if you have had so much experience, then . . . *sicuro,* you must be a very talented lady, but most of all very demanding when it comes to making love. Right?"

"Oh, sweet Mario, be yourself, relax, straighten your head out, *capisce? Solamente tuo.* Nobody else. And if you need lessons, I love to be a teacher anyway."

Once he understood my message, it was amazing to see the sudden change. He had adjusted his head and was now rapidly adjusting his cock. I had underestimated the size of his penis, because in no time, assisted by my soothing tongue and gentle fingers, he grew to be four sizes the original. *"Benissimo, bravo, Mario."*

I pulled his head down toward my vagina, and at the same time shifted my body around so I could go down on him myself to make sure the good work we'd managed so far would not fall down—under pressure. While I was working away to keep erect Mario's leaning tower of Pisa, he was proving that he was not naive in all ways of life. Yes, our young Mario was making very probing discoveries at his end of things, and for the first time this evening we were beginning to have some real fun. I don't know what Mario had had for dinner, but he certainly still had room for extra portions of Xaviera!

Just as we finished devouring one another (I must say the Italians certainly belong in the Top Ten Class for pussy-eating) and Mario was still hard and just about to put his lovely recuperated cock inside me, there was a knock on the door and Suzanne came dashing into my bedroom, babbling, "Hey, Xaviera, where the hell is the Koromex Jelly . . . that Jimmy has such a big cock, I can hardly handle him, but he is oh, so cute . . . though he doesn't stop talking about you, really digs you. Not a bad catch, a bit out of this world, but real great guy, lots of fun . . . Hey, when do you think you can join us—he doesn't want to come with either Kathy or me, until you're with us."

The most tactful approach this was not, and maybe the little bitch did this to turn Mario off from me. In any case, she *had* managed to push the wrong button. After rummaging around in my bathroom, she dashed out again with a tube of Koromex in her hand, and by this time Mario was already halfway dressed in his shirt and underpants. I did not quite feel like stopping him this time . . . anyhow the thought of making it with Jimmy was suddenly really blowing my mind.

Mario, sensing my thoughts, said to me on his way out, "Xaviera, I am sorry about tonight; I meant well, but I guess I am too much of a romantic. Anyhow, if you have nothing better to do next week, why don't I take you out for a nice dinner and then to the theatre, so I can straighten out my English a bit more and you can—ha, ha—straighten me out afterward, but, *cara* Xaviera, at *my* place, please—no more, the mob scene!"

"Of course, Mario," I said. "You can't imagine what a surprise the entire evening has been to me . . . really, *just one surprise after another.*" I couldn't tell him which part of the evening's various surprises he'd been, but anyway, he was a sweet young man and I didn't want him to remember this evening with any pain or embarrassment.

I'd put the negligee back on to accompany him to the

door, and now I drew him close and gave him a warm good night kiss, and at the same time, placed one of his hands on my ass and the other inside the negligee, on the top of my breasts. I wiggled about to see if I could stir him a little—and I stirred him a lot, but for now let the anticipation get him into top form. I ended the embrace, opened the door, gave him another kiss, this time on the cheek, and said, "*Caro* Mario, where there's life there's lots of hope, and there's plenty of life in your young body [I pointed toward the bulge in his trousers], so let us remember tonight fondly and have a truly wonderful night next week."

Mario looked down at his pants, blushed, looked up at me, smiled, and quickly said, *"Buena sera."*

"Buena sera," I said, "until we meet again."

Mario headed for the elevator and I turned around and headed for Kathy's room, completely dedicated to the principle that Jimmy was in there and that he and I were going to recapture the magic we'd had, with or without drugs, and fuck each other's brains out.

When I went through that door, I couldn't possibly have imagined the scene that greeted me. Edwin was on the bed with Kathy sitting on his chest, being vigorously eaten by him, while down below Suzanne was taking Edwin's cock into her mouth in large gulping swallows, up and down, down and up, while Jimmy was running the entire scene, at the same time taking time out to fondle Suzanne from behind with a hand which went through her legs and up into her young blonde cunt. Whenever he raised his arm to shout encouragement to everyone, he also raised Suzanne from underneath, and thus forced her mouth further down on Edwin's lucky prick, and . . . well, it was just wild.

"Hi, Xaviera," Jimmy shouted, "we're just getting into things here—working out our aggressions, don't you know." What I knew right off was that everyone had been popping amyl nitrates, and when Jimmy offered me one, I declined, content to stand by him and handle his fine big cock while he played group leader. . . .

"All right, Suzanne," he ordered, "let's have more of Edwin's stout fellow disappear into your mouth."

Suzanne took another inch of Edwin's penis which looked monumental, into her mouth. I didn't quite know where she put it, but it certainly disappeared.

"Now, Edwin, really," directed Jimmy, "Kathy hasn't moaned with pleasure for at least thirty seconds."

My God, my roommate, Kathy, who had done little more than drink and brood lately, was having the time of her life with Edwin. "Oh, Edwin," she purred, "if you'll eat me out again—the way you did before—I promise to *scream* for pleasure. But please don't stop playing with my ass, either."

Edwin, coming up for air, said, "I promise, I promise." Then, craning his neck and looking out from behind Kathy's body, he grinned at Jimmy and said, "How'm I doing, Coach?"

"You show great promise, my son," Jimmy said, "now get your head back into Kathy's lovable crotch."

Edwin obviously followed directions because almost immediately Kathy, her lovely body wiggling all over Edwin's willing face, was moaning, "Oh . . . oh . . . oh wow, it's *sooooo* good!"

This seemed to inspire something in Jimmy because he turned to me, with that infernal grin of his, and said, "Excuse me, my dear, but I have to do my own thing." He took his cock from out of my fond grasp and moved up behind Suzanne and, pulling her body toward him, he slid that wonderful cock into her without causing her to release an inch's grasp of Edwin's cock inside her mouth.

"Ummmmmm," mumbled Suzanne, *"za-wock* it to me, Wimmy." Her mouth was full of Edwin, so her bad diction came as no surprise.

But, hey, *I* was getting hot and bothered and my dear Jimmy was sticking it to someone else!

"Jimmy," I said, "I got rid of Mario to be able to make it with you! Now what the hell am I supposed to do while you're poking into Suzanne???"

"Hi, Xaviera," Jimmy said, obviously as high as a kite, "I promise you—you change your costume, and I'll give you the lead role in my play." Meanwhile he was bang-

ing away at Suzanne as though sex were about to be out-
lawed, and she had stopped sucking Edwin and she was
yowling, "Oh *migawd* Jimmy, I never had such a big one
in me!"

"Jim-my," I said in a loud voice, "will you please stop
fucking Suzanne and pay attention to me!"

"Can't just now, honey, but you go get out of that kinky
negligee and come right back in something respectable,
and we'll see if we can't do something for you."

Absolutely furious, I charged out of that room and into
my own. What the hell was going on here! It was *my*
apartment and *my* roommate and *my* friends in there fucking and sucking and no one, but *no* one, would listen to
me—they were too busy fucking and sucking!

I thought about it for a minute and then it struck me as
hilariously funny and I almost fell over on the bed with
laughter. First Justin, and then Mario, and then Jimmy,
and now me, complaining like a schoolteacher that they
weren't paying attention to me because they were busily
engaged in having some fun. Oh, woe is me, Xaviera,
what's happened to your sense of humor!

Jimmy the Great had said get a new costume, so I was
going to get me a new costume. I dove into my bureau and
searched for the sexiest bra and panties I owned. Then a
clinging long black dress, white scarf tied at the neck, black
stockings and garter belt underneath, long black gloves and
black leather pumps with crazy spike heels, and a ridiculously long cigarette holder to complete my ensemble. Before I left the room, I added lots of long golden chains
over my neck to dress up my costume, and now Dear
Jimmy, here I come . . . get ready to have your minds
blown!

I went back into the room and absolutely nobody paid
any attention to me. They were still at it, and the smell
of sex was beginning to permeate the room. I went over
to the light switch on the wall and flicked it up and down
so many times that even I saw stars.

"Your attention, please, ladies and gentlemen," I announced in a commanding voice, "Madame Xaviera is
about to do the dance for which she has been hailed in
two cities and three continents. Maestro James, please, if

you will, some appropriate music for my dance of dances!"

To my surprise, my complete surprise, everyone actually stopped what they were doing—cocks came out of cunts and cocks came out of mouths and mouths let go of cunts —and dragged themselves together and sat on the bed like meek little children and waited for me to make my grand entrance into Kathy's bedroom. Of course! They were all so spaced-out that it was easy for them to stop fucking and sucking and begin doing something else. Everything was a complete lark to them! Jimmy, his cock standing at half-mast, grinned at me and said, "Hey you, Xaviera lady, you just hold your butt right there until I get you the right music . . . You don't dance a step until the music's on—agreed? I'm your director and you dance one step before the music's on and I'll . . . I'll . . . well, you wouldn't want to see a grown man cry, would you?"

"Okay, Jimmy, let the music begin—so I can!" Oh boy, I hadn't had a single amyl nitrate and here I was, getting high like the rest of them.

Jimmy lumbered over to the phonograph and after looking over several records, put one on the turntable. It was a James Brown album, and it got me right into the mood and I began moving into the room doing the sexiest, slinkiest dance steps I knew, and some I didn't know I knew, and everyone applauded and I was really into it. I danced across that room, back and forth, as though I were Eve herself, trying to turn on the Snake, and by God, I felt sexy! Jimmy had come in and sat on the bed like everyone else, and I looked at all their faces and they were all staring at me as though I had invented burlesque. I realized it was the amyl nitrate working on them, but I wasn't going to stop until I had every one in that room dying to ball me, men and women alike, and so I danced close to the bed, then back a bit, then close, than back.

Jimmy was the one I really wanted to work on and I danced right up to him, almost into his face, then moved away, then back again, then away, until he was grabbing for me, always a second too late, and I was playing little games with the buttons on my dress, letting it droop off my shoulder to show part of the peek-a-boo bra, then all covered up again, my hand holding the dress together.

I don't smoke but I had taken this silly antique cigarette holder along as a prop, and now I wiggled and jiggled and bumped and grinded my way over to Jimmy again and, with sign language, demanded a cigarette. He gave me one and then I danced over him, awaiting a light, and when he bent over to get matches from his pants on the floor, I moved my spiked heel over to his hand and danced, flamenco-style, the heel of my shoe back and forth across his hand so quickly that my mind was telling me to stop it before I spiked him, but my body continued the wild, staccato movements until I finally undid my scarf and whipped it off my shoulders and looped it around Jimmy's neck, like a collar. Only then could I stop the mad dance over his hand, which, frankly, had terrified me as well, and instead lead Jimmy out into the middle of the room.

Holding him, my noble steed, by his white satin stirrup, I finally slithered out of my dress and heard a soft "Oh!" from the girls as they admired my sexy French bra. Then I pulled Jimmy between my legs and mounted him—my brain telling me, "Watch out for his back"—and padded him, spanking him, really, on the ass to give me a ride around the room. His back felt strong to me, and I could see that his cock was as hard as a rock, and I rode him around the room, reaching underneath to grab his cock, reaching behind to finger his ass, reaching below to play with myself as we continued this mad game.

Finally my horsie bucked, and rolled me onto the carpet, and got on top of me and fucked me until I saw stars.

This signaled an end to The Dance for everyone else, and Edwin had both Kathy and Suzanne splayed out on the bed and was popping another amyl nitrate into their mouths and eating both their cunts at once, at the same time mashing their bodies together so he could feel at least one tit on each of them and acting as though the two of them were really just one female.

Kathy, wild out of her mind, was yelling at Edwin, "You bastard, don't suck on her cunt so much, I need you over here," and Suzanne was replying, "Don't pay any attention to her, Edwin, you've got the sweetest snatch in creation right under your nose right now." Edwin apparently got bored by their in-fighting and since his cock was going to remain hard forever, he rolled over, pulled Kathy on top of him and onto his mad Irish cock, and Suzanne over his face so he could continue eating her, and went on taking care of both girls as though it were the simplest thing in the world.

Jimmy and I, between orgasms, had been watching this scene on the bed and now I pushed him back on the carpet and mounted his great cock again, and once more it was more than just fucking, there were feelings, caring for one another, anticipation of a marvelous come together— somehow we always came together!—and fucking away the problems of the world. His cock was pounding up into my belly and I loved it, I loved sitting on top of him without worrying about his fragile bones, squatting and bouncing and balling away above him until we both came again, both came in a searing explosion of sexual energy.

I must have passed out for a moment or so, but when I awoke Jimmy was out on the carpet next to me, and I watched, with both great interest and fascination, the proceedings on the bed. I don't know how many pills Edwin had popped that evening, but he was absolutely wild, a sexual superman.

Kathy, having been satisfied, was now pushing on Edwin's ass as he screwed Suzanne. "Okay, Edwin, hump Suzanne the way you humped me. Really sock it to her, Edwin! Give her that big thing of yours until she yells for mercy."

Edwin, for his part, suddenly rolled onto his back, holding Suzanne all the while, and placed her back on his cock. But mad Edwin had something far more elaborate in mind than merely fucking Suzanne. He moved her, like a rag doll, up and down on his cock and periodically lifted her up in the air, giving her a little toss upwards, then caught her and brought her down on his cock again.

"Oh, migawd, Edwin, be *careful* of her!" yelled Kathy, holding on to his balls and looking in awe at Suzanne flying above them.

Edwin caught Suzanne again and this time slammed her down on his cock, his own body arching off the bed, as he came in a noisy, tumultuous fashion. Suzanne, impaled on his dancing cock, was also coming, and Kathy more or less climbed over both of them and kissed and hugged them as though congratulating them on their brilliant teamwork.

After a moment, Suzanne gave a satisfied groan and rolled off Edwin to sprawl on the bed, and Kathy was obviously willing to take her place. She'd run into the bathroom and came out with a washcloth to clean off Edwin's penis, all the while kissing him all over, and Edwin, for goodness sake, still had the same hard-on as before. I was about to climb up on the bed to get into the act when I realized that Jimmy was now awake and fondling my ass, so I leaned over and whispered to him that it was time we all got together on the bed.

He more or less grunted his agreement, and in a minute it was me, not Kathy, who was riding atop Edwin's never-ending hard-on and Kathy was being lowered, bit by bit, over Jimmy's giant machine. "Oh, wow," Kathy said, a little girl expression coming over her face. "If I survive this, I'm going to just love it." But she needn't have worried, because Jimmy moved her up and down his cock so expertly that she was soon howling for pleasure while he just lay back and grinned at me.

To tell the truth, however, I couldn't afford to pay much attention to Jimmy's expert lovemaking techniques, because fucking Edwin was somewhat like playing football. He was squeezing my breasts together with one huge paw as though they were an accordion and with the other hand he was holding me by the ass and moving me up and down his magic cock. It felt terrific but for some reason I knew I wasn't going to come with him and I tapped Jimmy on the arm and quietly said, "You and me—together—again . . ." He nodded, but indicated Kathy, writhing on top of him, and then skillfully rolled over so that she was beneath him, but his weight was not on her, and moved her legs up over his shoulder and then, in three or four powerful lunges into her, brought her to a mind-blowing climax. She shuddered and groaned and simply slipped off of him, the most contented expression on her face.

There was a momentary—and that's all!—pause in the activities, and then I was wonderfully back in Jimmy's arms, his tongue inside and all through my mouth, his hands caressing my body in such a way that I felt that nothing sexual had happened to me today before this, that we had just joined bodies, and we moved into a beautiful fuck that had me seeing stars again.

I remember things going on after this, but I wasn't really with it. Whatever went on, it felt like Jimmy and me still together because when we kissed and caressed each other, it was so intimate, all our senses working, that it pervaded everything else.

For you see, there are times when lovemaking is all in the mind and even when Jimmy was giving Kathy the smoothest ride of her life, he was really fucking my mind.

For you see, to kiss someone can be a much more intimate act than fucking or getting fucked.

Because when you kiss someone, you see, you feel, you touch, you taste and you hear. . . .

I wish I could tell you that I saw Jimmy again and was able to help him out of his despair. But it isn't true. Not too long after this crazy evening, he was hospitalized again. He hadn't "flown" off a roof or anything like that. He had simply taken a good look at the world, and decided to leave it for a while.

If I can get back to America, I know who one of the first persons I'm going to visit will be.

Come back to Earth, Jimmy. We need you here.

The Girls in My Life

FIONA: The Reluctant
Debutante

Some of the girls I've known in my business had come from distinctly unglamorous backgrounds. In fact some of them do fit the stereotypes of the poor girl from a poverty-stricken family drifting into prostitution.

Fiona, however, was every svelte inch a lady. Born of a wealthy Milanese family—the family fortune was later dissipated by a gambling father—she received an elegant education, learning to speak French, Spanish, and English —though she was far more fluent in the first two languages.

After her schooling, Fiona got into fashion modeling, for which she was eminently suited because of her bearing, her divine figure, and madonna-like face. The only thing less than perfection about her face was a nose that was slightly—just slightly—too large, but she photographed like a dream.

When Fiona became friendly with me, she proudly showed me her model's portfolio, and I was slightly astounded. She'd been chosen not only as one of Italy's best-dressed women but had even made one of the "Ten Best-Dressed Women" lists for all of Europe.

How I came to meet Fiona would provide the script for a fairly bad movie. She had saved about three thousand dollars to come to the United States and see something

of the country. In New York she'd met an attractive young
Frenchman named Francois, whom she found charming
and intelligent and, supposedly, wealthy. He was going to
Las Vegas, and invited her to come along. Once there,
he virtually robbed her of all her money and gambled it
away at the local casinos. He also cashed in her ticket
back to Europe. Fortunately for Fiona, she at least had
a return ticket to New York.

(This same Francois, by the way, once showed up at
my place—this happened a few months before Fiona
met him—and had a big fat sexual evening for himself.
For which he paid with a big fat check. Which bounced
like a tennis ball. I had no way of tracking him down,
except to prowl the various clubs and discotheques at
which he then was known to hang out. And since that
wasn't my scene, I wrote Francois and his check off—bum-
mers both.)

In theory Fiona and I should have never met, since she
was referred to me by one of the staff of the really "in"
club in New York, Le Club. And I had never had anything
professional to do with anyone from that club. I don't even
know the gentleman who sent Fiona to me—he was a
friend of hers from Europe—but obviously he knew
enough about me to entrust Fiona to me.

Upon first meeting Fiona, I could tell two things about
her: that she was in desperate financial straits and that she
certainly didn't belong in the prostitution field. But I liked
her and since she had no money for a hotel room, I invited
her to move in with me for the time being. There's always
room at the inn—as the old saying goes—for someone in
trouble.

I made it clear to Fiona that staying with me was on the
house, and I hoped she'd be able to earn her passage back
by modeling. But it was the slack summer season and there
was no work for her.

So Fiona had a brief, abortive career as a call girl.
Basically she didn't seem to care for sex that much and
it didn't help that her English was frequently too limited
for her to relax with a client. I tried to teach her not only
some sexual finesse but to treat her bed partner as a fellow
human being. If she found it awkward to talk with him,

she could at least smile instead of always looking like a pale and wan madonna. Fiona seemed so removed from the rest of us sometimes that men didn't know what to make of her.

She and I got along fine, chatting away in Italian, but some of the other girls, since they couldn't converse with her very easily, ended up envying her for her great wardrobe. The clothes she owned were fantastic and chic—snakeskin skirts, antelope jackets, the most beautiful leather shoes and, always, bags to match her outfits.

It was obvious that Fiona was getting no pleasure from the pleasure game, and I eventually managed to put her in touch with a particular fashion photographer who had a preference for her type of model. She wasn't getting rich with the work he was giving her, but it was work she knew and respected and she was clearly happier at it.

By mid-fall she had a little career building for herself, and was enjoying New York more, when she was suddenly called home. Doctors in Milan had determined that Fiona's daughter—the child of a hasty marriage while still in her late teens—was dying of leukemia and so Fiona rushed home to spend all her time with her child.

We promised to write regularly and it was with great sadness I learned six months later that her child had died. Some months later, she returned to New York—strictly for a visit—and I was delighted to see her. And when I returned to Europe last spring, I visited her in Milan. She was a great hostess and guided me like a queen around Milan.

I was forewarned by her not to make any mention of her brief "poor girl" career in Manhattan since here in Milan she was a much valued member of the local jet set. I, of course, did not, but every once in a while some remark would send us both into a fit of giggling. Which always reminded me that Fiona had hardly ever laughed in New York City.

Ciao, ciao, bambina. Molto grazie.

IV. PUBLICITY TRIPPING

PHILADELPHIA STORY

Since the price paid for *The Happy Hooker*—$100,000 —was the highest ever paid for a paperback original, it was decided that I should go out and publicize the book. I was certainly willing to do so, and if I do say so myself, I became a damn good hustler when it came to promoting my book.

The last celebrity that Dell, my first publisher, had sent out on a major publicity tour was Joan Garrity, otherwise known as "J," the author of *The Sensuous Woman*. Her book has sold over seven million copies, I'm told, and while *The Happy Hooker* may never quite rival that, I'm certainly proud and pleased with the success of it.

My first out-of-town publicity stop was Philadelphia. No one in New York ever seems to talk about Philadelphia, much less go there, and true, it was certainly my first visit to the City of Brotherly Love. I wasn't there very long, but from what I saw Philadelphia is a nice-looking city with a good combination of old and new buildings.

I went to Philadelphia by Metroliner, which was another first—my first time on an American train. Previously all my traveling in America had been by car or plane. I don't

know about other American trains, but the Metroliner was
fast and clean and comfortable.

When I arrived in Philadelphia, I took a cab to the
television station that had invited me to appear on "The
Maclean Show." This is the kind of talk show on which
listeners phone in questions, and I was appearing with an
elderly psychiatrist who was also a professor. He certainly
looked the role—a little old man, somewhat roly-poly, with
a big nose and Shubert glasses worn near the end of his
nose. He was mostly bald and I judged his age to be
around seventy. When we were introduced, he spoke with
a heavy European accent and his manner was very Old
Worldish—almost courtly.

Most of the viewers who phoned in addressed their
questions to me, and I think I handled them well. It was of
course my first time at this sort of thing, but I'd been,
after all, in the "entertainment business" for the past few
years. Actually I'd performed as a young girl and am not
prone to stage fright.

The host of the show seemed to like the fact that I was
getting most of the questions, but I thought it was a little
unfair that the old professor wasn't getting a chance to
speak. Still, when he did get a question he would begin a
lengthy discourse on prostitution and morality and the
nature of female sexuality and the host would have to cut
him off. This happened three or four times and I felt
somewhat sorry for the professor because the host wasn't
exactly polite when he cut him off. I knew the old man
was being garrulous, but there should have been a nicer
way to limit his dissertations. Yet what could I do about
it? Apparently the professor would have required several
hours to get all his points across, and all we had was one
hour, with ten minutes out for commercials.

After the show, we said good-bye and each went our
separate way. I walked around to learn the city a bit and
then it was time to catch my train. While waiting at the
station, I was approached by a woman who said she'd seen
me on the show and wanted to compliment me on how
well-spoken I'd been. I'd been far more witty and articulate than the professor, she said, although she did feel
sorry for him having been cut off several times.

"I suppose some of the things he was trying to say might have been interesting if he'd been given a chance to finish," she said, "but . . . it really did take him forever just to finish a sentence."

I agreed with her, and since she was on her way to New York to do some shopping, we decided to travel together. And who should come along just then but the object of our conversation—the old professor himself. Like an elegant gentleman, he came over and kissed my hand, then that of my new companion. Introductions were made and he responded with a good deal of charm. We all boarded the train together and the professor and I ended up sitting together.

In contrast to his personality on the TV show, here he proved to be a most engaging conversationalist, and we had a very animated conversation. But imagine my surprise when he really began to analyze my character during the trip to New York!

I found that I had to watch every word I uttered because he seemed to find all kinds of meanings in each thing I said. It was fun trying to keep up with him, and at least I wasn't paying him fifty dollars an hour for the analysis.

"Why do you wear so much make-up?" he suddenly asked.

"Ach, I hate it—I loathe wearing all this make-up—but if I'm to go on a television program and be seen by thousands of viewers, I want to look my best for the cameras. Any woman would feel this way. By using make-up differently than you would for other situations, like going out to dinner or to a party, you're trying to project the right image for the cameras."

"Of course," he agreed, "you don't want to look dowdy or frumpy—and you do want to look as glamorous and sexy as possible."

"Then why did you ask me about the make-up if you agree with me?" I asked him, trying to throw him off-balance.

"What was right for the TV cameras is too much for the street," he pointed out, making me feel a little self-conscious. Then, as though he realized what I was thinking, he added, as though to cheer me up: "I think, young lady, that you are at the beginning of a great career as an author, or whatever exciting develops in your life. You seem to be an aggressive woman, self-confident, and with strong will power."

Then he really surprised me. "I read your book last week and felt I had to meet you," he said, adding the information that he'd cancelled three lectures in order to appear on the TV show. That made me feel particularly sorry for him since his experience on the show hadn't been very happy. But he didn't seem to mind.

Now came another surprise. "Would you mind if I give you a bit of advice?" he asked me.

"Of course not," I said, wondering, "What now?"

"Now that you are a so-called sex symbol, wherever you go women will look at you and say to themselves, 'Is she really as sexy as she's supposed to be? Can she really twiddle men around her fingers?' "

"So what would you advise me to do?" I asked him, now really curious.

"You are loving every minute of your success, and even though you told me you hate to wear make-up, I can see you basically love making yourself look beautiful, putting the eyelashes on and applying green shadow to your lids and then looking in the mirror and feeling on top of it all!"

He said this with real feeling and his enthusiasm made me feel good and laugh, all at once. He was reminding me of a cartoon character, with his big round nose and old-fashioned glasses and double chin and protruding belly, but he was really very sweet.

"You're right," I said, still giggling at being found out.

"You see," he said, sagely as possible, "you can't fool me . . . even though I am an old man now. I have had a lot of experience in these matters, and my advice is to stay *natural* and *spontaneous* and don't let success go to your head. Don't settle for being a sex symbol."

By now the train was coming into Penn Station and although I would have liked to talk some more with this kindly old man, I knew there'd be no time to have a serious conversation. But I have remembered what he told me and I think it was very sound advice. Sometimes things move so quickly in one's life that there's no time to reflect and remind yourself that the glamour of the moment is only temporary and there's still a real, everyday life to live.

So the irony of what was to be the start of a wild publicity trip was that the event itself—the TV show— really wasn't as interesting as my second encounter with the old professor. And it was a nice, gentle, start for me in my new career. I hoped that all the harassment was behind me and I was sure that I was entering a wonderful time in my life.

The Prostitute and the Public

QUESTIONS AND ANSWERS

During the lectures I have given, and when I went on radio talk-shows, I have especially enjoyed the question and answer sessions. Naturally, sometimes the questions were insulting and cruel and just plain stupid, but the majority of them were worth a serious answer.

Here are some of the more interesting questions I've been asked, on the air and in person, and my answers to them. In some cases they are my actual taped answers. Other times, my response here is the response I *wanted* to make then, but couldn't because my language would have been too frank.

Between each chapter of this section there will be a question and answer session. I hope you enjoy them as much as I did experiencing them.

Are there a lot of myths about prostitution?

I'll say there are. And in my opinion, that best-selling book by Dr. David Reuben, *Everything You Always Wanted to Know About Sex . . . but Were Afraid to Ask,* contained a hell of a lot of wrong ideas.

For example, I've been asked if prostitutes ever have orgasms and is it true that a good prostitute *never* should have an orgasm? It seems to me that Dr. Reuben believes the last part of the question to be the case.

Now that's absurd. Some prostitutes love their work and some hate it, while still others tolerate it. But it depends on how many people a prostitute sees every day. If she is a call girl and thus higher up in the hooker hierarchy, she only has to cater to four or five people a day to make a reasonably good living. So if the quantity of men is less, the quality of the love-making is higher and she can enjoy herself reasonably well. If she engages in intercourse and not just oral sex, there is a good chance that she will reach an orgasm. After all why not? Having sex three or four times a day isn't all that much. Some married or engaged couples have as much or even more sex during the course of a day. I remember when I was engaged to my fiancé, he and I would make love three or four times a day. So it's a silly myth that a prostitute cannot reach an orgasm or that a good one shouldn't reach an orgasm.

I must say, though, that if you're a street hooker and knock off twenty or thirty guys a day, then it does become impossible to enjoy sex, because you become numb after a while. You become indifferent to men, particularly when you're not very selective. There are too few good lovers left in this world to expect that twenty guys you just pick up on the street are going to thrill you. And emotionally it would be a miracle if she could reach an orgasm every time some guy laid her. The same holds true for male prostitutes or studs—they can make it, but their main goal is to make the customer reach a climax. All they're interested in is keeping their cock up and keeping it hard.

Sure it's true that all prostitutes, whether male or female, at least once in a while do fake it. This reminds me of one woman who called the radio program I was being interviewed on and said that all prostitutes were a bunch of fakers. She said that if men went to a prostitute, the first thing they'd ask her is if she loves them and will she reach an orgasm. And of course she will give them the answers they want to hear. So prostitutes must be fakers!

I answered her very politely and softly. First I asked her how old she was—that is, if it wouldn't embarrass her. She answered that she was fifty years old and had been happily married for over thirty years. I then asked her if there had ever been any other man in her life and the answer was no—she assured me she had never cheated on her husband nor had he ever cheated on her, as far as she knew. If she hadn't qualified her statement with that "as far as I know," *she* would have been a faker, but at least she knew there might be a remote possibility that he had slept with another woman once in three decades.

In thirty years of marriage, I asked her, had she *never* had to fake anything with her husband? She said she hadn't, that she loved everything about him. Of course they had had their ups and downs, but they still loved each other. Well, did she mean to say that every time she went to bed with her husband, during all those years, she reached a climax, and he reached a climax as well? I asked her if being a married woman didn't perhaps involve being something of an actress. To me, it seemed not having to deceive a man once in a while would be absolutely impossible. It was very apparent to me that in the course of my life I've discovered that it is easier to turn a man on, but a woman is sexually—well, different—and no matter how much two people love one another, sometimes the woman can't be aroused and thus she decides to fake it to please her man. And what about the times she wasn't feeling well or wasn't in the mood to make love—did she mean to tell me that everytime she made love with her husband she reached a climax!

There was a pause on the other end of the phone and the emcee, who was sitting next to me, smiled at me and nodded his head in approval. After a few moments' silence, the woman said yes I was right, and I in turn apologized for being so personal with her. I said I thought that maybe we women *should* learn to fake a little bit more, maybe we *should* be better actresses. And then perhaps our husbands and lovers wouldn't need to go to prostitutes.

There is an old adage which says a woman should be a queen in the kitchen, a lady in the living room and a whore in bed. And if only a lot more women would become whores in the bedroom, I think most prostitutes would be out of business.

However, these are hardly just the woman's problems.

When men come to a prostitute they do not only come for physical pleasure but also to talk about their troubles. And I've noticed that the first ones to accuse their wives of being cold and indifferent lovers are the men who think *they're* God's gift to women. They thought they were the best and greatest lovers on earth. And once in bed with me or one of my girls, it often turned out they were lousy lovers. Usually "slam bam thank you ma'am" types. And even though we were *merely* prostitutes, I and the other girls knew that the in and out approach isn't very satisfying to them, and certainly not to us.

So if I could, I would teach these men a lesson by telling them before you say your wife is dead in bed, ask yourself if you truly know what sex is all about. Most of them really need to be taught how to arouse a woman. I'd point out to a man that he may come home tired from work and there is his wife slaving in the kitchen and coping with the everyday problems of a housewife, and *he* doesn't want to hear her troubles with the kids and the car breaking down and perhaps *she* isn't interested in his problems at the office or how the stock market has gone down.

If only the two of you could learn how to relax for a couple of hours after dinner, and then maybe discuss your problems for a half hour. Then take a bath, either together or separately or even a nice cold bracing shower, which will usually freshen you up, and then make love and forget about the miseries of the day.

I've gone on at great length about this, but it really all does boil down to the issue of the relationships existing between men and women—not just those between Johns and prostitutes—and it's vital we think about these relationships.

Naturally there are other myths about prostitutes—about their hating men and all of them coming from poor, deprived or bad backgrounds—but I at least allude to these false notions elsewhere in the book, so I won't dwell at length on them here.

CHICAGO

I had come to Chicago to, among other things, appear on the famous Irv Kupcinet Show, and my official escort there was a top Dell regional sales representative named Dick. Besides being a very nice, attractive man, he gave me a lot of pointers on the "Kup Show" and on Chicago in general.

Being a born merchant, I guess, I immediately asked Dick how the book was doing and he said it was "selling like crazy"—good news to these eager ears. In point of fact, it was then Number Three on the local best-seller lists, and climbed to the top position a few weeks later. Call it author's ego if you will, but I like to think my appearances in Chicago had something to do with the book's gaining the top spot there.

I asked Dick if he usually shepherded authors around on promotional tours, and he replied that the only female author he'd taken around was "J"—Joan Garrity—the little ole "Sensuous Woman" herself. Well, this news launched a rather lengthy discussion about that book in which I was sometimes less than kind to the book and its author.

In retrospect it may have been silly for me to regard *The Sensuous Woman* and its author as competition. After all, it had been a huge hard-cover success before going into paperback, and Lyle Stuart, the publisher, had done a remarkable job in promoting it. By contrast, there'd been no time even to consider my book for hard cover because of the attendant publicity of the Knapp Commission investigations and the fact that I might have to leave the country sometime in spring of 1972. Still, I must concede that the mere mention of *The Sensuous Woman* could turn me into the "Sensuous Bitch."

For those six adults in America who haven't read or at least looked at *The Sensuous Woman,* it's a how-to-sex manual for housewives and in its own way it's a helluva cute book. However, to an experienced woman like me, it seemed like rather modest advice for women who need so badly to lose their hang-ups and inhibitions.

In any case, when Dick mentioned Joan Garrity I teased him about "falling in love with her," and he responded, "Nope, not in a thousand years could I go for her."

"Why not?"

"Well," he said, "not to be cruel, but she really reminded me of the housewives she's writing for. . . . She might be the most sensuous woman in town, but I'm afraid I like a woman with more obvious sex appeal."

I said that I'd heard from other people that "J" does have a way of talking to a man which will turn him on, make him feel like a king, the only attractive man left on earth—and believe me, this is no small talent. I'd also heard that "J" was always being asked in radio or TV interviews if she really wrote the book and whether or not she'd experienced all the incidents in the book, and sometimes she answered that some of the things had happened to friends.

Dick and I began kidding about "J's" famous jello bath —her favorite "thing"—and I said it all sounded pretty ridiculous to me. I may be a sexual romantic at times but I'm also practical-minded and by the time you'd go through the time and trouble to make the jello—and how many damn boxes of jello does it take to fill up a bathtub!—and before it hardened, you should be pretty much turned off by the whole thing.

At this point Dick observed that *The Sensuous Man* was really more of a competitive book for me, since it was being published just before mine. He also said a book called

The Sensuous Couple was soon to be published. We kicked that around for a bit, finally deciding that the best-selling book of all would either be entitled *The Sensuous Cat* or *The Sensuous Murderer.* The first would get the animal lovers in addition to the sensual-minded types, and the second would appeal to sensual mystery buffs.

"How about *The Sensuous Hermaphrodite*"? I joked. "*It* touches all sexual bases."

Dick laughed. Now we were getting really silly, and throwing out titles like rice at a wedding. *The Sensuous Librarian! The Sensuous Aero-Space Director! The Sensuous Spinster! The Sensuous Baby-Sitter!*

Dick said he'd heard that a rip-off of my book, entitled *The Sensuous Hooker,* was in the making.

"How about *The Sensuous Cock Sucker?*" I countered.

"Nope," he said, "it wouldn't get chain-store distribution." Then he added, "Not to speak of drugstores, train stations, airports, department stores, newsstand rack space, plus a few million other places."

"Oh," I said, "well, how about *The Sensuous Nose-Picker?*"

"You've picked a winner!" he applauded.

Ah, the "Silly Hour" was about to come to an end. By this time we'd reached the TV station where I was to do the Kup Show. I was excited by this because I hadn't been able to get on any of the network television shows for a variety of reasons—none of them very rational—and the Kup Show is very well regarded even if it isn't a network program. After Dick parked the car, we went upstairs and met Kup, who was most cordial. Dick wished me luck and said he'd be watching the show.

Of the show itself, I have many enjoyable impressions but there were too many people on with me for me to recall all that was said. I enjoyed Kup's questions—he'd read the book and his sharp questions reflected this—and a dialogue on human relations (physical, mental, emotional) I had with Dr. Desmond Morris, author of *The Naked Ape* and *The Human Zoo,* was *really* exciting.

Billy Daniels, the singer, was on and he was an elegant gentleman, even—or especially—when he broke up the audience by saying he was "all for prostitutes." After all, he quipped, he'd been one of their biggest patrons!

The star of the show, I guess, was Burt Reynolds, the TV and movie actor and upcoming center-spread in *Cosmopolitan* magazine. He is very attractive—reminds me of Marlon Brando in his younger years—but while I liked him, I couldn't escape the impression that he was somewhat self-conscious in his new role as a sex symbol. Still, he was very nice to me. A few weeks later, I got a call from him and he told me he was co-hosting the *Tonight Show* and had fought to have me on as the main guest. "The whole crew and whoever has read your book is dying to have you on," Burt said, adding the sad news that the Federal Communications Commission—as I mentioned in my Introduction—officially frowned on the idea. I asked him how come the retired Madam from Kentucky could get on both the Cavett show and the Susskind show, and he replied, "Don't ask me . . . the reasons, as told to me, were the title of the book and that you're too young and too controversial. . . ."

Another guest was Professor Irwin Corey, who is a good comedian, and an authentic *meshugana,* but on this evening at least I thought he made himself look like an asshole by his remarks, which struck me as being either far-out stupid or else just plain silly. What he seemed to be best at was interrupting. But at least he didn't make any of his inane remarks when Dr. Morris and I were talking. I think I would have punched him in the nose if he had.

Then the F.C.C. could ban me from television as being a dangerous person. . . .

After the program, I met Mrs. Kupcinet, who is a very sociable person, and Dinah Shore, who is Burt Reynolds' good friend, according to the gossip sheets and to anyone who has seen them together. No doubt about it, Burt must be the "someone who's in the kitchen with Dinah," who is, I hear, a really great cook.

I don't know how old Miss Shore is, but she looks sensational—that night she had on a beautiful white pants suit and nice tight sweater—and possesses the kind of charm and wisdom a woman can only have after living for some time.

There's no phoniness about her—she's honest and up-front with people—and no pretense so far as her relationship with Burt goes. She tells everyone she's in love with him, I gather, and I certainly hope it lasts. Sometimes these relationships are frowned upon because the younger man is regarded as nothing more than a gigolo, but no one who has been in Burt's and Dinah's company can deny they have some mutual admiration society going for them!

The Prostitute and the Public

QUESTIONS AND ANSWERS

Do you like men, or do you hate men?

More often than not, I adore men—and I love to make love to them. On the other hand, I have moments of hatred —but I usually am not able to stay mad for long, and there is nothing greater than "making up."

My attitude, however, has changed a little bit toward men, particularly since I was involved in prostitution for a few years. Possibly because of having been a prostitute and having gotten used to working on an hourly basis, I've become accustomed to short "relationships" with men. Now that I'm retired and traveling all over the world, I find myself in a position where *I'm* the one who picks men at parties, beaches, restaurants, discotheques. *I'm* the one who sets the pattern. I say to myself, "You're the person I want to fuck," and in nine out of ten cases, I get that man into bed. I feel like a victor, a conqueror! Then, after I ball him to my heart's content—either for a couple of hours or for the whole night (*if* I let him stay over for the whole night)—I am liable to turn into a piece of ice the next day, and tell him to get the hell out of my life.

This, obviously, has caused some strange reactions from my friends, because they cannot understand how I can virtually float around, pick up men and drop them again. I don't do this because I *hate* them, but merely because

269

I've been used only to short-term relationships. It is difficult for me to get emotionally involved now unless the chemistry really works and he is intelligent and stimulating enough to capture my mind as well as my body.

In a way my attitude is now more masculine. Now I am the hunter instead of being the hunted one. Most important, I no longer allow myself to be used.

Are you ever sorry you became a prostitute?

Well, yes and no. I've obviously had a great many experiences as a result of having been a call girl and then a madam, but I didn't come to America to become a "lady of the night."

I came here to get married, and when that worked out so badly, my pride was terribly hurt and I was tremendously depressed. So in order to prove myself again, I became promiscuous. I hated to be lonely, so I became one of the easiest targets in town for a man aiming to get laid that night. I loved sex, so why fool around—let's go to it.

But I kept hoping I'd find the right guy—someone who'd dig me for myself—but the kind of guys I mostly met didn't even have the decency to tell me the truth about themselves. I was still terribly gullible and I believed the stories they told me when they had to rush out of the apartment—usually to catch the last train to the suburbs, or something like that. But I believed their phoney stories because I wanted so much to see them again.

So when I drifted into prostitution, I found it was really more honest, at least. Then the men could level with me, and I knew I'd see them again whenever they could afford to see *me* again. "Okay, baby," men would say, "here's my story—I'm married, whether happily or not isn't important, but I have a good job and I love my kids and I'd rather pay than get involved with someone who might end up calling my wife, or maybe even blackmailing me." This certainly wasn't romantic, but more important—it was the truth.

No, I'm not *glad*—I can't be—I became a call girl, but I *am* glad I stopped being that naive little girl from Holland. There was no joy there.

Which do you prefer, Miss Hollander—to make love to a man or to a woman?

This is a difficult question to answer, because—as always —it depends completely on the person. But let me first give you a general idea of my love-making patterns.

I do like to make love to a woman, but I have a greater physical need for a man. Emotionally, however, when I am with a woman, it is because I choose her and the involvement goes beyond the physical appetite. Our relationship is longer lasting and deeper; I enjoy simply being with her, holding and caressing her and being kind to her. I usually play the male partner, and at times I definitely suffer from penis envy because I feel like fucking this woman all the way. Sure, there are dildoes, but there are times I would really like to have my own penis. If I just feel like having sex, I can pick up a man, fuck him and just as easily drop him again. I don't have to like him emotionally; it is very often a mere physical attraction—a matter of getting a good lay. Then it's over and done with.

I don't usually have Lesbians *only* calling up to be serviced. If they did, I would not charge. I only have the men pay—I guess, in that sense, I'm not a liberated woman!

How do you feel about the Women's Liberation movement?

Women's Liberation stands for an active movement to insure that women will no longer be second-class citizens. They look forward to the day when women will receive the same opportunity as men in jobs and education and equal salaries. And women will once and for all be recognized as an integral part of society and not be type-cast in the role of wives, mistresses and child-bearers. They will be recognized as having drives, needs and capabilities equal to those of men. In a sense, therefore, I identify with Women's Lib in the same way as a Gloria Steinem, Betty Friedan and Bella Abzug.

However, there are many prominent figures in the movement who use the movement as a sort of bellwether to castrate men. I'm not interested in castrating a man, which I believe is the worst type of paranoia. I do not care for dehumanization in whatever form it presents itself and this is my main argument against Women's Lib in regard to their attitude toward men. It is also my strongest feeling in sympathizing with many of their goals. I do not want to be dehumanized. I also want to be considered more than just the sum of my private parts.

Did you ever have a woman for a customer? What did she want?

Yes, I had women customers, but they came with their husbands or boyfriends.

The latest fashion these days is for married couples to call up and request a ménage à trois. Usually the husband calls the madam and asks her to send over a girl, preferably one who really digs what she's doing and loves to take care of the woman as well as the husband without faking it.

This was my particular specialty. I would go over myself and seduce the wife while her husband watched and masturbated. Most of the time, the woman gets a little uptight seeing her husband have sex with the prostitute, and will usually only tolerate the situation if she, herself, is being serviced by the girl, or if her husband just fools around with the girl—kissing her tits and fondling her. The female animal gets really uptight if her husband decides he wants to go all the way and ball the prostitute. At such moments, it's up to the call girl to straighten her out and say "Look, if you're having a good time, let him have his pleasure as well. After all, we may never meet again, so why get uptight? Let's all three enjoy together."

What is your favorite position when you make love to a couple?

My favorite position, in that instance, is when the woman lies on her back and I lie between her legs, with my head buried in her cunt, my belly on the bed and my legs spread-eagled. Then I suggest her husband stand behind me and fuck me, pushing his cock in from the rear and holding on firmly to my buttocks. This is a good three-way scene, where everyone can reach an orgasm at the same time, provided the woman, new at it, can relax and let herself go all the way.

The daisy chain is even better and more comfortable, where the man eats his wife, the wife—if she is that far progressed—eats me and I suck the man, or vice versa. I say, "Let all flowers bloom," if everyone agrees to it and enjoys what they're doing.

DON THE DEEJAY

My next stop was a large city in the Midwest, which shall have to be nameless for reasons soon to be apparent. The weather was kind of cold and miserable and here I was, wearing a low-cut dress and a muskrat coat! I was picked up at the airport by a meek, young Dell salesman who hardly said three words as he drove me to a radio-TV station owned by one of the local papers. At two o'clock that afternoon, I was to do an interview with a very popular disc jockey.

The man I was to meet proved to be a good-looking, wavy-haired, 29-year-old guy. Very groovy and aware of his attractiveness. Just as the salesman and I were about to go in the front entrance, he pulled up in his yellow Porsche and, honking his horn to get our attention, told us to wait until he parked his car.

Taking my coat as we walked in, he put his arm around my shoulder. We were about the same height and I could feel the warmth from his body. Before I knew what was happening, I was escorted into a studio outer room where the square salesman sat down and started to read the newspaper, trying not to pay any attention to the disc jockey—let's call him "Don"—and me. By this time, it was twenty to two and we had to be on the air by two.

We'd hardly been introduced when Don started to unzip the back of my dress. I whispered, "Hey, you can't do that, baby." He paid absolutely no attention to my protests and began playing with my breasts. He couldn't keep his hands off them, like a little baby playing with his toys. Since I was very turned on to Don, I got very horny as well, but kept looking at the clock ticking the time away. I also sneaked a look at the salesman, peering over the top of the newspaper at what was happening. I really didn't give a damn! I was supposed to be a sex symbol, anyway, so what the heck. While Don was playing with my breasts, he lifted up his sweater and opened his shirt so I could run my fingers over his hairy chest and caress his nipples as well. All of a sudden, the partially opened door swung wide and in walked two of his colleagues. Although I was a little embarrassed, they cracked up, telling Don that he was having the best of two worlds.

"You have a certain good interview coming up," one of them said, "and also a chick that will take care of you. But you'd better watch the time."

With all of this going on, Don told me a story which revealed what kind of a guy he was and how, since his program was that popular, he could conceivably fool around like this without worrying about getting fired. His story, Don said, indicated what one could and could not do on his program. (While he is putting on music on the air, he also raps with his audiences and keeps the telephone lines open).

On a Saturday night a few weeks ago, he told me, he'd gone with some friends to a party. It was a social "jet set" party—"very snooty and snotty," Don said—and he found the people about as boring as they were "beautiful." So without anything more entertaining to do, Don proceeded to get slightly smashed, though he was convinced he was still in control of himself.

He was wandering around the party, looking for some action, when he spotted this luscious knock-out blonde bird, a head taller than he was. Dressed in a long white gown that set off her tan, she could have been a model or a show girl or a creature sent from heaven, Don said, but what

she definitely was was the most stunning female at the party.
Oh, oh, Don told himself, I'm in love again!

The only problem was that the stunner had a date with
her, a kind of square-looking gentleman in his early fifties.
Don assured himself that he was taller, better-looking, and,
he was certain, far wittier, than this man—and the tall
blonde deserved to know him. Don had another drink to
fortify his "tall" estimate of himself, and when the blonde's
companion left her to refill their drinks, Don dashed into
the breech. He rushed over to the girl, introduced himself,
told her what he did, and finished his run-on sentence by
offering to take her home.

The girl looked flabbergasted and said, "Oh, no, I can't
do that. Can't you see I'm here with a date? I can't go
home with you." Okay, Don asked if they couldn't meet
sometime the next week, or could he at least have her telephone number? She became ice, Don said, turned her back,
and walked away.

"Yeah," said Don to me, "absolutely ice, but she was
still very beautiful." For the rest of the evening, he kept her
within his gaze. He had, he admitted to me, a very bad case
of "the hots" for her.

Don couldn't believe that there wasn't someway he could
get in touch with her. The party was almost over and a
lot of people were leaving and Don was getting frantic about
how he could possibly contact her. He sought out the
hostess of the party, but she didn't know where he could
reach the blonde. She had come with friends of friends.
"Even if we did know," the hostess said, very proper, "we
would not give you her number without her permission."

So that was that. Don just didn't know how to reach the
girl of his dreams. All he knew about her was her first name
was either Helen or Helena. He thought it was probably
Helen. What he associated her name with was Helen of
Troy so he romantically gave her the name of Helena.

He didn't follow the couple out the door to where their
car was parked, although that would have allowed him to
take down the license-plate number of the car. But not
having a detective's mentality, he didn't think of that or of
simply following the car.

The following Monday, Don decided to ask his listeners

to help. He said, over the air: "I'm lonely and I want a girl. I just don't want *any* girl. I want this particular girl that I met on Saturday night at a party. [He wouldn't mention the name of the people who gave the party but he mentioned the area and the street.] She has a dark suntan and her boyfriend is an older man in his fifties. Or maybe it's her fiancé. She's beautiful, she has big blue eyes, and she is probably a Danish or Swedish goddess. All I know is that her name is Helen. I will call her my Helena of Troy! Please, anyone who is listening out there in the audience who can help me—help me find Helen or Helena. I want her badly. I want to make love to her. I want to be with her. This is my cry to the sky. I am crying on my own program. I've never asked anybody to help me like this."

Then, after this remarkable speech, he went off the air and left the telephone lines open. Within the next half hour he got about six phone calls from people who knew a Helen or a Helena—girls who sounded as though they might have been she. But none of them *was* his Helena, Don knew.

Well, Don went back to playing records, but the next day he renewed his cry out for Helen, Helen, Helen. He figured by this time *somebody* out there would recognize his description of the tall, long-haired blonde beauty and tell him where to find her. Sure enough, during that program four more calls came into the studio. And out of the four, two seemed to be amazingly close to his description of the girl.

One call came from a male friend of hers, and the other one was from a girl who used to work with her and who knew her office number. So Don called that office number and indeed there was a Helen employed there. He even learned her last name. But she refused to pick up the phone and talk to him.

Next day he talked about her again on his radio program. This went on for about three or four days, with Don telling his audience that he was desperate because now he'd located Helen, but she wouldn't talk to him. He asked if there wasn't anybody out there who knew her home phone number.

Since by now most of his audience was alerted to Don's

cause, a call came in from a girl who said she was Helen's roommate and said that she would give him the number providing that Helen was told about it first.

Don said, "Oh, no, come on, give me the number. I know she likes me; I know she wants to talk to me. Come on, give me the number."

The girl said absolutely not. She said that if Helen knew he had the number without her having first asked Helen about it, she'd be furious. The girl said that the only solution she knew was to first ask Helen and then have her call the station. So he had to go along with this solution.

Don resumed playing records, happy as a lark and looking forward to hearing from his fairy princess. He couldn't wait to declare his love for her.

About ten minutes later the phone rang and, sure enough, it was Helen—and was she furious! She really gave him hell. She shouted over the phone, "How dare you say those things about me over the air—about how you want to make love to me! How dare you embarrass me like that!" She told him furthermore he was a bastard and a misfit. She told him she hated him and his program. She said she was sorry anyone had given him her office number and told him never to call her again.

Well, now it was Don's turn to be absolutely flabbergasted. He couldn't believe his ears. She kept right on screaming at him and said, "Don't you ever do that to any girl over the air again." She said her reputation was ruined. Then she slammed the phone down.

Don told his audience that he was completely disappointed and disillusioned. He felt like he was going to have a nervous breakdown because he'd really flipped over this chick.

Well, after the program, the phone rang in his office and guess who it was? Yep, Helen, and as nice as could be. She told him how sorry she was and she hadn't meant to hurt his feelings and all her friends were telling her how rude she'd been. She apologized and said maybe they *should* get together.

There was a long moment of silence on Don's end of the phone. Then he said, "Lady, do you know what I would like you to do? Lady, do you?"

. She replied, "No, Don, what do you want me to do—what do *you* want to do?"

"I'll tell you. Lady, you can go fuck yourself!" And with these words he hung up on her.

Well, it might have sounded ungallant of Don, but this "nice" girl, this sophisticated broad with her shitty attitude toward a slightly wild young man who wanted to be friendly, instead of being flattered by all this attention, had humiliated him and hurt his ego.

So it may have been ungallant of me as well, but I had found this a great story, and while he'd been telling it I had gone from fondling his chest to fondling something else. The Dell salesman, rightly feeling he belonged somewhere else, had made tracks for there, and by now Don's big schlong was staring at me from out of his unzipped pants and I was seriously considering giving him a blow job of the first magnitude.

Here was Don, with a large hard-on coming out of h pants, and here I was, on my knees, giving head, when h suddenly realized the time. One minute to air time! There was no time to have him come off—the show must go on!

He shoved his poor penis inside his pants, zipped up, grabbed his shirt, and dashed off. I followed, closing my dress and trying to straighten up my make-up where he had been kissing and smooching with me.

Don dashed through the door to the main studio with his shirt in his hand, me right behind him. We both were practically out of breath. The clock struck two, and you should have seen the change in him. A few minutes before he'd been joking around and acting crazy. He had been the big entertainer, the storyteller, and even the fool—but at the same time, the lover—and now, in a matter of seconds, he'd turned into the fabled disc jockey. He was completely straight-faced. There he sat bare-chested—ignoring the curious studio technicians—and acting like a perfect media person. It was too much. He asked very straight-forward questions and let me say what I pleased to the audience.

I was amazed at his discipline. His questions were excellent, and I tried to be equally professional in my responses. We made a perfect odd couple and we had a great time.

That night, I had to leave for Chicago and was tempted to take Don along—he'd made the offer—if only to complete the orgasm he and I half worked up, but Chicago might be strictly business all day long, and I couldn't afford to give in to temptation, however sweet.

Meanwhile, I had sweet fantasies on the plane!

The Prostitute and the Public

QUESTIONS AND ANSWERS

Is it true that all hookers are Lesbians?

My answer to this question is a firm "no." I would say that Dr. David Reuben in his book about sex makes yet another grossly wrong statement when he writes that all hookers are Lesbians.

It is indeed true that quite often a girl is asked by her customer to partake in a sexual act involving another girl, because a good many men tend to be "voyeurs." They like to watch two women making it with one another. And they generally insist that the two women don't fake it and will assist when one girl eats the other girl. So at the outset, two hookers might start out by faking the Lesbian act, and then it's like anything else. "Try it, you'll like it."

Provided the girls are clean, they might discover that they enjoy sex with another girl, but that doesn't mean they automatically become Lesbians. It just shows that if you teach a woman how to enjoy another woman sexually, she might really like it. For example, if you've never eaten caviar and you eat it, you might very well enjoy it just as much as smoking a cigarette.

There is of course the chance that you might dislike it. Some girls came to me and said, "My boyfriend doesn't want me to perform sex with women, so please don't ever put me in a room with another girl and customer in the bed." If I knew this, I respected her principles.

I've heard some girls say they'd like to try it and others say they like the passive role. They don't mind if another girl goes down on them, since that supposedly doesn't make them Lesbians, which is a wrong statement. Of course, there are some who are real Lesbians and are hookers as a way of living only, without feelings or emotions. But it's certainly wrong to say *all* hookers are Lesbians.

What are the things you would not do with a man?

There are very few things I haven't done with men. I've done practically everything. However, I would prefer not to shit or pee on a man or vice versa.

I basically like clean sex. Nothing turns me off more than dirt and the smell of shit, urine, a sharp body odor or bad breath . . . on a man or a woman. I can imagine that a lot of men, particularly Europeans, don't like to perform 69 with a girl, because the girls don't know what it is to douche, except perhaps French women, who use a bidet regularly. But to douche is something most foreign girls have never heard of. Maybe only if a doctor prescribes it, will they do it. European women say that douching takes away the natural resistance of a woman against any disease in her vaginal area.

In countries like France, Italy and Spain, certain men love to have their wives and girlfriends unshaven, with long hair under their armpits and on their legs. To them that seems to be extremely sexy. A bit of body odor turns them on even more. So deodorants are hardly ever used. But there is nothing more irritating than, for example, eating a fishy-smelling cunt or sucking a non-circumcised cock with a taste of perspiration and left-behind urine. Ugh . . . give me a clean, circumcised cock any time! Please!

What type of girl do most men want as a prostitute and what are their most frequent requests?

I'd say as a rule the average man doesn't ask for a big-breasted woman, as most people assume. Men are mostly attracted to a girl's legs and then look for a girl with a nice ass . . . you know, a nice, soft, sexy ass, preferably not too skinny, something to hold on to. Tits are usually the third thing they look at, and last, but not least, the face, unless a man lays down a lot of money and wants something of a social relationship with her as well, say a dinner date. He will then prefer a charming girl with good looks as well as a certain amount of intelligence.

But most men who visit houses of prostitution are extremely horny, have a limited amount of time and would take any type of a girl I'd suggest, provided they were not homely, of course. They basically wanted the girl-next-door type, however, sexier, yet wholesome. I used to try to stay away from a girl who looks too much like a real whore, but sometimes a shy man gets turned on by an aggressive, whorish-looking chick.

I did have one girl who looked rather sluttish. She wore a wig or a hairpiece, one or two pairs of false eyelashes, a lot of black make-up on her eyes and she was known to wear the shortest, tightest pair of hot pants around her long, sexy legs and shaved pussy. She was insatiable and she was always at my house from ten at night until two or three in the morning.

She was absolutely fantastic in scoring at bachelor parties or big group scenes. She really enjoyed sex and her specialty was blowing guys. She had a way of turning a man on two or three times in one evening. She'd be good, not only for sloppy seconds, but also for final thirds. She could knock 'em off in five minutes. She was one of the few girls who would climax by just sucking a guy off. Somehow, nobody ever complained that she rushed her customers or looked too vulgar, because she really loved her work. She wasn't exactly the type you'd send to the Waldorf Astoria or to the 21 Club to take care of a hundred-dollar John, but she did very well in my house among several other girls.

Most men require a blow job—fellatio—because that is something they hardly ever get at home and if so, very few women know how to give a good blow job. They either scrape the cock with their teeth or don't know what to do. A lot of women are too uptight to have cunnilingus performed on them, or for them to perform fellatio. To them, it's something dirty.

Sex is basic with most women. They feel they are within their rights to refuse to do anything that they consider unusual or contrary to the norm. To them, sex should be a matter of in, up and out. Even though their sexual fantasies might differ, neither husband or wife wants to lose the respect of the other. So most men consider a blow job *not cheating* on their wives. After all, they're not sticking their penis into a woman's vagina. They don't even kiss the prostitute. Those men want to get their climax over with in a quick, selfish way, and yet enjoy a very exciting, one-way treatment.

If, however, the customer requests the 69 position, then he can give the girl satisfaction as well, provided he knows what he is doing. Seven out of ten men are not expert pussy-eaters. They just chew the clitoris like it was a piece of gum. Some men keep fumbling around near the right place and don't know where to put their tongues. They merely tickle you to death. They can't find the "man in the boat" and for that, a woman's tongue is still the best to please another woman.

Another thing a lot of men foul up on is that once they try to perform 69 or go down on a woman, they not only miss the clitoris by miles but they also use their hands in a rough way and stick their fingers with—who knows—dirty nails right up the ass or plunge into the woman's cunt with such a lack of sensitivity that, in many cases, a prostitute would much rather eat cookies or give a blow job than have a man handle her like that. So usually a hooker will tell a John once she finds out he is no expert, "Look, take it easy or leave me alone and let me just do you."

It might seem rude to the customer, but I think it's better that way than have him fool around like a kid in a candy store, provided he pays more and wants to learn. Very often it seems that the man who pays more money expects less, and the man who pays less money expects more (his money's worth!).

Who do you prefer making love with—men or women?
When I was in the business, I would only make love to

a man and have him pay me, but when I was with a woman, I could not accept her money. I love to *give* pleasure to a woman, provided I really dig her emotionally as well as physically, but I really prefer to consummate sex with a man. I could do without making love to a woman for quite some time, but I cannot do without a man for more than forty-eight hours. Then I get frustrated.

What form of sex do you like most? Which position?

I like the 69 position—the French style—where both partners please each other orally. The man is turned around on his left side, with his head facing the woman's cunt, while she lies on her right side with her mouth facing his cock. This, actually, is great foreplay for the final sex act, but even during foreplay, each can reach orgasm, and very intensely. As far as my body is concerned, I prefer to reach a clitoral orgasm as opposed to a vaginal climax. I hardly ever get turned on until the man has warmed up my clitoris. To perform the sex act in the 69 position gives me complete psychological satisfaction, as well as physical fulfillment. To me, there's nothing better than to have a man eat me and stimulate my clit, while I suck his cock and caress his balls. I will usually reach my orgasm at the moment I feel he is about to come, too. I prefer to do this with somebody I really like, with whom I've enjoyed a longer lasting relationship.

A great thing to do is to first have oral sex and then immediately afterwards, if the man is a strong bed partner, to have him put his cock into your cunt, and to get fucked.

I also very much enjoy the position where the man lies underneath me and I sit on top of him. Just before I reach orgasm, I lie flat on his body, stretch my legs and close them, so that his penis, my clitoris and my cunt are simultaneously rubbed together.

What type of penis do you prefer—a big one, average or small? Why?

To tell you the truth, I prefer a big one—the bigger, the better. But it depends on the man. If he's shaped big, he *can* be rough in bed and hurt a woman, while other men are gentle. It's not so much the length that's important to me, but the width, and I think it's a myth when doctors say that the size of a man's organ has nothing to do with the woman's climax.

I've come across women who are built very small and tight. They, of course, couldn't handle a man who was large, but an average woman can take on a well-constructed man. And if the man seems to be too big, then it's just a matter of lubricating her or, maybe, using some vaginal jelly to get her going. I know from experience that once the man is inside her and everything is going smoothly, she will certainly enjoy her sexual activity, and a bigger cock to the smaller, skinnier one. Obviously so, because there is not as much friction with a small cock inside your cunt —once you've known the feeling from a big one filling up your vagina.

Do you think you are a sexually liberated woman? What is your definition of that?

I definitely think I'm a most sexually liberated woman, which is why I'd like to write or give lectures on that subject, answering people who have sexual problems. I do think the definition of a woman who is sexually liberated is one who is willing to try anything and everything once in sex, without discrimination because of age, color, race or gender. She should try it all once, without hang-ups, but with some imagination and flexibility, of course.

It is also important that the woman enjoys, or at least tries to make it good, without regrets or guilt feelings.

Another factor that will make a woman more sexually liberated is to perform the act of love with a partner of her own sex. In other words, I'm talking about bisexuality— giving and receiving pleasure, one woman to another.

Generally speaking, however, giving pleasure to your sex partner and participating and enjoying it all yourself as well, is one of the traits of a liberated woman.

What do you think about group sex? Are you for or against it?

I have done some research on this subject, but it is very difficult to answer properly until I know more.

I do consider group sex good for certain people, particularly for married people who may be slightly bored with each other but are not willing to undertake the final step toward separation. Boredom is still one of the overriding factors which will drive a great many married couples into group sex.

If a swing occurs spontaneously (after dinner or a party, for example), that's one thing. It's an impromptu act, a "let's get together" scene. But if, as a hard and fast rule, we get together at Tom, Dick or Harry's house every Saturday night, and we swing and fuck together with the same group, then I think this could lead to a sick situation, or at least a boring one.

Another vital factor in a group sex scene is that both the male and female partner should have equal fun. However, quite often the woman's body deteriorates after childbearing, while her man is still trim and attractive. What usually happens is that while the man can readily find another girl to fuck, the other swingers are not too interested in fucking his wife. This leads to a "politesse fuck"—a courtesy fuck. Any other man present, if he is a gentleman, will more or less feel obligated to fuck this physically less attractive woman, even though he is not physically attracted to her at all. This *is* a sick scene. If the woman doesn't get a polite fuck, frustrations set in. The physically unattractive wife feels left out, it is painful for her to recognize her husband is enjoying sex with another woman while she is not really getting her end of it, and in her mind, his current behavior is much more a matter of cheating than his occasional jaunt behind her back.

Group sex is good and can only work if everyone amuses himself, each couple secure in the knowledge that they came together and will leave together. There's no taking the partner away for more than just a swing. In other words, there are no emotions involved. It's like going to a prostitute without paying. You do your thing, enjoy a good fuck, you say, "Goodbye, see you the next time around," and go home. In that context, I'm willing to bet that group sex has probably saved quite a few marriages.

THE SCREWED-UP JEWISH
TELEVISION PRODUCER

I was back in Chicago to tape the Marty Faye television show. At that time I still wasn't used to the rough, sarcastic attitude of some television "luminaries." While no one had been able to talk me into a corner, some interviewers had sure tried hard to make a fool of me. On the other hand, I usually found that, whatever the show, the cameramen and crew were really nice to me, and sometimes these guys would be somewhat hilarious in their off-camera behavior.

Before the show, I noticed there was a thin, meek-looking guy in his early thirties, with short brown hair and horn-rimmed glasses, hanging around from the very first moment that I walked into the studio. I was wearing a short skirt— a miniskirt, maybe not fashionable anymore, but it was bright and it would look good on color television—and a tight-fitting sweater. So I attributed his presence to a little horniness on his part. But he finally got the courage to come up to me with the question he obviously had been dying to ask.

"Miss Hollander, I don't quite agree with your saying in your book that most Jewish men are so screwed up."

Laughingly, I asked him what was *his* problem?

"Oh, no, I've got no problem. I just think you're wrong.

I think that a lot of Jewish men are perfectly normal and happily married. I just wanted to make a comment on your book."

I looked at him suspiciously and thought to myself, "There's something bothering this man, or why else would he come to me?" As they say in French, *Qui s'excuse, s'accuse*—"He who excuses himself, accuses himself."

Just before the taping, I asked one of the studio people who the little man was and learned that his name was Irwin and he was connected with the station as a producer of special events programs.

Then it was time to go up for the taping and I stepped up on the rostrum, sure that Irwin's eyes were following each step I took. As I anticipated, Marty Faye's TV technique was to be nasty-funny-sarcastic, but he didn't make a fool of me, or shall I say I didn't give him a chance to do so. I remember even blushing once at some rather raw remarks he made—the kind of talk no one expects to hear on television—but I also remember how proud I was when I walked off the stage, saying to myself, "I think I got my message across to the audience." Indeed, the live audience gave me a nice round of applause and seemed quite pleased with my contributions to the show and how I managed to feint Faye's rather nasty questions. As I was leaving the station, I made a stop at the soft-drink machine to get myself an orange drink and who should come out of the studio, dashing up to me, but Irwin!

He didn't say anything, just stood there shy and bashful. So I finally asked him, "What *is* it that's bothering you, what's your problem?" Meanwhile, the Dell representative who was supposed to take me to the next show—a radio show—was pulling me by the arm and saying "Come on, Xaviera, we have to go." But I felt I had to talk to this little guy because he obviously needed help. So I excused myself for "a minute or two" and took him aside—he obviously wanted to talk to me without anyone else listening in.

We went out into the hallway and I said, "Come on, Irwin, tell me what's wrong."

"You see, Miss Hollander," he began, "I didn't want to admit it, but I think you're right. You might understand the situation I am in . . . It's *true,* Jewish men do have some kind of a problem—at least I do."

Then he proceeded to tell what was wrong. "You see," he began, "I got married about two years ago to a very pretty girl from a poor, Jewish family. We were engaged for about two years and she was the first girl I had ever slept with.

"You know, I myself come from a well-to-do family. I don't hold such a terrifically important job here, after all, but it's honorable and I love my work. Actually, my parents are supporting us.

"My wife was very sexy and horny for about a year before we got married. She was a virgin and during our engagement we used to make love quite often and she used to reach an orgasm and I was very happy with her. Then we got married, and it all changed suddenly."

"What happened then?" I asked, now really sympathetic.

"Well, we actually got married . . . you know, got the license and exchanged rings and vows and were really married; and we took off that same afternoon for a three-week honeymoon in the Bahamas . . . Well, *that* very night, she turned into a piece of ice when I tried to make love to her.

"She said, cool as ice, 'I'm sorry, darling, but I had to fake it all the way through. I really wanted to get married, and I didn't care to whom. It just happened to be you. I didn't want to be a poor little secretary anymore, slaving my hours away behind a silly typewriter, taking orders from a sloppy boss, and now that we're married, I might as well tell you the truth . . . I'm just not that passionate. I was a great actress, I guess. I don't enjoy making love to you and I never really did. I just hated working . . . I'll try to be a good housewife, I really will, provided you give me the security I want.' "

"At least she has been honest with you," I said quietly, "though a little bit too late."

Actually his sad little tale had sent a streak of anger running through me. In my opinion, this woman was a far worse prostitute than I'd ever been. She married dishonestly, not only for money but also to achieve the security and sanctity of marriage. These are the broads who are only looking forward to the house in the suburbs, the furs and diamonds, and in the case of a divorce, the tremendous alimonies.

Many such women, once they're married, neglect their husbands completely, or else honor their sexual obligations towards their husbands once in a blue moon. Others just have sex to produce children. They usually repress their natural sexual desires and their feelings, if they have any for their husbands at all. These are the women, the wonderful princesses, who, once settled down and with all the goodies they want to own, will hardly ever please hubby's sexual desires—up until the moment they see that beautiful big diamond ring from Tiffany's on a girlfriend's finger, or their girlfriend's new mink coat. Then, oh boy, watch out for the sexy approach, because then Momma is out to score! And he—schmuck of all schmucks—without knowing it, is being taken for a sucker again.

These women, I feel, are *negative* prostitutes. And they are the worst type of prostitutes. Sometimes a housewife can be a bigger hustler than a regular hustler.

Anyhow, here was poor Irwin, telling me his sad story, and I really felt sorry for him. He needed my help, or at least some advice. So I asked him, "How is your sex life lately?"

Poor sad Irwin! She was still the only woman he'd made love to. And now the rest of it poured out—his sexual troubles. On top of everything she'd been a virgin and he'd been just as green as she. Other than the usual two or three positions in intercourse that most inexperienced lovers assume, they'd never had oral intercourse or tried any other variations. Up until the moment he had picked up my book, he never had even looked into any books about sex. So Irwin obviously had been oblivious to anything that might show him there were other ways to have sex. He hadn't seen sex magazines. He hadn't seen any stag movies. Of course he'd heard of them, but had never seen any.

So I decided to play God. I instructed him, very firmly: "Either send your wife to a psychiatrist for treatment—I ordinarily don't believe it helps much—or else try to cultivate a more varied sex life for yourself. Try to stimulate your wife a lot more by reading certain sex books and really practice what you learn. Become a dynamite lover! But if nothing else helps and the situation stays miserable, be honest with yourself and go for a divorce. Really Irwin, why stick around if there is no healthy relationship?"

Irwin looked miserable at my advice.

"Sex," I said, now on my liberation podium, "isn't a matter of sticking your penis into a woman and leaving it there for a while, or else simply banging the brains out of your partner and then saying, Ah, ha, I made it! It's a matter of getting turned on emotionally to your partner and of achieving the know-how in lovemaking. Why should such an important human activity be left to what you've heard or else the few obvious things everyone reads about! Try to be such a good lover that your wife loves sex with you, Irwin! Don't be timid, be brave—you can only complain about her if you don't try to make her your very willing bedmate.

"But if you really try, and it doesn't work, then be honest with yourself—there *is* no marriage! You've only one life to live, and you should be living it with someone else . . . at least that's my advice."

"My God, Xaviera," he cried, "you're a regular Doctor Joyce Brothers! You really have helped me."

"I hope so, Irwin. You're a sweet man, and you've acted honorably, and you deserve a better break in life than a clamped-up wife."

I really had to go then, to make the next show, but when I left Irwin, his eyes were shining—that poor, distressed man was really touched by what little advice I'd been able to give him. And in turn he'd made *me* wet-eyed —and I sincerely hope Irwin was able to turn his wife around. If not, I hope he threw the " 'nice' hooker" out the door!

The Prostitute and the Public

QUESTIONS AND ANSWERS

Is there any one particular kind of girl, in terms of background, who is more likely to become a prostitute?

Perhaps at the street hooker level, but not among the better class of call girls.

Some girls who worked for me began their careers as stewardesses on lay-over time; others were secretaries fed up with a nine-to-five monotonous job; married women out to make some extra pocket money or compensate for the salary lost when their husbands lost their jobs, or to pay for an upcoming divorce; or models or actresses without work, usually in the summertime, or girls from abroad like myself, with immigration problems and/or language barriers. What they wanted most was money and independence and not being tied down to a nine-to-five job. I feel that working in a horizontal position and making love beats the hell out of clerking at Macy's, or taking dictation. Those girls certainly were no misfits or didn't come from run-down families.

In your former occupation, you knew some pretty tough characters. Were you very often frightened?

Yes, there were a few times—mostly before I was a madam—when I had good reason to be frightened. And the experience I had in Miami, which is in this book, certainly had its frightening moments. But the real fears I have have nothing to do with isolated experiences.

There are three or four things I'm deathly scared of in

life. One, is to grow old and lonely and miserable or to be dependent on my children, if I ever have any. I would like to have kids but not to rely on them for security in my old age. What I want is to be independently wealthy. I want most of all to have something of my own. Not necessarily to be a millionaire, but to own a house or an apartment. Some place I could sublet and have an income from. I don't want to always have to work my brains out. I'd hate going back to a nine-to-five job. I would like to take a crack at being an entertainer. After doing lectures and tours, I was thinking that perhaps I'd like to star in a one-woman show. I have a good sense of humor and like to convey messages to people. Not just about prostitution—right now, that is the least interesting thing in my life—but what turns me on is the psychological makeup of people. That is what I've tried to do in both my books. I'm sorry some people have been shocked by the stories in these books. I sure didn't make them up.

Another fear I have is of being invalided or crippled. Again I'd hate to think I was dependent on anyone. I'd hate to die in a painful way, but on the other hand I'm not afraid of death. I'm not afraid of committing suicide. In fact, I've tried to kill myself twice. If I ever get that depressed I might even try it again. But I won't do it over any man, but simply because I want to die.

To repeat myself a bit, I really am very much afraid of being poor. I'd only like to be wealthy in the sense that I can afford to live well, in the style I've been accustomed to most of my life. I don't want to die in the poorhouse. I don't want to ask charity from anyone, whether it is the government or an individual. I can't understand the bums who get seventy-five dollars a week for doing absolutely nothing. Or if they can find a job they don't hold on to it. Maybe this is a way of life they enjoy or perhaps they're just apathetic. I want to be ahead of the game.

If you ever have a daughter, would you mind if she became a prostitute?

At first my reaction would be, "Yes, of course I'd mind. I wouldn't want my child to become a prostitute," but then after thinking about it twice, I'd say to myself,

"If she's attractive, if she likes sex, men, independence and money, and if that is what she likes to do, well, let her."

But only if she did it with class. There is nothing more terrible than a cheap prostitute. I would leave it up to her. I'd prefer, however, to see a daughter of mine seek some other way of life. It may be the oldest profession in the world, but unfortunately it is still looked down upon—a so-called degrading way of life. Until people change their minds about this business, I'd rather she would choose another "respectable" profession. But if prostitution made her happy, I'd give her my blessing. I certainly wouldn't say, "Don't do it." But I'd certainly advise her to get out as soon as she'd achieved what she wanted.

In the last century, when girls or boys said they wanted to become actors and their parents had their hearts set on a medical career, say, the children usually met with strong opposition. It was the same thing if a young man or woman wanted to pursue a career as an artist. In those times, that was something strange and untoward, until they became successful, when the parents could be proud of them.

To have a successful prostitute for a daughter is not usually something a parent would be proud of, not even my own mother, who is a rather understanding woman.

Do you believe in romance? Are you a romantic person and, if so, how is it that you are in such an unromantic profession?

Yes, yes, yes, I believe in romance. Hell, I can be terribly schmaltzy. For instance, certain pieces of classical music, such as a violin concerto by Paganini, or Tschaikovsky, or a cello concerto by Bruch, can set me in tears almost immediately.

I *can* be romantic, emotional or hyper-sensitive, but I must admit I was in a business which, generally speaking, did not seem to be very romantic. However, I tried adding some romance, some atmosphere, to my kind of work. I did try to be charming and friendly to everyone who came to my house—to men who had troubles at home or at work; men who were on the verge of nervous breakdowns; and one, even, who was about to commit suicide.

I ran across all types—men who did not know what to do with themselves anymore; they had broken up with their wives and were estranged from their children. Others were just lonely and miserable and had no place to go, while still more had gone through serious business problems. There were, of course, a great number of men who were just out for a good time. I wasn't running a clinic!

With the first type of man, I'd just sit and talk and in some cases, wouldn't even charge, because usually, he had been a good customer until—bam—the ground gave way underfoot and he was without a job or income. This happened with quite a few stockholder friends I had, when quite a few houses simply closed down. I couldn't reject these men just because they were not able to pay. They needed to talk to someone, and one day I knew they would get back up the ladder and compensate me for my kindness.

It is a known fact—and as the old-fashioned expression says—that a good prostitute has a heart of gold. Well, this still does exist. Many times, prostitutes make the best girlfriends. They are, quite often, much more understanding than the average girl, because they experience so much and learn a lot about people. These girls are usually very honest and don't tolerate bullshit, dishonest stories or lying in any form. Again, I'm not talking about the hard-core street girl, but the honest, up-front call girl who has time for each person she services, who gives him his money's worth, emotionally as well as physically.

These girls have certainly added some romance, and I, too, am very romantically inclined. I hope I'll meet the right man some day, a man who I'll really dig. He will have to be intelligent, mature, bright and have a good sense of humor. I would love him to be artistic, or at least have an interest in the arts, but most of all he will have to be human and humane.

JERRY AND ELLY

I was in Phoenix, between major stops in my tour—I had one radio show to do there—and I had some time to myself. I didn't know anyone there, apart from the Dell representative, but I remembered that a good friend in New York had once lived in Phoenix and said that if I ever visited his old hometown, I should look up his best friend there, a very successful lawyer named Jerry.

I don't usually call strangers, but I thought it would be nice to have someone to meet for dinner, or whatever. So I looked up his firm's number and gave it a whirl.

His secretary was the suspicious type and it wasn't till I made it quite clear that I wasn't looking for a lawyer, that I was the friend of his best friend, that she let me speak to him.

He was most cordial over the phone. He'd read my book, so had his wife, and why didn't I come right over and say hello?

Wasn't he busy? I asked.

"Not too busy to meet a famous lady from New York," he replied. Wow, they grow 'em friendly out West!

Actually his office was quite close to my hotel, so after getting directions, I strolled over there.

Jerry was a man in his late forties, well-built, with a most

pleasant—not handsome, but attractive—face. He was bald-
ing and wore long, curly brown sideburns. He dressed very
well and obviously did very well. His office was large and
furnished in excellent taste.

On his large desk, there were three pictures, one of his
wife—a woman around his own age, kind of pretty—another of his daughter, I guessed, and the third either his
son or son-in-law. There was also a picture of this fabulous
house. My friend had told me Jerry was wealthy, but this
looked like a palace!

Jerry showed me another picture of his wife, standing in
front of their house, and I noticed she must have had a
fantastic body, because she was wearing a dress and no bra
underneath and her breasts were standing high and firm and
I could see the nipples through the dress. She certainly
didn't look like she'd ever needed silicone shots. When I
complimented him on her figure, he said, "But, of course,
it's all real, and that is why I'd like her to meet you as well.
Your book has turned the both of us on so much, we're
thrilled that maybe we can get together . . . You know,
Xaviera, the picture of you on the back of your book
doesn't really do you justice. You are far more attractive
in real life, and I sure hope you can find the time to meet
my wife."

I said, "Why not? I'll be in Phoenix for another evening,
although I have a radio interview scheduled for later on
tonight and a supermarket book-signing stop for tomorrow.
Except for that, I'm available. I'll leave it up to you."

"Swell, let me call my wife and discuss this with her.
Meanwhile, how about having a drink with me somewhere
other than here at the office?"

At this point, I was becoming a trifle confused. First he
wants me to meet his wife, now he has time for drinks.
I thought he was so busy, with the phones ringing constantly, that if he could leave the office at all, it'd be for
a short interval to have a drink with me or a quick lunch.
Yet before I realized what was happening, he'd left a message with his secretary that he was going to be out for the
better part of the afternoon. By now it had dawned on me
that I maybe was going to have more than just lunch
with this man. Since I'd had a lousy fuck the night before,

with a TV producer in Kansas City, I suddenly began to look forward to making it with Jerry. I remembered that the Dell representative, who was a cute guy, had offered to buy me dinner, but I thought, "What the hell, I could have a little afternoon fling with Jerry and still have time to have dinner after the radio show."

We went out to a nice restaurant and all through the meal, though Jerry was being very entertaining, I knew we now both had sex on the brain. I felt like having a little excitement, and I was getting really very horny and turned on by Jerry. My cunt was all juiced up and ready for action.

He could have blindfolded me and I would have followed him anywhere, but in this case, it was a lovely, genteel hotel. We didn't have to register or anything. It was most likely a room permanently reserved for his private use and I must say it was done very discreetly. There wasn't any danger of being found out by anyone. No matter what or with whom it happened, he'd still be Mr. Big, an upright, important citizen.

Before going to the hotel, I had told Jerry I needed to stop off at a drug store. I wanted to feel clean all the way after a morning of travel. As we stopped in front of the drug store, Jerry gave me ten dollars without asking me anything. While he was waiting in the car, I went inside and purchased a small portable douche bag and some vaginal douche liquid in raspberry flavor. Now I was ready for whatever the afternoon had in store.

When we got to the hotel room, I went into the bathroom and took a shower (luckily I had a rubber band with me to tie back my hair). Then I douched. I even had a portable toothbrush with me, somewhere in my big handbag. Jerry was very happily surprised that I was such a nut about cleanliness and he took a shower as well.

Then we went at it, like two horny fools. I must say Jerry was a terrific lover. He ate me for half-an-hour and then we performed 69, upside down, inside out. He ate me again and again with his quick, quick tongue. He certainly knew how to find the right spot to turn me on. He pushed his right hand index finger into my rear end, and another one into my vagina, and with his other hand, while eating me, he was massaging my clitoris.

Meanwhile, I was sucking his big hard cock. He was moaning and groaning furiously with pleasure, and each time he held back, pulling his cock out of my mouth to keep from coming, I'd be about to climax all over his face. It was a nice raspberry-tasting liquid that came out of my vagina—like a delicious dessert after lunch, Jerry said, complimenting me. He loved every bit of it. He had to —I had my legs tightly squeezed around his head.

I remember very well the third time I came, he was ready to explode in my mouth. His balls were getting harder and harder and his cock started moving and penetrating back and forth faster in my mouth and in the palms of my hands. But he still was able to hold back.

After he'd made me come three times with his mouth, tongue, and his fingers, vibrating my clitoris quicker than anybody I'd ever been with, I felt like really fucking him. I jumped on top of him and pushed his body flat down beneath me with just his swollen penis standing up. My legs were spread over the bed and I was going to prove to him that I, too, knew what rhythm was all about, especially when I sat on his cock and rocked up and down on it. Then I lay down on top of him with my legs completely straight and close together, squeezing his balls and his penis so tightly that he could hardly move. I was the one who was conducting the orchestra this time. From *adagio* to *crescendo* to *forzando*. Back and forth with my arms underneath his shoulders, all the time blowing kisses in his ears, or kissing his hot mouth, we worked ourselves to a fabulous, simultaneous orgasm—a fantastic explosion with perspiration dripping off our bodies, making them all the more supple.

We were so sweaty and hot that we both took a shower again, together this time, and then started all over again. This time, I tried sitting on his face, half-way hunched downwards so I was on my haunches, half-sitting and half-standing. Jerry was on his back, his legs up a bit, and I balanced myself on top of him, pushing my cunt up and down his upper chest, so my clitoris would tease his mouth. I went up and down, up and down, and we could hear my pussy going squish, squish. While his tongue flicked away at my clit, I held my balance with one hand, holding on to the bedboard, and with the other I tickled his nipples and caressed his navel and groin areas.

After I came once again all over his face, we quickly turned around, and I put two big pillows under my stomach and stretched out on top of them. But instead he moved me to the foot of the bed, and with my ass sticking up in the air he slammed his tremendous cock into my waiting cunt. It was just grand being balled almost non-stop by Jerry and his beautiful thick cock.

That afternoon, Jerry managed to come three times and I lost count. You can well imagine how exhausted we were. But it was very satisfying.

When he drove me back to my hotel, Jerry told me he had been very excited by me and had enjoyed every second we'd spent together. He said he had a special request in mind that he couldn't express until he'd gotten to know me better. He had wanted to find out, he explained, whether I was really all that good in bed and whether my book was just a phoney story or the real thing. I was the best lover he'd ever had, and the book had to be for real.

I thanked him for the praise and said he did "pretty nice work" himself. But what about this "special request"?

So he elaborated. "My wife has only once in her life had a woman make love to her. This was in Spain quite a few years ago. We picked up this young eighteeen-year-old girl, a prostitute as it turned out, who was introduced to us by some Flamenco dancer. My wife was slightly aroused by making love to a woman, but the girl was too innocent, young, and inexperienced. She didn't really turn Elly on. Also, we were all very drunk and Elly doesn't even quite remember what happened. But she has expressed the wish to be with a woman at least once again."

I didn't say anything, and he went on.

"Xaviera, your book is the only book that has ever really turned her on—I mean sexually. She would desire a woman like you very much. Honestly, I didn't quite know at first how to put it to you . . . Now after our session, I feel a lot easier discussing it."

"Exactly what do you have in mind?" I said.

"Would you like to come over to our place tonight after the radio show—that would be approximately ten o'clock —and have a scene with me and my wife? I will come and pick you up and take you to our home. It's about forty-five minutes from the city and I will arrange for you to be back in town at what time you have to be tomorrow."

I told him that besides my radio show I was supposed to appear in a shopping center and sign some of my books early the following morning. He said there'd be no problem. So I decided right then and there to go ahead with the game and go and please his wife. The idea appealed to me. Her stunning body was what turned me on most . . . her face looked sort of pretty from the photographs.

That night, during and after my radio program, some nasty old ladies called the station with some religious objections, saying that it was a sin to have a prostitute on a radio program and that it was a sin their sons were probably listening to me. Some even started quoting the Bible, about this and that. I answered them by borrowing a line from the Book of Matthew, which, as I paraphrased it, says, "Thou shalt not prostitute thy daughter . . ." but, I argued, it doesn't say, "Thou shalt not prostitute thyself." This didn't make too much sense, I realized, but it got those ladies in a huff!

Also somewhere else in the Bible, it says that the civilians and the harlots are the first ones to enter the Kingdom of Heaven. So that meant, as far as I could see, that the poor and humble along with the hookers and the whores had a secure place in heaven. I doubted, I said, that the same could be said for religious lunatic ladies. This wasn't the way, I knew, to make friends with those callers, but at least it got some laughs.

Jerry came by to pick me up in his Mercedes and we had a pleasant drive out to his home. Along the way, he said, "Xaviera, I know you're out of the business, but this is a very big favor you're doing me and I'd like you to know I appreciate it." With that he took out an envelope and when I looked inside, I saw three one-hundred dollar bills. "I can't accept this," I said. "Please, no money."

"You didn't ask for it," he said, "I'm offering it—as a

present. I didn't have time to buy you one and this is my humble substitute."

"Okay, on that basis alone I will accept it. Thank you, you're very kind."

"No," he said, "it's *you* who are being kind."

Jerry drove his car up a beautiful driveway and when we entered the house, I realized it *was* palatial. The furniture was obviously done by a decorator. Evidently these people weren't to the manner born, but they'd learned about elegance and culture. I noticed that they also fancied art and owned quite a number of originals, but here, or so it seemed to me, it was obvious they weren't quite sure where to put what. However, they had a collection of paintings of their family, spread over one wall. That was attractive in its way but somewhat static. This place, I couldn't help thinking, would make a great brothel—with paintings of the girls on that wall!

Jerry's wife, Elly, finally appeared from somewhere in the house and I'd been right about her body. It was fantastic, or so it seemed—she was wearing a long, luxurious, multi-colored nightgown. She was no longer pretty, being somewhat faded looking, but seemed very pleasant. Jerry left us at the bar to get acquainted, saying he had some business to talk over on the phone and would be "a while."

Elly discussed my book with me in a rather constrained way. Contrary to what Jerry'd told me, she'd only read parts of the book and seemed mainly concerned with whether or not it was all true. I assured her it was. She also wanted to know if, despite all my experience, I still enjoyed sex. I told her it made me enjoy sex even more, since I pretty well knew the score by now, and was pretty selective as a result.

"I just don't understand it," Elly said with a sad shake of her head. "I enjoy sex but I'm still, after all these years, very uptight about it." She then went on to tell me she'd made love with a woman one time in her life, but she was pretty drunk during the whole thing and couldn't remember one bit of the affair. Jerry wanted her to try it at least once, she said.

I, of course, knew this, and nothing she was saying was

very encouraging for this evening's little adventure. It was going to take quite a campaign to get her into a properly swinging mood.

We were still seated at their bar, a huge elaborate affair, us talking at one end and Jerry making his phone calls at the other end. Elly went into the kitchen to get some snacks and chocolates and cookies and brought them out along with a fresh orange juice.

I was being treated with great tact and courtesy, I felt, and Elly didn't seem morbidly curious about my kind of life and she certainly wasn't hostile or condescending. After all, I was there on Jerry's invitation and he must have called her and announced what was to happen this evening. However, I knew he hadn't told her that we'd spent the afternoon in bed together and I certainly wasn't bringing her up-to-date about it.

When Jerry finally hung up the phone, I could see by his grinning face and eager eyes that he was very much in the mood for another session. He and I had worked out a code in the car: the moment he'd say, "Xaviera, would you like to freshen up a bit?" it would be the time for me to go to the bedroom and get ready for the big seduction scene. Just how, and when—well, it would be up to me to approach Elly.

To my surprise, however, we continued to chat for another half-hour at the bar about my publicity trip and the book and then it was Elly who suggested we all go for a "skinny dip" in the pool. Jerry gave me directions on how to find my bedroom, and it was only then that I realized the immense size of their house—a palace so large and expensively furnished that it seemed ludicrously big for two people whose children had grown up and now had families of their own. This house would be perfect for orgies, for bacchanals, for tremendous parties, instead of just being a huge home for two people on their own.

Jerry had assured me in the hotel room that he loved his wife deeply, but simply needed variety at times. That at least was a positive factor in their relationship, especially when two people grow older. Having all that money and a good marriage certainly made their life more comfortable. I hardly knew them, but it didn't appear to me as if they had a lot of friends . . . somehow I saw loneliness in their eyes, as well as boredom.

Upstairs I found my room without any trouble. It was handsomely furnished and on the king-size bed there were fresh, crisp, bright-striped sheets, and fluffy bright towels in the bathroom. The pink wash basin was heart-shaped and had golden spigots, shaped like a swan's head. I quickly unpacked my small suitcase, put my toilet articles out, took a shower and douched, brushed my teeth, wrapped a large orange towel around my body, and barely ten minutes later I was padding barefoot through the big, marble living room towards the bar. Jerry and Elly weren't there, so I went looking for them. As I familiarized myself with the house, I realized that they must have two pools, one indoors and one outdoors. I saw the outdoor one first and it was empty, or looked that way from where I was standing in the house. After five minutes of searching for them, I found the other pool, and Elly and Jerry were standing on one side of the pool, both wrapped in big towels. Jerry encouraged me to get right into the water. "Have no fear, honey, it's nice and warm," he said. Needing no further encouragement, I dropped the towel from around me and did an elegant skinny-dip off the side—there was no diving board—in good form, if I do say so myself: arms stretched forward, head in between, body smooth and flexible, knees slightly bent. Jerry applauded the dive, and Elly stood there smiling at me, and I challenged them to join the fun. Jerry removed his towel and dove into the water near me and a second later was standing right next to me. He didn't touch me, and we both stood there, watching Elly.

Still on the side of the pool, Elly dropped her towel and she had on a crocheted turquoise bikini underneath. I must confess her body was every bit as fantastic as I'd expected and I certainly got very turned on to her. She didn't dive into the water, she walked in very ladylike, via the steps, and sat down on them. Neither one of us was wearing a bathing cap. With my hair, long and straight to my shoulders, it didn't matter if it got wet, but hers was light blonde and curly, and I could tell she'd just been to the hairdresser that day. So, in order not to spoil her hairdo, I surmised, she just sat down on the stairs, her body half-covered by the water.

Jerry and I swam for about fifteen minutes straight, racing back and forward like a couple of bare-assed kids—crawl, butterfly, backstroke—making our bodies feel smooth and strong. Elly just watched us. Then, slightly out of breath, Jerry and I moved to either side of Elly and talked softly to her for a while, both of us trying to excite her mind as well as her body. Jerry started to massage her back—he'd mentioned to me on the way to his house that his wife loved a good backrub—because that would be a good way to turn her on. However, he hadn't anticipated the swimming pool scene, and this might be a new way of getting her started.

The water made us all feel light and it was amazing how lovely our bodies looked. Jerry's cock looked twice as big as usual in the water. Elly had a wonderful body with a very flat belly, and for a woman of about forty-eight, she really looked sensational. I even envied her breasts because, through her bikini top, I could see how high and firm they were. Jerry could see how I was digging his wife and, in particular, how I dug her big tits. This is something I really like—a woman with firm, big breasts. A mother complex, maybe?

When Jerry insisted on her swimming in the nude as we did, she slowly pushed her straps down her shoulders and we entered the water together. The water was warm but I could feel her body shiver in my arms when I placed one arm around her midriff while with the other I massaged her back. I softly scratched her shoulder blades with the tips of my long nails. She was getting excited, I could see —there were goosebumps on her arms—but when Jerry finally, gently, undid the back straps of her bikini halter and removed the top completely, it was me who was suddenly excited. I couldn't help but stare at her nipples, large and erect in the center of a pair of beautiful big boobs, so beautiful that many a young girl would have to be envious of her. This woman's body was out-of-sight and this was only the beginning of our play. I could hardly wait for her to strip off her panties.

As Elly's slender legs were stretched out in the water, she

pushed up her flat belly above the water to leave a puddle
of water around her navel. She seemed shy and almost
childlike. She turned around in the water and, resting on
her arms, turned her back to us, her head just above water.

What was most appealing to me—even more than Elly's
great body—was her shyness. There is nothing that turns
me on more than genuine innocence, and I could see she
wasn't faking it. So Jerry and I decided to have another
race while Elly worked on straightening out her head, because she obviously was trying to overcome her embarrassment at the situation.

She surely knew what was going to happen next. Once
her bra top was removed, she certainly would have to take
off her bottoms as well, and from there on, we'd see what
would develop in the pool. She was of two minds, I was
sure, like a woman who's afraid of being raped and yet is
secretly looking forward to the experience.

When Jerry and I finished doing a few more lengths of
the pool, we swam to the spot where Elly was standing
by the steps. We hadn't planned it that way but we embraced her simultaneously and kissed her—one in each ear
—and then together pulled off her bikini. It happened so
abruptly she didn't even have a chance to protest.

I could feel her hips shiver in my arms; she was obviously dying to have it happen to her and looked positively
naughty now, like a little girl about to do some mischief.

Once her bottoms were removed, she revealed a splendid
triangle of black pubic hair. I noticed that she had trimmed
it, but it was still nice and full. In the water it seemed
even bigger and darker, and her tits looked fuller and firmer.
Very groovy.

When I looked down at my hands, I saw that they were
all crinkly from the water. We must have been in the pool
for nearly an hour and pretty soon I'd have to start making
advances to her and get her out of the water, because I
wanted to do more than just kiss and caress her breasts
while we were in the pool. I was looking forward to doing
my thing "all the way."

I remember pushing Jerry away, rudely almost. I realized
a moment too late I shouldn't have done this because he
might feel left out, and I knew he was going to feel even

more left out of the game later on in bed, when Elly would be my victim all the way. But it was time for some action.

I put myself in front of Elly and held her by the shoulders with one hand, while pushing her bottom up with the other, and began to kiss her hair, earlobes, and neck. Her hair was still mostly dry because the upper part of her body had remained out of the water. I pushed her buttocks up higher and ordered Jerry to support her underneath her back, and then I dived in the water and began to kiss her triangle, putting my tongue all the way into her wet cunt, blowing water and hot air.

Now I told Jerry to hold her even higher so she could lay flat on her back on top of the water, and I made him push her pelvis and her pubic arch even higher so that it was stretched above the water while she was spread-eagled with her legs sort of floating on the surface. I then kissed her from her neck to her nipples to her navel, all the way down, and pulled her legs further apart, wrapping them around my body.

With one hand teasing her clitoris, bright pink and very easy to find, and the other hand up between her buttocks, I kissed her between her legs. Her heavenly porch opened and closed itself with every fast movement of my tongue. And since Jerry used all his fingers on me that afternoon, I figured he must have tried this with his wife and she'd enjoyed it. So now I had my hands inside her every place they might be able to do some good. I could feel the spasms of her body as she reacted to my mouth and exploring hands.

Jerry was obviously a much more experienced lover than his wife. She had been married for twenty-eight years, she'd told me, but it was nice to know there were still certain things she didn't know and was willing to learn.

So the time had come for us to get out of the water and continue the lesson in a drier place. We dried each other off with the big towels lying around the poolside. I slowly toweled Elly off, touching every part of her body. She cuddled up in my arms and smiled girlishly. The two of us walked back into the house in a close embrace, like two young lovers.

We'd forgotten all about Jerry, who was picking up the

pipe that he'd left by the side of the pool. Once we were in their bedroom, I took the towel from Elly's body and kissed away the last drops of water from her belly, which lay between her navel and her mons veneris. She propped herself up on some pillows and got comfortable; meanwhile Jerry came in and sat down next to us on the bed, staring at us. I shooed him away and he went around the large room, adjusting the lights, and then lit the fireplace, which crackled cosily. Then he put a record on the stereo. The music wasn't to my taste, but I know he meant well.

There was just enough light to see what was happening. I didn't make a move to go down on Elly right away because I wanted first to put her in the right mood, so I began caressing her. Shyly, in a soft voice, she asked me a question about my book, a copy of which was on her night table. "What scene excited you most when you wrote the book, Xaviera?"

I answered and it seems that we were both turned on by the same scene—the one that took place in a nudist camp. Here I'd described the woman I called my "Red Flame," whom I seduced by the side of the swimming pool, and what had turned Elly on most was where I wrote about performing cunnilingus on the "Flame" while her husband watched us (he later on gives her a finishing fuck). I remembered this scene very well and it was particularly vivid after the tender way Jerry and I had prepared Elly a little earlier out at the pool. For that matter, maybe the scene in the book had made her suggest that we all go skinny-dipping to start things off.

When I picked up her copy of the book, I noticed that the chapter where this nudist swing scene takes place was rather dog-eared, so obviously this really was her favorite part in the book. On a hunch I took the book and began to read the scene aloud, in what I hoped was a sexy voice and as if it were really happening at that moment.

I sat on the edge of the bed holding the book with one hand and with the other, I was playing with Elly's breasts. Between pages, I blew soft kisses in her ear.

Meanwhile, inspired by my dramatic reading abilities, Jerry's cock was growing to gigantic proportions, almost bigger than it was that afternoon. This turned me on plenty, but Elly turned me on even more, and since I'd already had so much cock today, I decided not to make her upset by fucking Jerry but rather to concentrate my attentions solely on her.

Jealousy, by the way, is something which often happens when three people swing who are not used to swinging. The man loves watching another woman make it with his wife or girlfriend, but that is all he can do in most cases. He has to be strictly a voyeur, because the moment he shows affection to the other girl in the triangle, his wife gets jealous or angry. Jerry, though, was being very tolerant, staying away from the two of us.

After I'd finished reading part of that chapter, I could feel Elly trembling with unconcealed excitement and anxious as hell for me to make love to her, just as I'd done with the "Flame." Jerry had started jerking himself off meanwhile— his cock, rigid and stiff, his hand tightly wrapped around it, moving up and down. He was willing to remain a spectator and this was perfectly alright with me since, when I concentrate on a woman, the man ceases to exist for me —except at the end, when I get very horny and want to feel a hard, big cock inside my body.

So I spread Elly's legs apart, then placed them around my head, and started chowing down on her, forcing my mouth onto her clitoris. Her clit was nice and big and, fortunately, the "man in the boat" did not give me any trouble. I found him right away with my forefingers, as I held the lips apart to reveal the wet, bright pink interior.

I felt a tightness when I moved my fingers into her smooth, lubricated cunt, meanwhile holding onto her clitoris with my tongue and the sucking movement of my mouth. With one hand, I pushed my finger (with the one short nail, for just this purpose) in deeper and deeper, and then quickly out again. Then my fingers caught her cunt lips gently between thumb and index finger, and I massaged them with a circular motion that became lighter and lighter, and the lubricating cunt juice began to flow wetter and wetter. With my forefinger, I tickled the end of her clit so that the "man in the boat" would really begin to get excited and I could feel him dance like a boat, bobbing up and down upon the wild waves in the ocean. He began to dance faster and faster, like a *"harvah,"* as they say in Yiddish, until finally, I could feel her shake and tremble, even deep inside her warm cunt where my other finger had once again penetrated.

She was tight for a woman of her age, especially one who'd given birth to two children. Elly was almost as tight as a girl who'd just lost her virginity.

Her body began to contract as if having spasms; she pulled my face deeper inside her and then it came—an overwhelming orgasm, and her moistness dampened my hands and face. In that moment, I was sure, she was utterly satisfied. Her body was drenched with perspiration and her hair was damp with all the curl out of it.

Jerry was extremely excited but he kept very quiet about it, and the two of us watched him as he finished masturbating and almost proudly dropped the thick, white load from his swollen cock on his own belly, and sat back sighing, relieved.

As for Elly, I even had seen the nipples of her breasts stand up erect just before she came. This by the way, is how you generally can tell if a woman really has reached a climax, or if she's just faking it. Just before she comes, her nipples may become quite extended and after she has reached her orgasm, she sometimes gets goosebumps all over her body. Her nipples will remain hard for a little while, and then go soft again.

Jerry went into the bathroom and Elly took this opportunity to whisper to me that it had been an awful long time since she'd been "really turned on like tonight." She said she had never been unfaithful to her husband, but somehow, she just had become less passionate over the years. This didn't mean they didn't love each other any more, but they were just sexually bored with one another.

The fact that Elly was so easily aroused by me could very well be a psychological factor but it was clear that she *was* very much turned on and also intrigued because it was something altogether new. She begged me please to let her make love to me this time. This hadn't been part of my lesson plan, but it showed a lot of progress and I readily agreed to the switch in roles. She kissed me, sucked my tits, caressed my body, and even went as far as to go down on me. She wasn't really good at it—couldn't find my clit—but with my guidance she became more skillful. At first I couldn't reach a climax, but finally I achieved it by having her climb on top of me. I had her mount my knee like a rider straddling a horse. I pushed her body up and down, squeezing her legs tightly. I came by squeezing my clitoris against her thighs, legs around legs, holding on in a passionate grip. From her cries, I guess we both came simultaneously.

Jerry was now back and acting very neglected. Twice was enough for his wife. Had he forgotten he'd had me *three* times that very afternoon? I wasn't really in the mood to fuck him because my head was all filled with wanting his woman again, over and over. And besides, he'd brought me out to ball her, hadn't he? I just wasn't ready for cock yet.

However, to avoid a scene, I told him that tonight I would be something of a voyeur myself and that I would "teach them some new tricks." We began with the position where a big pillow was placed beneath her ass and her legs were placed high up, wrapped around his shoulders. As it happened I did help out by putting my tongue up his ass, giving him an excellent ream job by sticking my tongue as far into his rear as I could while he fucked her.

Next I taught them the "zig zag" way, which calls for her to lie on her right side and he on his right side, so they were together, spoon-fashion, but instead of their legs straight behind one another, she would make a turn and throw her left leg at a 45-degree angle backwards and then move her body away from him, her head almost outside the bed, while he would push her ass very tight against his crotch, slamming his cock into her. In this way he could penetrate deeper into her.

She really kept fucking and fucking him at a rapid speed, until I imagine she'd gotten a bit tired, and twenty minutes later, now with her perched up on top of him, still neither one of them had come.

As the resident lay analyst, I decided that what was missing was intrigue. His wife, who had been with him so long, couldn't turn him on as much as I had that afternoon.

After Elly had fucked Jerry for about an hour in all

kinds of positions, she climbed off of him and felt her pussy with her hand, asking him kind of wryly, "I thought you just came, or didn't you?"

This was amazing. Here was a woman married to a man for twenty-eight years, who had never had sex with another man, and who still doesn't know what kind of sexual rhythm her husband has or whether he's come or hasn't come. She obviously had no idea how he clicked; she was just his faithful old love-machine.

If a man told me he came, I would know it. I could tell by the sweat on his body, the spasms of his movements, by the tempo of his breathing. I could even tell sometimes by the pulsations of his penis inside me. Certainly I'd feel the jism in my warm cunt. I wouldn't have to check with my hand to make sure.

I felt sorry for her and said, "Elly, suppose I take over and eat you up a little? You just lie back, relax . . . you must be exhausted. I will close up your nice little pussy again, and you'll get all excited and gush your hot juice again. Meanwhile Jerry can fuck me through the back entrance, and that way, we can all come together."

I moved Elly to the middle of the bed. We turned off all the lights this time but lit a candle instead, and then I started eating her more ferociously than ever. God, was it exciting feeling her clit growing bigger in my mouth!

Jerry first massaged my clit with a gentle motion, and then he got behind me and entered me from the rear, my hips in his tight grasp. Held that way, his cock seemed like a sharp knife going through me, even bigger than that afternoon. He certainly got to me with it.

The bed was rattling while Jerry banged away at me and Elly was letting go little screams of pleasure as my tongue gobbled up her little knot. Jerry's cock occasionally would slip out, leaving me unfilled, teased, waiting, but not for long.

Now and then I could feel the head of his cock probe into my ass, and with the help of some human spit and some Koromex Jelly, he managed to go that route without hurting me, while I was still bent forward on hands and knees chomping up Elly.

And so, with Jerry's cock buggering me from the rear-end, his left hand caressing my nipple, his right fingers playing with my swollen clit, we all reached our orgasm at the same time and fell in a heap on the bed utterly tired, but very satisfied.

My goodness, it had been a long day, but Jerry managed to get me to the supermarket on time the next day. Among other things, I was asked if I was enjoying my stay in the Southwest. With a broad smile, I replied, "Yes."

The Prostitute and the Public

QUESTIONS AND ANSWERS

Miss Hollander, we've heard you want to give lectures now that you've retired and your book is a success. What would be the subject of your lectures? Would you enjoy lecturing, and do you have a message to convey to young people in particular?

Yes, I'm preparing lectures and taking as my subjects: the myth and reality of prostitution; female sexuality; the psychology behind sex; sexual aberrations; what turns people on and—just as important—what turns them off. Sort of "how to—do, feel, enjoy . . ." lectures, really. However, my basic theme would start with prostitution itself, and from that platform, I would cover all the other subject material.

The message I would hope to convey, especially to the American woman, would be how to "Hang up your hang-ups!"—be more understanding, be more tolerant and sexually-liberated—how to really relax and enjoy sexual activity and pleasure, both from her own personal standpoint and that of her partner.

Sexual revolution is taking place right now. Sex is great, joyful and clean, and is no longer considered forbidden or "dirty." I want to bring about some new sexual enlightenment. The proof that society is ready for sexual advice is shown, for instance, in the statistics for divorce, separation, patients using tranquilizers and visiting doctors and psychiatrists with their emotional ailments, which are usually related to sexual hang-ups. The root cause seems to be an inability to adjust to a sexual relationship caused, in many cases, by too little sex education within or outside marriage, and the very mistaken impression that sexual enjoyment and fulfillment is the exclusive privilege of the male.

Psychiatrists, however, are on their way to a better understanding with their patients. For example, in a recent article, one psychiatrist describes a new form of sexual therapy—weekend encounter groups, which are taking place in some of the major U.S. cities, where sex is utilized to treat such problems as frigidity, impotence and premature ejaculation—so-called sex clinics.

How come you're thinking about going on a lecture tour, giving talks on subjects like female sexuality, liberated sex, the myth and reality of prostitution? What can you teach people about sex that we can't? For instance, as a happily married housewife, I can just as easily describe how to please a man as you can. Why is it that they would choose you and why are you such a success?

It's very easy to explain. You, as a housewife, supposedly faithful and monogamous, know maybe how to please one particular man, your husband. But that's just one type of man. There are hundreds of different guys, with different sexual fantasies, sexual traumas and sexual appetites. I've dealt with masochists, sadists, fetishists, impotence, voyeurs, exhibitionists—all types.

My range of experience in life is a lot larger, and I think I have a lot more material to discuss and contribute than just how to turn your husband on. There's more to sex than just being aware of what makes one man tick sexually.

I'm sure it would take you a long time to discover how to treat other types of men, and I'm just as sure you don't want to find out about it. You'd better leave the lecture to me!

Do you really feel more "respectable" now that you're retired?

Hell, yes.

I noticed one thing—when you're up, you're everybody's

favorite. When I was down—i.e., in the eyes of society, a known hooker or ex-jailbird—I was no longer good enough to be invited to any social gathering. This wasn't due to the law chasing me around, because certain acquaintances knew where they could get hold of me any time. They were afraid I'd come to a party and start passing out my business card, looking for business. Secondly, they were afraid to introduce me as "Madam X." "What does Miss Hollander do for a living?" "I am running a brothel," I'd always answer, since I hate to lie.

But now that I'm retired and have become a celebrity, the author of a famous best-selling book with publicity tours and lectures included, I get invitations from people like Ben Gazzara, Terry Southern, actors and authors asking me to their parties and even asking if they can include my name on their invitation lists. Journalists ask my opinions about Women's Lib, politics, Vietnam, etc. Various people want to include me in fund-raising parties. "We're giving a party here," "We're giving a party there," "Can we use your name, please?" N.O.W., the National Organization of Women, an organization which used to be very much against prostitution—or as they used to call the profession, the Oppressed Sisterhood—wrote me a letter. It came from a representative in Connecticut, asking me to deliver a lecture on female sexuality, and saying that there'd be a thousand women present to hear my views. The fee was only fifty dollars, but the lecture would be, for me, a matter of prestige. When I told the lady I was about to leave the United States forcibly, she even went so far as writing a long letter to the head of the U.S. Immigration Department, petitioning to keep me in the country. Once X. was nothing but a stupid hooker, but now she's a celebrity fully able to discuss not only what she wrote about, but many other things as well. I can now talk knowledgeably about what turns people on, what makes them tick, their sexual problems, how to save a marriage, etc., from my experiences with thousands of men and women over the last few years.

ST. LOUIS BLUES

St. Louis, Missouri, is—to the best of my knowledge—
the only American city where there has been an attempt to
ban my book.

I wasn't there when this happened—I'd already departed
these shores—but I do remember St. Louis as the city to
which I seem to have brought the most controversy. I
recall one live radio program I was on where the calls
were coming in like an avalanche of outrage. How dare a
prostitute (retired or not) be on the airwaves! How dare
anyone publish her book! How dare such language be allowed on the air!

As a matter of fact, I didn't mince terms on the air but
I certainly didn't use four-letter words or any vulgarisms. I
used clinical terms like cunnilingus, fellatio, oral sex, and
the like, and if this offends people's morality, they must
be living in the Dark Ages. I simply have to attack this
kind of morality, or at least try to straighten it out as a
warped way of thinking. If discussing our double standards
and hypocrisy in sexual matters freaks out people—shocks
them—it simply means they're so square in their attitudes
and uptight and frustrated in their ability to express their
emotions that it's long past the time they were told the
truth over the public airwaves. Their problems are that

their receivers—their brains—have gotten rusty as a result of intellectual pollution, otherwise known as stupidity.

These same people probably got equally agitated when, a few weeks prior to my visit, they read in the papers that a liberal high school teacher—a female—had engaged a prostitute to come and give a lecture at a local high school as part of the school's sex education program. This had created a terrible fuss, but the newspaper reports had neglected to mention that this same teacher had, as part of the same program, arranged to show a stag movie in which every conceivable way to have sexual intercourse was shown. She had also shown a film on childbirth.

The films hadn't gotten her into any trouble, but the scheduled visit of a prostitute sure did! She was fired for her planned action. For all I know, she may have been reinstated by now—I certainly hope so—but it's really something to think about. Which might be potentially more unsettling for these kids—seeing a film *made* for prurient interest full of fucking and sucking and probably joyless sex, or hearing a hooker explain her way of life? Personally I think that kids who've reached the age of sixteen or seventeen are probably pretty well-informed about sex, and neither the film nor the prostitute's lecture would bother them in any way, but the idea of a human being talking to kids about her life strikes me as strictly educational. More so, certainly, than pictures of people being brutally killed on TV or in films.

The next day I went to a radio show which was nice and close—just a block away—from my hotel. Again the disc jockey was a little Jewish guy. (Don't ask me why, but I always seem to run up against little Jewish men; it seems I always get to like them and we get along extremely well.) But unlike Don, the wild man and the wildest deejay in the Midwest, this one seemed very troubled and intro-spective. And what was memorable was not the show I did with him—which was kind of uneventful—but the therapy session we had before and after the show.

He seemed a little nervous, so I asked him if anything was the matter. Shortly before the show started, he finally got it out. "Miss Hollander, you're about the only person I'd dare explain my problem to. I'll be honest with you. I've been married about eight years and I've been very selfish because of my career. I've neglected my wife's interests and hobbies. We've gone to parties together and it's always been *me* who's been the center of attention. Everybody would say, 'Hey, how are you?' You know, I'm the big deal famous disc jockey and she is nothing other than Mrs. So and So.

"She is a very pretty lady, very faithful and very much in love with me. The pure 'Jewish American Princess,' but the type of 'princess' who is an exception to most of them: she also gives as well as she takes. In other words, she is a good housekeeper, wife and mother of my two kids. She saw to it that I ate the food I really like, and made sure in the winter I wore my coat closed and wore a scarf around my neck, and thick gloves.

"I went from one mother to another. From the *Yiddisha* momma, who was my mother, to my wife, the Jewish American Princess. And if she wasn't a princess, I certainly made her a princess. I spoiled her—but materialistically, not with my love.

"Yet, I did love her, but I also neglected her in my selfish way. She made love to me any time I wanted to, but I do remember there were moments that *she* was in the mood and I didn't have time for her or show interest in her."

While listening to this man, I felt a lot of empathy with his wife. When I'd been engaged to Carl, I went through the same thing. I was in love with the man, giving and doing everything for him. Whenever he felt like going to bed with me, I submitted, even though my heart was breaking sometimes, or I was sad. But whenever I needed sex, especially when our relationship was going badly and sex was about all I had to look forward to, he was the one who refused me and said he had no time because he had work to do. So in this instance I could feel for both parties involved—this disturbed guy and the wife he says he neglected—since I understood both points of view.

We'd been talking about ten minutes and I still didn't know what was really bothering him. I asked him what exactly the problem was. "I've got to tell you something I don't even dare tell my close friends or colleagues here," he answered, after a moment's hesitation. "Last week, my wife came to me and she was pretty upset. She said, 'I'm going to see my psychiatrist and I've got to talk to him urgently. I'm all confused!' With just those words she went out, leaving me guessing. A week has gone by with me still up in the air about what's going on, but tonight before I came to the radio station, she confessed that she'd been having a love affair on the side. The first time in eight years' marriage that she'd slept with another man!"

I knew his wife was, as he said, a pretty girl, because there was a picture of her on his desk. And judging from her picture—she had a natural smile on her face—I imagined she was a friendly, easygoing person. So having an affair must have meant his neglect had driven her up the wall.

He went on: "We have a neighbor called John, who used to pay a lot of attention to my wife whenever we met on the street or in the supermarket. And he's, of all things, a Catholic—in other words, a *goy*.

"We didn't socialize together—you know, we Jews usually stick together, just like anywhere else in the world. So I was literally amazed when she told me she had had an affair with this Catholic man—had been his mistress!

" 'Darling,' she said, I must confess that I've been cheating on you. We've been married eight years and I'm still very much in love with you, but something is wrong—our marriage is going on the rocks. We've had too many arguments lately . . . You've been so busy building up your career and being the famous man, the center of attention, you've left me far behind you. You've hurt me so much . . . unknowingly, and I know I can't blame you too much because that's your character. You don't mean to hurt people. You're outgoing and spontaneous and I'm more the introvert, who likes to stay at home and bake cookies, and prepare your breakfast and a kosher dinner.

" 'Darling, I am a woman and I want to prove myself again. I need love and affection and you've neglected me altogether. I've been thinking a long, long time about it and I've flirted with men at parties, but something always said

"No, no don't do it." I was always afraid I'd hurt our relationship. I do believe you've been faithful to me . . . but I've gone out and slept with a man. And this man—I might as well tell you who it is—is our Catholic neighbor, John.' "

At this point, my friend said, he could have hit the ceiling. But he somehow kept calm, and the next thing she told him amazed him even more. " 'I must say that the first thing I noticed when I went to bed with him was that he's not circumcised, obviously because he's a *goy*. It was different than yours, because there was something extra to it. And he's been very nice to me. I did enjoy sex with him and I've reached climaxes over and over again. But even so, there was something empty about the relationship. He's married and I'm married and, after a few times with him, I felt he was just using me. He didn't love me as much as I wanted him to.

" 'Each time, after we'd slept together, I noticed his attitude change. Well, what was I after all, just an inexperienced neglected Jewish housewife, who'd never slept with anyone other than her husband! You know that you and I didn't have very much experience. . . .

" 'He taught me a few new things in bed, but I'm too ashamed to even tell you about them or to even try them with you, because actually we haven't even had sex much together lately.

" 'I've physically enjoyed every bit of him, but it started to hurt more and more when I realized he was using me, and was just having some fun in teaching me the ropes. It was all part of his game—the game of hunting new women, preferably frustrated little housewives. Anyway, to me, it was good for my ego, even though it only lasted a month. That's exactly how long it lasted and I've only seen him during the day. He used to sneak over on his lunch hour while you were on the radio. Sometimes I'd even leave the radio on while you were on the air and it was just like you were there and saying to me, 'Go ahead and do it.' "

This was the end of the confessional between him and his wife. He'd left right after they'd had this discussion, and came to the radio station. Confused and shattered, he didn't even know how he drove over without crashing the car.

After he'd told me all this, he then said, "Yeah, I guess you, as an honest prostitute, must have come across a lot of men with problems."

"Yes, I have indeed, but the amazing thing is that I have come across lots more unhappy people, not by being a prostitute, but by rapping with press people and fans on this publicity tour. Somehow, they seem to become more relaxed and open and if they have any problems, they usually tell me about them. They generally start out by asking me to autograph their books for either their boy-friends or girlfriends or relatives, and then before I know it, they've started telling me their problems. They confess to me about their lives and their love affairs. That's why I could never be like Germaine Greer and say about my publicity tours: 'I hated every moment of it, the getting up early in the morning, and the rushing around, what a con-stant hassle.'

"I've learned so much about people and about what makes them click, during all my various visits to the many different cities in the U.S.A. No matter how successful a person you are, inside that person the heart can be bleeding. . . ."

"I know," he said. "That's the way I feel right now."

I wanted to ask him what he was going to do about his wife, but it was time for us to go on the air, and during the program I understood why his interview with me seemed to be kind of half-hearted on his side. I'm sure his revela-tions to me before the show had drained everything out of him.

When the show was over, I asked him how he thought it had gone, and he smiled weakly and said, "Fine. You've become very good at this." We were standing there, a bit awkward with each other, so I asked him the question I felt he wanted to be asked. "What are you going to do? Have you thought of calling your wife and talking it over?"

"Yes," he said, "but I can't bring myself to do it just now. I need some time to think."

"If you love her, as you say you do, and you've ad-mitted that you neglected her, I hope you're not equating her little affair with your years of neglect."

"I know I've been wrong on that score, but *I* haven't been fooling around with anyone."

"No, you've been too busy building your career."

"Ouch," he said, smiling painfully. "You don't pull your punches."

"No, and if your wife had had it out with you a long time ago, she perhaps wouldn't have been driven to have this little fling of hers. Which is all it was. . . ."

"Maybe to you . . . you're used to these things. . . ."

"Listen," I said, getting annoyed with his self-pity, "I'm no Women's Libber, but we've all got to get over the idea that we own each others' bodies! So your wife fucked this neighbor—I think you mind his not being Jewish more than you mind her fucking him!—but she still loves you. Whatever she hoped to find in having an affair, what she ended up with was knowing some good new tricks in bed."

"Yeah, and how can I make love to her knowing where she learned those tricks? I've got feelings, too . . . ."

"If you'd spent more time with her, and made love to her more, you'd have discovered those tricks together. In any case, if you love her, you'll enjoy her new sexual knowledge. Stop acting like a regular Victorian."

"You're right. I'm hurt and I'm being stupid. If she can forgive me my years of working so hard to 'make it,' I *should* be able to forgive her a month of infidelity."

"Why don't you have a couple of drinks to relax and then call her up? I'm sure she's worried about you. It took a lot of courage for her to tell you. . . . Just think, what if she hadn't told you?"

"Yeah, I didn't think about that. That would have been a helluva lot worse, for her to have gone on living a lie. . . ."

"Well, good, I'm glad we've had this talk."

"So am I. . . . I'm just sorry I caught you on a night you were so upset."

"Don't worry," he said, graciously, "the program went all right—at least your end of it."

"Thanks," I said. "I have to run along now. Meeting someone for dinner."

"Goodnight, Xaviera, and thanks, really. I'm very grateful."

Then he paused, and smiling that small smile of his

again, added, "Just don't expect me to say hello to that neighbor of mine when I meet him in the supermarket."

"Take some karate lessons, and give *him* a lesson in 'Good Neighborliness,' " I said, waving goodbye.

I don't know if he made the call to his wife. I had to leave the next morning, and didn't have time to call him.

I can only hope our little talk helped him to help himself. He deserved better—he really did!

The Prostitute and the Public

QUESTIONS AND ANSWERS

What kind of person are you, really?

Who am I? I often ask myself that question. People ask me if I'm happy, satisfied or content. Or they ask me if I'm a Lesbian, or if I hate men, or am I masochist, or a sadist. My answer is that I'm a little bit of everything. I am happy at most times . . . and sad occasionally. I'm emotional and sensitive, very much so, but I can also be tough as nails. I'm an exhibitionist because I like to walk around in the nude, as long as I am young and well put-together, and feel comfortable that way. I'm not ashamed of people seeing me in Eve's costume. I have been known to do a strip-tease in an inside swimming pool down in Miami, at the Jockey Club, while thirty square people were watching with their eyes glued against the glass of the pool enclosure. I love to shock people—shake 'em up—so in that sense, I'm an exhibitionist.

On the other hand, I also like to be a voyeur at times. I recall a scene on a beach in Puerto Rico, a short time after my book came out. I went down there with Larry and a great photographer, a Dutch woman who wanted to take a set of publicity pictures. We went out early in the morning to take some nude and semi-nude pictures for a German magazine, *Quick*. The beach was deserted, most people were still sound asleep. There was a wooden fence separating the beach from the shore area. This was the beach right near the Americana and San Juan hotels.

I kept the bottom of my bikini on and removed the bra. Antoinette, the Dutch photographer, must have been a little bit of a Lesbian, because even Larry noticed that she sometimes got very turned on watching me in action as a model. She made me jump and stretch and bend backwards and forwards, in and out of the water. While I was doing all this, I happened to glance at the wall. I looked both ways and when I looked to the left, and where the wall was at a right angle, I noticed a young Puerto Rican. My guess was he was a street laborer. He was in his mid-twenties, fairly good-looking, wearing a denim overall. He got very excited watching me. I had to look through the splits in the fence twice to see the expression in his big, black, bright eyes. His curly hair and forehead were wet with perspiration. I had been on exhibition for about ten or fifteen minutes. No one else knew, just he and I—we had some real vibrations going between us.

Neither Larry nor Antoinette had noticed. She was too busy taking pictures and Larry was keeping watch against anyone coming on the scene unexpected. But somehow he didn't look behind the wall. I remember how turned on I was, exhibiting myself in front of this man, particularly when he started to masturbate and exposed his big, hard cock to me.

At that point, Antoinette asked me to remove my underpants. Larry told me not to. If it hadn't been for him, I would have done it—knowing that the young guy behind the wall would have climaxed immediately. That was all he really needed to come.

We took pictures for about an hour. By then, some men came out to jog on the beach and I had to quickly put my bra back on. Some of the joggers would stop for a while and peek around at me, before proceeding with their morning exercises. Every time Larry moved near the wall, the Puerto Rican voyeur would hide, but I'd follow him with my eyes. By the time the pictures were all taken, the guy must have come three times. I myself saw him ejaculate twice. I was surprised that Larry and

Antoinette didn't notice that my head was turned toward the wall most of the time the voyeur was watching me and jerking himself off.

To me, being an exhibitionist and, at the same time, a voyeur turned me on so tremendously that when we had finished shooting the pictures, Larry and I went up to our room, whereupon I virtually raped him. After I had fucked him real good, I told him what had happened. Larry became furious and asked why I remained exposing myself, practically nude. So I told him the guy wasn't committing any crime, that he was just playing with himself, and hadn't bothered anybody. I found the entire scene amusing and it had stimulated me to look even groovier for the pictures. I had moved and stretched my body better, like a panther, because I had been turned on so—like a bitch in heat— and my bikini pants were soaking wet. I would have liked nothing better than to run behind the wall and screw that young guy, but I knew, of course, that I couldn't do it.

I am also a masochist and a sadist at the same time. How is this possible? This was brought out one day when I was making love to Larry.

We'd had some emotional problems, but up until that time, physically everything was fine. We didn't make love that often—maybe two or three times during the course of a weekend—but on the particular weekend, I really felt in a masochistic mood. Nobody usually ordered or slapped me around, but I needed it badly—not only the fist on the table, but also on the ass wouldn't be a bad idea! My special role with my customers had sometimes been the masochistic-sadist treatment, where I usually played sadist —I was the master. Sometimes I dressed myself in black leather, or even rubber suits, with high heels, black stockings, a black G-string with matching garter-belt, black bra, and, if necessary, even long, black gloves. I usually also wielded a cat-o'-nine-tails, a whip or a paddle, in case the customer begged me for that.

However, this time, the opposite happened. *I* begged Larry to pick up a piece of thick, strong rope which was lying next to my goodie bag, in order to tie me down. I really felt like being overpowered and was dying for him to fuck me all over, to rough me up, humiliate me, force me. Although at first, Larry was a bit hesitant—he'd always been gentle with me—he went sheepishly to the corner of the room, picked up the rope and, once in bed, changed into the role of the master. He tied me down thoroughly, with my hands behind my back and legs together. I loved every bit of it. I still recall how I loved the tingling feeling when the rope closed around my fists, and the noise of him spanking my ass until it was red. Then I begged him to hit me with the cat-o'-nine-tails until my buttocks were glowing hot. All the while, I was helplessly tied down.

I then begged him to fuck me in the ass. He did so with his hard penis while I was bent forward on my knees. He penetrated me deeply from the rear, almost cracking up my bridge while he slammed it to me Greek style. It was painful, but I do remember climaxing on the spot, the moment his penis touched my buttocks. He also played very roughly with my clitoris while I was hunched forward on my knees. My nose was touching my knees; my arms were folded backwards; and the ropes were cutting into my wrists. This proved to me that I was definitely a sado-masochistic combination.

I have found out in slave scenes that I enjoy inflicting pain and humiliation mentally, as well as physically, as much as I enjoy receiving pain. Not so recently I had one of my slaves—who also, at times, likes to be the master in these scenes—a very talented man, I might add, tie me down and start to boss me around. However, the phone began to ring and things didn't work out so well. He took off the ropes so I could answer the phone and then he started a complete mental torture with me, without even touching me or tying me down. He just made me do things, with his voice, his eyes, his whole mannerism. He was my complete master, like *L'Histoire d'O (The Story of O)*.

I begged him, by pretending I was tied down, to let me suck his cock while I was bent backwards on my back, with my knees pulled up behind my buttocks (his orders), my hands holding onto my feet. I had no pillow under my head (he had thrown them off the bed), and he sat on top of me, on my chest, his legs on either side of my head, with his penis hard and erect—obviously very tempting for me to suck. Every time I'd try to raise my head (my hands were held behind me by his firm grip around them), his knees would put my shoulders down so I couldn't move. Every time I managed to pull myself up a little bit more, he would pull his cock back unexpectedly. By now, I was extremely excited. The anticipation for more torture drove me into ecstasy. Occasionally, he would let me suck his cock for a few seconds before pulling back again. I remember watching us in the mirror in the soft light.

He then ordered me to lie still while he got up and took my whip. I was in for a real treat! The clicking of the whip turned me on tremendously and the cat-o'-nine-tails was slapping on my behind. First the slaps were hard and painful, then they became softer. Then he tickled me between my legs, with the whip teasing my pussy and ass. While he teased me, he spanked me with his other hand as punishment.

If you've never tried this scene, you're better off not judging it. Too many consider the sexual minority groups, which I wrongly described as freaks and weirdos in *The Happy Hooker,* as real sickies. I herewith apologize for this label. Society must learn to better understand these groups and, where possible, accommodate them. I still have to learn a whole lot more about myself. We simply mustn't judge others too quickly.

HECTOR THE HYPNOTIST

In Detroit nothing really exciting happened. It's a city of cars and more cars. I did get excellent press coverage and as a result of my visit there, a few weeks later I heard from one of the nation's leading lecture bureaus. It was an offer to give a lecture in Detroit's Town Hall. However, time didn't allow for this before I left the country.

In Detroit I also met Hector the Hypnotist.

I had been on a TV show and was in the process of saying goodbye to the people connected with the program when a short, intense-looking man came over and introduced himself to me and Fred, a Dell sales representative for the Midwest who was my host in Detroit. He was Hector Harris, he said, and he handed both Fred and me his card. It read: "Hector Harris, Director, Harris Institute of Hypnosis, Dallas, Texas." I looked at him again and was slightly amused to realize he was wearing a very obvious toupee. Truth to tell, he looked slightly mad, with his pale blue eyes and intense expression and rapid manner of speaking.

We talked for a few moments and at least Mr. Harris seemed rather entertaining, even though he kept giving me his bloody card, until I began thinking I must own more of his cards than he did. In fact, he even went so far as to open my handbag and put two or three cards in there. I let him know I wasn't amused by this because I feel what's in a woman's handbag is very much her own business, but Hector wasn't at all fazed by my scolding him.

Finally I asked Hector if there was anything I could do for him because we had to be moving along to another show, and he responded that he could do me a great deal of good.

"How so?" I asked him.

"I can get you a lot of press coverage in Dallas and the Southwest," he replied. "In addition to my institute, I am a public relations specialist."

"Well, that might be fine," I said, really not taking him very seriously, "but you'll have to work through my publisher. Call them in New York, and we'll see."

"Very good. I will follow through post haste," said Hector, asking me for my phone number in the city. I reached into my handbag to get a pen and paper to write down my number for him, and Hector immediately took this opportunity to reach in himself and help himself to a copy of *The Happy Hooker*, immediately insisting I autograph it for him. I had the choice of being angry or amused with him, but he was so intense about things it was simpler to be amused. So I signed the book for him and said I'd look forward to hearing from him.

Of course I never expected to.

However, a few days later, back in New York, I received a long-distance call—Mr. Harris was calling long distance, collect. I didn't think it was very polite of him to charge me for the call, for openers, but I decided to accept it. There was nothing to gain by standing on ceremony about a collect call from Texas.

Hector was very enthusiastic over the phone, practically shouting in my ear. "Okay, it's like I told you—I've organized a great thing for you. I'll give you the details in two days—I have to speak with your publisher first. They should pay your fare here. You'll have great television and radio coverage. And newspapers, too! I'm going to hypnotize you and let the press see how well I can do with a little hooker, who will be converted into a lecturer, or whatever it is that you want to be converted into!"

"Very good, Hector," I replied, "I'll be interested in seeing what happens." At the same time, I was thinking to myself, "I think this man is cuckoo. What nonsense he spouts!"

However, being a saleswoman and promoter myself, I decided to call Dell and see if there was anything of substance to Hector's promises. He did come from a part of the country that I wasn't scheduled to visit and if he could deliver what he promised, I'd be willing to go.

When I called the publicity director at Dell, she said, yes, she had spoken with Hector and, in fact, he'd called several times, and always collect! Well, what did she think about him? Her answer was more or less what I'd expected: that he made her more than a little nervous because he carried on, over the phone, like such a nut! But, to my surprise, his plans seemed genuine enough and Dell was going to go ahead and sponsor the trip. They would pay the plane fare and, since Hector was offering me his house to stay in—this was news to me, by the way, but seemed okay, better than staying in a hotel room—the trip wouldn't be so costly because there'd be no hotel bill.

The only question left to settle, she told me, was did I really want to go with this character?

I thought about that for a minute, then answered, "Yes, the publicity will be good, and we had no trip planned for that area, so I think I should go. Anyhow, I'm somewhat curious about this whole hypnosis bit, and that should make it more interesting."

"All right," she said, "I'll make the arrangements."

I guess I hadn't thought much about it, but I *was* curious about Hector as a hypnotist. As a child, I had been fascinated by the idea of hypnosis because my father used it in his practice of psychiatry. He also used it, as a medical doctor, in delivering babies. On several occasions, he had tried to hypnotize me—as an experiment—but I fought him and wasn't a good subject.

However, he taught me to hypnotize frogs and chickens by placing them on the floor on their backs and making them look at a long straight line until their eyes got tired. It also helped to push a certain small vein in their bellies—particularly with frogs.

I remember one day—I was about eleven years old at the time and, like many children that age, a bit of a sadist—

when I'd hypnotized a frog for hours, playing cruel little games with him, waking him up, then hypnotizing him again, then repeating the process. The day before I'd asked my father why people liked to eat frogs' legs and he said they were very tasty and considered a delicacy. I asked how they were cooked and he said they were boiled in hot water or oil. Evidently the idea of how the frogs were prepared in restaurants stuck with me, because I now woke up my little frog and took him into the bathroom, put him in the sink and turned on the hot water. The poor little creature gave a loud quack, turned stiff and died.

The moment the frog died, I began to laugh hysterically, but soon I got really very frightened because I knew I had done something wrong and my father, who was the gentlest of men and would never harm an animal, would be very distressed with me. As I was having these thoughts, my mother came into the room looking for me and discovered the dead frog in the sink. She became furious with me for my cruelty and slapped me across the face. Then my father came in to see what all the commotion was about and he ordered me into my room and locked the door. I kept a diary in those days, and my punishment, my father decreed, would be to write the words, "You are not allowed to kill frogs. You can only hypnotize them," one thousand times in my diary. Only then could I leave my room.

Needless to say, I didn't hypnotize any frogs after that, and my only other experience with hypnosis was a few years ago, when I was in Las Vegas with an old boyfriend. We'd had dinner at our hotel and I was very anxious to see a floor show featuring a famous female hypnotist. I wanted to be hypnotized, I told my boyfriend—who thought I was kidding at first, but finally he agreed to take me.

When we got seated, the hypnotist was asking for volunteers from the audience and I was among the first to raise my hand. I remember going up on the stage, taking a seat and right from the start resisting her. Her voice seemed very loud and monotonous to me and the lights were bright and uncomfortably sharp. Even though we all closed our eyes, the lights on the stage seemed uncomfortably bright to me. From what I gathered, everyone else was hypnotized in a very brief time, but I kept fighting and fighting it and she was getting annoyed with me.

My body felt limp but I kept half-opening my eyes, sneaking looks at her and at the other people on stage, and the hypnotist caught me doing this and scolded me. "You're cheating," she said. "Get off the stage and go back where you belong! You're no fun."

So I got up and went down the steps and returned to my table, but don't ask me how I found my way because for the next three-quarters of an hour, I really *was* half hypnotized. But I do remember the hypnotist telling one young man—he was a truck driver, he told the audience—he was carrying a bird, a falcon who was dangerous because it bit people, and would have to wear a hood over its head. But, the hypnotist told him, he would have to talk to the bird to comfort and reassure it that he was still its friend. And the truck driver did just what the hypnotist told him to do. Another subject, a young woman, was told she was carrying a pet canary and to talk to it, and another person was "given" a parrot to talk to and even began sounding like a parrot himself.

Watching all this, I was glad I had resisted, because she really did ask people to make fools of themselves. One man was told he was nude, and he became very embarrassed. The hypnotist told another man that she was standing there nude herself—I should mention that she had an extremely voluptuous figure—and what did he think about that? Well, his imagination began working overtime and he obviously was having some sensuous thoughts as a leering, horny expression came over his face. Later on, she made him feel guilty for wanting to attack her.

I must say, as I was becoming more awake, that I also found some behavior the hypnotist induced in people to be in rather questionable taste. She told one girl she was a go-go dancer and had her strip down to her underwear, and she made another girl rush off the stage and down to her boyfriend and begin making love to him. The girl started loving him up so furiously I thought she would rape him right there, but the hypnotist had her stop before she was guilty of indecent exposure, and return to the stage. So by the time the show was over, I was glad I had resisted and hadn't been made to perform for the titillation of the audience. But my fascination with hypnosis remained, and I was still quite willing to try it again, but only under the right conditions.

All this is by way of saying that my curiosity about hypnosis was a considerable factor in my decision to see what Hector the Hypnotist could do for my book. So a week later I got off the plane in Dallas Airport and was met by Hector and a small entourage. He had on a new toupee and was wearing, on his arm, a big sexy brunette with large dark-rimmed glasses. She had simply tremendous tits which stuck out like balloons and was wearing a red, white and blue miniskirt, revealing thick but well-shaped legs. Her face, behind the large glasses, was very pleasant—almost childlike and innocent.

On Hector's other side was an old, bald photographer who was busily snapping away, and another man very interested in astrology—at least he immediately told me he knew an old witch who was very anxious to do a chart on me. There was also a newspaperman in this strange little greeting party. It wouldn't be a boring trip—I soon enough realized that—if this weird menage of people was any indication.

One moment I was being greeted like a queen, with the photographer and the witch's chum fighting over who would have the privilege of carrying my bag, and the next minute I was embarrassed even to be among these people because Hector had whipped off his toupee and started acting like some insane film director as he led us out of the airport. I didn't know if he was kidding or not, but after a moment's astonishment we all started laughing, and for the first time I felt fairly comfortable with these people.

On the other hand, driving with Hector out to his house in the Dallas suburbs was a genuinely terrifying experience. He was a terribly reckless driver and, to make matters worse, it had begun to rain and the roads were wet and slippery. As he drove, Hector kept talking in a loud voice and shouting and carrying on, constantly gesturing while taking one hand off the wheel to make a point, and alternating his foot between the brake and the gas pedal. Hector kept yacking away, and no one seemed to dare talk back at him. I soon enough got the idea that Hector was boss among this little crowd, a regular little King Shit.

After a while I just tried to tune Hector out and began a conversation with Jill, his sexy girlfriend. I couldn't understand what she was doing with this zany character, but I soon realized that she really admired him and thought he was a truly fascinating man. He'd done "amazing things" with hypnosis she told me in an awed voice, ranging from a football player he'd hypnotized into a great performance to a singer he'd hypnotized into winning a song contest. Another feat he'd accomplished was to convert—ah, Hector's favorite word!—a nervous, stuttering salesman into becoming one of his firm's best income producers.

Then there were the people—men mostly—who he'd hypnotized into giving up smoking or drinking. One guy, an absolutely nervous wreck, Jill said, whose career was in shambles because of his heavy drinking, was treated so successfully by Hector that not long after they completed their sessions together, the man was appointed president of his bank. Obviously Hector was a talented hypnotist, and I was now very interested to learn how good a subject I'd be for him. I wasn't interested in his "converting" me into a good lecturer or anything else—after my various TV and radio appearances I felt quite confident in front of an audience—but I was really intrigued by the idea of hypnosis itself, and how I would react.

I didn't have long to wait. When we got to Hector's house, we had something to eat and then we all went right up to his office to see if he could succeed in hypnotizing me. To my surprise, this irritating little gnome put me at ease right from the start and, with my full cooperation, put me into a total hypnotic state.

Hector made me completely relax and just let myself fall forwards and backwards, with him always catching me at the last minute. He then made me try to pull my arms apart, without success because they seemed to be riveted together. Then he made me do a strip—off went my clothes, until I had nothing on but my bikini pants. The next moment, I found myself jumping and stamping on the floor—doing some kind of Indian dance. Hector had me do all kinds of crazy, silly things but all the while I was wide awake, looking at the others, but feeling absolutely no embarrassment. And they just sat there, amazingly quiet. Jill was positively entranced, but she refused to be his next subject and so did the others. When Hector took me out of hypnosis, I felt completely relaxed and we decided—Jill, Hector and I—to go out to dinner to celebrate. The others were going home.

Before the photographer left, however, he took some more publicity pictures of Hector and me—some with Hector wearing his toupee and others without! This struck me as very funny because before he hypnotized me, I'd begged Hector to remove his toupee because I thought it was a joke and would make me laugh. And when he took that thing off, he became an entirely different person. Hector's pale blue eyes seemed to pierce right through me and with just his index finger, pointed between my eyes and forehead, was able to put me in a trance almost immediately. His small body seemed to grow in strength and size as he commanded me to do the various things.

We went out for dinner at a little Italian restaurant, and as I was drinking some water, Hector said to me, "Let me do one more thing to show you I'm a good hypnotist."

"Sure, go ahead. What do you want to do—make the water to taste like milk?" He replied that that wasn't such a bad idea. And, indeed, he then mumbled a few words, touched the glass, looked in my eyes deeply, and the next sip I took *did* taste like milk to me! Hector then asked the waiter for another glass of water, so I could taste the difference between the two glasses of liquid. To say the least, I was pretty impressed with my friend Hector. However, whatever bad habits he could cure me of, I certainly didn't want him to talk me out of sex!

Since it was quite late when we'd finished dinner, we went right back to his place. Jill seemed a bit hesitant about going back to the house, and she whispered to me that she'd never slept with him. And, what's more, she was having her period.

Well, sleeping with Hector certainly wasn't anything I'd expected to do, either, but I decided to just be cool and see what developed. Jill kind of turned me on, because she seemed so young and naive and sweet, really. So if I had to sleep with him to sleep with her, that might not be so bad. (I'd already forgotten about her having her period.)

Hector had the whole night mapped out anyway—we would all go to bed together and have a grand time, and Jill and I reluctantly agreed. As for me, I rationalized it by telling myself that I was thanking him in advance for his help on my book. Tonight I'd fuck his brains out, but that would be that.

Just as we all got into bed, Jill sheepishly told him she had her period and was flowing very heavily. This, of course, turned me off her because I was not in the mood to drink tomato juice that night. So what else was left to do but suck her gorgeous tits, meanwhile working on horny Hector. But he wanted all the attention, and was such an egomaniac and tyrant in bed that it was horrible to perform with him.

Actually, I was too tired to even think straight—he'd been endlessly talking and talking the whole night long, and at one point I said to him, after an hour of fooling around, "Look, Hector, this isn't what I came to Dallas for. I'd like to relax because I've got a pretty hectic schedule tomorrow." But he wouldn't let go of Jill and me until he, the little King himself, came three times. He screwed the hell out of me and Jill had a sore mouth from sucking him—her contribution since she was temporarily out of the fucking action.

If it hadn't been for Jill's being so sweet and passive, except for her very active mouth (she did a good job as far as that's concerned, *not* on *me*—she was too shy for that—but on Hector), I would have certainly kicked Hector's ass out of the bed. But I kept reminding myself that this was a way of thanking him for arranging all the TV and radio exposure and taking us out to dinner, and that I might as well be nice and show my gratitude by pleasing him.

Actually, it was unusual for me to think this way. Straight girls often feel that after a man takes them out for dinner—wines and dines them and takes them to the theatre—they ought to go to bed with him, because they think, "That's the least I can do for him after he has spent fifty or a hundred dollars on me tonight." But this ought not to be the feeling. With the Women's Liberation philosophy in mind, a woman should be able to say, "Okay buddy, you want to take me out, you want to spend money on dinner and the theatre? All right, but I tell you up front, I won't pay you for it with my body afterwards—or else I pay for my own meals."

If I went to bed with a man before I became a prostitute, it was because I was lonely or because I was horny; I wanted a man's cock, not his buying me a meal. Dinner I could buy for myself. So it was ironic that I was now thinking in terms of showing my gratitude to Hector by fucking him. He must have been a much better hypnotist than I'd realized.

In any case, by the time Hector, hypnotic humper, was done three times, even he was slightly exhausted and Jill and I gratefully got up from his bed. Jill got dressed and put her glasses back on, once again looking like a schoolgirl. I wasn't quite sure what her story was. Why had she gone to bed with Hector—she didn't owe him any favors? Did she really have her period—I couldn't tell, since she kept her panties on during the entire session. Was she uptight and was she as innocent as she looked? I must say she gave a pretty damn fine blow job for a supposed amateur.

From what she'd told me earlier in the evening, she had a straight job during the day and had two children to look after. Her husband had deserted her, she said, and now she lived with her mother. I wasn't sure if any or all this was true, although I had no reason to doubt her.

The next day I had a crazy day, running from program to program, and was really grateful when the day was over. I'd invited Hector and Jill for dinner and as we were walking into the fancy restaurant Hector had selected, I heard several men greet Jill as "Bambi." So I asked Hector, when Jill excused herself to go to the ladies' room, "Did you know that they call Jill 'Bambi?' "

"No," Hector said, "not up until tonight."

Then I spotted, sitting at a nearby table, three guys who I knew from New York because they were former customers of mine. They were all from this area. (I certainly used to have clients from all over the U.S.A.!) They greeted me and invited me over to their table for a minute. I excused myself and went over to say hello.

"How have you been?" one of them said. "Are you opening a franchise here?"

"Are you crazy? I don't know what you are talking about. Why do you say that?"

"Because you're having dinner with our good friend, Bambi, over there." And with that, we all looked at Hector and Jill, who both seemed shocked by this conversation, which they could hear.

"Shhh," I said, "don't talk so loud. She's Hector's girlfriend. You mean to say she is a hooker? Aw, c'mon, I don't believe it—she seems so innocent and has two kids."

"Hey, baby, those are the ones to watch out for. They're the best. Bambi is a twenty-five dollar hooker—she really hustles hard because she does have two children to support, and she keeps a straight job to please her mother. But in her free time, she drives all over the city in her little Volkswagen and visits her clients. And her price is only twenty-five dollars!" I threatened jokingly to tell her how well off these guys were, so that she could at least raise her price to fifty dollars. They laughingly agreed.

"Okay with us, she's sure worth it because she gives the best blow job in town!"

So you see, I'd been fooled by a so-called innocent girl. If it hadn't been for her big, challenging tits and the blow job on Hector, I'd never have thought from just looking at her that she might be a hooker. If it hadn't been for the fact that her bra pulled her breasts up so high, I'd have really believed she was some little schoolgirl, with a few extra years on her.

However, when I went back to Hector's table and he asked me what *that* was all about, I replied that it was just a case of three guys mouthing off—they thought Jill was someone else, and they also wanted to make it with her. We all laughed at this, but I also got a wink of thanks from Bambi-Jill.

That night, when we went back to Hector's place, I promptly excused myself from any fucking-sucking sessions on grounds of being utterly exhausted—which was true enough—and went off to my own room. I don't know what Jill did with Hector, but from the yelps of delight, all his, coming from his bedroom, she must have blown him from here to perdition.

I did one more show the next day, and Hector was unhappy with me because I hadn't plugged his institute, but
there'd been no opportunity to do so. He drove me out to
the airport, however, and all in all, it had been a pretty
interesting time. Before I left, I whispered into Jill's ear,
"Your price has gone up—inflation, you know—charge fifty
dollars."

"Okay," she giggled. "Thanks a lot."

The Prostitute and the Public

QUESTIONS AND ANSWERS

Looking back, what's the strangest, most exotic aspect of prostitution that you can recall?

There could be a variety of answers for this one, but I would have to say the strangest fact of prostitution today is the number of prostitutes who are actually trans-sexuals—men who have had their sex changed and became women! For example, some of these are homosexuals who started out as transvestites, parading around in female clothing and, in some instances, becoming female impersonators on a professional level. Then they have gotten silicone shots or hormone (estrogen) injections and, slowly but surely, almost became actual women in desires and looks. The only thing those men needed to make them completely feminine was the removal of their penis and the insertion of a vagina. If only the Johns knew that quite a few prostitutes nowadays who they pick up on the streets were actually transvestites or even trans-sexuals! Men who've had their penises removed or flapped inside, and had artificial vaginas created.

I heard about one of Paris's most famous call girls, a trans-sexual, who was so gorgeous that she could hardly handle all her customers. She fucked so much that she absolutely wore out her artificial vagina and had to go back to the doctor three times in one year to insert a new plastic

343

cunt, so she could keep on fucking! I cannot guarantee how much of this story is true! There is another trans-sexual in France, whose name is Coccinelle, and who became very famous about ten years ago as one of the first successful trans-sexual operations. She was a great night-club performer.

While talking once to one of my girls who was an independent hooker (she had also played several roles in stag movies), she told me how she had worked on a customer once together with a trans-sexual prostitute. Eventually, the customers find out. She said that usually, in bed with a John, there is somehow a very indifferent feeling from the trans-sexual which the John senses. A trans-sexual is still basically a man and he/she can't fake orgasms well enough when they're in bed. They can't make the same noises women make when they fuck. They might have high-pitched voices, but still there is often a sort of weird, raspy quality in it. Their breasts are hard as rocks from the silicone and feel artificial. If a man took a good look at their vaginas, he would certainly see, in nine out of ten cases, a rather weird-looking pussy, and this sight alone would be enough to turn him off.

The girl with whom I spoke used to have to take part in the sex scene herself. She was the one who really had to turn the man on. And then the trans-sexual would end up fucking him. Somewhere in the middle, there was usually a complaint from the John and he'd usually ask to finish fucking her the next time around. He'd want to make it with the *real chick,* and by saying the real chick, he really didn't know he wasn't making it with a real woman, because my friend would never reveal that he had fucked a converted woman. But somewhere in their minds the Johns knew there was something rotten in the state of Denmark. That's what you get when you try to fool the whole world!

It is a known fact that some homosexuals go through serious nervous breakdowns either before or after they undergo the complete operation. Before, because they are unhappy in their own skins, being a man and really wanting to be a woman, and after, because they are not always able to reach any kind of orgasm any more, or the operation was not a complete success and left them sort of hanging in between. Quite a few trans-sexuals have committed suicide within a couple of years following their sex change.

I know one trans-sexual in Holland, a lovely girl now, who even as a man always liked women and never had sex with other men. He simply wanted to be a woman himself and when *he* became a *she,* she became a very notorious Lesbian. That is, in my opinion, really far-out!

A lot of gay studs don't even want to have a complete operation. They just become whores who fold their penises backwards; some, indeed, get silicone shots to look like real women. When they go out on the street, dressed like hookers in miniskirts, high heels and wigs, and they pick up a John, they just pretend they have their period once they are in bed, and keep their panties on. Since they don't ask for much money—fifteen or twenty dollars—they just give a blow job, which they enjoy tremendously. They suck those men off, usually without ever being found out. Sometimes, however, when such a customer finds out, it can be a very heavy scene and I've heard of quite a few male chicks who ended up getting punched in the face, or knocked out by the John who wanted the *real thing.*

What unusual changes do you foresee if prostitution ever became legalized?

If prostitution were ever to be legalized, then anyone earning a living that way would have to pay income taxes. It would be no more than reasonable then that there should be such provisions made as hooker pension funds, schools for the retraining of hookers who are over-age so that they can qualify for straight jobs, jobs that could utilize their knowledge of human beings. Also, day-care centers for children wouldn't be a bad idea, so that more mothers could become hookers for a few hours a day.

L.A.

Looking back on it, I could regard my whole publicity tour of America as a grand ego trip. Despite the hustle and bustle and travel and occasional hassles, I enjoyed most of it enormously—as I knew I would even before the very first leg of the trip. I knew I would be successful promoting something I believed in, and in some ways the toughest part of the trip was getting along without too much sleep. But I had just graduated from a line of work in which I'd gotten used to very little sleep.

Los Angeles—a beautiful city without a heart. I saw quite a lot of the city, particularly since it involved miles and miles to get from one place to another. I've never been in a city with so many highways, so much concrete.

I arrived there on a Saturday morning, carrying a heavy winter coat I certainly didn't need in Los Angeles. But I'd just come from the very cold East, so I had to carry two entirely different wardrobes with me—one for winter and one for warm weather.

I was met at the airport by a group of Dell salesmen, one of whom had even brought his wife along to meet me. Since it was a Saturday and I had not been booked on any weekend programs, I actually had some time for myself and was able to spend a lot of time with friends. By Monday I was so rested and felt so energetic that when the Dell people came to the hotel for a six o'clock breakfast with me, I complained, looking over my schedule for the day, that they hadn't arranged a full day's program for me. Later in the morning I was supposed to have a second breakfast with a newspaperman who wanted to interview me. At noon I was scheduled to appear on a radio program. After that, I would be through for the day.

Laughingly, the Dell people told me to put on my bikini and work on my tan, and get in touch with them later in the day. Nothing doing, I told them, I was here to hustle my goddamn book, not to go sunbathing. I said I'd spent most of the weekend resting. Dell hadn't arranged for me to come out to the West Coast just to sit around, I reminded them, and why was it that here on the Coast, where there were so many people and radio and TV stations, that they couldn't get me booked for more shows and appearances? In a slight state of shock, they all sat there and brooded about this for a while. Then the youngest salesman there mentioned Dick Whittington, the disc jockey, as a good person for me to appear with. I'd heard Whittington myself on the radio and I thought he sounded groovy. So it was decided to let this young man try the Whittington show and some others, later in the day, after my morning's activities.

However, later on, when I *heard* this salesman talking over the phone, I had to question the quality of his salesmanship. He'd dial a number and get somebody on the phone from some radio program. Then he'd tell them he was from Dell Books and he had Miss Xaviera Hollander, author of *The Happy Hooker* in town and she was available for an appearance. Obviously they'd ask him what the book was about and he'd say, "Oh, it's a book about prostitution." What's worse, he'd say this in a very dull and flat voice, no enthusiasm, nothing. He was probably talking to some little drudge of a secretary and she'd say we're not interested and hang up the phone.

So I told him, "Look, I beg your pardon, but would you mind dialing the number of 'The Dick Whittington Show' for me, and this time I'll do the talking." He asked me what he'd done wrong.

"First of all," I said, "may I please give you a lesson

about selling something? If you want to promote something, you have to give the person you're talking to the impression that you're at least interested in it or know something about it. Sound a bit enthused about it, tell them that the book's been publicized all over the country and that Miss Hollander, the author, has been appearing before the Knapp Commission in New York. Tell them its not only about prostitution but sex in general. Tell them it's very controversial. It is, you know!"

"Oh," he said, and dialed the show for me. When I got Dick Whittington's secretary on the telephone, I didn't waste my time explaining too much. She told me that he was on the air and asked what my book was about. I didn't bother giving her a long, monotonous summary of the book but instead told her the key facts, adding the important information that the book was already a best-seller all over the country.

About two minutes later I was speaking to Dick Whittington, and if anyone can be turned on by a voice they certainly could by his. I explained briefly who I was and he became very enthused, saying he'd read about me in *Time* magazine and although he hadn't gotten around to reading the book yet, he was dying to talk to me. He said to come over right away if I could—I said I could early in the afternoon—and sure enough he later devoted an hour of his program just to me, and wanted me to come back again. I thought that was a great compliment, especially from a man who had had so many famous and controversial guests appearing on his show.

Dick Whittington, you may be sure, is a very groovy guy. He is in his thirties, is very direct and has a great sense of humor. He wasn't biting or sarcastic, and even told his audience that he was a bit afraid of me. He also said that he was very turned on by me, and he wished his listeners could have a look at me because I looked like anything but a hooker. "She's cute and sexy and has a wonderful sense of humor," he said. Boy, talk about ego trips!

Dick also said he thought prostitution should be legalized, and this probably inspired a lot of the phone calls he got, both during the program and afterward. I even went so far as to give the audience my telephone number at the hotel where I was staying. It was the Beverly Hilton and my room number was 1-2-3. This sounds funny and I thought it would get a laugh if I mentioned it. I also got myself some free advertising by announcing that I was going to appear at the Pickwick Arms Bookstore to autograph copies of my book. Dick didn't mind a bit, and he even mentioned it again the next day on his program.

Dick and I really had a nice 'n loose time on his show. He messed up two of his commercials because everytime he would mention something liquid, especially if something was good on your tongue or in your mouth. I would whisper something to him that really cracked him up. I certainly would have hated to be the sponsor of those commercials, though I suppose the fun we had with them actually drew attention to the products. After the show some of Dick's colleagues paid me some very nice compliments, telling me I was a real charmer. So it had really paid off, making my own phone call.

The next day I was paid another extremely nice compliment by one of the Dell managers in Los Angeles. "You are a tough cookie to do business with," he said, "but you are a charming, convincing and delightful saleswoman. You could certainly give a lesson to some of our salesmen here." He even told me I should get a medal for the way I was hustling my book! "You are a better hustler on your book," he said, kidding, "than you were with men." I didn't know about *that,* but it was an interesting thought.

That afternoon, I appeared at the Pickwick Arms Bookstore. Everything was very well arranged. About four hundred copies of my book were stacked up on display, and I was comfortably seated at a table with a large glass of fattening Orange Julius in front of me, autographing books. I must say I enjoyed meeting the California public that afternoon a lot more than I had enjoyed meeting the people passing through New York's Penn Station about two weeks earlier. I don't mean to generalize about the difference in the attitudes of people on the West Coast and those on the East Coast, but here's my experience for what it's worth.

It was a very cold day and I was seated at the entrance

to this bookstore in Penn Station, sitting under a big card-board sign with my picture on it, advertising my book. I was wearing a turquoise dress, closed up to my chin, with long sleeves and I sat there, signing away and shivering from the cold.

After I'd been there about an hour, I had sold approximately one hundred books, of which ninety-seven copies went to men. If a woman came by with her husband, and they saw the sign saying who I was, she'd usually grab his arm and pull him away, preventing him from even taking a closer look at me or the title of the book. I also recall two older ladies who gave me a very dirty look as they walked by, one saying to the other, "She's nothing but a slut." Then there was the young Chinese couple who started to giggle when they passed by. I don't think they understood that I was promoting my book, and they were laughing because I was beginning to resemble a *frozen*—not *fallen*—woman! More nonsense: some men walked by me two or three times, back and forth, observing every movement I made, but too compromised by my presence there to stop and buy a book. Some men simply looked at me, and seemed to get all juiced up, but they probably thought it would be too much like patronizing a prostitute to stop and buy the book from me directly.

Yet more nonsense: there was one woman who had first given me a dirty look, but then walked to the back of the store, got herself a copy from the shelf, quickly paid for it and, the salesgirl informed me, covered it up with a magazine she was carrying. Some other people who bought the book couldn't wait for the girl to put it in a brown paper bag. In some cases, the cashier asked people if they would like to buy the book from me directly and have it autographed, but they recoiled in horror. Poor things—they were going to have to read the book in secret and hide it in the office or at home!

By marked contrast, I received an entirely different welcome at the Pickwick Arms. True, Dick Whittington had helped to see that I got a warm reception. Even the women listeners who'd called up the station weren't hostile, and I had hoped that meant they wanted to meet me and buy my book. Sure enough, the moment I walked into the bookstore at five o'clock sharp, I was welcomed with a loud, "Hurrah, there she is!" People were queuing up in front of the store—women, boys, girls, elderly people, tourists. I even met some Dutch people who'd moved out to California many years ago because they liked the climate, and some other people spoke German to me.

I especially remember two very attractive women, both in their late thirties, who came up to me and stood there, smiling. Finally one of them—she had a very sexy look in her eyes, by the way—said her piece: "Miss Hollander, I want to compliment you on what you've done. If I were ten years younger, and I had gone through what you did, with your fiancé and all, I'd have probably done the same thing. I have a very good job as an architect, but I wish I had the courage to do what you've done because I love sex just as much as you do." She told me she respected me for my honesty, and hoped I'd "make a million dollars with the book!" She also said she was going to give the book to some of the men who'd used her during her life, and maybe it "would open their eyes." Very pleased, I gave her my very best wishes in that regard.

Then there was the group of girls—four roommates—who came dashing into the store, yelling, "Where is she? We want to invite her for a spaghetti dinner tonight!" When they saw me, they rushed over, saying they'd bought the book as soon as it came out, but now they wanted to buy two more copies to have them autographed. And they began raving about how much I'd taught them! I was sort of tempted to accept their dinner invitation, but I wasn't sure about my plans for the evening, so I had to decline. The gesture was nice, though.

At one point a young housewife came up to me, holding her eight-year-old son by the hand and carrying a four-month-old infant in her other arm. She had large curlers in her hair and was wearing Bermuda shorts, and looked like a good little *hausfrau* and mother. As it turned out she was full of fun and extremely good-natured, and she had her eight-year-old hand me a copy of the book and, looking at his mother for approval, declare: "Mommy wants you to write something dirty for daddy, so he can read it. Here, on the first page, please . . . maybe daddy can learn something from your book and mommy says she'll let me read it when I

get to be a big boy!" I thought this was so adorable that I
stopped autographing books and had to hug this kid for
being so cute. Instead of something risque, I dedicated the
book to the mother, the father, the little boy and the baby,
and she was so pleased that she kissed me on both cheeks!
She said she hoped one day I'd have a baby and find happiness. She also told me I'd given her new insight on men and
also on prostitution, and that she'd certainly learned a lot
about keeping her man happy from my book.

So you can see why I found the business of the book-
autographing party a very gratifying experience in Los
Angeles. This was also my experience, with some degrees
of difference, in San Diego and San Francisco. Of course
each day I was out there the book became better-known, but
there certainly seemed to be a lot less hypocrisy in people's
attitude toward the book than I'd observed while stationed
in chilly Penn Station. Maybe the West Coast life-style makes
for a more relaxed and liberal attitude; maybe it's just the
weather. I don't pretend to know the reasons for it, but it's
true just the same.

When I got back to the hotel that evening I was more than
a little tired, and my writing hand felt as though it had a
permanent cramp. The desk clerk told me I had received "a
bushel of phone calls," and gave me the messages. It was
slightly mind-boggling, what my being on Dick Whittington's
show had caused in the way of public response. And the
minute I got upstairs, the phone was ringing madly.

This call was from a hippie with Indian blood, he said,
who wanted me to go to a party with him—plenty of "drugs
and freaky scenes," he assured me—and I declined, with
thanks. Then there was a call from Raoul, a cute kid I'd met
in the bookstore that afternoon. Could he come over and
see me? I recalled his dark good looks—he had an olive
complexion and deep brown eyes and black, curly hair—
and I was really tempted. But no, I was going to be a "nice
girl" and go to bed early.

"Call me tomorrow," I said, "and maybe we can get
together."

The next call was from a former client of mine, an extremely rich kid from Texas. He wanted to "paint the town red," but I told him I wasn't up to any whooping it up, since I had to be up early the next morning. He immediately offered to come over—he'd buy an orchestra, or something, to amuse us for the rest of the evening. Again, showing admirable will power, I declined with thanks.

Between calls, I managed to order up some dinner, and so I took a number of calls with food in my mouth. This wasn't polite, I know, but neither is a growling stomach. One call was from a guy named Paul, who had a fabulously sexy voice. He'd heard me on the radio and had read my book and, by any chance, was I alone?

Oh, oh, I thought, here's another horny-handed guy inviting himself over.

But no, Paul wanted a nice bedtime story. After speaking with him, even for a few moments, I recognized that he was a masochist, and sure enough, he was soon begging me to humiliate him over the phone, to yell and scream at him and insult him.

I asked him what he did, and the information simply gushed out of him. He was thirty-one and "fairly good-looking," he said. Sometimes he acted, but his real ambition was to be a producer. He had some credits, but nothing substantial, although he certainly qualified as a part-time producer. He had an "active sex life," he told me, but what he needed was a domineering blonde type—tall, voluptuous, strongly built, with long waving hair.

I said I'd have to excuse myself as I didn't meet some of those qualifications and, besides, I was really very tired.

Wouldn't I tell him one cruel little story?

No, I said, I just wasn't in the story-telling mood.

Could he call back tomorrow? Or could we have lunch? Or dinner?

Once again I declined, with thanks. I was genuinely sympathetic toward this poor guy, but my acting as an answering service was really wearing me out. So I rang downstairs and told them to hold any additional calls. I went to sleep, content I'd put in a productive day, despite the evening's telephoning. . . .

I put in a full day the next day, had dinner with some friends, then had a late date with the nice young man who'd called after meeting me at the bookstore. He turned out to be a rather skillful lover, which surprised me for one so young—but then, as I've said, kids really do know more about sex these days!

His cock was big, tremendously long and very well-shaped, and just what I needed. But what was absolutely fantastic was his love-making in the 69 position. His mouth was gentle, but his tongue was as fast as mine and he knew right away how to find my most sensitive areas, right away what turned me on. And Raoul gave me a massage, kissing my whole body as well, starting with my toes, which can be very sexy.

When he left early in the morning I was so glad I'd received *his* call, at least—all work and no play makes Xaviera a very horny girl!—and later in New York I received a very sweet love letter from him.

The next day I intended to make a phone call to Bernie Cornfeld, the financial *wunderkind,* who perhaps could tell me the whereabouts of a friend of mine from New York, David Stein. Cornfeld's financial empire in Europe was in serious trouble, I knew, and he'd taken a house in Los Angeles, so in late afternoon I gave him a call and the phone was answered by a pleasant-sounding young woman who said Bernie not only knew I was in town but had been expecting my call.

This surprised me, as I'd never met the man, and I asked if David Stein was staying with Mr. Cornfeld. Yes, she said, and Bernie was having some people over that evening and would I like to join them?

Well, yes, I certainly would.

Delighted with this unexpected invitation, I dressed for the occasion in a new light-green pant suit which set off my newly-acquired tan, and had the hotel get me a taxi. The driver, a nice-looking boy in his early twenties, whistled between his teeth when I gave him the address I wanted.

"Man, that must be the groovy 'in' spot these days! I've already taken two great-looking chicks up there tonight—

birds who just flew in from New York. They told me that Cornfeld had sent them their airline tickets and that they can stay there as long as they want . . . guy must have a lotta bread, huh?"

"Yes," I answered, giggling a bit, "I gather he is a very successful baker." As we drove up a winding road to Bernie's house, it seemed as though each successive house was bigger and more sensational, and of course Bernie's house, at the very top of the hill, was the most spectacular of all, with a fantastic view in what was obviously the most glamorous location. The house had belonged to George Hamilton, the driver told me, adding that the movie star was a close buddy of Cornfeld's. So as I paid the fare and got ready to enter the house, I was full of anticipation—was this going to be a great orgy, a super-intellectual meeting of the minds, a collection of movie stars, or what? After all, I'd been told that anything goes in Los Angeles. . . .

As I entered the house, I saw my friend David playing pool in an adjoining room, and I went over to him and received a warm greeting. He then took me into a huge dining room where, at the head of the table—which must have had thirty chairs around it—was the Great Man himself. Bernie is a short blond man with a reddish beard who is, I estimated, in his early forties. He was very cordial, giving me a kiss on the cheek, and introducing me to the man sitting next to him—"Rabbi" Al Capp, the famous cartoonist.

I knew Mr. Capp had had some problems with the law himself recently, so I took a chance and said to him, "Hi, how are you, you dirty old man . . . We've both hit the newspapers recently, haven't we?" He took my kidding good-naturedly, booming that deep laugh of his, and I added that I was looking forward to being on his show back in New York. As it happened, Capp was staying in Los Angeles a lot longer than I was, and so I wouldn't get to be on his show, after all. But I enjoyed meeting him—he was very friendly, almost the fatherly type.

The rest of the people at the table were young, attractive Jet Set types—the men good-looking and the girls blonde and lovely. They were just finishing their coffee, and Bernie told me that there'd be movies shown in a few minutes in his basement theatre.

XAVIERA

Hmmm, movies? I wondered if these would be some extravagant stag films or what?

Well, it was a Charlie Chaplin film, but the theatre was quite something—a huge carpeted room—and the audience was certainly interesting. In walked Candice Bergen and, a few minutes later, Tony Curtis. I had a conversation with him later, and to my disappointment, he was just an average-looking, quiet guy with curly hair and nothing special about him. What I mean to say is that I thought he'd be terribly handsome, but he's not—or didn't seem so to me—just kind of boyish, and certainly very well-mannered.

While still watching the movie, a really pretty blonde sat down next to me, introduced herself as Katrinka from Sweden and we struck up a kind of whispered conversation. At one point, she said, "How long will you be staying here?" This confused me at first, then I realized that she assumed I was one of Bernie's many house-mates. "Only this evening," I said, "since I haven't been invited to stay the night."

"Oh, I'm sure he'd—"

"I'm teasing you," I said, "I'm really only here for this party." Then I explained why I was in Los Angeles and we both had a good giggle.

When the films were over, we went upstairs and settled in one of the living room's several leather couches. I liked Katrinka and I liked her even better when two very good-looking friends of hers came over to be introduced to me. Their names were Jack and Frank.

Hmmm, which one did I like better? Jack was about ten years older than his buddy, Frank, and just a mite too serious-looking for my taste. So I would concentrate on Frank, who was almost indecently good-looking.

No way. Frank had a date with him, and so did Jack, and neither chick was letting go of her man.

However, we did have a good talk—both were connected with making films for television, and Frank did some acting as well—and they were both bright, hip guys. Katrinka said we should all get together, but I told her that I was scheduled to leave the following night and didn't think I could change my plans.

This prompted her to remind Jack that he was also flying

to New York the following night, and why didn't he check to see if we were on the same flight?

We weren't, and Frank added that he couldn't change his flight—he had to wait for some film to be delivered to the airport and take it to New York—but he'd be happy to take me out to the airport.

"Hell, yes," said Jack, "I'll drive out with you and we can have drinks and a little fun at the airport."

Their girlfriends didn't seem very thrilled at our travel plans, but I was glad to know I'd spend my last hours in Los Angeles with friends. They said goodnight, after having made arrangements for the next night, and I scouted around to see if anyone else at the party interested me as much as Frank had, but there wasn't anyone.

Oh well, I'd had a good lay in the hay the night before, so I mustn't be greedy. After saying goodnight to Bernie and David, I called for a cab and enjoyed the twinkling lights below and the beautiful drive home. In some ways it was the best part of the evening.

The next day was a continuous pub crawl—"pub" standing for publicity in this case—ending with an early dinner with some journalists. Then—zap—back to the hotel to pick up my bags, and then—zip—out to the airport with Jack and Frank, in Jack's snazzy Lincoln Continental. I was feeling pretty frazzled when we left the hotel, but soon relaxed between the two men in the comfortable front seat of the big car.

Gosh, I thought, I'll get back to New York early in the morning and it may not be until tomorrow night until I have some sex. Almost three days without sex—I might dry up and blow away! So right then and there I decided to blow away, all right . . . *then and there*.

Since Jack was driving, I would first have a little fling with the dreamboat, Frank, sitting next to me. He seemed a little startled by my first advances, but very soon his pants were definitely too tight for him. With one hand resting on what was now a healthy Hollywood hard-on, I used the other to loosen his tie and open the top buttons of his shirt. His chest was hairy and warm and I was getting more turned on by the minute. I began playing with his nipples and he opened his shirt so I could play with them even more, squeezing and sucking on them, then gently biting them until they were as stiff as possible. But even though Frank was very aroused by now, he just sat slumped back against the seat, letting me do all the work, as though he were embarrassed by me doing all these dirty things in the front seat with his good friend, Jack, driving the car.

I looked at Jack, who was doing his best to concentrate on the road and not on us, and said, "You don't mind, do you, if we make out a little?"

"Be my guest," Jack laughed, as though this sort of thing happened every time he got behind the wheel.

So Frank and I crawled into the back seat, like a couple of kids, and I proceeded to make a real joy ride out of it. Frank, who still seemed kind of shy, finally took off his jacket and then I pulled his hand over to my body and moved it around and around on me, and then under my short dress and next to my bikini panties. He was finally getting the idea—he may have been good-looking but he sure didn't seem very experienced—and was moving his fingers underneath my panties and right where they belonged. In fact, with a little direction from me, he was soon massaging my clitoris very nicely and I could get back to my own, equally serious, task—which was to let his poor penis come up for air.

I unzipped his fly and pulled down his trousers and shorts to see what I could find, and—lo and behold!—there was a beautiful throbbing penis, with a nice thick head, down there just waiting to be properly sucked. So while Frank, now getting with it in the best Hollywood adventure traditions, was really moving his fingers inside my cunt, I was producing my own shoot-'em-up.

By feeling Frank's balls, I knew he was close to coming in my mouth, and while I didn't want to deny him that, I did want a first-class fuck so I asked him if he could hold out, and he moaned, "Yessss . . . I think . . . I hope so. . . !

"Think of sad things," I told him, "think of funerals and disasters and all sorts of sad things. You just mustn't come so soon."

So Frank and I took off most of our clothes and lay down

together and moved into a good, deep, long fuck. True to his word, Frank was able to hold off a while and we screwed for at least fifteen miles before he came. By then I'd had an orgasm every seven and a half miles or so, and was pretty satisfied.

"Well, well," said Jack from the front seat, "I wish I could have that on film. . . . We'd pack 'em into the theatres."

"How much more time do we have?" I asked him, now sitting up and carefully leaning forward so I could talk with him without being seen by people in other cars. I was feeling really crazy, and was quite willing to take him on as well.

"Lots of time—we're very early," he said. "But why do you ask? Is there something you forgot to do?"

"No," I said, smiling puckishly, "but maybe you should leave the driving to Frank and we can see if you 'try harder'. . . ?

Jack laughed. "Thanks, Xaviera, but I'm afraid I'm too conservative to do it in the back seat of cars any more. I really do require a bed."

"The back seat's really quite spacious," I said. "Are you sure?"

"Sure he's sure!" said a voice from behind me, and a revived Frank was pulling me back to him, and this time we had at least a twenty-mile fuck, since Jack was kind enough to drive around the airport until we were done. We were lucky that it was a pretty dark night, and nobody in another car saw us, and there were no ten-car collisions.

It isn't something I'd recommend to everyone, but it was a nice way to get to the airport.

What's more, I was able to sleep all the way to New York, enjoying pleasant little dreams of Frank and Jack, Jack and Frank. Next time I'd learn just how "conservative" Jack really was!

V. WINDING UP

The Girls in My Life

ANNE: A Precious Friend

One night, mostly out of curiosity, Larry and I decided to visit one of the swinging spots in the neighborhood, Captain Kidd's Pub. Friends had mentioned the place to me and I was intrigued by what I'd heard. The bar is located in the East Twenties. The front section is reasonably well-appointed and mostly frequented by neighborhood people, usually middle-aged men who have a few drinks and watch television or talk sports. In back, however, is an area with private rooms filled, on certain nights, with a great many swinging young people anxious to cash in on the excitement which the older folks up front seem to have lost long ago.

In order to join this group, Larry and I introduced ourselves to a genial-looking man in his thirties, sitting by himself at a corner table. He had us fill out an application form. We each paid a membership fee of five dollars and were allowed admittance into the large back room which held dozens of tables arranged in three lanes.

Evidently this was some kind of party night as most people were in far-out costumes or else wearing masks. There was confetti spread all over the place and paper streamers of various colors hung from the ceiling, and the whole atmosphere seemed festive enough.

At first glance, at least, there seemed to be only couples,

so we looked around to see if any of our friends were here tonight. Sure enough, voices called out to us, and even with their masks on, I recognized some swingers I knew. One or two members of this crowd teased me and Larry, because they recalled how jealous he'd been when I once made it in a "scene" with a gorgeous gym teacher and his girlfriend. We chatted with them for a few moments and then moved on.

I was having ambivalent feelings about this place. It seemed relaxed and congenial, but it also somehow reminded me of a supermarket where people go to shop for people. Here you either took them with you or else arranged for home delivery. Also, this really wasn't Larry's kind of scene, and after a relatively few minutes there, I'd have been quite willing to leave if he brought up the subject.

On the other hand, I sensed some kind of challenge just being there. I noticed the way people were staring at us because, I assumed, we were newcomers. Also, Larry and I were tanned and rested and I think we made a pretty handsome couple. So we were being looked over because we were potential new playmates for some of the people—new meat on the rack, as it were—and while this might have been flattering, it just wasn't. I felt like saying, "Yes, folks, I'm all there. All 120 pounds of woman, with smooth skin, good boobs, and a hot cunt."

It's funny how an increased sense of awareness can suddenly color one's perceptions. If I looked inviting to some of the men who seemed to want to get acquainted, they now looked and sounded vulgar to me. Larry and I walked around, looking for a free table, and although I smiled at people, rather automatically, I must confess, I had an urge instead to laugh at some of these ninnies because they were trying so hard to have a good time. Some of the women, now that I could observe them more closely, simply looked ludicrous in their manner of dressing, their fat asses stuffed into hot pants two sizes too small. But I kept a kind of frozen smile on my face. I hate making fools out of people even when they seem determined to do the job themselves.

Finally Larry and I found ourselves a small table close to the band, and we gratefully sat down after having virtually walked through a gauntlet of sly, intended-to-be sexy, invitations and not a few gropings by hands reaching out to touch our bodies. I guess we should have had the sense to leave, but I didn't feel like being compromised into leaving. After we relaxed a bit, I danced with Larry and suddenly spotted a very good friend of mine, Anne, in a corner of the room, sitting by herself.

My first instinct was to rush over to her—I was very fond of her and hadn't seen her in quite a while—but I remembered that a friend had recently told me Anne was dying of cancer and had only a short time to live. I didn't know if I could bear to be reunited with this close friend of mine, knowing what I did.

Anne and I had met on Fire Island one summer. She was a Parisian, of royal descent no less, a lovely girl in her mid-thirties. We had a very emotional relationship during that summer vacation, and in the beginning of my career as a call girl, Anne and I had done a bit of hustling together. She had kept her straight job as a legal secretary while by then, I'd given up mine as a United Nations secretary.

Of course, I would go over and see her! She was a close, close friend. I quickly explained the situation to Larry, excused myself, and literally rushed over to Anne. Yes, it was so good seeing her again, and she was obviously surprised and delighted to find me suddenly there next to her. Luckily the crowd was, if nothing else, pretty tolerant so they didn't think it strange to see two girls hugging and kissing each other. Then I took her over to the table to introduce her to Larry.

Anne and I had had some wild experiences in swings with one of my previous boyfriends, Paul Lindfield. I recall he once put the two of us into a bathtub, then watched us make it—it's rather difficult to perform cunnilingus in a bathtub full of water. Other times, and other baths, Paul used to have tremendous fun drying the two of us with a large bath towel. He would then push Anne and me into bed and, cheerfully aided and abetted by our horny friend, Marvin, we'd all engage in a lighthearted swing with no emotional involvements. Paul also received a small souvenir from Anne: two little crabbies (lice) that began to multiply in a short period of time. I still remember quite vividly seeing Paul getting all agitated and upset when he caught one of the little buggers in his pubic hair, which he kept combing and

combing to get rid of them. The little beasts fell off the
comb into the sink. I then carefully wrapped them in a piece
of toilet paper and flushed them down the john, where they
journeyed in peace through the sewers of Manhattan. After
this, Paul and I stayed clear of Anne for some time, but we
never let on that he'd caught body lice from her. When I met
her this night, I thought about the incident but wouldn't
dream of mentioning it to her, even though I thought of it
as funny. Obviously she wouldn't have been amused.

When Anne had been well, she was an extremely horny,
fun-loving girl. She got married when she was twenty-three,
to a man from Johannesburg. He died in a horrible accident
a month after their wedding—he got electrocuted when he
was arranging the lights on their Christmas tree in Durban,
South Africa. Anne never quite recovered emotionally from
the loss. Shortly after his death, she left South Africa and
moved back to France, where she lived for several years.
Being intelligent, adventuresome, and gifted, she decided to
leave France and try her luck in New York. After coming
to New York, she secured a job as a multilingual secretary
in a large law firm and acquired her immigration papers.

For fun and pleasure, she used to visit gay bars, as she
was bi-sexual and tended to be "butch." She also liked going
to swings and probably, I assumed, this was why she was at
Captain's Kidd's this evening. She always enjoyed sex and
men regarded her as being a real dynamite piece. The only
thing that sometimes jarred men was her overpowering personality and high-pitched, staccato way of speaking. Her
voice never seemed to match her warm and sensuous body.

In any case, this particular night, for a brief period of
time, she was my best, most tender, friend again. I took Anne
out on the dance floor, leaving Larry behind, understanding.
I closed my eyes and reminisced about the lovely moments
we shared in my small, cozy, apartment. I used to caress
her big, firm breasts, suck her nipples and the aureoles
around them and lick her neck right under her short hair
and bite her earlobe, while gently pushing my leg between
hers and mounting her. I can still remember feeling the
moisture on my leg after she came simultaneously with me,
clinging together as if we never wanted to let go.

This night, when I opened my eyes to look at her closely,

I realized again how much shorter she was than I. And her hair, cut very short, almost mannish, immaculately groomed, was being all messed up by my wild, affectionate fingers running through it. We danced endlessly on the dance floor, forgetting everything around us except our rediscovered closeness. Her hands reached upward, caressing my face and neck, and then she gently bent my face down to hers, so that we could kiss. Her lips were soft and moist, tasting a little salty. Her eyes were troubled and seemed to ask something of me, wordlessly. They also reflected admiration.

It was only then that I realized the little creature I was holding in my arms, whose body pressed against mine, was truly a dying woman. She seemed to guess what I was thinking and she nodded her head. Now her tears flowed freely as they fell on my shoulders, dripping onto my breasts. I could feel her body shake and tremble while her nails dug deep into my flesh. Her tears to me somehow resembled a chain of pearls, made of love and fear for what the future had in store. "This is the only happiness she might know for a long time," I thought.

I gently lifted up her wet face and pressed a kiss on her eyelids and then on her full mouth. She eagerly opened her lips wide to admit my warm tongue to explore her mouth, as it once used to explore her vagina, knowing and remembering every part of it. Her eyes remained closed and I could see sharp lines round them, lines she never used to have. The same lines, less obvious, appeared around her mouth and nose. She had changed, *"ma petite Anne, ma chèrie,"* for pain had left its mark on her once smooth, almost boyish face. The happy glance I'd detected in her twinkling eyes when I first met her tonight was no longer there. Gone. The sparkle was gone and the pain-killing medicine had stopped doing its work.

Soon nature would slowly but savagely take complete charge of her shapely body. It would destroy the fire that was once in her eyes and consume the rest of her. She told me that already her body was covered with cancerous lumps. Her once beautiful breasts were now filled with hard tumors. Her vagina could no longer be penetrated because it would be too painful. This as a result of extensive surgery she had undergone in the last year, involving all her major female organs, of which most had been removed.

Anne no longer felt a real woman—*une vraie femme*. She laughed, almostly wryly, as she told me of this, but her soft words hammered into my head and made my heart throb with pain. How much did I now, suddenly, adore this miraculous, frail, brave woman whose body pressed against mine and who still carried herself so proudly.

Obviously very few people knew of her condition and they knew even less of the pain she suffered whenever the medication wore off. She continued to work as a secretary, although to get through a morning was frequently pure torture for her. But her spirit had continued to triumph over her malignant, diseased body.

The music had stopped long ago and the dance floor was deserted, except for Anne and me. Suddenly, we felt as if hundreds of eyes were peering at us, for we had forgotten everyone else. I have no idea how long we had stood there. Anne straightened her back, lifted up her head, and with a warm, friendly kiss, she bade me goodbye. Straight as a soldier, she moved through the room full of people, probably none of whom realized this brave little woman carried death in her body.

I looked around the place, feeling desolate yet enriched, for having known a woman like Anne, content that we had shared a few moments of happiness and affection. *Au revoir, Anne? Partir c'est mourir un peu.*

LONG "KISS-TANCE" CALLING . . .

When I finally returned to New York after my publicity trip through the United States, there were a number of telephone messages waiting for me. Three of them were from the same person, a woman called Claudette in Los Angeles I didn't recall ever having met a Claudette in Los Angeles or anywhere else. I did indeed meet three or four girls while staying in Los Angeles, but none of them was named Claudette. Her message was to call her back collect, so—why not?

I picked up the phone and placed the call, and the woman who answered had a beautiful semi-low voice. Judging from her voice she might have been in her early thirties, and she sounded lovely.

Right off I asked her, "How did you get my number?"

"I've *just* finished reading your book," she replied, "and discovered much to my disappointment that you had left Los Angeles already. I heard you on the Dick Whittington Show . . . if only I'd read your book sooner, I would have contacted you in L.A.

"I sure as hell had a hard time getting through to you. First I checked it out with the local distributor of your book and he told me you'd already left the city and would be finishing your whole publicity trip in three days. He advised me to call your publisher in New York and they referred me to your agent and—*voila,* that's how I finally got to you."

"Oh, I see . . .that's interesting, but still this is an expensive call just to say hello. What's on your mind? Can I help you with something?"

"Mmmm, to tell you the truth, I got very turned on by your book. It also made me think about my own life and somehow I suddenly felt the urge to set up a similar business as you had out here on the West Coast."

I was surprised and must have sounded it. "Why, are you a hooker right now, or what is your story?"

She laughed very sexily and said, "Oh no, nothing like that! I used to be a fashion model and over the last five years I have worked as a fashion designer for several stores, doing pretty well actually. In my type of business you get to know an awful lot of different people, mainly businessmen—buyers from out of town—who come to L.A., usually without their wives. Those guys are pretty wealthy types and sometimes they come in groups for conventions or like that. Most of them are from the New York area . . . they represent stores like Saks Fifth Avenue, Bonwit Teller, Lord & Taylor or Bergdorf Goodman.

"They come out here to buy California fashions or go to trade shows. They generally attend to business during the day, but you know how things go, later on in the evening . . . they often invite me out for dinner. I am a single girl . . . what do I have to tell you this for . . . and obviously they all want to end up in the sack with me. And if the fellow is an important connection for me, I usually agree. What the hell, I like sex and these are basically easygoing guys. Of course I have never charged them—you know, my reputation as a designer. I would not even dare to ask them for any bread, so I just go along with all their wishes and all that jazz."

"So why not continue that way if you're having fun?" I said.

"Well, I heard you on the air and I've read your book. That whole story sure as hell turned me on and I started wondering. Maybe I am in the wrong profession."

"How old are you, Claudette, if I may ask?"

"I'm thirty, not the youngest anymore, but I also am, in all immodesty, pretty well put-together, or as these New York guys say, well-stacked. Anyway, after reading your book I've decided I definitely am not going to sleep with any of these buyers for free any more . . . on the other hand, I felt uptight about how to approach them on the money bit. So I sat down yesterday afternoon with three of my best male friends, all in the same business as I am—and all very well-off—and we discussed your book. I told them I wanted to open up a house like yours."

"Oh?" I was wondering where this long-distance conversation was going to lead.

"Of course they thought I was crazy at first. But then it began to dawn on them that it wasn't such a bad idea after all, since they know lots and lots of horny buyers coming to L.A. every week, always in the mood for a girl and never knowing where to go for a piece of ass—pardon the expression. So . . . *that's* why I called. I need some advice, or maybe approval, on your part, because me and my friends think we've pretty much figured it all out. They'll put up twenty thousand dollars so I can make a down payment on a three-bedroom condominium and furnish it nicely and ooh la la, I'm in business, no? But the problem of course is how to go about getting the girls to work for me. . . ."

"Whoa, Claudette, you are really going too fast for me. You have never even turned one trick in your entire life and —'ooh la la'—you want to be a madam overnight?"

"Yes," she said, "that's right."

"Maybe you should try it out first and see whether you like the life of a prostitute and how you like the attitude of men toward you in your new role. It seems to me you're doing just fine, in my opinion, as a fashion designer. Where do you live, for instance?"

"I have a beautiful pad in Bel Air—you can compare that to Beverly Hills in L.A.—and I would never want to give that up, nor my job as a designer. But I am just fed up with letting all those money possibilities go by. Besides, now I've warmed up my three investors, they really want me to get going with it."

"I hope they are legit and don't end up pimping off you —remember you are new at this ball game."

"Oh, no they are one hundred percent legit. I know them well."

"But Claudette, money investment is not really all that important. If you have a nice two-bedroom apartment or even a one-bedroom place where you convert the living room into a bedroom, that will do. I honestly don't think you need a twenty thousand dollar investment."

"Oh, I don't care, I only want the best for my clients. If you can help me find some groovy girls who want to work for me, I will arrange the rest. Believe me, I will treat them well. . . . Actually I've already planned to let them live in my new house and I'll also supply them with a car."

"Hey, Claudette, you must be crazy to do this."

"Why do you say that?"

"First of all, I don't think you should be doing this at all. Secondly, if you do what you say you intend to do, your girls will do nothing but take advantage of you. If you are going to be *that* generous, and give them free room and board and transportation, they will surely wind up stepping all over you. What's more, men want variety and if you have the same three girls living in, once they've seen them all, they'll want something new and what are you going to do with those three girls—kick them out on the street?

"You'd be much better off getting a few girls' numbers who have their own place but are still willing to spend some time, say a few nights a week, at your place. Through those girls you undoubtedly will get to know others, by word of mouth. . . . By the way, how will you go about building up business in the first place?"

"Oh, that's no problem whatsoever—My friends know tons of people coming to town, as I told you before, and they'll just lay it on the line to them. . . . I'm sure they would much rather come to my cozy place and have a good selection than hang around the bars and pick up some trampy-looking chick.

"Look, Xaviera, to make a long story short, your book made a different person out of me and once I set my mind to doing something nobody can stop me, and all I ask of you is to help me find some girls. I realize you don't know L.A., and I also gathered from your radio conversation that you are now strictly an author, but could you please at least give me some ideas?"

"Honestly, Claudette, I can't help you with any phone numbers . . . while I was staying at the Beverly Hilton in L.A., I *did* meet a few girls at the bar. They recognized me and congratulated me on the book and we talked a bit, but I had no reason to take down their numbers. But they'd be easy to find, I guess. One of them was a really lovely blonde Dutch girl. Her name was Anne-Marie—and she introduced me to three of her friends . . . listen, you have a pencil and paper?"

"Yes, just a sec. Okay—shoot."

"O.K., write down Anne-Marie, Dutch, blonde, approximately twenty-six; then there was Sheri, a dark-haired girl with short curly hair and kind of chubby, and the other name I remember was Anne-Marie's closest friend, Deborah, a real flaming redhead with sex virtually drooping out of her eyes. Claudette, honestly my head is not into that game anymore, and that's all the help I can be. So why don't we change the subject, from business to yourself— tell me what you look like, et cetera."

"O.K. Meanwhile, thanks for the information and someday I will drop you a line and let you know what has come of my great ideas. . . . As for my looks, I am fairly tall, about five-feet nine, have long, shoulder length, auburn-red wavy hair, with a natural gray streak in the front, green eyes and an All-American cutey-pie tip-tilted nose. I have been told that I have a very sensual mouth—and my pride are my sparkling white teeth, with not one cavity! My breasts are big and firm, 36-D, and I have long slim legs. I think my ass is just a tiny bit too heavy, but men tell me they love it, 'gives them something to hold on to.' "

She paused a second, then continued, "I've got to watch my weight, however. I just love candy and it takes a lot of will power to stay off that sweet stuff."

Then her voice dropped to a husky low timbre and she almost whispered in my ear, "Xaviera, when I looked at your picture on the book, I knew it had to be you. . . . I

was really turned on by reading about your love affair with
Helga, the first girl you ever fell in love with. You know,
I can really almost identify with Helga, the way you described that whole scene and the way she looked. I even
believe I look something like her, although I have reddish
brown hair and she was a brunette. And you know, when
I was a teenager, the same thing happened to me as to Helga
—a woman seduced me and I didn't know whether I should
enjoy it or not. It was all so strange and new to me. I had
had sex with boys at that stage, but honestly I was so uptight
about this female thing that ever since that first experience
I've been fighting the Lesbian tendency I obviously have,
but wanted to deny. For a good many years I put it away
in the back of my mind, like a big bad secret and now at
thirty, after reading your stories—so damn honest!—all of
a sudden I felt what I had been missing all those years.
Despite all the sex I've had with men, what's been lacking
is a deep emotional involvement, and I think that maybe
only a woman like you will be able to provide me with that."

"Claudette, darling, face reality—we are many miles
apart, and here you are, a career woman, ready to plunge
into the tough business of prostitution. I must warn you
that you may become hard and indifferent toward women
as well as men, I just have to warn you about that. So why
don't you content yourself with being just as you are—if
you want, try finding a woman like me. The memory of
your one love affair is so many years old you really ought
to renew the experience before you come out with those
statements about needing a woman to love.

"Still, I must admit *you are really turning me on.* I am
lying on my bed, watching myself in the round mirror on
the ceiling and listening to your lovely voice. Wish you were
here. Dammit, if only we had met in L.A! I am wearing
nothing but a light blue jean shirt barely covering my naked
ass and all the way open in front. . . . What are you wearing?"

"Oh, I am so juiced up," she almost cried in my ear now.
"I can't believe that anyone can get me so turned on by
phone—just thinking about you there in New York with
nothing on but a shirt, and your hot juicy cunt ready for

me. . . . I am a bit confused as to what I would like to do to you or be done first. . . . Oh hell, I'm dressed in a pair of light blue slacks with a little shift blouse on top of it and my pants just stimulate me right near my crotch because they're really tight and because of that, my cunt is constantly in contact with the soft material."

She paused, then continued, "And now I am unzipping my pants and slowly rolling them down. I am sort of hanging down in one of those big fluffy orange swivel chairs, which is on a thick white rug, and my little silver-gray poodle is licking my bare toes, and I wish it were you! I would give anything to just be able to spend this night with you."

"Claudette, listen to me, let me seduce you by phone— I'm going to get that lovely cunt of yours so juiced up you will barely be able to stand talking to me any more. Hold the phone in one hand, pressed against your ear, and move your other hand slowly toward your belly. . . . Now stroke your navel with your soft fingers and now crawl lower, toward where I guess your bikini panties are covering your lovely, lusty love box. . . . Now pull your slacks down all the way. C'mon, step out of them and also lift up your blouse. Are you wearing a bra?"

"No, no, my tits are big but really firm, and I luckily don't need a bra . . . oh my nipples are hard and yummy, dying to be kissed by your mouth, oh, if only I could feel your mouth around my tits, they'd be all yours! Yes, yes, I have pulled my pants down, and the dog is lying on them and sniffing the crotch. . . . The little darling must smell the love juices that I started producing when I still had them on. . . . Come on, please Xaviera, tell me more, tell me all about all the exciting sexy things you're going to do to me, the things I've missed for so many years."

"Right, darling. Now you slowly, really slowly, pull your blouse over your head and take it off as well. All you are wearing now, I suppose, are panties, and keep those on for now. Ummm, you must look very sexy, hanging loose in that chair. Now I'm going to go and stand behind your chair and caress your neck, gently massaging. . . . Now come the tender strokes of my warm tongue, around your ear lobe, in your neck, and now I am standing right next to you to press a full moist kiss on your mouth, exploring every part of your lips and mouth. Now I bend forward onto my knees and bury my head in your lap, my arms wrapped around those gorgeous hips and ass of yours. Your thighs are divine and your legs so gorgeously long and now they are spread apart, forming a triangle with the floor. Your breathing becomes faster now as my tongue moves lower and lower, away from its hideout place, your warm safe belly. I am now coming closer and closer to your pink panties—I guess they are pink?"

"Yes, yes, they are white and pink, a mixture! What else will you do to me? Can I play with myself? I am *so* horny just listening to you, please can I just rub myself down there while you keep on talking to me? Will you do the same and think of me?"

"Yes, yes, of course, do that. I want you to insert your finger deep into your cunt, but only after you have put it in your mouth and sucked it all the way deep inside your mouth, making it nice and warm and wet, ready to stimulate that darling lovebird of yours. I meanwhile have removed my shirt as well, and with my legs slightly pulled up I am also starting to please myself, looking up in the mirror watching every movement I make, naturally thinking about you, that precious woman of mine. . . . But now, here I am back with you in the same room again, and I am on my knees on the floor, in between your long legs but down at your feet now, and I start sucking your big toe and then your other toes, one by one. This sends lovely chills through your entire body, and your hard nipples show goose bumps around them, and your legs start shaking just enough for me to notice, and you tighten and open your cunt so I can just peek inside.

"My, my, your pubic hair really matches your other hair, auburn with a streak of red in it. Curly and lots of it, yet trimmed on the side, I'm sure, because you like to wear bikinis. . . . Now I am working my way up your legs and I finally reach that fantastic end of the two-way road, your mons veneris, a voluptuous full cunt, with the glistening juice inviting me to bite into it. Now I start sucking your clitoris, gently so as not to hurt you—just moving that little, but rapidly growing, knot left and right, around and around in my mouth, getting the sweet taste of it. I drink more of your wonderful nectar until my cheeks and mouth are all wet. Then you assist me, so while my long tongue finds its way inside your cunt, you are continuing the vibrating movements with your own hands, rubbing and squeezing that clit to ecstasy. . . . Darling, remember today you have made up your mind, you want a woman as a lover and there is nobody that can please another woman better this way than a woman. Today is our festival!"

Meanwhile, while talking and listening to Claudette's heavy and faster breathing over the telephone, I was rubbing my own pussy frantically. I have put some Koronex jelly into it, to make it all a lot smoother, and as I can hear over the phone, my lover on the other end was about ready to have her own orgasm, surely masturbating right along with me. . . . So I whispered in her ear a few last sentences to get her really hot and buttered up: "Oh, yes, yes, yes, now I have taken you away from the chair and have pulled you down besides me on the thick white rug and with your legs wrapped around my neck I tongue-fuck you all the way, while pushing my two middle fingers in and out of your juicy cunt faster and faster, better rhythm than a man's cock would give you. I can feel you tighten and loosen your vaginal muscles . . . meanwhile with my other hand I am playing with myself and now . . . now, *there* it is, that long expected great, groovy orgasm, all over my face, and my own hands squeezed in between my legs, my whole body shaking from the beautiful spasms of my own excited eager cunt!"

By now, Claudette must actually have reached her orgasm, and so had I. There was silence on the other end of the phone, and it took me a minute as well to catch my own breath. I was tired from talking and my tongue felt like leather but by God, how I wished I really could have drunk her pussy just as I'd described myself doing.

When we both came down to earth from our long kiss-tance fantasy, Claudette guaranteed me that the moment she had a chance she would fly to New York and then . . . really do it all. She wanted to kiss me, caress me, hug me, learn how to please me and then, last but not least, fall asleep in my arms.

But we never met . . . .

The Girls in My Life

LINDA: The Fastest Mouth in the East

Linda and her boyfriend, Allen, were introduced to me by my photographer friend, Freddy, on a cold winter's afternoon. That is, he had called up and said he was sending over this girl I should meet. No more explanation than that. Allen, Freddy said, was a musician without a job and Linda "was a freaky girl who liked sex." This hardly made them seem unusual to me, but I said okay, I'd talk to them.

About six o 'clock on a Sunday afternoon, the doorbell rang and it was Linda and Allen. They came up and after a few minutes of conversation, I decided I liked them. Linda came on very strong, while Allen seemed rather shy at first, but they were sweet kids and I told myself I'd help them if I could. Little did I realize that Linda would prove to be the most sexually talented person I'd ever met!

She was around twenty with a pale face, accented by two heavy rouge spots on her cheeks. And thick layers of eyelashes. And lots of black and white eye shadow. No lipstick, no bra, no stockings—and it was so cold that day—and no panties. She was wearing hot pants and each time she spread her legs, even slightly, she revealed a shaven pussy. Her legs were just beautiful and she seemed to have large breasts.

So there was Linda—long brown hair, with a hairpiece added, that exotic face, a tight-fitting black sweater, hot pants and beaten-up black boots. She had a heavy Brooklyn accent and absolutely no inhibitions.

Allen looked, well, artistic. Thick curly black hair, worn long, dark romantic eyes and a sensitive mouth. He was much better spoken than Linda, and obviously better educated. He also dressed almost completely in black.

With me at the time were Larry and Kathy, my roommate, and we all sat fascinated as Linda told us her story. "Xaviera, Freddy said you are the greatest and that we should look you up. So here we are, man . . . ."

With that, she pulled her sweater out from beneath the big belt she was wearing and let it hang outside her hot pants instead of inside. With a heavy sigh she then said, "What else is there to do besides having a little fun," and with this she continued her story, her hand now placed squarely on Allen's crotch.

He didn't seem to mind.

"Allen, my old man here, and I have been living together for the past year," Linda continued. "The problem is that he is still married and his two adopted children live with his wife. That bitch is pestering the hell out of us —she is suing him for a huge alimony even though she has a good job. But Allen is out of work now—he has a great act, but there's no work for musicians unless you're with a band and it's hard to join a band nowadays, no matter how good you are.

"I have been a professional ice skater, but I'm not working now. So we are just grooving and fucking ourselves silly . . . but we are running out of bread and we don't have any money past next week. The rent is due and our stomachs are empty most of the time."

I looked at Larry and he looked at me and neither of us knew what to think about this strange young lady. If I knew Larry, his impulse would be to get up, go into the kitchen and whip up plates of bacon and eggs for these two kids, but Linda just went on talking and no one moved. We were all riveted to our chairs—no one wanted to miss a word.

"Luckily," said Linda, "my mother works as a hatcheck girl in a fine restaurant downtown, and so once a week the owner allows us to come down and have a dinner on the

house. That's the only hot meal we have all week. . . .
Look, Xaviera, I'm not here to bother you with our financial problems, but Freddy said you might help us out somehow. We know the business you're in, and we dig it. After
all, Allen here and me are swingers and freaks, right,
Allen?"

Before Allen got a chance to say anything—confirm or
deny that they were "swingers and freaks"—Linda unzipped
his black corduroy pants and took out his penis.

"You see this little thing here?" she said. "Well, just wait
and see what I do with that cock—miracles!" By now Kathy
was in semi-hysterics, giggling like crazy behind her hand
at Linda's behavior, and moving her chair closer to the
couch where Linda and Allen were sitting, the better to
observe Linda's "miracle."

Larry and I were suddenly holding hands like two kids
at the movies, and doing our best to suppress a giggle.
Despite our sophistication, we have never seen anything like
this. Linda is now leaning over and sucking Allen's cock
and even though Allen's cock is not immediately responding, it is obvious that she is—well . . . well . . . a born cocksucker.

Now Allen's cock is at last responding to her expert
mouth, and growing to at least twice its original size. Linda
has her sweater off now and is sitting there, bent over Allen's
cock, moaning and groaning as she ferociously sucks him.
Her large tits are on either side of his leg as she hovers
over him, one leg crossed over the other, her hair over
her face, sucking him toward climax. Her hand is now inside
her hot pants and she is fingering herself to an orgasm.

Suddenly Allen stands up, his prick also standing up, tall
and cocky, picks up Linda in his arms, and sets off for
where he thinks the bedroom must be. Now that Larry and
I are over our shock, we are very turned on by this performance and we quickly follow them into the bedroom.
Everyone rips off his or her clothes and now we are all going
at it. Larry is kissing my breasts and then I am madly
sucking him as Linda is still doing to Allen. All four of us
are now into a wild orgy, but the main event is Linda
sucking both Allen and Larry's cocks—I have generously
donated Larry's cock for the occasion—while I muff dive

into her completely shaven pussy. It is a wild experience, as I have never sucked a bald cunt in my life and even though she is obviously super clean, it does not turn me on as much as a cunt with short, trimmed hair. I just want to see some hair there—not a kinky, bushy crop necessarily, but just trimmed short.

Meanwhile Kathy, who sometimes couldn't care less about sex, is standing in the doorway, chain-smoking cigarettes and watching us all with wide-open eyes. We invited her to join the fun several times, but she won't budge. It dawns on me that she probably is thinking that I do not usually let myself go in public with Larry—our sex life is almost always quite private—but today Madam X has made an exception and gone public.

By now Linda has taken care of Larry and is back exclusively on Allen's cock, sucking it as though it were the greatest candy cane, and the two of them have a simultaneous orgasm, she just by sucking and hugging him.

Fantastico, Linda, you are . . . you are hired—as the greatest cocksucker in the world.

When we all got dressed, and were back in the living room, Linda wanted to know how the audition had gone. She asked me with a wink, "Well, did we pass the test—do you think Allen and I could work for you?"

She jokingly refers to Allen as her "superstud," and it soon becomes clear that he would like to be taken on as a male prostitute. This certainly was not in my mind at all, so I replied, in all honesty, that while he was a good-looking boy, I didn't think he would ever be a great stud simply because his cock is not big enough to meet the requirements of those few of my customers who want a boy to have sex with them. Then, too, I am almost always asked, I have to explain to them, for boys with the biggest possible endowments. Also, Allen simply takes too long to warm up and, most important to me, I don't think he particularly cares for men and would perhaps not be able to get it up at all with another man.

Allen didn't seem at all unhappy with my line of reasoning, nor did Linda. Indeed, she is telling me, "You haven't seen a thing yet! Wait until you come down to one of our regular orgies, where Allen ties me up and beats the shit out of me. He really digs that, makes him feel real good and supermasculine. . . . I dig it, man, all the way . . . *oy gevalt,* for an Italian cat like him and a Jewish broad like me, we certainly form an odd couple. Don't you think so?"

I smile and nod my head. Yes, I think so.

Now that Linda is going to work for me, we are going to have to have a little talk. Not about sex, because this sex kitten doesn't need lessons from anyone in that department. But she is going to have to dress differently and look differently. If she is going to become a call girl, she must not look whorish—which she now does. Different clothing and different make-up—that is the prescription for young Linda.

We discuss this, and there seems to be no problem. I will advance her some money for new clothes and I assure her she will do well in this field if she doesn't come on too strong. It's agreed that she will start the next night, so that is all settled.

Allen gives me a warm kiss goodbye, and says to Larry, Kathy and me, "Thanks so much for entertaining us."

"The pleasure was ours," I say. "You two have certainly entertained *us.*"

Linda started the follwing night. Allen did some food shopping with some of the money I gave her, she explained, because they had nothing in the house. She cooked them a "great Italian meal," she said, and promised to bring over her special antipasto or spaghetti with garlic sauce real soon. I told her the antipasto would be wonderful, but I didn't think the spaghetti would be such a good idea on a business night.

Linda was now wearing more suitable clothes, but she still had on a half-ton of make-up. Instead of three layers of eyelashes, she now "only" wears two, and instead of pitch-black eye shadow and eye liner, she has put on charcoal eye

make-up. So her face still looks whorish and unnatural, but
to my surprise, her natural "come on" as a person soon
makes her an instant hit with men, and in a relatively short
space of time she is the biggest scorer in my house. She is
rapidly known for her speedy success with men because there
are indeed very few men who can resist her speedy blow
jobs for more than a few minutes. They may be thinking
about fucking her, but her rapid tongue and succulent mouth
are going to get to them before they get to her. Not that
Linda has anything against balling customers as well—in
fact, she was there when I needed a girl to take it the Greek
way—but she just loves to give head, and this is the only girl
in my experience who can virtually come each time herself
by sucking on a man's penis. That's how much pleasure it
gives her.

Some months later—it was now summertime—I had a
house full of men and no room for them. Linda did yeoman
work for me by taking two young stockbrokers into the bathroom and blowing one while he sat on the sink and then,
having decided the bathroom cramped her style, took the
other guy out on the balcony and had him lie down in one
of the lounge chairs to enjoy the best blow job in town. He
came so noisily I thought that half of New York must have
heard him yowling, "I'm commmmming!" But fortunately
for me in that apartment (this was the apartment previous
to the penthouse on Twenty-fifth Street) my upstairs neighbor was a very groovy, swinging guy, with a bedroom full
of mirrors himself, and he simply leaned over his own balcony and said, "Bravo!" Knowing Linda, if he could have
dropped his cock over the balcony, she would have given
him more reason to shout "Bravo."

By this time Linda had gone through the Xaviera Hollander finishing school, but the education didn't really take.
She looked sensational in bra and panties and long black
stockings held up by a garter belt, plus high spike heels, and
she looked very well in almost any kind of dress because
she had a good bust—this is one lady who really needed
a bra—and dynamite legs. However she preferred that

original all-black outfit of hers and no bra, and I had to scold her several times for showing up like that. Still and all, once she went to work with that magic mouth of hers, it was hard not to be glad to have her aboard. If *The Guinness Book of Records* had an entry for "Fastest Blow Jobs," I'm sure Linda would rank in first or second place.

Another thing that bothered me about Linda was her constant complaining about having no money. I knew that Allen was playing in a top nightclub in town and supposedly making very good money, and I knew Linda was making a buck, yet she continually was moaning that she had no money, especially whenever I suggested she add something a little more stylish to her wardrobe. Eventually I learned from her that Allen was handing over his entire salary to his wife, and Linda was helping out in that department as well, so they were paying dearly for their freedom.

One night I bumped into Allen and Linda at the restaurant where her mother worked. They were still following their practice of a "freebie" meal every week. I hadn't seen Allen in months and he looked just great—his hair was a bit shorter and there were some interesting gray streaks in it, perhaps the result of his problems with his wife. He also had grown a full mustache, which looked well on him and made him seem more mature. He was wearing a well-tailored suit, which also added to his good looks.

This was in marked contrast to Linda, who was in her usual black ensemble and had her eyes smeared with black stuff again. I couldn't help but remark about how she loved to molest that nice face of hers, and she replied, "Allen loves me in sexy hot pants and lots of make-up. Then he knows everyone will look at me and he gets a kick out of that. He's pretty funny, my old man, isn't he? Wants me to be as whorish as they come, so why not . . . ?"

I didn't have a good answer for that, so I wished them *bon appetit* and moved off to my own table with Larry. Linda and I continued to have problems about the way she dressed at my house, and eventually we just drifted apart.

I hope they're happy, Linda and Allen, and I will never ever forget my introduction to them.

And I will always remember how Linda was dressed on

at least one night—in black underwear and those stockings and garter belt and high heels, about to give a man the blow job of his life—every man's dream fantasy come true. But even so—I preferred my girls to look a lot more demure and not like the ultimate whore.

THE PRODUCER'S HOAX

One day in April, 1972, I had a call from my lawyer. He said that a man had called him from Chicago and requested my number. Of course my lawyer refused to give him any information until he had spoken to me first and cleared it with me. The man who'd called claimed to be a film producer who had gotten my lawyer's name and number through a friend of Robin Moore, my co-author. It all seemed rather complicated, so I said to give him my telephone number and to have him call me direct.

Moments after I'd hung up the phone with my lawyer, it rang again and it was our friend, the producer. He had a European accent and I immediately placed it as either Danish or German. After about five minutes shilly-shallying he finally informed me he was Irving Rubeen from Copenhagen, he had a movie company in Holland, another movie production company on the West Coast and offices in New York City. If he was legit, it all sounded rather intriguing and exciting. *The Happy Hooker* was already a solid success and of course we were eager to have a good film sale. Also, since I was facing "voluntary" departure from the country and had a limited time to stay in the United States, this would be the perfect time to make a final decision on the movie. When I left, I'd at least know what was going to happen—whether or not the book was actually going to be made into a movie.

Mr. Rubeen ended our conversation by telling me that he wanted me to fly out to Hollywood and that his secretary would get in touch with me. When I asked him how I could get in touch with him, he said he was leaving to negotiate some business back in Denmark and would be difficult to reach, but his secretary would get back to me within the hour.

About an hour later, a Miss Woodson called, said she was his secretary, and told me she wanted me to fly to Hollywood the next Saturday. I asked her why the big rush for me to go to Hollywood and she explained that they wanted to base a screenplay on my book and wanted me to eventually play the lead. My head spun a little when I heard this. If true, it seemed to me like the beginning of a new career and since they had a movie company in Europe, it would be possible to make the film there, where production costs were so much lower than in the States, if I did have to leave here.

An hour later, Miss Woodson called again and asked me to come to Chicago the following day. I asked her why, since I'd agreed already to fly to the West Coast. She said that I must come to Chicago because she wanted to meet me first. Miss Woodson explained she was initially responsible for the actors Mr. Rubeen hired and she had to arrange a screen test for me. This sounded a little strange to me—how could a secretary know whether or not a person was the right type to be an actor or an actress? Nevertheless I accepted her explanation. The old ego was acting up again—this wasn't our first movie offer, but it was the first to give me some personal participation. It was a new world for me, and if nothing else I wanted to know more about it.

Miss Woodson had said she'd meet me the following afternoon, and when I looked at my calendar, which was full of radio and television promotional work, I saw that I'd arranged to go to Washington, D. C., that morning at ten. It would mean a busy day flying from Washington to Chicago, but I'd agreed to come. Miss Woodson said to be sure and travel first-class and she'd reimburse me when I arrived; she also told me she would make reservations for me at a top hotel and that we'd meet in the lobby around five o'clock. She'd recognize me, she said, because she had read my book and would know me from the pictures on the covers.

After I finished my interview in Washington the next day, I went straight to the airport and got on a flight to Chicago. The weather, when I arrived, was horrible. While it had been warm and summery in Washington, Chicago was miserable, cold, and rainy. The air traffic was all jammed up and we circled Chicago for about an hour. I was supposed to meet Miss Woodson at five o'clock and I was already an hour late.

At the airport I had to wait another half-hour to get a cab to the hotel and finally shared a taxi with three salesmen who were there to attend some electrical appliances convention. One rode in front and the other two in the back, with me. En route to the hotel, I flipped out these guys with my crazy stories. They were young, green, and horny, and to make the cab ride more interesting, for them *and* me, I moved my hands quickly from crotch to crotch and worked them into nice big erections. They were more than a little smashed, and all of them—including the guy in the front, whom I hadn't touched—were soon comparing notes on who had the biggest one, who the longest, etc. I almost never play games like this in taxis, but I guess this one time I just wanted to be what is called a "cockteaser." The two guys in the back were so horny by now that they tried to molest me right in the cab, and if I hadn't reasserted control of the situation, I'd have gotten raped somewhere or other by three men, or at least two.

Somehow I enjoyed the struggle, though, because all the travelling around made me kind of giddy. Who knows? Maybe a little bit of sex wouldn't hurt. But I had to look nice and not at all messed up. So, stop the kidding, Xaviera! By the time the taxi finally arrived at the hotel, I managed to pull up my pantyhose (how unsexy can those passion killers be), brushed my hair and then allowed our merry group of would-be gang-bangers to pay the cabfare.

In the lobby I didn't see anyone who might look even remotely like a Miss Woodson. There were three elderly

ladies in a corner chatting and giggling, no Miss Woodson
there—Miss Woodson had sounded young over the phone.
I assumed she must've tired of sitting around the lobby
waiting for me and had made some other arrangements. I
went over to the reservation desk and was reassured to find
there had been a reservation made for a Miss Hollander.
But the room had not been paid for, so I wasn't about to
check in as yet.

My next stop was to go over to the check-out desk and
to the bell captain, and ask if a Miss Woodson had perhaps
left a message for me. The answer was "No, no messages."
I decided to sit around and wait, thinking that maybe she'd
been delayed as well. But then again, she had called me from
Chicago and there was obviously no reason for her to leave
the city.

After waiting in the lobby for three-quarters of an hour,
I decided to call my New York apartment and speak to
Larry. He was there and advised me to fly back right away
because *Time* magazine wanted to do an interview with me
and they needed to take some pictures the next day. However, I felt kind of reluctant to go back since I'd come all
this way. I waited a while longer, then left a note with the
bell captain for Miss Woodson, telling her I'd been there
and was going to catch an eight-o'clock flight back to New
York. Disillusioned and tired by this time, I called Larry
back and told him I'd be taking the next plane back to New
York, at eight o'clock.

I cabbed out to the airport, exchanged my ticket, and was
about ready to board the plane when I heard my name being
called on the intercom: "Miss Hollander, telephone. Please
go to the Information Desk." So I did, figuring it was Larry
with an important message for me.

However, to my great surprise, it was our Miss Woodson.
By this time I felt tired and abused and I snapped at her:
"Look, I've come all the way from New York to Washington
to Chicago and you didn't even leave a message at the hotel
for me, and I don't think I should come back now. I'm
going back to New York where I have certain commitments
to fulfill. I'd counted on meeting with you for an hour or so
and taking a late plane back. I'm tired and irritated and I'm

going to take a plane back to New York in five minutes!"
She sounded very agitated by my news and told me to hold
on for just a minute and seemed to be having a conference
with somebody else. When she got back on the phone, she
told me that Mr. Rubeen had postponed his trip to Denmark
and was very insulted that I wouldn't come back. "You know
how movie producers are!" she said, adding: "They don't
come to you; you have to come to them, baby."

Now she sounded overwrought. "How *could* you do this
to us after all the trouble we took to arrange this meeting?"

Mr. Rubeen seemed to be giving her hell in the background, and now she was virtually begging me to come back
since he seemed furious at her for the screwed-up arrangements. She said they'd reimburse me for any expenses that
I had or might incur, whether it was the cab or plane fares.
Money was no object. "Please, cancel the appointment in
New York," she said, "or if you can't we'll get you on the
last plane to New York."

By this time, it was almost eight o'clock, and I didn't
think there was a chance in hell I could make *that* plane.
So I agreed to come back for a few hours. There were other
planes I could make, if necessary. I called Larry back and
said: "Tell the people from *Time* to get the interview with
me via phone and forget about the pictures. Just give them
some of my old ones." Larry sounded a little worried about
me because he now thought my trip to Chicago had to be
some kind of a farce. He was also worried about my being
so tired and upset.

But back I walked through the Chicago airport to get a
cab to the city. It may have been my imagination, but the
airport now seemed several miles long. My feet were hurting
and a corn on my left little toe was killing me. I had a run
in my stocking, and I didn't feel one-tenth as attractive or
interesting a female as I had even at the end of that wild cab
ride.

I finally got a taxi and headed back to the hotel. I didn't
have to share this time, since there were plenty of cabs
available. It's lucky that the cab driver shut up at first since
I wasn't in the mood to talk to anybody right then. Eventually he said to me that my face was awfully familiar. I said

that was possible because I'd had my picture in the Chicago
Tribune about a week earlier and that I'd written a naughty
book, *The Happy Hooker*. He gave me a big smile and said,
"At first I thought it was a book about those poor drug
addicts, hooked on heroin and all that stuff, but when I read
it, I found it one hell of a good book. I don't usually read a
lot of books, but that is a *hell* of a good one! My wife is
learning from it every day and I'm practicing every night."
He laughed at his own joke, and when I left the cab, he
slapped me on my shoulders—for good luck, I presume,
though I'm not sure which of us he was wishing good luck.

This time, I'd made sure I'd be able to find Miss Woodson.
She'd told me over the phone that she'd be wearing a green
leather suit and I saw her standing near the entrance of the
hotel. Miss Woodson, a lovely young black girl, was talking
to two tall, tough-looking guys, but she spotted me right
away and came over to me. After she greeted me, she introduced me to the two guys, who shook hands like a vice,
and whisked me away. Miss Woodson couldn't have been
more than twenty-two years old and she was carrying a
movie script under her arms, which she handed to me, saying it was mine "to read and study" for my test. We then
went over to the check-in desk. She advised me to pay for
my own reservation, get the key, and wait up in the room for
Mr. Rubeen. When she saw my surprise that I had to pay,
she hastily said that Rubeen would later pay back all my
expenses in one.

I paid the hotel bill of twenty-five dollars—without luggage you have to pay in advance—but it would seem as
though the bureaucracy in hotels is as bad as anywhere else.
When I wanted to pay in cash, they didn't want to accept
my money without identification. Since I didn't carry any
identification with me, payment by check proved impossible.
The room was booked under the name "Hollander" and all
I had with me was a copy of *Show* magazine, with my
photograph on the cover, saying I was Xaviera Hollander,
"The Happy Hooker." But that was not enough for our
bureaucrats. They wanted more identification, such as credit
cards, passport, driver's license, social security card. I had
none of these with me.

We had to go to the bell captain, who had to go to someone else again, and after hopping around from place to place for about half an hour, we finally got to speak to the manager of the hotel. I was getting pretty aggravated and felt like punching him in the face. He finally told me it was okay to pay by cash!

With my money finally accepted as legal tender, we went upstairs to my room—which turned out to be a crummy little hutch. I was frankly surprised. I thought, "Oh, boy! This is real style for a rich movie producer."

However, I wasn't going to let myself get upset—there was a Miss Woodson, after all, and I was supposedly going to meet Mr. Irving Rubeen. Let's face it, I was just a little girl out to make a big score, maybe become a movie star and act the part of her own book. What did I care about a mere twenty-five dollars and some airfare and fatigue?

Miss Woodson left me alone with the instructions to look over the script she had given me, saying that Mr. Rubeen would show up in about twenty minutes. For three-quarters of an hour, I sat there reading the damn thing and getting bored stiff. It was all about sex and girls on the beach making it with guys of all sizes and colors. All I'd be doing was moaning and groaning and getting banged on the beach. I thought, "This must be one of those Danish dirty-movie producers—my God, I don't want my book to be converted into one of those hard-core porno films. The only thing that will have anything to do with my book is the title . . ."

Since I had nothing better to do, I kept reading the script and God knows it didn't get any better. At last there was a knock on the door. I opened it and there stood Mr. Irving Rubeen!

He certainly looked like a movie producer—in his late forties (or early fifties even), thick, bushy, silver-gray hair worn half-way down his neck, large brown eyes, heavy black eyebrows, and a round face, like a baby cherub. He was wearing red pants and a red, turtleneck sweater with white shoes and socks. He wore a big diamond ring on his pinky and a diamond-studded watch on his left wrist. To me, he certainly looked as if he had money. He seemed friendly and yet, when interrupted, he was very brusque. His English

was perfect, however, with far less trace of an accent than
- over the phone.

We discussed a few chapters of my book and then he
came to the point. He said that he'd talked to Robin Moore
already. At first, they'd had a great many communication
problems, since whenever he tried to reach Moore at home
in Connecticut, or at his office in New York, he was never
there. "So I finally spoke to his friend and associate, Jack
Letheran," he told me. "I even talked to your literary agent,
John Starr, and it's agreed that I should buy the book and
we're almost all set. All I've got to do is draw up the con-
tracts and have them signed. I came to you last, because I
thought you might be too 'hot' to get involved with, too
many people might be watching you. I wanted to take a
good, close look at you and instead of going to Copenhagen
as planned, I decided to stay one more day."

I was very flattered to hear this. Still, I couldn't understand why neither Robin nor John Starr had ever mentioned
anything about this man to me. Why did he have to call Jack
Letheran and my lawyer, instead of asking my agent, John
Starr, for my telephone number, or even Robin Moore, for
that matter?

Well, whatever had happened, we'd finally gotten together,
that's what counted. We talked about Hollywood and Los
Angeles and whether I'd ever been there. As it happened I
told him, my publisher had just sent me on a terrific publicity tour which had given me a chance to see quite a bit
of the country. I said I liked the West Coast, being part
orange juice (I drink it day and night). The weather was
nice, the people friendly, and I'd met this wealthy guy in
Beverly Hills, Bernie Cornfeld, who was then living in
George Hamilton's former house.

Irving then jumped up and said, "I know Bernie, good
old Bernie! He's a great pal of mine. You know, actually
my girl, Miss Woodson, used to be *his* private secretary and,
in fact, she took care of getting girls for him and somehow
managed to keep his hectic love life reasonably organized—
so he wouldn't have two dates at the same time."

Then he added: "Little Miss Woodson is now living in a
two-hundred-thousand-dollar house which used to belong

to one of the Gabor sisters, and actually me and my friend Bernie financed her house . . . You see what can happen when you're a twenty-two-year-old girl, involved with a big producer, and you're a smart cookie. You live up to your promises and you make friends. That's what you should do, Xaviera. We want you to come out to the West Coast and see what life is like out there."

If I was going to stay in America, I told him, I wasn't really interested in living in Los Angeles because the distances between one place and another were so tremendously great that, apart from the big, palatial houses and the parties, it didn't seem a very exciting place for me to live. San Francisco was a lot prettier, with its beautiful midtown area. On the other hand, to make a movie, I'd be happy to live in Beverly Hills for a little while.

Irving then told me that he'd known Bernie Cornfeld for a good many years and that Bernie was currently involved in a hotel operation in Acapulco, together with Hugh Hefner.

I mentioned that I'd heard Bernie was having problems with the Internal Revenue Service over alleged fraudulent stock manipulations in his overseas company called IOS.

"Yeah," Irving said, "Bernie's got a few troubles. But he ain't exactly broke yet."

"When I saw him in L.A.," I added, "there were some pictures lying around of his fantastic chalet in Geneva— some pad!"

"He's had to give it up," Irving told me. "But you're right—it's like a palace. I spent a month there myself the summer before last."

Well, if nothing else, Irving seemed to know Bernie Cornfeld very well and it was certainly true that Bernie knew a lot of important fat cat people in the movie industry. I was beginning to feel a lot better about Mr. Irving Movie Producer.

Was it true, I asked Irving, that Bernie was one of the world's great Johns—that he'd been known to spend thousands of dollars on girls?

"Oh wow, yeah . . . like dig it, baby. One night me and Bernie and J. Paul Getty's son were going out to an exclusive nightclub in Paris and Bernie had arranged for one hell of a knock-out girl to join him. He had paid a thousand dollars, mind you, a grand up front for the whole night. Then Getty Jr. walks in with a gorgeous doll, and Cornfeld right away turns to him and says, 'Look, I'll buy her from you for the night.' So he gives Getty's girl fifteen hundred bucks and sends his first date home in a cab. But he doesn't give her cabfare, because that was included in the price. Getty, since he suddenly doesn't have a date anymore, has to call up another girl for himself and this time *he* lays out two thousand bucks. . . ."

I laughed, having enjoyed, but not quite believed, this fantastic story, and then Irving switched the conversation back to the movie deal. We talked about me playing myself in the picture, so I immediately asked him if it were going to be an X-rated movie or a straight movie, and I was pleasantly surprised to hear that he wanted to make it a "fairly straight" picture. He would, he said, try to avoid using real sex as much as possible.

I asked Irving to be somewhat more specific, so he described what was going to be his approach to the film.

"You know," he said, "my favorite scene from the book is where you take on that twenty-nine-year-old kid who's afraid of girls—you know, the one who's sent to you by a psychiatrist—and you pop his cherry. You remember that scene?"

"Yes, it's my book and I remember the scene very well," I reminded him, but then I wanted to know how that scene, which is really quite graphic in the book, could be done in good taste on the screen.

"We handle it this way," Irving Movie Producer began to explain. "We open with a scene of you and the guy—you're in a sexy negligee and he's standing there in your living room with his shirt half-way open but you're just talking. Okay, we do a dissolve or something and there you two are, in the bedroom now, and he's got his shirt off—that's all— and he's lying in your arms. The lower part of his body won't be seen, so we leave it to the audience's imagination what's going on down there. Suggestive, but in good taste . . . Now the camera moves in on your face and bare arms— implying more intimacy, you dig. Okay, now a socko surprise—a film within a film. You and the kid are in bed looking at slides being flashed on the wall of the bedroom. The slides show a nude couple having sex in various positions and your voice-over explains to the kid what's going on. . . ."

He paused, I guess to get my reaction to the scene unfolding before me and I said, "Well, it sounds different . . . but what's the point of the lecture?"

"That way we can get in some graphic stuff without being pornographic . . . hell, it'll really be educational, and we have to avoid getting anything worse than an 'R' rating so we can get the right bookings."

"What else?" I said.

"What do you mean, 'What else'?"

"My God, is that the whole film?"

Irving was not amused. He went on to describe other ideas he had for the film—simulated sex scenes, a "wildly erotic" soundtrack played by a leading rock group, special lighting effects—a whole lot of movie talk that, frankly, sounded like a foreign language to me. The important thing was that he had done a lot of thinking about the film, was ready to talk contract, and wanted me in it.

"When do I have to be out on the Coast?" I asked him. "You know I may be deported before too very long."

"Don't worry, we have our lawyers looking into that business," he snapped back. "I wouldn't be talking to you right now instead of being in Copenhagen if I thought you wouldn't be available. So look, you'll come out to Hollywood this weekend and stay with Miss Woodson. By the way, it's her twenty-third birthday on Saturday and you'd better give her a little present."

I hardly knew the chick, but okay, if it would make everyone happy, I'd take a little present along.

"You'll stay in that beautiful house of hers in Beverly Hills as her guest. She will take you shopping on Monday and then you go to the hairdresser, get your hair fixed real nice, and she will get you three or four wigs. We will buy an entirely new wardrobe, bikinis, shoes, skirts, slacks, and things like that, and then you'll have to do the screen test. You know, you'll have to walk in and out of a door. You'll have to show what kinds of make-up fit you best, how you step in and out of a car, walk up and down stairs, drink a glass empty and pour coffee in a cup, cut a cake, those kind of things. Time after time, you'll have to repeat all this until you are a success."

In other words, it would be a test to see how I'd behave, look, and move. I'd never done this kind of thing before but it all seemed interesting and certainly a challenge.

"You might have written a good book," Irving continued, "and you might look nice in your publicity pictures, but we don't know how photogenic and flexible you are in front of a movie camera."

"How long will all this take?" I asked him.

"You should be back in New York by next Wednesday."

Well, this sounded pretty reasonable in terms of my time. And besides, it'd be something of a vacation from my life in New York—even though there was lots of work involved —and might end up being a lot of fun.

By "fun" I wasn't necessarily thinking of sex, but suddenly, now that the business conversation had more or less ended in some kind of agreement, Irving seemed to be paying an awful lot of attention—that's visual attention—to my legs. I was wearing a miniskirt, a green dress with red cherries on it, and I'd taken off my pantyhose while waiting for Irving to arrive. In any case, I was grateful to have panties on because something in Irving Movie Maker's behavior was setting off a warning bell in my defense mechanism. I'd been a madam, after all, and had several movie producer clients who were rather kinky. "Shit," I thought, "am I going to have to behave like every Hollywood starlet and fuck the producer to get a break?"

Irving didn't disappoint me. He asked me to spread my legs so that he could "take a better look at me." I felt like asking him if he'd care to take a Pap smear but figured he wouldn't take too kindly to my sense of humor. What the hell, I told myself, if he needs these cheap kicks, let him have a small thrill.

Irving's big brown producer's eyes began rolling around, a bit comically almost, in his reddening face. He was still seated, but one leg kept popping over the other and I could tell he was taking the whole thing a lot more seriously than he should have been—I began to wonder whether Irving and I were about to make a Marx Brothers comedy or a bad X-rated film. Fortunately, there was indeed some comic relief. All along, the telephone had been ringing every half-hour and each time it was Larry calling from New York, worried about me and anxious to know exactly what was going on—and this time, thank God for Alexander Graham Bell, it really did keep cool the Chicago situation.

Here he was again, my dear faithful Larry, and I told him not to worry. "I'm with my producer, and he's very nice," I said. "And please don't call every twenty minutes. It's all right, really. We're discussing the screen test and I need some time without interruption from anyone to find out if I'm making the right move. Okay? I appreciate your concern, but everything's under control."

Larry—I know him so well—didn't sound convinced but I reassured him everything was okay. Meanwhile Irving was growling, "Tell that guy to stop calling. What's his problem?"

I got off the phone, and after listening to some more of Irving's grousing, I decided it was time to ask him some questions. Namely, what movies had he produced so far? "*Airport*," he answered with an arrogant gleam, "you heard of it?"

"You were the producer of *Airport?*"

"Well, you wouldn't have seen my name above the titles, but believe me, if you want to talk about the financing, *I* was the producer of that flick. . . ."

Well, of course I had no way of checking out on the spot whether or not Irving actually had been the "money man" for *Airport*. So I asked him what movie he was working on at present and what he was doing in Chicago. Both questions were answered by Rubeen telling me that he was working—"on a crash basis"—on the production of the movie about the Clifford Irving hoax.

"Isn't the book supposed to come out first before you can make a movie?" I asked him.

Rubeen said that this was going to be the exception because of all the publicity. In this instance, they would start the movie right away and have the book come out simultaneously. This sounded rather unusual to me, but I'm not familiar with the wheeling-dealing world of movie money, so I let it go. I was feeling really weary and excused myself to go to the bathroom and freshen up a bit. I was hoping he'd take the hint and go away. Not a chance.

All the way to the bathroom, I could feel Rubeen's eyes on my back, legs, and ass. How was I going to deal with this guy and not jeopardize my film? Jesus, why is everything so complicated?

In the bathroom, I washed my face and hands, put on some cologne to freshen up, and marched back into the room hoping that Irving would drop the Crude Producer role and let us proceed on a no-bullshit basis. No way. He immediately tells me to lift up my little skirt and "show me what you look like."

"I'm blonde, have green eyes, and I'm really very tired," I told him.

"Look, honey, if you're going to play yourself, I got to know what your body looks like. I told you no total nudity, but parts of your body are gonna be shown and I wanna know what those parts look like. I'm gonna have a lot of bread tied up in this flick, and I gotta right to protect my investment!" He glowered at me, protecting his investment.

I glowered back at him. I do not like to be shouted at, particularly in lousy Chicago hotel rooms by a movie producer who's been less than gracious all night long. Never once did he offer to buy me even a cup of coffee or some food. Where the hell was *his* professional courtesy! I'm part of his investment, aren't I?

"Mr. Rubeen," I said, as calmly as a combination of anger and ambition would allow me, "I thought the whole idea of the screen test, which of course I might fail, was to prove I'm more than suitable for the role. . . ."

"I am the producer of this film . . . I am boss of this fucking film . . . and if you want to be in this film, you do as I say! Right here. Now! In this hotel room."

Irving was becoming more aggressive. "I want to see and feel your flesh," he ordered me. "Show me your ass and cunt."

"Jesus, Irving," I thought, "if you want to go to bed with

me, why not ask for it like a man instead of acting like a nut?"

For the next half-hour or so, I got a complete physical from Rubeen, but no sex. I had a few small bruises on my body and he wanted to know the history of each of them. In fact, Irving Movie Maker seemed to be far more interested in doing his own kinky thing than in getting into bed with me.

He began asking me questions about my career as a madam and whether or not I was still active. I told him a few things but emphasized that my retirement from that life was very real. What did I want out of life? he wanted to know. Some question. He might as well have asked me to explain the meaning of life. Or to define the universe. Still, if he wanted to talk instead of screw, that was more than fine with me.

Gradually I was able to turn the conversation—my physical examination had ended, and apparently the patient had graduated with good marks and a clean bill of health—back to the movie. While I asked some questions of Irving, I apparently had his permission to get dressed again.

When would there be a complete treatment for me to read? I wanted to know.

"I have writers working on it," Irving said.

"Well, it's got to be an improvement on the one treatment I've already seen—that was totally unacceptable."

"I don't know about that one—what was it like?"

"It made me out to be a wild Dutch broad who was fucking a high New York judge, the whole Knapp Commission, and most of the district attorney's office. And at the same time I'm a notorious madam, I'm just a dumb bunny who falls flat on her face while running out to get a cab!"

"Hell," Irving said, "that sounds like a dumb-ass approach to your life story. I don't see the point of making such a 'down' picture—the idea is you're a glamorous and supersensual lady. . . ."

"Well, I'm glad you agree with me that the film ought to have something to do with the real 'me.' "

"Who is the real 'you'?" Irving asked me. "Are you really a romantic woman, or are you really frigid?"

"Me! Frigid? I should say not!" I might have some personal problems, but frigidity wasn't one of them.

"No," he said, suddenly kind of pensive, "I believe you're a very emotional woman, with passionate feelings and desires, when it comes to the right person. And I think you're a woman who has been pushed around too much lately. A lot of people—yeah, quite a few people—have taken advantage of you and used you. Am I right?"

"Yes, absolutely." I couldn't figure this man out. One minute he's a weirdie; the next he's a sensitive, decent guy, almost fatherly to me.

"I want the film to show that I'm more than a pair of legs, tits, and an ass," I said, "and I'm deliberately using that expression because too many men *do* view women that way, whether it's a prostitute or a straight chick . . . so I want this film to have not only sex in it, but real romance as well, and emotion, and, maybe most important, a lot of humor. It should be a happy movie. . . ."

"Look, baby," Irving said with enthusiasm, "I think you're one hell of a groovy kid, and *you're* the one who is going to sit down with me and tell me how you want the movie to be done."

"That's great," I said.

"Now for the rights to the book and your participation in the film, we're going to offer two hundred thousand dollars—how's that sound to you?"

"Well, I leave these matters up to my agent and lawyer."

"Sure. Fine. And *my* lawyers will work on your problem of staying in the country. You know, we've been doing a lot of research on you—it's already cost me several thousand bucks to learn all about you."

"I don't understand—what are you talking about?"

"Look, honey, I've had private investigators doing their thing all over New York to check on the reliability and truth of both your book and your business. I needed to know whether or not the book was a big phoney, whether you'd really written and lived it the way you say you did."

"I still don't quite understand—how'd you get a hold of my girls?"

"Don't worry," Irving said, "we've got our connections. We have spoken to approximately ten girls—not me, but some of my people . . . you know a bar or restaurant on the East Side run by a Greek fellow?"

"Which restaurant?" I interrupted him. "That could describe a lot of places."

"It's somewhere in the East Fifties near Second or Third Avenue."

"Does the name start with a 'P'?" I asked, testing him.

"Yeah, I seem to recall it's Pemble's or something like that. . . ."

"That's right. So what happened at Pemble's?"

"My people got friendly with the crowd at the bar and casually mentioned your book. In no time at all, we met two girls who knew you. What's more, they spoke very highly of you, and through them, we met some more. One of them was a black chick named Carmen. She said she didn't work for you anymore, but the two of you had started out in the hooking game about the same time. You really dug her once, and she liked you very much, too."

"Yes, she's a beautiful girl."

"Yeah, well, as I say, I wasn't there . . . then there was another one called Ellen, or Helen maybe, who goes by different names—like, uh, let's see, one begins with an 'S.' "

"Signe?"

"That's her. What is she—a madam?"

"I don't know . . . I'm out of all that stuff so I really don't know what's *what*, anymore . . . When I first met her, she was having a lot of trouble with her boyfriend, some Italian pimp who used to beat the living shit out of her. Last time I saw her was at my lawyer's office about a year ago. My criminal lawyer was representing him. Her pimp—or whatever he was to her—not only used to beat her up but also got into all kinds of fights, was involved in drugs, armed robbery, et cetera—a real lulu."

"Yeah, yeah, we know all about it. She said you were awfully nice to her and helped her out with some money and Johns when she had to start her career all over again—after she finally ran out on her boyfriend and left behind all her addresses and money and things."

Well, that was gratifying. I was happy to hear that the girls had a good word for me. I'd never dreamed that when I was being fair and square with them—even giving them their money when someone stiffed them or a check bounced

—my reward would be their help, however accidental, in getting a movie contract. The ball sure takes funny bounces.

Meanwhile Irving was continuing his report from his investigators, which included talking about me with some ex-madams, and I was thoroughly convinced he'd done his homework on me. I finally told him that I was impressed with all his research and was very glad it had turned out well for me.

"Look, we're gonna do it your way, but I just wanted to show you that I've had my men out. One of these chicks, DeeDee I think her name was. made a thousand bucks because one of my guys had this filthy rich millionaire in town who wanted a broad. So he got fixed up with DeeDee. Had I known you before, I'd have recommended you but you were too hard to get hold of with all your publicity trips. I know a lot of guys, mostly bankers from abroad, who're willing to shell out a thousand for a real knock-out chick. Any guy I recommend to you is worth a grand per night. Here, let me give you some names. . . ."

"No, no thanks, really. I'm retired and plan to stay that way. I fuck for fun now, that's all, and I don't want anything to do with Johns, even rich ones. I've got this new career and—"

The phone rang again, and this time it wasn't Larry. One of the tough-looking boys I'd met in the lobby talking to Miss Woodson had called earlier to say he'd bought two copies of the book and would I autograph them for him? He'd come to my room or else I could go to his room to sign the books. I thanked him, but said I was busy and couldn't break away. Now he was on the phone again with the same request. I asked Irving if he knew anything about this guy, but he shook his head. So I said, "Look, I really can't do it tonight. I'm still tied up. Maybe tomorrow morning . . ."

Tomorrow morning, hell. I wasn't going near either of those guys even in daylight. They were about the meanest-looking thugs I'd ever seen.

I put down the phone and turned back to Irving, who was suddenly looking at me as though he'd just taken a Horny Pill. I tried to say how tired I was and tomorrow's another day and there'll be plenty of time for this later on and—well, Irving just wasn't having any. What he *was* having was my clothes off, and I took them off so he wouldn't rip them to shreds. In another moment he was chowing down on me as though oral sex was about to go out of style and instead of being stimulated I was feeling very, very up-tight. He didn't turn me on physically, at all, and with each passing minute he was getting progressively weirder.

Instead of making love to me, Irving began biting me and pulling my legs apart and twisting my arms—punishing my body like the true sadist he was. I didn't know which he was going to twist out of a socket first—my arm or leg. And all the while he was beating up on me, he was throwing off his clothing, his eyes once more rolling in their sockets and his entire face having taken on a maniacal look. Now completely naked, he was attacking me with this huge, thick, ugly cock in his hand. In most cases an erect penis is a wonderful sight to me, but that thing in Irving's fist was like some blunt instrument with which he was going to stab me, right up to the womb.

I hadn't taken my diaphragm along, since I had had no intention of getting laid—much less raped—so I pleaded with Irving not to attack me. "Please, Irving, don't fuck me. I don't have my diaphragm with me and this is a dangerous time for me," I said, trying to hold him off.

Irving, his face really out of control now, probably didn't even hear what I was saying. He threw me on the bed, twisted me onto my stomach, and rammed himself up my rear end. I started bleeding, but that didn't bother him. He kept twisting my arms and legs and throttling me, on the bed as well as on the floor. At one point Irving flipped me over and jammed his big dick into my vagina, which hurt like hell because I was tight and dry and in no way ready for him. He still hadn't come, and before I could try to stop him, he'd pulled out and was going into my mouth so deep that I could hardly breathe. I was gagging like crazy, but this is how Irving Movie Maker completed his rape of my body.

Or so I thought. Irving wasn't yet done with me. He still hadn't come and this made him go even more berserk. He had me stretched out on the floor, straddling me, his knees locking my arms to the floor, and he was slapping my face until there was no feeling left there. I had somehow managed to endure the sex without screaming, but now I heard myself screaming bloody murder and Irving put a pillow over my face to stop me. He stopped me, all right. Either I stopped screaming or I would have stopped breathing.

Meanwhile Irving was back inside me, riding me like some crazed animal, and when I felt he was about to come I mustered all my strength and tried to throw him off. In the process I almost kicked him in the balls—which would have been a nice turn of events, but as strong as I was managing to be, Irving was right back on top of me with his big fat cock back inside of me, pressing himself into my body, and finally dropping his load.

I felt sick and abused and filthy. Irving had left me a wreck. My entire body ached and my hair felt half-way pulled out. And while I was trying to pull myself together, Irving was getting into his clothes about as fast as Superman gets out of his. He seemed terribly anxious to leave, and the madman look had completely left his face. In fact, he looked at me as though *I* might be a menace to *him*. My God, how could he get pleasure out of the horrible scene he's into when he looks so worried about it afterwards?

I guess this realization gave me courage and I yelled at Irving as he seemed to be about to rush out the door. "Hey! You just wait a minute! You did all this to me, and now you're running off into the night. You straighten out the bill, this room, my airfare, and the rest. I didn't come here to be fucked and raped by you, did I?" There he was, almost out the door, and I was standing there, bare-ass naked but defiant, his rotten sperm still dripping from between my legs, and he kind of meekly came back and sat down on the couch. I wanted to really sock it to him, but first I had to clean up. I couldn't stand the way I felt, so I "ordered" Irving to stay there while I washed up. I honestly didn't expect him to be there when I got back, but right then and there the most important thing in the world for me was to feel like a human being again.

But when I came out of the bathroom, feeling slightly better, there was Irving waiting for me. I dressed—fortunately he hadn't ripped apart my dress—and addressed some questions to Irving, who answered them as though he were the tamest pussycat in town.

Of course he had his addresses for me—here was one for Amsterdam, one in Copenhagen, and two American addresses, one in Los Angeles and the other in New York. Irving dutifully wrote them all down. We also talked about possible licensing arrangements and he said he'd be cooperative about anything I wanted.

I was beginning to understand Irving, I thought: he was one of those men who need to freak out now and then, when his sexuality takes over all his normal instincts—not that he was any great gentleman to begin with. But he did go to all this trouble and expense to meet me, and we're going to make a movie together. My "producer's couch" adventure had been more horrendous than most, but I was ready to make a movie if Irving was. What was really happening was my usual capacity for passing over bad scenes very quickly. With life able to give us so many good moments, why dwell on the really depressing ones?

Irving, having furnished me with addresses and a number of reassurances, was ready to bug out, so I had to remind him about my expenses. "Oh, yeah," he said, "that's easily taken care of. You call my office in New York and ask for Mr. DeRivera. He'll reimburse you for everything. Write down everything . . . Hey, make sure you go back to New York first-class and even take a limousine to the airport if you want to. Charge everything to us. Okay?"

"Okay," I said. "I hope to see you again."

"What are you talking about? I'll see you this weekend in Hollywood."

With that, Irving took his leave of me, reminding me that Miss Woodson would be calling me in New York to make the arrangements for my stay in California.

I went back into the bathroom, ran the hottest bath I could, and proceeded to soak myself in it for a very long while. Although it was already two in the morning, and I was due to fly out at seven, my weariness was such that I figured it'd be somehow simpler to get three or four hours sleep, get back to New York, and then collapse for the rest of the day. I just wanted to get out of Chicago and the clutches of Irving Movie Maker and his mixed-up moods.

After soaking myself until my skin was pink and crinkly, and almost falling asleep in the bathtub, I finally got out of the tub, having convinced myself that the whole day had been a bad adventure that I'd never have to repeat again.

I phoned downstairs to the desk and said I'd be checking out very early in the morning and to please call me at 5:30. Fine. No problem. However, there was a long distance call to Los Angeles on my bill, plus a fancy dinner charged to me—no wonder Irving hadn't brought up the subject of food!—which had to be taken care of. Okay, I said, I'd pay for these items providing they'd accept cash this time without a fuss. Cash would be fine, the man at the desk said. He had great respect for cash.

After combing my hair and applying a cold washcloth to some of the many bruises beginning to appear all over my body, I was finally ready to go to bed. So of course the phone rang. My first reaction was not to answer, but then it dawned on me that it was probably my good silver fox, Larry, calling to see if everything had gone all right. I picked up the receiver but it wasn't Larry it was the young hood who had called twice earlier. This time he sounded really threatening, telling me, "Hey, baby, we ain't nobody's fool. We know you're alone now, so no more excuses. Me and my friend, we want to come over and get that sexy book signed . . . and you'd better sign it real quick."

Thinking back on it I guess I should have been frightened, but I was too angry to feel fear. "Listen, 'baby,' just keep your cool. I'm not signing books for anyone this time of the night—I'm too goddamn tired to play games with you and I'm too goddamn tired to do *anything* but go to sleep. I've been up since early this morning and I'm entitled to my sleep!"

His voice came back at me, softer this time but just as mean. "Come on, that's no way to talk to me, honey. You ain't talking to some little peanut boys . . . so if you don't want to have us drop in on you, you'd better get your ass over here and real fast, or else—"

I didn't hear his last words because I slammed down the receiver. I got into bed, leaving one small light on, and tried to relax myself into sleep.

But I couldn't turn off. It had been such a wild day, and

here I was getting invited to autograph parties in the middle of the night. I just hoped those guys wouldn't check with the desk and be waiting for me in the morning.

There was a loud knock on the door and voices outside which put me into a state of terror, but since I knew who was out there I wasn't going to answer. I could always call for protection from the hotel. Or could I? How could these guys dare to come banging on my door at this hour? Maybe everybody was working together against me.

I kept quiet, my hand on the phone, and they seemed to have gone away. Then they were back again, banging on the door. This time I wasn't so frightened since I more or less expected them to try again. The door looked pretty strong and I was ready to call the desk if they kept it up, so I just kept quiet and tried to remain calm.

My friends didn't come back and I was finally able to get some sleep—maybe two hours of it—before the desk clerk called the room to wake me up. I showered, dressed quickly, and went downstairs to the lobby to check out. I was relieved to get out of Chicago as fast as a cab and plane would take me.

I arrived in New York absolutely destroyed, with no luggage except the bags under my eyes. Larry was at the apartment when I got back and became enraged when I told him what had happened. Why hadn't I called him, he demanded to know. It was a good question. I hadn't called him because things happened so fast and, besides, I'm a big girl and should be able to handle almost any situation. Still, Chicago hadn't represented any situation I'd care to face again. I could have used Larry there, that's for sure.

I told Larry I had to go to sleep or else I'd fall apart, but before he left I'd given him all the information about Irving, his company's name, the various addresses, his lawyers' telephone numbers, and all the rest. By the time I woke up in late afternoon, he'd checked everything out and even without him saying anything, his face told me the story. It was all a hoax. A cruel, bizarre hoax.

The closest thing to reality was that Robin Moore's office had received two calls from our Irving, but Robin himself had never talked to the man. Rubeen had then called Jack Letheran and asked him to come to Kennedy Airport immediately and meet him in the hangar housing his private plane. The purpose of this rush trip out to JFK? To hand Rubeen a copy of *The Happy Hooker*. Why didn't Letheran ask Rubeen simply to buy a copy of the book? Well, I guess he was as gullible as I was—in any case, he did make the trip out to JFK and there was no Irving and no private plane belonging to Irving.

Larry, I must hasten to say, had never swallowed the producer story and now he really gave me hell. The next time a movie producer wanted to speak with me, he would come to me—not vice-versa—and Larry would be there and whether or not we cut a deal, I'd be safe and be treated with dignity.

I still don't know what really went on in Chicago. What motivated Irving to go to all that trouble? I'd helped him with some names of restaurants and persons, but he really *had* had his people speak to people who know me. Just to get me to Chicago? Was Rubeen working with those two guys, or what?

Larry's theory is that the whole thing was a Mafia plot, and those two guys were "hit men" out to "get" me because certain Mafia muck-a-mucks were afraid I'd name them as customers to the district attorney's office in New York. (Apparently it's alright to cheat the public and kill people, but not to be a bad family man and visit a house of prostitution. Some code of morality!)

Yet Irving Movie Maker *did* know so much about me and clearly *had* thought about making a film about me. Or was I just being gullible again? Maybe Irving and his pals were just out for a gang-bang and specialized in luring attractive female celebrities into hotel rooms where they'd more or less be victims. . . ? It was all so crazy. Did Irving need to impress girls with his status as an interested producer so he could then sadistically rape them? If he didn't live in Chicago, it seemed a lot of work—at least I hadn't paid for *his* airfare—for one violent orgasm.

My own theory is that Irving and his two pals specialize in these elaborate gang-bang conspiracies, and the timing that night was simply off. So his two henchmen didn't get to come up and visit me sometime. I may be trying to put a "good" face on it—after all, they had to spend money to set it up—but I don't buy the "hit men" theory. The long arm of the Mafia doesn't have to reach me in Chicago when I'm already available in New York.

All in all, it was a pretty scary twenty-four hours. I'm sure I made a lot of mistakes during that period, but I'm alive—and that's the most important thing.

The Girls in My Life

LOUISE: Philanthropist

Louise and I have been great friends since the start of my career as a call girl. We then lived one block from each other in Murray Hill and both worked at the same time for Georgette Harcourt.

Despite her occasional work as a call girl, Louise lived her own peaceful existence. Money was important to her only because of her children—she didn't have legal custody of them, but they visited her every weekend and she couldn't exist without those visits—and because her job, a modest public relations post with a firm representing artists and performers, so involved her with the young, aspiring artists and musicians (a lot of them rock musicians and singers) she met during the day that she was continually trying to sponsor them and help them get concerts and showings.

And not only was she generous of soul but she so often would use her own money to help these struggling young artists advance their careers. She asked no thanks or reward for her efforts. When these artists did get ahead, her satisfaction at having helped them seemed reward enough. Then, too, there were more than a few affairs between Louise and her young artists. That's some reward, I guess.

The big event in her life, though, was the weekend visit of her three sons, whose ages ranged from six to fifteen.

There's a certain weekend scene in New York that sophisticated New Yorkers can readily identify: it's the divorced parent of either sex, reunited with her or his children and obviously doting on them with the kind of affection made more intense because of the separation which precedes, and will surely follow, their visits. Louise and her kids would be typified this way on any weekend—Louise and the three kids romping through Central Park; Louise taking the kids to the U.N. or to Lincoln Center or to something nice 'n corny like Radio City Music Hall. Whatever the kids wanted, whether it was balloons in Central Park or some nifty toy in F.A.O. Schwarz, they got it. Sure, she spoiled her kids, but as she pointed out—"only two days a week."

The obvious thing to say about Louise is: isn't it too bad she doesn't meet some really nice guy deserving of her who could afford to adopt her three sons. Well, life seldom follows the old kind of Hollywood movie scripts, and it just hasn't happened. Louise is well into her thirties, and doesn't lie about her age. She makes no pretentions about being younger than springtime, but her delicious personality and keen mind do make her seem youthful and refreshing. In fact most men are so taken by her charm that they forget she's slightly over the hill and has weight problems.

In fact, weight was Louise's eternal problem—she had always verged on being plump, but sometimes her weight went up and down like an elevator. Whenever she managed to do some serious dieting, she of course looked younger and more attractive; but whenever de ole debil, "More Pounds," got a hold of her, she would look matronly.

Still, regardless of weight problems, there were two things that never changed about Louise—her remarkable bosom (for any customer who called Georgette or, later, myself for a nice girl with big boobs, we'd call on delightful Louise and her 38-D attributes) and her remarkable disposition. I know she was ambivalent about being a call girl, even on a part-time basis, but she never burdened anyone with this fact. Just as she helped her artists, she was a friend to everyone. In some of my darkest moments, when I was sorriest I'd ever come to America, she was always there for a cup of tea and some reassurance. To me, the most beautiful thing about a human being is his or her ability to transcend personal problems and do something for a friend. It's a rare, rare attribute and Louise had more than her share of it, this really unique, human quality.

For me this wonderful quality of Louise's was always evident in her face, her wonderfully expressive face. When she was being most concerned with a friend, at her very, very nicest as a fellow human being, her face always seemed to remind me of Giuletta Massina when she played the title role in *Nights of Cabiria,* one of my all-time favorite films. I remember so fondly Louise's own round face, with her short hair and those superb big brown eyes and her mouth, always about to be twisted in a gaminelike smile. And Louise's habit of lifting one eyebrow, almost sarcastically, as a kind of editorial comment on a situation, which also accented the small scar on her cheek.

So let's never feel sorry for someone who is so much better equipped than most of us to deal with life. Louise loves people but she also loves sex, and I doubt if any sexual encounter has been much of a burden for her. If anything, she can be absolutely impetuous when she sees someone she wants. I have known her to see an attractive man in a bar or restaurant, or even a nice-looking guy at a bus stop, stop and chat with him, end up having a drink together, and then invite him home.

Louise, to say the very least, was not very business-minded. She needed warmth and affection, and lots of sex, and if these encounters provided her with nothing more than a few tender moments, she enjoyed each of them to a high degree.

I've kept in touch with Louise by mail and recently received some interesting news from her. She's no longer a freelance call girl—some of her young musician and artist friends have begun to make it, and they want Louise to represent them, so she's been able to open her own small public relations agency. Business isn't booming, she says, but it's healthy enough to keep her at home nights.

Well, not *all* nights. Louise still loves sex and young men —a swinger from way back, she is far happier swinging for free rather than for business purposes.

On the other hand, her finances are in better shape as well because she's met an attractive, affluent man in his forties who helps her out. Equally important, they really dig each other, but it's a free sexual relationship because Louise, like me, has to have that diversity of mixing with new people, falling in love with sweet, young innocent types, all types, being alive each hour you're awake—and then having really sweet dreams. Yet we both need that safe harbor—in her case her steady, generous boyfriend; in my case, Larry—to get back to.

Louise, may I be like you one day. You have been good to many of us—your once-upon-a-time colleagues, "the girls;" your artist friends; your swinging friends; and, of course, utmost in your mind, your wonderful children.

SOME UNFUNNY THINGS HAPPEN
ON MY OUT

April 1972. *The Happy Hooker* selling like hot cakes. Publicity trip finished. Meetings with District Attorney and Police Commissioner almost coming to an end. Spring arriving. Perfect setting for a happy ending . . . no?

No.

After my book had been out a few months and I had been on many progressive radio and television talk-shows, it was Assistant District Attorney Conboy who felt that I had outlived my usefulness as a star witness. The grand jury didn't think I would be a good witness, either, particularly not after all the statements I had made on sex and prostitution—as if that had anything to do with my being an honest witness!

I'd also spent time at the Police Commissioner's office, since people there were convinced I knew all sorts of dark secrets I'd withheld from the District Attorney's office. However, I didn't have any more information for them and I was growing very annoyed at their constant "bribes," if you will, of being allowed a few more months in the country. I finally said, "I am sorry, gentlemen, but I think that will be it . . . for now and forever . . . I have come to the conclusion that I am pretty well fed up with living in this country, at least for a while. I would like to come back one day, but certainly with a better reputation . . . gentlemen, try your luck elsewhere. I've had it. I'm only too glad to leave, and the sooner the better."

So now it was Xaviera Hollander versus the U.S. Immigration people, and I knew I wasn't going to win that battle, although recently a lawyer who's an expert in the field has told me I should have gone to court to stay in the United States, instead of voluntarily leaving so I wouldn't be deported. But at the time, I really had no heart for the battle.

One day, while in Mr. Conboy's office, I was formally arrested by two burly Immigration officers, who clearly wanted me deported as soon as possible. And my bail was set at ten thousand dollars!

I didn't even have that kind of money in the bank, and Mr. Conboy, recognizing the absurdity of the situation, I guess, helped get the bail down to $2,500—which still seemed absurd to me. What was more, the banks were about to close. I called Larry, but where *was* he! Well, somehow my dear friend got my bank to stay open after the official hours and got the bail money—that is, the new sum. And if I left within ten days, then I would get the money back. As it happened, I didn't have to leave quite so soon—my lawyer got a postponement—but I've never had that bail money returned.

Other problems arose. The Internal Revenue Service started investigating a good many people and that is a subject I want to say something about.

What happened? Well, just after the D.A. had finished with me, I received a letter from the Internal Revenue, notifying me that two special agents were assigned to my case—in other words, the I.R.S. was on my tail. They also sent me a letter requesting my financial records for the past four years. This surprised me, since I had filed the proper tax forms for previous years, except for 1971, and there was still time for that.

These I.R.S. men went to well-known Johns in New York City with my horrible police mug-shot. The customers were asked if they had ever seen me before and many had not. And some who knew me also knew I had written the book, *The Happy Hooker*, and playing dumb, they would say, "But isn't that the girl who wrote that best-selling hooker book, who's been all over the newspapers?" Most Johns are as loyal to me as I would be to them, and because of their own tax problems would never admit to having spent outrageous amounts on any hooker.

The I.R.S. went as far as trying to gain entrance to my apartment, using all types of pretenses. The only thing that I would tell them is: "Here is the name of my accountant. I am very sorry but I cannot talk to you, so please get lost." They never did go to see my accountant, which leads me to believe that their intentions were not honorable. I also understand that Ted Ratnoff, fleeing from America to England, realizing that his arrest was imminent, tried to take revenge against me with the I.R.S., and supposedly wrote letters accusing me and some of my friends of all types of financial transactions. Interpol finally arrested Ted the bugger on a warrant from the United States, and he now is free in England fighting extradition to the U.S.A.

Some irony. I was fighting to stay in America, and Teddy is fighting to stay out. I was granted immunity from any charges, but had to leave. Teddy has all kinds of charges facing him in America—partly as a result of Larry's and my testimony—and so far they can't get him back.

I would like to settle with the I.R.S.—I'd rather pay taxes than fool around and get in trouble for tax fraud. To pay taxes on my book is obviously logical, but the way they investigated me on the prostitution business was ridiculous. After all, it *is* illegal and yet you have to pay taxes once they find out, without being able to deduct all the real business expenses, such as lawyers, paying off crooked policemen, moving costs and so on. I'm really not kidding. In this regard, Uncle Sam is a bigger pimp than anyone!

And little did I know that several months after I had already left the country, there would be a letter addressed to my former Manhattan address simply stating that a lien and levy of $101,088.25 had been put on the royalties income of my book. I had filed, as mentioned before, my income-tax papers through 1970 and was willing to work out any moneys owed as well as my 1971 tax, but how was I supposed to do this when I wasn't allowed back in the country? And how was I supposed to live if they were going to intercept all my royalty income?

While still in the States, the epitome of all my problems came into being through an interview I had done with Channel 7's "Eyewitness News." The filming took place in my apartment, and they asked me many tough questions to which I gave straightforward answers, but I did refuse to discuss anything about politicians or any other important clients. A week later, this innocent taping would cause me untold anxiety.

To my great astonishment, while watching the news, I saw myself again—this time, however, with my voice over-dubbed by an announcer stating that I was a cold, mercenary woman, accused of being a conspirator with the Knapp Commission and having among some of my top clients politicians attached to the Lindsay, Rockefeller and Nixon administrations. I can categorically say that this is not true. I do, indeed, have many social friends from all walks of life and some of them might come from Washington, but they are strictly *social* acquaintances. I still don't know why Channel 7 did this to me, but undoubtedly pressures were brought to bear to get me out of the country as quickly as possible.

A few days later, I was notified by the D.A.'s office that too many pressures were being put on by Washington, D.C., and that I should condition myself to leaving the country damn soon.

The story had been spread around—I believe by Ted Ratnoff—that I was seeing one of the hierarchy from the White House, who supposedly had given me a three hundred dollar check. Again, Conboy insisted that I had received a check, and that I must reveal the name of the payer. It wasn't true, and I refused to lie. It never happened.

The Girls in My Life

LEAH: The Naked Lioness

As I am writing this final nosegay to the girls in my life, it is November and, as mentioned earlier, I am residing in Toronto, giving this book the so-called Finishing Touch.

My new publishing company has not only given me an advance twice as large as I received for my first book but they have also given me superb service as far as editing the book is concerned. For periods of days and, during one stretch, of weeks, I have been more or less locked up in a lovely hotel suite with my lovely editor, Bob Abel. He was my editor at Dell as well, but he switched jobs, and not really by coincidence, I switched publishers. In any case, it's a famous tradition—writers following their editors to other publishing houses.

Bob is also famous, at least with me, for another reason— he is the only man to have spent such extensive periods of time with me and not had sex with me. Temptation came, and *how* . . . not only from me, walking around in just a man's shirt, three-quarter's open, but even more so when a knock on the door last night interrupted our work session. I was rewriting and Bob was going over the rewrites and a friend—a girl named Lola who's the public relations director for a local film company—was typing up the final edited version, when in walked, or rather, in charged, this super-sexy blonde creature named Leah.

Leah is not really a great beauty—though she photo-graphs very sensually—but she just radiates sex. About five feet, four inches tall, she has it all. Her figure is about as divine as a figure can be—her boobs are absolutely knock-outs (my last pun of the book)—and I mean it as a high compliment when I say she looks as though she has just stepped out of the pages of *Penthouse* magazine. Not *Play-boy,* because Leah is sure not the girl next door, not unless the wildest exhibitionist in the Western Hemisphere happens to live next door to you.

Actually, Leah is European. She is originally from Czech-oslovakia, an orphaned child who grew up in grim circum-stances, with a foster mother who seemed to take great de-light in beating her. Leah has traveled extensively through-out Europe ever since she was fifteen—she is now all of twenty-one—and speaks fluent Czech, Russian, Hungarian, French, German and very sexy English. Quite apart from her wild sexual escapades, she is a talented artist and sculp-tress, and if she ever stops being a kind of nomad, may make a name for herself in this area.

But right now she is just a bird of fancy. I knew her from New York, where in early 1971 she had occasionally worked for me. But Leah doesn't seem to care too much for men, and usually managed to get involved in a three-way scene where I would go down on her and this would arouse the guy so much that he achieved his orgasm in a quick, tumult-uous fuck with me. For her part, Leah loves to be eaten and her clit, though hidden away in a snug part of her almost child-like vagina, once detected grows twice its size and her cunt becomes a snug harbor of passion.

Not only does Leah love to make it with me but she might be called my little slave girl because, and perhaps as a result of her rough childhood, she is a bit of a masochist and likes being spanked and having her hands tied behind her back. Leah really is a far-out lioness, however, of the vegetarian species. She refuses to eat meat or fish or men, though not in that order. She also won't wear fur coats.

On this particular night, Leah came roaring into the suite and I introduced her to Lola. Bob had already met her on an earlier visit, and his comment, after she'd left, was that she was the closest thing to "a walking sexual fantasy" he'd ever seen. "Bad for the brain," he kidded, heading for the refrigerator to make himself a Scotch and soda.

Almost immediately, Leah and I started kidding around. I told her to show Bob and Lola her great tits, and—poof!— up went her sweater and there were those two luscious mounds of flesh topped by two cherry jubilee nipples. They looked so good I immediately started nibbling on them, until Bob said either everyone was going to nibble on them or else I'd better get back to finishing the chapter I'd been working on. And since it was more important for me to get the book done than to fool around with Leah's magnificent mammaries, I went back to work.

But not for long. Leah began fooling around again, when I was on the phone, and I pushed her away, telling her to show my friends her "cute cunt." And—poof! again—she had her tight hip-huggers down around her thighs and was displaying her snatch, only half-covered by kinky golden blonde curls. "Daaarlinks, when you are eating me, you are eating the cleanest pussy in town," she crowed in her Czech accent. "I will never taste fishy. You know why? Because I am vegetarian and never eat fish!" She broke up at her own joke, and I hung up the phone and rushed over to keep the rest of her clothes on.

A little later, however, when Bob was off in the corner struggling with one of my indefinite antecedents—or was it a dangling participle?—and Lola was banging away at the electric typewriter, Leah and I sort of snuck into my bedroom to do our own banging away. In less than a minute we were both nude and in the 69 position. Leah was eating me with a fervor no vegetarian should have, and I was being more delicate, intending to work her up gradually until I could make her scream for pleasure.

We were both getting pretty worked up when there came a knock on the door, and Bob's voice: "Ladies. Ahem! Will you please stop what you're doing in there so we can concentrate on what we're doing out here! These working conditions are unfair and inhuman . . . at least open the door."

"It's not locked," I mumbled, between love bites on Leah's crotch.

So in marched Bob and Lola, intent upon doing their best to distract us. Bob shouted out film directions—"Okay, Xaviera baby, we're coming in for a close-up—smile and look up longingly at the camera . . . oops, Leah, we've lost your right boob . . . twist a little to the left . . . very fine . . . ass up in the air a little more, please . . . that's it, good girl! . . . Xaviera, not so much noise, please, there's going to be poetry on the soundtrack—either T. S. Eliot's *The Wasteland* or a poem by Robert Burns. . . ."

Meanwhile, Lola, who can be a pretty funny girl, was fiddling with my big powerful AM-FM radio, trying to find the appropriate music. "Xaviera," she yelled at me, "pay attention! Do you want rock 'n roll or folk music?"

"Just don't play any of that fucking church music," I said. lifting my head from between Leah's yummy thighs. "*He* always wants to play church music!" By this I was referring to Bob's fondness for choral music, which I don't especially enjoy. *Especially* when I'm playing 69 with my gorgeous piece of ass, Leah!

Bob and Lola kept it up for a few minutes more, and the little I really heard of it, it was awfully funny. But Leah and I just kept working on each other, and we managed a fairly good orgasm—though, honestly, I think she managed to stay a lot more with it than I did.

"Aw shucks," said Bob, "I had another ten thousand feet of film in my Brownie camera."

"Don't worry," said Lola, "I'm sure that at the slightest request, they'll do a second take."

"I don't know," said Bob, "at this point they've already done a lot of rewriting of the script."

"This is bad for my heart," said Lola.

"Ain't where I'm suffering," grumbled Bob, fairly merrily, as he went back to his—or rather, my—dangling participles.

So I closed the door, locked it this time, and did a second take.

Leah not only is a great-looking chick with a crazy cuckoo mentality, who undresses in a jiffy in front of big crowds, or small gatherings, or groups of one, to shock and turn them on, she also is quite often called my younger image, because whoever sees the two of us together says there is a striking resemblance. The same blonde straight shoulder-length hair, the same mischievous eyes, bangs over our foreheads and an exceptionally happy disposition and good sense of humor.

Leah is presently staying in Toronto to finish her studies in art and sculpture. Actually, she isn't a hooker any more and just like me, loves people, traveling and exciting things to happen. Wherever I have gone in recent months, she has managed to keep track of me, because she really likes me. So we decided last night to take off a few weeks in December, when this book supposedly should be finished and at the printer's. Leah and I will then fly to Europe and visit cities like Paris, London, Amsterdam and, last but not least, Rome, where her biggest ambition is to have me take some great nude pictures of her in front of the Vatican.

In order to do that, she will cover her naked voluptuous body with a big black cape and at the opportune moment, preferably with some monks or priests standing right behind her, she will then throw off her cape and I will snap my camera.

Then, who knows—we may take this occasion to stage the first orgy ever held in front of St. Peter's!

EPILOGUE

When I look into the mirror, I say to myself: "Kiddo, you have certainly changed since leaving Holland. A few character lines around the eyes. The fresh Dutch apple pie look is partially gone. A mature woman who has seen a lot looks back at me, instead of the dewy-eyed girl who set out to see a bit of the world.

Still, what is most important to me, there is still a ready smile on my mouth and a naughty twinkle in my eyes.

Reflecting back upon my frenetic days as a madam, I tend to forget the bad times and relive and enjoy the good experiences. I am managing to forget the dishonest people, the corrupt police, the so-called friends who let me down the moment I was in trouble. But I will never forget—no, *not* the parties or the sex—but rather the men and women who have put their confidence in me. I flatter myself that I was patient and helpful and anxious to help a lot of people. My reward? I hope I learned from where they went wrong in life.

Now, looking back, truly the worse thing was not the troubles with the police but the failure of people whom I trusted and regarded as close friends to remember my name, much less my phone number, when the bad times descended upon me. To them, I had become a social pariah, but when my book was published and I was about to throw a big party, they were suddenly good friends again. Who needs them? I have found new friends.

I am happy to be out of the business. I suppose it was inevitable if I was to grow as a person. But since it happened while I was still a young woman, it has meant an exciting new career for me—including the respectability denied a madam—and it's grand to be ahead of the game again, to be on stage again—and not have to worry about cops waiting in the wings, or friends who are distinctly fair-weather types.

With or without me, the business of sex goes on. In fact it's rather amazing that the introduction of The Pill and evolving social attitudes have helped usher in a sexually liberated generation and generally more relaxed codes of sexual behavior, yet . . . prostitution is booming. And people like me writing about their sexual experiences and the editors of the glossy girlie magazines can expect to cash in tremendous amounts of money from that part of their audience—it isn't the entire audience, to be sure—whose need to read about sex never manages to be satisfied. Something is wrong here: sex has been with us since the human race began its existence, yet I would estimate that 90 percent of human beings still suffer from enormous inhibitions in this area.

The old quote, "A good girl shouldn't and a bad girl should," still is operative. People: Get off that moral pedestal of sexual behavior! Everything goes as long as both partners enjoy what they are doing. It's that simple. It's basic. Dig it.

As for the future, I have no long-range plans other than what I am doing: travel, new adventures, new friends, new books. If you were to ask me whether or not I would like to get married and have children and really settle down, my answer is—ready or not, here it comes—a loud *Yes!* Surprised I might have such old-fashioned ideas left in me? Well, despite the great times I've been having in Europe and Canada and the Caribbean—hmmm, does sound like fun, doesn't it?—my primary wish is to really settle down with one man, who I can love and care for. I love children and I love to be needed. If I can find that one man I am looking for, who can please me as a partner in life, as a lover in bed, and as a husband and father who understands what the responsibility of having a family is all about, I will be only too happy to give up the Great Xaviera Hollander Man Hunt real-life series I have been starring in for these past five or six years.

My sexual hunger will be fulfilled by one man only, because I will have found peace of mind—found myself as well as a man I can truly love. If that moment ever comes, I wouldn't require mass orgies or twenty different positions to enjoy a deep, abiding sexual relationship.

But then, you may ask: How long will this last, this seventh heaven, if she ever finds it? How realistic is it for her to expect to settle down after the wild life she's led?

I honestly can't answer such questions. I just know that I'll do my damnedest to try and avoid the pitfalls I've learned so much about in recent years. I will simply try my utmost to make something out of the relationship, whether married or just living together.

Meanwhile, not to worry—I am still a happy bachelor, not quite ancient enough to qualify as an old maid or spinster. I am still relishing my new-found freedom and still living up to my Fun Principle: Never a Dull Moment. I feel like a bird whose wings have been clipped, but have now grown back. So I fly where 'ere I want and, one day, hopefully back to the United States for at least an extended visit. But I love living both in Canada and Europe—though I sure miss the sun at the El San Juan Hotel—and now I also have a regular job as a columnist for *Penthouse*.

I really enjoy this type of work, since it means even more communication with the world, answering letters from men and women who feel they have sexual problems and do not want to talk them over with some psychiatrist. The amount of mail I have received in the course of just a few months is astounding. I am honestly flattered and sincerely hope my monthly advice will afford some reading pleasure as well as offer help to my readers.

Other things in the offing? Plenty, but nothing definite as of this writing. There are movie deals, Happy Hooker games, Happy Hooker lingerie, Happy Hooker records, Happy Hooker perfumes and colognes, Happy Hooker cookbooks—a lot of interesting possibilities.

XAVIERA

Do you have any good ideas? Please let me know. I love to get your mail.

Talking about mail . . . keep an eye out for my next book. It's to be published later this year and it's called *Letters to The Happy Hooker*. I think you'll enjoy it. It's a collection of the many, many fascinating letters I've received from readers around the world as a result of my first book. Plus some select adventures depicting what happened when I answered some of those letters. Hmmm, interesting, those. . . .

Goodbye for now, folks . . . stick around, and Keep in touch with the Dutch!

Xaviera Hollander
Toronto, Canada
December 1, 1972

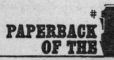
THE TRADE

H. B. GILMOUR

**The explosive behind-the-scenes novel
that explores and exposes the world of the Bestseller!
A shattering insider's look at the passions, politics and people
who make and break the books that become #1!**

WARNER PAPERBACK LIBRARY

78-009 / $1.50

NOW IN PAPERBACK!

THE EXPLOSIVE NOVEL OF THE RUTHLESS MA-
NIPULATORS WHO RULE THE STOCK MARKET
JUNGLE—"FASCINATING"—*The New York Times*

THE DINOSAUR FUND

by VARTANIG G. VARTAN
Author of **50 WALL STREET**

Meet the "instant money men"—those whiz-kids of Wall
Street, who make Cash McCall look like a piker.

"THE DINOSAUR FUND succeeds as well as anything in
print at conveying the atmosphere of that strange world
where life is infused into new fortunes with a few beats
of the stock ticker. It is a world of immense wealth, of
private airplanes equipped with tiled showers, and Roman
Baths in inner offices. . . ."—*Time Magazine*

THE DINOSAUR FUND

A Warner Paperback Library Book

78–063 / $1.50

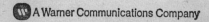 A Warner Communications Company

How Today's Swingles Live Together And Love It!

Apartment To Share

Everything You Need To Know To Win Today's Roommate Game

By Gwen Gibson Schwartz

A modern guide to the joys of group living. Learn how hip singles avoid costly mistakes and solve the unique problems of today's roommate game.

☞ The Protocol of Pot Smoking.

☞ What happens when four guys share an apartment with three girls.

☞ The over-dependent roommate

☞ What goes on when a boyfriend spends the night in the same bedroom with two girls.

Dozens of candid case studies reveal how now-generation roommates meet, manage and move on. How they handle men, money and meals . . . and how they master the lively art of communal life.

76–185 / $1.25

WARNER PAPERBACK LIBRARY

Ⓦ A Warner Communications Company

Available wherever paperbacks are sold